P9-CKQ-106

From Head Shops to Whole Foods

Columbia Studies in the History of U.S. Capitalism

Columbia Studies in the History of U.S. Capitalism
Series Editors: Devin Fergus, Louis Hyman, Bethany Moreton, and Julia Ott

Capitalism has served as an engine of growth, a source of inequality, and a catalyst for conflict in American history. While remaking our material world, capitalism's myriad forms have altered—and been shaped by—our most fundamental experiences of race, gender, sexuality, nation, and citizenship. This series takes the full measure of the complexity and significance of capitalism, placing it squarely back at the center of the American experience. By drawing insight and inspiration from a range of disciplines and alloying novel methods of social and cultural analysis with the traditions of labor and business history, our authors take history "from the bottom up" all the way to the top.

Capital of Capital: Money, Banking, and Power in New York City, by Steven H. Jaffe and Jessica Lautin
Creditworthy: A History of Consumer Surveillance and Financial Identity in America, by Josh Lauer

From Head Shops to Whole Foods

The Rise and Fall of Activist Entrepreneurs

Joshua Clark Davis

Columbia University Press   New York

Columbia University Press
Publishers Since 1893
New York   Chichester, West Sussex
cup.columbia.edu
Copyright © 2017 Columbia University Press
All rights reserved

Library of Congress Cataloging-in-Publication Data

Names: Davis, Joshua Clark, author.
Title: From head shops to whole foods : the rise and fall of activist entrepreneurs /
    Joshua Clark Davis.
Description: New York : Columbia University Press, [2017] | Series: Columbia
    studies in the history of U.S. capitalism | Includes bibliographical references
    and index.
Identifiers: LCCN 2016050678 (print) | LCCN 2017011171 (ebook) |
    ISBN 9780231543088 (e-book) | ISBN 9780231171588 (cloth : alk. paper)
Subjects: LCSH: Business enterprises—Political aspects—United States—History. |
    Small business—Political aspects—United States—History. |
    Entrepreneurship—Political aspects—United States—History. |
    Social movements—Economic aspects—United States—History. |
    Business and politics—United States—History.
Classification: LCC HD2785 (ebook) | LCC HD2785 .D33 2017 (print) | DDC
    322/.30973—dc23
LC record available at https://lccn.loc.gov/2016050678

Columbia University Press books are printed on permanent and durable acid-free paper.
Printed in the United States of America
COVER DESIGN: NOAH ARLOW

For my mom and dad

Contents

Acknowledgments

There is no way I can acknowledge and thank all the people who have contributed to this project since I began it more than a decade ago, but I will do my best. Any omissions I make here are entirely my own fault.

Peter Filene could not have been a more supportive and generous adviser. Over six years of writing and research, Peter gave me invaluable comments, revisions, feedback, and ideas I needed to complete the first major draft of this work. Just as importantly, I was very fortunate that Peter believed in the value of historical research on very unconventional topics—including natural foods stores, drugs, and head shops—when many historians suggested to me that such topics could not or should not be researched. Jacquelyn Hall, Bill Ferris, John Kasson, Jerma Jackson, and Bill Chafe gave me ample support and insight. Their wonderful blend of approaches to understanding the past—the history of social movements, American studies, African American history, labor history, folklore— allowed me to write a book that connects many fields that typically remain unconnected.

Friends and colleagues, of course, have been just as important in completing this work. Over the years, a number of them have read and commented on drafts or simply discussed ideas with me, including Jim Berkey,

Angus Burgin, Asher Burk, David Cline, Catherine Connor, Marko Dumančić, Marcie Ferris, Raphael Ginsberg, Paige Glotzer, Will Griffin, Elizabeth Gritter, Emily Hilliard, Mischa Honeck, Seth Kotch, Michael Kramer, Joseph Lacey, Jessica Levy, Jan Logemann, Gordon Mantler, Michael Meng, Kelly Morrow, Betsy Nix, David Palmer, Robin Payne, Peter Pihos, Brad Proctor, Jason Perlmutter, Kerry Taylor, Mary Turnipseed, and Brandon Winford. My dear friend Andrew Bell would have loved to see this work in print if he were still with us.

At conferences and presentations, I have been very fortunate to get feedback from a number of very insightful panel chairs and commenters, including Nathan Connolly, Sara Evans, David Farber, Larry Glickman, John McMillian, Derek Musgrove, Natalia Petrzela, and Russell Rickford. Christopher Dietrich's comments on and suggestions for various chapters, especially the introduction and conclusion, were invaluable. Anonymous reviewers at *The Sixties: A Journal of History, Politics, and Culture* gave me very constructive feedback for my work on head shops, as did Jeremy Varon in his capacity as editor.

I could not have completed this book without the unceasing help of the library staffs of the University of North Carolina at Chapel Hill, Duke University, and the University of Baltimore. A number of research assistants have also helped me tremendously with this work, including Lyndsay Bates, Susannah Roberson, and Liz Tompkins. Sarah Summers did an excellent job transcribing several oral histories I used for this book. I have also been very lucky to have institutional support at various times from the University of Baltimore; the Center for the Study of the American South and the Southern Oral History Program at the University of North Carolina, Chapel Hill; and the Thompson Writing Program at Duke University. My colleagues at the University of Baltimore have been incredibly supportive as I complete this manuscript.

A number of small businesses I patronized over the years inspired my thoughts on this topic and, although I was not aware of it then, gradually led me to write this study. As a teenager in Decatur, Georgia, outside Atlanta, I made regular visits to the black-owned record store Vibes Music and More operated by Jae "Majiq" Warren and to glorified head shops such as Junkman's Daughter. I also discovered vendors selling Afrocentric goods and black-nationalist books in flea markets such as the Mall in downtown Atlanta. Years later, as I began my graduate studies in history, I found myself wondering where these businesses came from and what their histories were. In the process of writing this book, I visited activist businesses founded in the 1960s and 1970s that are still operating as of 2017: Charis Books & More and the Shrine of the Black Madonna in Atlanta, Rainbow Grocery in Decatur, Marcus Books in San Francisco and Oakland, and OK Natural Foods in Baltimore. These stores have defied the odds and stand as testaments to a previous era of activist business that stretches back more than half a century. In Baltimore, I have spent countless hours eating, writing, reading, and drinking coffee at Red Emma's, a radical bookstore and café that epitomizes the best of what the new generation of activist businesses has to offer. I have also shopped at Whole Foods Market, where I have had nothing but positive experiences with the company's hard-working and kind employees. Anyone who reads this work should realize that my criticisms are not directed at the vast majority of the people employed at Whole Foods but rather at the company's executives, especially founder John Mackey.

I am very grateful to have interviewed a number of owners and employees of activist businesses for this book, including Lex Alexander, George Bishop, Lewis Brandon, Doug Brown, Paul Coates, Charlie Cobb, Casey Czarnik, Paul Hawken, Andy Kowl, Dan Lackey, Stephanie Marcus, David Matthis, Don Moffitt, Daphne Muse, Judy Richardson, Karen Saadeh, Mark Skiles, Jay Thelin, and Edward Vaughn. This work benefitted immensely from the time and energy that each of these individuals spent in sharing their personal histories with me. I thank each one of them. I had originally hoped to interview John Mackey, but he declined my request.

I am fortunate to have assembled my manuscript just as Columbia University Press was launching its Studies in the History of U.S. Capitalism series. I could not have asked for a better home for this book. I am thankful that the press has embraced this book's unusual focus on business, social movements, and counterculture. I am also very grateful to have worked with two wonderful editors: Philip Leventhal, who guided me through the review process and the first round of major revisions, and Bridget Flannery-McCoy, who intrepidly assumed editorial duties in the second half of the publication process. Their help has been absolutely indispensible. I must also thank the quartet of historians who have served as the series editors—Devin Fergus, Louis Hyman, Bethany Moreton, and Julia Ott. All four have given me invaluable professional and intellectual guidance, and I am especially thankful that they workshopped the entire manuscript at a crucial intermediate stage in the process of bringing it into shape for publication. Louis in particular deserves many thanks for all his work as the lead editor for this book. In addition, Charlie McGovern, a reviewer for the press, gave me critically important comments on the manuscript, as did two anonymous readers.

Of course, I also thank my family. My brother and sister, John and Rosemary, have discussed history with me for years. No one has talked about this work with me more—or debated, cajoled, and supported me more—than my loving partner, Lauren Du Graf. Even as Lauren was completing her dissertation, she made sure that I did not let up on myself in finishing the manuscript. I owe her so much. Finally, I have to thank my parents. For as long as I can remember, they encouraged me to love history. I was very fortunate to grow up in a household where discussions of the past—not only the stuff of traditional textbooks but also the details of daily life that are frequently excluded from those books—happened on a regular basis. I probably wouldn't have become a historian without my parents' love of history or their constant support in the pursuit of my goals. I dedicate this book to both of them. Although my mother is no longer here to read this book, I know it would have made her happy to see it in print.

Abbreviations

ABA	American Booksellers Association
AFWA	Alternative Food Workers Alliance
AMIBA	American Independent Business Alliance
BALLE	Business Alliance for Local Living Economies
CO	Co-op Organization
CR	consciousness raising
DDT	dichlorodiphenyltrichloroethane
FBI	Federal Bureau of Investigation
FDA	U.S. Food and Drug Administration
FEA	Feminist Economic Alliance
FEN	Feminist Economic Network
FFCU	Feminist Federal Credit Union
FWCC	Feminist Women's City Club
HIP	Haight Independent Proprietors
LeMar	Legalize Marijuana
NCUA	National Credit Union Administration
NNBL	National Negro Business League
NORML	National Organization for the Reform of Marijuana Laws
NOW	National Organization for Women

OM	Organic Merchants
PTA	Paraphernalia Trade Association
SDS	Students for a Democratic Society
SNCC	Student Nonviolent Coordinating Committee
UFW	United Farm Workers
WITCH	Women's International Terrorist Conspiracy from Hell

From Head Shops to
Whole Foods

Introduction

Ron and Jay Thelin found taking LSD for the first time absolutely transformative. LSD, the brothers believed, could "change the consciousness" of
the nation and inspire Americans to reject the aggression they thought had
driven the country to war with Vietnam. As Jay explained, "We can no
longer identify with the kinds of activities that the older generation are
engaged in . . . They have led to a monstrous war in Vietnam, for example.
And that's why it's all related—the psychedelics and the war, the protesting, the gap in the generations." In January 1966, the Thelins opened the
Psychedelic Shop in San Francisco's Haight-Ashbury district with the primary hope that they could "provide materials that would allow you to have
a good trip" and safely experiment with acid. The Psychedelic Shop sold
pamphlets and books on LSD as well as religious texts from Asia, brightly
colored posters, beaded necklaces, and smoking papers. When California's
legislature voted to outlaw LSD, Ron co-organized the Love Pageant Rally,
which drew hundreds of people to protest the move by dropping acid in
unison in Golden Gate Park. Yet the more the Thelins' shop attracted customers, the less the Thelins seemed to care about making money. After a
year in business, they replaced a large portion of merchandise with a meditation room. The store welcomed anyone in the Haight to spend as much

time as he or she wanted in the store's Calm Center without having to make a purchase.[1]

The Psychedelic Shop was not alone in blending business goals with political objectives. In the summer of 1968, veteran members of the Student Nonviolent Coordinating Committee (SNCC) opened the Drum and Spear Bookstore in Washington, D.C., specializing in works by writers of African descent. In addition to its brick-and-mortar store, Drum and Spear ran a brisk mail-order distribution business for other black booksellers and by 1969 even launched its own publishing company, with headquarters in Washington, D.C., and Dar Es Salaam, Tanzania. Drum and Spear was commercially ambitious, yet it was operated by a nonprofit organization, Afro-American Resources, Inc. "We don't define profit in terms of money," said SNCC activist and store cofounder Charlie Cobb. "The profit is the patronage of the community, which allows the store to self-support." Most critically, Drum and Spear aimed to provide its customers with "access to the right kind of information about the black movements, people and their history."[2]

In 1972, Coletta Reid and Casey Czarnik launched Diana Press, a print shop in Baltimore with the primary goal of "freeing women entirely from male printing establishments." Reid and Czarnik joined forces with several other women active in local lesbian-feminist groups to form a collective to operate the press. Each woman in the multiracial collective earned $100 for a month's work and reinvested most of that salary back into the business. As one staffer recalled, the press "didn't worry about making money, or our profit margin." Within a few years, Diana Press had become one of the leading publishers in the women's movement. "Although we are committed to remaining financially viable and independent, we are also committed to producing books that speak to the real needs of women— not to male assessed market potential," the company's catalog declared.[3]

And in 1978, John Mackey and Renee Lawson—who had met while living at a vegetarian cooperative house—launched a vegetarian and organic food store called SaferWay in Austin, Texas. Mackey described his politics as "social democratic," and he felt "alienated from society." He and Lawson bonded by "question[ing] our nation's values. While the Vietnam War was foremost in many of our minds, human rights, food safety, and environmental deterioration were major concerns as well." The young couple opened SaferWay seeking to "make our country and world a better place to live." Mackey was a member of several cooperative groceries and believed that "business and corporations were essentially evil because they selfishly sought only profits." The name "SaferWay," of course, spoofed the supermarket company Safeway and indicted the social, economic, and environmental dangers of corporate chains. Within two years, Mackey merged SaferWay with a competing store to form a new business he and his partners would call Whole Foods Market.[4]

Operating in different areas of the country and selling different products for different reasons, these businesses shared a critical commonality, one that placed them at odds with conventional notions of capitalism: the people who ran these enterprises touted social and political change, not profit, as their primary objectives. These four stores, for all their unique features, represented a much larger movement of thousands of such businesses across the United States.

I call the individuals who operated such businesses "activist entrepreneurs." They emerged from social movements of the late 1960s and the 1970s believing that American society was sick from inequality, conformity, materialism, hypocritical moralism, and alienation. American business not only exhibited the symptoms of these social illnesses, they argued, but also reinforced and often created them. These unconventional business owners sought autonomy and independence from such sicknesses. With their small, politically informed, and often struggling shops, they offered alternatives to what they saw as the homogenous, discriminatory, and spiritually bankrupt consumer culture of chain stores, modern industrial production, and multinational corporations. Activists conceived their storefronts as antidotes to the alienation produced by America's dominant business and consumer culture. Just as New Left groups such as Students for a Democratic Society (SDS) and SNCC extolled "participatory democracy," activist entrepreneurs espoused what I call "participatory economics": the idea that citizens could regain power over their lives by making their daily experiences in capitalist society more humane, authentic, and even politically progressive or radical. (In speaking of "entrepreneurs," I recognize I am deploying a term that was not common in the 1960s and

1970s, either in business or in activist circles. Although activist entrepreneurs didn't call themselves such, the term conveys their particular blend of social movement participation and business ownership.)[5]

Activist entrepreneurs re-envisioned the products, places, and processes of American business. First, they sought to introduce products that promoted progressive and radical politics as well as cultural pluralism in the marketplace. The businesses in this book grew out of the New Left's "movement of movements," which included civil rights, Black Power, feminism, pacifism, environmentalism, the hippie counterculture, and other movements. Second, these entrepreneurs conceived of their storefronts as political places or "free spaces" that incubated a culture of activism and solidarity. Third, many activist enterprises reconceptualized processes of doing business by promoting shared ownership, limited growth, and democratic workplaces. In turn, they rejected capitalist norms of limited proprietorship, profit maximization, rational economic behavior, and hierarchical management. Activist businesses accorded varying levels of importance to these three factors. Black-owned bookstores and head shops focused primarily on their products, but they also emphasized places and, to a lesser degree, process. Most natural foods stores were concerned with products above all else, but co-op groceries were also deeply engaged with process. Feminist businesses came the closest to placing an equal emphasis on process, products, and places.[6]

Their differences notwithstanding, activist entrepreneurs partook in a shared but largely forgotten experiment in the 1960s and 1970s to create small businesses that advanced the goals of political change and social transformation. Although social movements may be best remembered for marches and mass meetings, activists also eagerly harnessed small businesses as a critical tool for disseminating their ideologies and doing organizing work. A consideration of activist enterprises thus forces us to rethink the widespread idea that the work of social movements and political dissent is by definition antithetical to all business and marketplace activity.[7]

The businesses in this work furthermore belie the common but mistaken notion that political activism and counterculture occupied two separate spheres in the 1960s and 1970s. Indeed, activist businesses were both political and cultural institutions. Some activist entrepreneurs understood social change primarily as political, whereas others understood it primarily as cultural—but these views represented two sides of the same coin. And with their progressive and radical politics, activist businesses provide a sharp contrast to the common narrative of business as an overwhelmingly conservative, profit-making endeavor in postwar America.[8]

The title of this book serves two purposes. By using the phrase "from head shops to whole foods," I am referencing the wide range of businesses this book examines. But, more importantly, I am highlighting a marked transition away from the collective goals of political progress that some, although not most, activist enterprises made between the late 1970s and the end of the twentieth century. The most prominent and powerful retailer to emerge out of the activist business tradition is Whole Foods Market. Over the course of the 1980s and 1990s, Whole Foods abandoned both its initial enthusiasm for collective political change through socially minded commerce as well as its skepticism of unfettered capitalism. Even though the company selectively employs countercultural, spiritual, and sustainable business practices, it now focuses overwhelmingly on conventional corporate business goals of double-digit growth, national market share, and an optimal share price for its stock, which it has sold publicly since 1992. The company is renowned for its high prices, conflict-ridden parking lots, and founder John Mackey's conservative economic views, in particular his public denunciation of labor unions and the Affordable Care Act as well as his libertarian claims about the evils of government. At best, Whole Foods offers consumers opportunities to improve their health and reduce their ecological footprint through individual acts of self-reform. It may be the most prominent descendant of activist business in America today, but it is a neoliberal offspring that its forebears would not recognize as legitimate.

In the twenty-first century, activist entrepreneurs' most enduring legacy is the language of liberation and social change they passed on to countless businesses, many of which have little enthusiasm for the work of social movements. Examples of this influence include tech companies in Silicon Valley that seek to flatten their organizations and encourage their employees to embrace mindful meditation; self-described social enterprises and "mission-driven" businesses; artisanal and boutique retailers that promote "buying local" and celebrate their independence from chain stores and mass production; and even big-box retailers that now gladly sell products they once scorned, including black-authored books and organic foods—all legacies I examine in the conclusion. Despite their widespread influence, activist businesses of the 1960s and 1970s are rarely remembered for the impact they have had on contemporary companies that celebrate ethical business and community engagement.[9]

Meanwhile, a new generation of committed leftist businesses calling themselves the "solidarity economy" or "new economy" has emerged to continue the work begun by earlier activist entrepreneurs. Although this revival has slowed the decline of activist storefronts in the past several decades, it has not stopped that decline. Solidarity businesses are fewer in number and less visible than their predecessors were in the 1960s and 1970s. Corporate co-optation of some of activist businesses' most popular features has made their offerings less distinctive and less appealing to customers than they once were. Ironically, the appropriation of activist enterprises' ideas by the business mainstream has made it more difficult for the new generation of activist businesses to thrive.

This books focuses on black nationalist bookstores, head shops, feminist businesses, and natural foods stores. I chose this particular set of activist businesses due to their prevalence and impact. Roughly 100 black bookstores, 150 or more feminist businesses, 700 natural foods stores, and thousands of head shops operated in the United States in the 1960s and 1970s. Activist businesses were established all over the country, but they were concentrated in cities and college towns. Areas near universities seem to have been particularly conducive to activist storefronts. Not only did these areas often have cheaper rents than other areas major cities, but they were home to large numbers of politically engaged young people who were prime candidates to work and shop at activist businesses.[10]

For reasons of space, I had to leave out a variety of less numerous but still significant enterprises aligned with other social movements in these years, including Chicano and Asian American movement businesses, such as Piranya coffee house and the Amerasia bookstore, respectively, both in Los Angeles; bookstores that emerged out of the gay liberation movement, such as the Oscar Wilde Bookshop in New York; labor movement businesses such as the gas station and grocery store operated by the United Farm Workers in Delano, California; craft stores operated by the fair-trade and civil rights movements; and even Marxist businesses, such as the Socialist Workers Party's Pathfinder bookstores.[11]

In chapter 1, I start by investigating the intellectual and political origins of activist businesses and analyzing them within the context of the New Left, postwar criticisms of consumer culture, and an even older tradition of social movement businesses in the United States. This chapter offers a conceptual framework for understanding the shared ideological foundations of a diverse range of activist businesses and addresses activist entrepreneurs' larger implications for capitalism as well as the criticisms these businesses faced.

Chapter 2 examines Black Power activists who founded scores of bookstores throughout the country in the 1960s and 1970s, hoping to prompt both a "revolution of the mind" and a transformation of business culture in black communities. These activists hailed bookstores as information centers where African American community members could meet to learn about and agitate for radical movements for racial equality and black progress. African American booksellers sought to promote the goals of the Black Power movement by affirming racial pride, celebrating black history and identity, and promoting connections with Africa. As Black Power declined in the second half of the 1970s, however, these bookstores were compelled to deal in an ever broader range of black-authored works, many of them less political in nature.

Chapter 3 examines countercultural entrepreneurs who sold paraphernalia for smoking marijuana or enhancing LSD trips at small stores called head shops. Head shop owners hoped their stores would provide hippies with desperately needed public spaces where they could gather in peace without being harassed. More importantly, these entrepreneurs believed their products allowed people to alter their minds—and even their societies—through meaningful drug use. In addition, many head shops supported the antiwar cause and collaborated with the organized movement to reform America's drug laws. Yet as head shops became increasingly popular, law enforcement, legislators, and parents' groups assailed them as promoters of a dangerous drug culture with no redeeming social or political value. Such attacks on head shops represented one of the early salvos in the cultural and legislative war on drugs that would escalate in the 1980s.

Chapter 4 investigates a wide range of businesses that feminists created in the 1970s, including credit unions, printing presses, bookstores, and mail-order catalogs. Arguing that male-controlled, American corporate capitalism was one of society's most powerful perpetuators of sexism and patriarchy, feminist entrepreneurs believed their products and services promoted women's liberation in the wider public and offered women economic independence from men. These businesses were particularly interested in creating democratic workplaces through collectives and other participatory organizational models, and they sought to operate storefronts as autonomous "free spaces" for feminists, lesbians (including lesbian feminists), and women more generally. Yet feminist entrepreneurs faced a range of challenges, including fierce movement debates about their businesses, the difficulty of sustaining collectives in the long term, and the decline of second-wave feminism in the 1980s.

Chapter 5 examines natural foods stores that sold vegetarian and organic products with the goal of advancing environmentalism, animal rights, and pacifism. Natural foods sellers promoted their trade as an ethical alternative to supermarkets that exploited workers, invested in environmentally destructive agriculture, and sought to maximize profits above all else. Like feminist businesses, natural foods stores eagerly practiced cooperative ownership and collective management. By the late 1970s, the natural foods market had become more lucrative than anyone could have imagined a decade earlier. As a new generation of companies such as Whole Foods Market aggressively pursued profits in the 1980s and 1990s, however, they would move far from natural foods sellers' earlier values of democratic workplaces and collaboration with social movements.

Chapter 6 and the conclusion trace activist businesses through the 1990s until today. They explore not only the significant but contradictory impacts these enterprises have had on American business culture, as seen in a revived appreciation for small business and the emergence of a so-called solidarity economy, but also corporations' generous appropriation of the themes of liberation, social consciousness, and ethical business. Activist entrepreneurs' influence on American business may be much less radical than they had originally hoped, but their dream lives on—albeit fragmented and diluted—in the language, products, and goals of countless American companies today.

I

Activist Business

ORIGINS AND IDEOLOGIES

The owners of such deeply unconventional businesses as the Psychedelic Shop, Drum and Spear, Diana Press, and SaferWay all voiced a shared critique of the dominant commercial and political order of postwar America. These young activist entrepreneurs were born during or after World War II and grew up amid an American consumer culture more dominated by chain retailers, national brands, and advertising than ever before. By the mid-1960s, the new medium of television—what one historian has called the "first exclusively commercial medium in history"—made its way into 94 percent of American households and urgently beckoned young viewers to consume. From 1950 to 1970, businesses' total expenditures on advertising in the United States nearly tripled. Especially for those who grew up in the suburbs, the dominant form of public space was the corporate shopping center, which had replaced the public square as the center of life beyond the city limits. In the quarter century following World War II, chains came to dominate American retail as their share increased sharply from about half to nearly three-quarters of all general merchandising sales. With the help of a powerful new communications medium and the growth of chains, "big business" became much bigger in the postwar years.[1]

Meanwhile, the idea that a mass marketplace could produce shared abundance and reduce social inequalities—what the historian Lizabeth

Cohen has called the "Consumers' Republic"—held incredible sway for millions of American adults. By the middle of the twentieth century, government, labor, economists, and industry reached a consensus that bigger businesses produced better products, sold them more effectively than smaller firms, and provided more benefits to consumers than small companies could. America's massive industrial output and high levels of standardization in production, retailing, and advertising helped build a consumer culture that was unparalleled in size and abundance. Public-policy makers and citizens celebrated mass consumption as a leveling force that could fulfill "loftier social and political ambitions for a more equal, free, and democratic nation" when coupled with adequate social spending, state regulations, and protections for labor. Countless Americans—including Vice President Richard Nixon in his famed "Kitchen Debates" with Soviet premier Nikita Khrushchev in 1959—pointed to America's mass-consumer culture as the ultimate expression of the country's global supremacy.[2]

Yet at almost the exact moment that the tremendous postwar prosperity was reaching more and more Americans, a number of critics began to question the impact of this culture of abundance on the country's democratic values, its pursuit of social equality, and its spiritual well-being. In the second half of the 1950s, best-selling liberal writers, including Sloan Wilson (*The Man in the Grey Flannel Suit*), William Whyte (*The Organization Man*), and Vance Packard (*The Hidden Persuaders*) depicted American business and consumer culture as unfulfilling, conformist, and manipulative. Leftist writers—careful readers of Karl Marx, if not necessarily Marxists—took these criticisms even further. They condemned modern American businesses and consumer culture for fueling a form of psychological estrangement much deeper than simple dissatisfaction. They called this condition "alienation," a term they borrowed from Marx's early writings on *Entfremdung* in *Economic and Philosophic Manuscripts of 1844*. Alienation, Marx argued, was a profound form of spiritual discontent and dehumanization that workers experienced in their lives as they sought to comply with the dictates of industrial work, class hierarchy, and capitalist bureaucracy. Because the complete text of these essays became available to many readers only after the first full English translation had been published in 1959, the idea of alienation was still relatively fresh to American leftists in the 1960s.[3]

Although Marx located alienation primarily in the lives of industrial workers, leftist thinkers in the 1950s and 1960s increasingly argued that alienation plagued all Americans and that virtually no one could escape the dangerous influence of modern consumer culture. C. Wright Mills and Herbert Marcuse were advocates of this interpretation who enjoyed an enthusiastic reception from young American readers in the 1960s. Mills, a heterodox leftist sociologist at Columbia University, wrote eloquently in *White Collar* (1951) of the stultifying effects of modern middle-class work that sapped Americans of their independence, and he despaired of the "alienating process that has shifted men from a focus upon production to a focus upon consumption." And Marcuse, a Frankfurt School theorist, declared in the introduction to his best seller *One-Dimensional Man* (1964), "Free choice among a wide variety of goods and services does not signify freedom if these goods and services sustain social controls over a life of toil and fear—that is, if they sustain alienation."[4]

Other thinkers on the left, without necessarily using the term *alienation*, also denounced what they saw as the profoundly dehumanizing and psychologically corrosive effects of modern American capitalism. This group included anarchist thinkers such as Paul Goodman, who in his best-selling work *Growing Up Absurd* (1956) condemned "the economic lunacy" encouraged by television; Murray Bookchin, whose book *Our Synthetic Environment* (1962) was an early leftist criticism of the environmental dangers of corporate capitalism; E. Franklin Frazier, the African American sociologist and author of an incisive critique of African American business and the middle class, *Black Bourgeoisie* (1957); and the feminist and former labor journalist Betty Friedan, who in her work *The Feminine Mystique* (1963) denounced advertisers for "persuading housewives to stay at home, mesmerized in front of a television set, their non-sexual human needs unnamed, unsatisfied, drained by the sexual sell into the buying of things."[5]

Under the influence of these thinkers and a range of social movements, many young Americans came to view business and consumer culture with deep skepticism by the late 1960s. According to one study, more than half of American teenagers had been "favorably impressed with the business system" in 1951, but by 1971 that figure had sunk to just 35 percent. "Why does youth consider Big Business 'immoral'?" the editors of *Fortune* magazine asked with palpable anxiety in a special report titled *Youth in Turmoil* in 1969. Speaking for many American marketers, corporations, and retailers, *Fortune* feared they might lose an entire generation of shoppers to growing discontent with the social and environmental costs of the country's business enterprises. The editors of *Fortune* seemed perplexed by the deep alienation that critics attributed to American capitalism and dismayed by the growing perception that the country's consumer culture was rife with inequality.[6]

Indeed, a wide range of Americans were excluded from a postwar consumer culture that celebrated the white, suburban, heterosexual, and law-abiding family of four as the normative social and economic unit. Most flagrantly, African Americans were denied equal recognition in this consumer culture. Across the country, black consumers often shopped in segregated retail districts, and in the South many white businesses still refused to serve blacks through the 1960s. Even stores that did accept black customers often treated them dismissively or with open suspicion and hostility. The vast majority of advertisements ignored African Americans and other consumers of color, and the few ads that did feature blacks often ridiculed and disparaged them. The black nationalist writer, publisher, and bookstore owner Don Lee (later Haki Madhubuti) rejected altogether the idea that white-dominated consumer culture had any relevance for African Americans: "The important issues as a result of the mass media are hot pants, bell bottoms, hogs, Hondas, night life and other mediocrity to keep our minds off dealing with the killers of the world."[7]

But it was not just African Americans who felt that their country's consumer culture excluded them. Women, after all, faced pervasive credit discrimination and were regularly denied loans if they were married. They also endured a barrage of sexist advertising, which overwhelmingly depicted them as homemakers and mothers while ignoring professional women and adult women who were unmarried. As Betty Friedan argued, "The perpetuation of housewifery, the growth of the feminine mystique makes sense (and dollars) when one realizes that women are the chief customers of American business." Gay and lesbian Americans were virtually invisible in their nation's consumer culture. Latinos, Asians, and Native Americans appeared only occasionally in advertising and usually as caricatures. Even unconventional lifestyles invited scorn. Individuals who consumed illegal, mood-altering substances were roundly condemned as self-destructive and dangerous, even as advertisers glorified cigarettes and alcohol as carefree pleasures. Even consumers who made unconventional dietary choices were made to feel deviant. Vegetarians and advocates of organic foods in the 1960s were widely considered quacks. A Bank of America market study described natural foods consumers as "aging arthritics, would-be Tarzans, and all manner of food faddists." In the eyes of the *East–West Journal*, a major promoter of natural foods, the "conspiracy of agri-business and the federal government" perpetrated "nutritional, economic and cultural exploitation."[8]

As these contradictions became clear to many young Americans, some of them began to wonder what was lost in their country's compulsion to consume. Amid a public discourse that celebrated the American "free market," businesses' cultural and social inequalities struck many young Americans as deeply hypocritical. Yet not all young people rejected business wholesale. In fact, some began to explore its ethical possibilities. Could entrepreneurs, these individuals asked, operate in a manner that was democratic, authentic, humanizing, and just? Could a business function as a public space that served the good of its local community and not just the good of its owners? And if so, could such a business still make a profit? These were the questions that motivated activist entrepreneurs.[9]

ACTIVIST ENTREPRENEURS AND THE MOVEMENT OF MOVEMENTS

Activist entrepreneurs explored these questions within the context of the ascendant left social movements of the 1960s and 1970s. Although these movements emerged from different political traditions and sought to address different concerns, they shared the objective of making American society more equal, democratic, and humane. They in turn fueled the rise of additional social movements that flourished in the 1970s, including the gay liberation, antinuclear, animal rights, and drug legalization movements.

These activists expanded traditional left analyses of consumer society's material inequalities to articulate a broader indictment of the social, spiritual, and psychological harm that modern corporations inflicted on the American people.[10]

The pioneering New Left organization SDS articulated one of the era's most significant critiques of American big business with its publication of the Port Huron Statement in 1962. Believed to be the most widely distributed document of the America Left in the 1960s, the statement is best remembered for introducing to tens of thousands of readers the concept of participatory democracy as a corrective to a calcified American political system. Less remembered but nonetheless influential was the Port Huron Statement's criticism of America's "remote control economy"—namely, the dominance by business, government, and labor elites that "excludes the mass of individual 'units'—the people—from basic decisions affecting the nature and organization of work, rewards, and opportunities." The SDS instead proposed an economy in which "work should involve incentives worthier than money or survival. It should be educative, not stultifying; creative, not mechanical; self-direct[ed], not manipulated, encouraging independence[,] a respect for others, a sense of dignity and a willingness to accept social responsibility." In this economy, the SDS envisioned, democratic institutions would address seemingly "private problems—from bad recreation facilities to personal alienation" not as individual crises but as "general issues" best resolved through collective struggle. Not surprisingly, two of the key influences on the statement were Marx's *Economic and Philosophic Manuscripts* and C. Wright Mills's work, both of which appeared on the SDS's official reading list for members.[11]

Mills's criticisms of the dangers of bureaucracy and what he called the "labor metaphysic"—the American Left's historic belief that the working class was the primary agent of social and political change—in particular shaped activists associated with the New Left. Before the 1960s, American socialists, Communists, and social democrats worked primarily through highly structured and centralized organizations while emphasizing a primarily materialist conception of historical change. By contrast, the New Left sought to combat the ways in which bureaucracy and centralized power of government, business, and even some of organized labor combined with racism, sexism, and other forms of oppression to undermine democracy and breed alienation. For these young radicals, Americans' individual struggles with alienation were rooted not only in class conflict but also in a range of collective political, economic, and moral problems. As the feminist Carol Hanisch famously declared, "The personal is political." Although collective empowerment was critically important for both iterations of the Left, the New Left was much more concerned with individual freedoms and expressions than its predecessors were.[12]

Within this context, it is no coincidence that corporations became targets in a number of social movements' pivotal actions in the 1960s. The lunch-counter sit-ins at Woolworth stores that began in February 1960 in Greensboro, North Carolina, for instance, launched a new phase of direct action in the civil rights movement. One of second-wave feminists' earliest public direct actions was their protest against sexist beauty norms and the "Consumer Con-Game" at the Miss America Contest in Atlantic City in 1968, sponsored by Pepsi-Cola. Protests against corporate production of the pesticide dichlorodiphenyltrichloroethane, better known as DDT, and the publication of Rachel Carson's groundbreaking book *Silent Spring* (1962) stand out as seminal moments in the rise of the modern environmental movement. Criticisms of consumer culture grew so great that the president of Conference Board, America's leading organization of corporate executives, declared in the recession year 1976 that "the immediate origins of [businesses'] difficulties lie in the social revolution of the 1960's and 1970's."[13]

Despite their critiques of corporations, activists established small businesses in the 1960s and 1970s more than ever before. Far fewer activists of the era, compared to their predecessors in the so-called Old Left, believed that the Marxist dream of destroying capitalism was possible. Yet young activist entrepreneurs were still keenly interested in decentralizing and democratizing power. Like many of the era's movements, they favored political projects over political parties. They believed that democratically structured small enterprises could empower people to achieve real liberation and escape the depersonalizing alienation produced by undemocratic, bureaucratic institutions such as big businesses and large political parties. In this regard, activist enterprises reflected an anarchist influence on the era's left movements that was much less pronounced among the Left in midcentury.[14]

Activist entrepreneurs' harnessing of small businesses for political purposes illuminates a forgotten dimension of dissent in the 1960s and 1970s. For many thousands of Americans, activist business was a serious attempt to develop both new forms of enterprise and community as well as a new vehicle for political and social transformation. Critics alleged that activist businesses reduced collective struggles for democracy and equality to individual acts of opting in to political change and that they promoted lifestyle and cultural choices over direct challenges to the dominant political system. The entrepreneurs in this work, however, did not believe they had to make such binary choices. They hoped to bring about political transformation and a more pluralistic marketplace by operating small businesses *in direct collaboration with*, not instead of, collective social movements.

Head shops aligned with the counterculture, antiwar, and drug legalization movements; black-owned bookstores promoted black nationalism, pan-Africanism, and anticolonialism; feminist enterprises participated in the women's and lesbian liberation movements; and natural foods stores collaborated with the environmental, animal rights, and peace movements. Furthermore, activist businesses had a broad appeal that frequently transcended the ideological fault lines within movements. Liberal feminists started businesses, but so did radical feminists; culturally oriented black nationalists launched storefronts, but so did the Black Panthers they often disagreed with. As such, activist businesses provide a nuanced view of the inner workings of social movements that traditional ideological analyses often do not.[15]

Activist entrepreneurs also complicate the dominant historical interpretation of businesses' political engagement in the 1960s and 1970s as overwhelmingly conservative. Progressive and radical small businesses provide a sharp contrast to a prevailing narrative that focuses on corporations' campaigns for deregulation, tax reform, and free-market fundamentalism in the postwar years. Activist businesses rejected not only these businesses' economic views but also many corporations' conservative interpretation of Christianity they deployed to buttress their marketplace ideology. By contrast, activist entrepreneurs drew on a range of non-Western religious traditions in their business activities, including Buddhism, Hinduism, and

Islam. Although activist enterprises represented only a modest portion of the overall number of businesses in the United States, their mere existence demonstrates the range of political possibilities available to the era's business owners.[16]

The 1960s and 1970s represent a period when activists experimented with business more than ever, but the history of American social movements seeking change through small enterprise started long before then. At antislavery bazaars and so-called free-produce stores from the 1820s until the Civil War, abolitionists sold fair-trade goods as well as memorabilia and literature condemning forced labor. Labor organizations—including the Grange and the Farmers' Alliance in the late nineteenth century as well as the American Federation of Labor, the Congress of Industrial Organizations, and the Industrial Workers of the World in the twentieth century—established cooperatively owned stores. Feminists established "suffrage shops" where they sold memorabilia and literature to support their cause in the 1910s. Marcus Garvey's United Negro Improvement Association celebrated business enterprise as a critical vehicle for pan-Africanism in the 1920s, while a number of African American civil rights and labor activists, including W. E. B. Du Bois, Ella Baker, and A. Philip Randolph, endorsed cooperative businesses as tools of economic democracy in the 1930s and 1940s. A wide variety of religious groups—ranging from the pacifist Shakers to the black nationalist Nation of Islam—sought to advance their spiritual and ideological work with retail businesses.[17]

Even anticapitalist thinkers promoted businesses that were democratically structured. Marx, Friedrich Engels, and Vladimir Lenin all endorsed worker-owned cooperatives, and small private enterprises operated openly in such countries as the Soviet Union, East Germany, and Maoist China. Marxists established their own bookstores in the United States by the turn of the early twentieth century, and Communist parties operated cooperative cafeterias in the 1920s. Activist businesses of the 1960s and 1970s built upon this groundwork but far exceeded their predecessors in number, influence, and geographic reach.[18]

Nonetheless, the misconception that individuals involved with social movements and counterculture in the 1960s and 1970s avoided business activity remains surprisingly durable in both historical discourse and popular memory. Historians have written of a New Left that regarded "consumer society as the enemy of both authenticity and social change," of hippies who "scorned materialism and consumption," and of students who "distrusted the corporations." Other historical interpretations have stressed that major corporations co-opted countercultural motifs for their advertising and used them to craft a looser, liberated workplace culture and management style. Upstart chain retailers such as the Gap, with no real connections to a social movement or counterculture, eagerly traded on themes of generational conflict, youth rebellion, and flower power in these years. One scholar has even argued that the countercultural authors of *The Whole Earth Catalog* incorporated the values of the military-industrial complex into their work. Although these interpretations have stressed how corporations sought to appropriate the work of the New Left and counterculture, they have largely avoided the question of how activists went into business for themselves.[19]

My goal in the chapters that follow, by contrast, is to reveal activists' largely forgotten strategy of establishing their own independent businesses to advance the work of their movements and to counter corporate power in the 1960s and 1970s. Contrary to popular opinion, Americans involved with social movements and counterculture did not reject business altogether, even as they sorted through its contradictions. In fact, they exercised more control of their businesses' commercial possibilities than scholars have previously recognized. They were highly skeptical, for instance, of what Thomas Frank has described as Madison Avenue's attempts at "the conquest of cool" and "hip consumerism." Corporate efforts to capitalize on the era's insurgent politics and sense of rebellion struck observers from the New Left and underground press as transparent, exploitative, and insincere. "You are beginning to talk like us, to sympathize with our frustrations," wrote the *Big US*, a radical underground newspaper in Cleveland, in an "open letter" to Time, Inc. "But it won't work, man. We know what you're up to. You are not joining us because we've turned you on to a better way of life; you're joining us to lead us—lead us away from the left, back into the fold of capitalist apple pie Americana." As *Ramparts* and *Rolling Stone* editor Ralph Gleason wrote in an editorial denouncing Columbia Records' notorious "The Man Can't Bust Our Music" advertising campaign in 1968, "The name of the game, seen from one point of view, is to steal the rhetoric of the revolution.... [T]here's money in revolution and Columbia is smart."

People involved with social movements and counterculture were well aware that their rebelliousness could be converted into corporate profits. Not only were they prepared to resist such attempts at co-optation, but they also believed they could create their own businesses that faithfully promoted the values of social movements and the counterculture.[20]

PRODUCTS, PLACES, AND PROCESSES: THE QUEST FOR PARTICIPATORY ECONOMICS

Unlike most conventional businesses, activist entrepreneurs sought to achieve three fundamental nonfinancial goals in the 1960s and 1970s: to advance and disseminate the ideologies and values of a range of social movements; to create "free spaces" where marginalized people and activists could publicly assemble and collaborate; and to offer an alternative to chain retail by making small business more democratic, participatory, collaborative, and spiritually fulfilling. In so doing, they sought to transform American business by remaking its products, places, and processes.

Activist businesses sold products that were imbued with progressive and radical values. Drum and Spear sold "books, pamphlets, and documents which inform and educate our community towards its own interests and concerns." The organic food pioneer Erewhon sold "the highest quality biological food" that could "effect a biological, psychological and spiritual change." The clothing and crafts maker Liberation Enterprises sold "items [that] will serve as consciousness-raisers, by making the feminist spirit more visible." Activists businesses of all kinds believed their products had political power and offered customers paths to enlightenment and justice. Corporate retailers avoided many of these products as they emerged in the second half of the 1960s, both because they wanted to avoid any association with radicalism and because they believed such products were unprofitable. Almost all feminist businesses, head shops, black bookstores, and natural foods stores were initially independent retailers. Only in the second half of the 1970s and thereafter did chain stores gradually seek to compete with independent activist businesses and to sell some of the products they had pioneered.[21]

Most activist entrepreneurs were just as keenly concerned with where they conducted business—their places—and not just with what they sold.

They thus hoped to create democratic, participatory, and inclusive store-fronts that functioned as "free spaces" for employees and customers alike. They envisioned small businesses as vehicles for a spatial politics of libera-tion and resistance, and they sought to build a different marketplace than the one found at the local shopping center, in the supermarket, and on tele-vision. These spaces would make up an integral part of an alternative pub-lic sphere where marginalized peoples, activists, and countercultures could exchange information, discuss ideas, do organizing work, and build com-munity. A term popularized by civil rights and feminist activist Pamela Allen, *free space* became critically important for a wide range of activists who hoped to create distinctive milieus for their movements or what some simply called "movement culture." Other free spaces included union halls, politicized fraternal organizations, and progressive and radical houses of worship.[22]

As free spaces, activist businesses welcomed a variety of Americans long demeaned by American corporations, including women, people of color, gays and lesbians, and various nonconformists. The workers at the Femi-nist Federal Credit Union in Lansing, Michigan, considered their business "a woman's center . . . with bulletin boards and posters about Feminist news and activities." Staffers at Drum and Spear similarly sought to make their store "accessible to low-income black people, so that you didn't have to be academically grounded before you could come into this bookstore. . . . People who had never been inside a bookstore, they would want to come on in and see what was going on." An employee at a San Francisco hash pipe factory praised her workplace as "a free atmosphere" in which employ-ees were encouraged "to speak out." As another employee, a long-haired, eighteen-year-old hippie, explained, "It was probably the only place I could get a job, looking and living the way I did." This was an era in which many conventional businesses shunned activists and hippies, at times even bar-ring them as customers from stores or summoning police to harass them for loitering nearby. People who had difficulties finding jobs in the main-stream economy because of their radical political values, activism, or coun-tercultural leanings as well as because of widespread sexist, racist, and homophobic hiring practices found employment opportunities in activist businesses. Today, the idea of free space lives on in the more common term *safe space*, a similar concept of creating areas that welcome people who face widespread harassment and oppression.[23]

Free spaces also functioned as hubs of "movement culture." These businesses were political education centers where activists and marginalized peoples became friendly with employees, attended political meetings, distributed and picked up alternative media and political literature, and read and posted messages on bulletin boards. For the uninitiated, this activity meant gaining exposure to new ideas, texts, leaders, and ways of living. The more politically seasoned would use free spaces to meet and interact with people who already shared their ideals. Activist businesses aimed to give movements a degree of autonomy from the dominant economy against which they rebelled. They also functioned as beachheads from which activists could promote their political values and offer people alternatives to the forms of business and community that prevailed in broader society. Activist storefronts were supposed to draw people into these movements and to mobilize them in the name of their causes.[24]

In addition to their products and places, activist entrepreneurs were deeply concerned with their processes or how they conducted business. Many of them sought to democratize and humanize workplace social relations, to increase individuals' control over their labor, and to make businesses more genuine and sincere in line with New Left social movements' emphasis on authenticity. Co-ops and collectives were owned by their members and operated on a "one member, one vote" management system. Meanwhile, individually owned activist businesses borrowed a variety of features from collectives, including shared authority; minimal rules and social controls; political and friendship bonds as key factors in recruitment and advancement; a privileging of value-based incentives over material gain; a flattening of social hierarchies; and a sharing of labor that democratized the distribution of tasks and responsibilities among workers. Although only some activist businesses espoused all of these principles, virtually all of them implemented at least some collectivist principles in their operations, especially value-based compensation, the minimization of rules, and the privileging of political bonds and friendship. According to one worker in the feminist Women's Community Health Center in Cambridge, Massachusetts, collectives offered "the only work situation that has the potential to be non-exploitative and non-oppressive in every aspect. Working [in] a collective is working for oneself. It is the only place to do unalienated labor." Activists viewed their businesses as "prefigurative institutions" that served as models for the democratic society that social movements hoped to build. Similar interpretations described activist businesses as "counterinstitutions," "parallel institutions," or "parallel structures" that sought to create alternatives to prevailing forms of retail business and public space. As workers of the Chicago Women's Graphics Collective, makers of feminist and antiwar posters, explained, "Collective working and living is [sic] important in creating the revolutionary society within the old."[25]

To be sure, the pursuit of participatory economics could incur significant costs, especially in collectives. The following chapters reveal a series of shared problems that activist entrepreneurs faced. The participatory work of forging consensus could be tedious and incredibly time consuming. The direct, extensive communications it entailed often made decision making emotionally demanding, if not impossible. Collectives' heavy emphasis on consensus and ideological unity often made their memberships politically, economically, and educationally homogenous. Many collective members were white, highly educated, and economically privileged. The high expectations for ideological commitment meant that workers often volunteered for free or logged long hours to earn virtually nothing. This meant that working-class people could not afford to sacrifice their already limited earning power by volunteering. These shortcomings at times limited the reach of participatory economics and curtailed its effectiveness as a social movement. A deep fear of disagreement and conflict motivated some collective members to conceal their true feelings about important decisions, often just postponing deeper interpersonal disputes that would later turn into larger conflicts. Yet for all the pain such nearly interminable political discussions inflicted, they nonetheless held a hallowed position in social movements. As one SDS pamphlet proclaimed in 1965, "Freedom is an endless meeting."[26]

Activist businesses' emphasis on prefigurative institutions, shared authority, and mutual aid reflected an ideological debt to anarchism. Anarchists may be best known for opposing state power, but, like Marxists, they have also long condemned capitalism as a force for oppression and inequality. Unlike right-wing libertarians, they do not regard capitalism, unregulated markets, and individual power as the ultimate sources of human freedom. Activist entrepreneurs' strong preference for small businesses and their concerns about the dehumanizing, alienating effects of large bureaucratic structures also reflected anarchism's influence. These interests were often imbibed through contact with pacifist and antiwar groups that had been exposed to anarchism. Granted, small numbers of activist entrepreneurs, especially head shop owners, did flirt with anti-government, libertarian ideology. On the whole, however, activist businesses' suspicions of government reflected the subtle but widely unacknowledged influence that anarchism exerted on a wide range of social movements in the 1960s and 1970s.[27]

This deep suspicion of government was quite different from most con-ventional businesses' suspicions of the state. Whereas corporate business leaders condemned what they saw as excess regulation and an overly bur-densome tax code, activist entrepreneurs took issue with the state's repres-sion of political dissent, criminalization of social deviance, failure to address social inequalities, and privileging of large corporations through subsidies, policy, and tax breaks. Head shop owners, for instance, pushed for the decriminalization of marijuana and the release of drug offenders from prison, and natural foods grocers decried the U.S. Department of Agricul-ture's active role in promoting chemical pesticides and subsidizing large-scale, corporate farming. Feminist and black nationalist entrepreneurs viewed the state as a primary perpetrator of sexism and racism, respectively. A wide swath of activist businesses condemned economic collaboration between the state and defense companies as a corrupt military-industrial complex. At the same time, state officials and law enforcement often looked unfavorably on activist businesses and subjected many of them to surveil-lance, arbitrary and illegal arrests, confiscation of their products, and the revocation of business permits.[28]

State-sponsored backlash against activist businesses can be seen as a sign of how much they threatened accepted norms of political expression and business enterprise. Government harassment, in turn, gave many activist entrepreneurs more reason to criticize state intervention in their affairs. Of course, such attitudes coincided with antigovernment sentiments that flourished among social movements and the counterculture as protests against the Vietnam War grew. Law enforcement's frequent clashes with protestors and regular searches of activists and hippies for drugs as well as an increasing number of political prisoners also gave rise to growing suspicions of the state. Demands for the legalization of mind-altering substances and especially of marijuana, which I address at length in the chapter on head shops, also fueled antigovernment attitudes among many activists. To be sure, few if any activist businesses were resolutely opposed to the state. Although activist entrepreneurs selectively objected to government intervention in their enterprises, they continued to push the state to address their demands for racial and gender equality, gay rights, environmental sustainability, and business regulation. At the same time, they hoped to create free spaces that were refuges from state persecution.

Activist entrepreneurs also envisioned their businesses as free spaces for spiritual enlightenment. To many of these entrepreneurs, modern American capitalism and consumer culture represented nothing less than a form of spiritual death, a deeply penetrating form of alienation that denied people their humanity. They likewise rejected organized Christianity, considering it a source of repressive moralism, unfeeling spirituality, and hypocritical double-talk on the major issues of the day. Instead, they incorporated elements of non-Christian spirituality into their operations.[29] Many found inspiration in Hinduism, Islam, and most of all Buddhism. They were particularly enamored with the Buddhist concept of "right livelihood," the idea that people should earn a living ethically by helping others and avoiding hurting living creatures. Right livelihood gained wide circulation among activist entrepreneurs through such popular books as E. F. Schumacher's *Small Is Beautiful: A Study of Economics as If People Mattered* (1973), Michael Phillips's *The Seven Laws of Money* (1974), and Baba Ram Dass's (Richard Alpert's) best-selling paean to spirituality and mediation, *Be Here Now* (1971). These manifestos for humanistic economics resonated deeply with the owners and employees of activist businesses. In Austin, Texas, for instance, members of an umbrella organization for local cooperatives vowed to "maximize respect, concern, sensitivity and attentiveness to other people" and to "never sacrifice human relationships to efficiency" in the course of running their businesses.[30]

Even the naming of activist businesses asserted explicit cultural and political claims. This practice extended beyond the specific storefronts I look at in the following chapters to include the very categories into which entrepreneurs grouped themselves. The term *black bookstores* declared that black people, contrary to many racist stereotypes, avidly read and wrote and were devoted to the tasks of intellectual and economic self-sufficiency. The term *feminist businesses* announced that women could run enterprises and organizations without any help from men. The label *head shops* claimed them as the go-to businesses for "heads," or people who sought to alter their consciousness through illegal drugs as opposed to people who were part of the "straight" society. The term *natural food stores* announced that these businesses championed ecology and presented themselves as alternatives to the oft-derided "plastic" consumer culture of supermarkets and industrial agriculture. The arrival of these businesses as recognizable segments in the American marketplace is significant. Whether these entrepreneurs qualified the term *business* or avoided it altogether, they believed that redefining the very language they used to describe economic exchange was an essential aspect of the larger quest of developing an alternative form of capitalism.

Although activist entrepreneurs aligned themselves with a variety of movements, all of them were both politically engaged *and* countercultural to varying degrees (table 1.1). Black nationalist bookstores and feminist businesses were almost inseparable from the social movements they represented. Many head shops and natural foods stores, meanwhile, understood their efforts to transform the dominant values of American culture as a part of creating a counterculture. Nonetheless, head shops also worked closely with the drug legalization movement, and natural foods stores, especially co-ops, collaborated with the ecology and animal rights movements. Employees in many businesses discussed in this book participated in the antiwar movement. By the same token, black-owned bookstores sought to cultivate an alternative culture in the form of the Black Arts movement, and feminist businesses sought to develop a counterculture of women's art, music, and literature. Perhaps more than any other institutions of the era, these businesses brought together social movements and countercultures into the same spaces.

TABLE 1.1 Activist Businesses

Business Type	Social Movement Ties	Critique of Capitalism	Products	Places: Free Spaces for Marginalized Peoples	Processes: Democratic Ownership and Labor Practices
Black-owned bookstores	Black Power and black nationalism; pan-Africanism; Marxism; Third World solidarity	White consumer culture denies blacks visibility, economic opportunities, culture they can call their own.	Black-authored books; texts about black nationalism, Black Power, Africa, the Third World; African clothing, art, and music	Welcomed blacks, especially black activists, when many businesses excluded both	Virtually all independently owned; some established by nonprofits, community centers, and houses of worship
Head shops	Hippie counterculture; drug legalization movement; antiwar movement	American consumer culture is inauthentic, alienating, conformist, plastic, undemocratic.	Drug paraphernalia and occasionally drugs; underground newspapers; Asian religious artifacts; antiwar memorabilia	Welcomed hippies, antiwar protesters, and drug users, all unwelcome at many businesses	Virtually all independently owned; some collectives and nonprofits
Feminist businesses	Second-wave feminism; lesbian feminism; lesbian liberation; antiwar movement	Male-controlled corporations and consumer culture perpetuate gender roles and patriarchy and subject women to economic dependence.	Woman-created products; T-shirts, books, posters, jewelry promoting feminism; woman-controlled financial services	Woman-controlled spaces that welcomed women and feminists; particularly important as spaces welcoming lesbians	Virtually all independently owned; large proportion collectively owned and managed and explicitly nonprofit
Natural foods stores	Environmentalism; antiwar movement and pacifism; animal rights; hippie counterculture; anarchism	Agribusiness is environmentally destructive and cruel to animals; chain supermarkets are unhealthy, unnatural; farm and grocery labor is exploitative.	Foods made without pesticides and preservatives; vegetarian foods; non-American food, especially from Asia	Welcomed vegetarians; people from non-Western cultures with non-American diets; pacifists; hippies	Virtually all independently owned until 1980s; many consumer co-ops, some worker owned; some collectively managed

ACTIVIST BUSINESSES AND CAPITALISM

Activist entrepreneurs were steeped in social movements and political work, but some leftist and countercultural observers questioned what they saw as these entrepreneurs' dangerous flirtation with, if not capitulation to, capitalist profit motives. Left-leaning journalists and self-styled underground newspapers periodically cast activist businesses' motives in a negative light. In "The Age of Acquireous," a cleverly titled article from 1970, San Francisco's newspaper *Good Times* recognized "long hairs selling useful items like health foods" but excoriated "others selling items with no redeeming value, e.g. phony hippie jewelry." Retailers of both useful and useless countercultural products reaped "huge profits" and were "largely apolitical," if not "taking sides against the revolution." As another underground paper declared in an editorial title "Money vs. People" in 1969, "There is NO revolution. Only a new, generation of 'hip' artsy-craft entrepreneurs vamping every human experience [and] perverting it into monetary abstraction." As I show in the following chapters, black radical activists penned strident critiques of "black capitalism," and numerous feminists denounced the role of business in the women's movement. By the late 1970s, natural foods sellers fretted over the commercialization of their business, and some countercultural critics worried that head shops were surrendering their political values.[31]

These critics realized the potential contradictions between activist entrepreneurs' stated political ideals and their pursuit of profit and growth. They questioned whether activist businesses' profits benefitted their workers and their communities or if the gains accrued strictly to the owners. Some wondered whether activist businesses treated their employees any better than other small businesses did. These critiques had merit in certain cases. Some activist entrepreneurs did depend on low wages or even volunteer hours to make ends meet. *Good Times* went as far as to denounce hippie businesses as "great labor rip-offs" that underpaid their staff while promising higher wages that would likely never come.[32] Moreover, activist enterprises did not always remain politically engaged as time passed. In some cases, they simply drifted out of movements. In others, they consciously disassociated from them. As the hippie counterculture became less political over time, so did many head shops and natural foods stores. The declines that black nationalism, feminism, and the antiwar movement experienced in the second half of the 1970s were also factors in activist businesses' decreased political engagement.

Critics were particularly concerned with the possibility that financial success would transform activist businesses into exactly the kind of big business that their owners and employees claimed to despise. They doubted that any business could grow while serving its community and providing its employees a modicum of equality and freedom in the workplace. Some activist business owners feared that major financial success was incompatible with producing political and cultural change. Natural foods businesses' "number one purpose is to help effect a biological, psychological, and spiritual change in people who are dropping out [of society]," remarked natural foods pioneer Paul Hawken. "I don't know [if] big business can sell organic foods to the people. I doubt it. . . . We need small family distributors and small family stores, and we need a marketing system that is going to be very direct." Yet many criticisms and fears of activist businesses significantly overstated their potential or desire for growth; Whole Foods was virtually alone in transforming from activist storefront to successful chain retailer.[33]

In fact, many activist entrepreneurs were terrible at running their companies, at least according to traditional measures of business effectiveness. Many devoted too much time to political work, countercultural community building, partying, or getting high to build successful businesses. Most kept poor records and did little inventory or financial planning, had limited access to credit, and kept irregular hours. Not surprisingly, the majority of activist businesses did not last longer than five years. They thus may seem to offer little of value to us decades later.

Yet activist entrepreneurs of the 1960s and 1970s demonstrated that advancing political change through business, although difficult, was not impossible. When activist businesses sold large quantities of products long before they were readily available from mainstream retailers—such as the book *Philosophy and Opinions of Marcus Garvey* or the feminist health manual *Our Bodies, Ourselves* or anticolonial fair-trade goods—they did not systematically transform American capitalism. But they nonetheless used the marketplace to introduce millions of Americans to radical forms of political thought and action.[34]

Activist entrepreneurs fiercely criticized capitalism, but they also believed that their businesses could serve the purposes of social movements and progressive change by emphasizing cooperation over competition and solidarity over sales margins. Many of them wanted to create a new marketplace of nonprofit and low-profit businesses that rejected capitalist objectives of maximizing profits. As the editor of *Northwest Passage*, a New Left and countercultural newspaper in Bellingham, Washington, explained, countercultural "freak businesses" were not intent on eliminating capitalism. Rather, they sought to earn just enough to support their owners and staffs "while offering both them and their customers alternatives to the ValuMart ripoff madness" perpetrated by a popular regional discount chain. For these entrepreneurs, their greatest power lay not in doing away with capitalism but in creating alternatives within the market economy to the ever-larger, more structured, and purportedly more rational American corporations, whose ultimate responsibility was to maximize profits for shareholders. Like the movement of consumer activists that surged in the late 1960s and 1970s, activist entrepreneurs felt they had a political duty to counter corporations' excessive power.[35]

Indeed, many activist entrepreneurs believed that they could create and sustain businesses that were minimally capitalist or even not at all capitalist. Such arguments rested on the simple but far from universal observation that the United States had a mixed economy and that "capitalism," "economic activity," and "business" often overlapped but were not identical phenomena. Businesses and economic activity, after all, had thrived in various parts of the world for centuries before the emergence of merchant capitalism in medieval Asia and Europe. Three of capitalism's central defining features—the private ownership of capital, the employment of wage earners who do not own the means of production, and the accumulation and continued reinvestment of surplus in the pursuit of ever-greater profits—described most, but by no means all, American businesses by the twentieth century.[36]

Like owners of conventional companies, some activist entrepreneurs aspired to maximize their profits and to expand. But other activist businesses operated in spite of capitalism. As worker- or customer-owned businesses, for instance, cooperatives and collectives were at most minimally capitalistic. Many activist businesses measured their success primarily in terms of advancing their movements' political goals, not in terms of financial growth. In so doing, they pioneered a variation of the "stakeholder theory" articulated by business scholars in later decades. This theory held that owners and managers are obligated to balance their financial interests against the interests of employees, customers, and their local communities, even if doing so reduces profits.[37]

Some activist entrepreneurs sought to challenge capitalist imperatives of management ownership and profit maximization by engaging in a process that the sociologist Erik Olin Wright calls "eroding capitalism." Creating enterprises that challenged capitalism while operating within a capitalist-dominated economy was quite difficult. Activists struggled to resolve the differences between political efficacy and business success. Financial survival premised on limited growth was challenging, even more so when coupled with political objectives. Many activist enterprises that resisted conventional capitalism failed to cover their costs and eventually had to shutter their operations. Other companies, such as Whole Foods Market, started with activist goals but eventually discarded those ideals in favor of the traditional capitalist goals of maximizing profits.[38]

Yet other activist businesses staked claims to being noncapitalist by incorporating as nonprofit corporations under 501(c)(3) of the Internal Revenue Code—or, in the case of credit unions, 501(c)(14). These enterprises were legally bound by the rule of "nondistribution constraint" to reinvest any profits back into their organization instead of distributing them to owners or investors for their financial gain. Despite their noncapitalist approach to surplus, nonprofit organizations in the United States have a long history of business activity. For-profit activist businesses meanwhile borrowed practices from nonprofit and social movement work, including bartering, engaging volunteer labor, soliciting donations from community members, and securing grants from foundations.[39]

Co-ops and collectives tended to be either nonprofits or minimally for-profit businesses that distributed the small amount of surplus they earned back to their member-owners. Workers at the Oakland feminist bookstore collective ICI: A Woman's Place, for instance, published a brief how-to guide for aspiring booksellers titled *Starting a Bookstore: Non-capitalist Operation Within a Capitalist Economy*. As the guide explained, the bookstore's workers "served the needs of the community according to ability and personal interest and thereby qualified for a reasonable share [of earnings], small but adequate food, shelter, clothing, but without interest in or ambition toward personal accumulation of wealth and useless possessions."[40]

The central contradiction in activist business was that entrepreneurs who objected to capitalism still had to make money to survive. It was not, as some critics claimed, that these entrepreneurs exploited idealism and faked political engagement in order to commodify dissent and earn great riches. Activist entrepreneurs who criticized capitalism could not totally ignore economic realities if they wanted their enterprises to survive in the long term. Indeed, the greatest threat to activist entrepreneurs was not being co-opted but simply going out of business. Many activist enterprises stayed in business for only a few years, and most of those that emerged in the 1960s and 1970s did not make it to the 1980s.

Yet this impulse to minimize or even eschew profit did not represent a form of economic fatalism. Some activist businesses that pursued modest profits or even mere subsistence managed to survive for decades. Eroding capitalism, it would seem, was difficult although not impossible. Movement veterans understood that the eventual death of their political organizations did not necessarily signal the failure of the larger struggles for which they were fighting. The Populist Party, for instance, failed in its presidential bids in the 1890s but succeeded in popularizing ideas such as the graduated income tax, the eight-hour workday, and direct election of senators—ideas that other parties eventually adopted and made law. Activist entrepreneurs similarly recognized that their businesses might not survive but that their cumulative political and cultural influence could long outlast the enterprises themselves. As Susan Sojourner, an employee at the Washington, D.C., feminist bookstore First Things First explained, "We feminist businesswomen see the work that we do as furthering the movement, spreading the word, servicing the needs of movement women, and changing the idea of new women who don't now identify with the movement. . . . Profit is indeed not our single or primary aim." Although activist entrepreneurs may have been unusual in how they defined business success, their definitions were very much in line with prevailing sociological interpretations of how to measure the effectiveness of social movements. In short, business success might look one way to an economist or corporate manager but an entirely different way to an activist.[41]

Even activist businesses that failed financially deserve the attention of historians of capitalism. If we focus only on the stories of business success, we ignore the lived experiences of the vast majority of small businesses in the United States, more than two-thirds of which do not survive even a decade. The businesses in this book force us to recognize that entrepreneurs are motivated not just by careful financial considerations and market analysis but also by stubbornness, idealism, and even willful defiance of economic practicalities. Triumphalist narratives of small businesses as reliable generators of economic gain and increased equality lose credence when we give failed enterprises their due consideration. If anything, activist businesses remind us that American capitalism is as much a history of failure as a history of success.[42]

For all their potential pitfalls and contradictions, many activist enterprises succeeded in contributing to social movements and political change, provided their customers free spaces, and established democratic workplaces. Few activist entrepreneurs ever thought their work could take the place of the traditional organizing work of social movements. Rather, they saw their businesses as providing these movements with critical assistance in the creation of political change and as operating especially as ideological gateways that could expose nonpoliticized individuals to social movements' values and goals. Many of the people involved with activist businesses remained direct participants in political movements. Natural foods sellers organized to push the federal government to change its environmentally destructive subsidies to corporate agriculture; head shops pushed government to legalize marijuana and other drugs; feminist businesses fought for the Equal Rights Amendment and the equal-credit laws; and black booksellers participated actively in black nationalist organizations such as the National Black Political Assembly. Activist entrepreneurs who had grand, utopian ideas of upending American consumer markets and realigning them with the values of the New Left and the counterculture inevitably fell short of their goals, yet they achieved some modest success at creating alternatives to what they saw as a corporate-controlled marketplace that perpetrated political and social oppression.

Activist entrepreneurs rejected postwar economists' and business leaders' consensus belief that small businesses were outmoded, inefficient, and backward. They instead insisted that their independent storefronts could succeed without significantly growing and scaling up. Their embrace of small business was in part a defiant response to the decline of independent firms in postwar America. As late as 1939, independent stores accounted for more than 75 percent of all retail sales in the United States. But by the end of the 1960s, that share fell to a little more than 50 percent of overall sales and to even lower levels in sales at department stores and variety stores. This decline inspired concerns among a number of progressive and radical American thinkers. Chief among these admirers of small business were C. Wright Mills, who expressed that admiration especially in *White Collar* (1951), and the urbanist Jane Jacobs, who in her book *The Death and Life of Great American Cities* (1961) celebrated independent small businesses as community anchors in Manhattan's neighborhoods. Activist entrepreneurs agreed with Mills and Jacobs that independent businesses afforded Americans a modicum of freedom, community, and authenticity in modern life, especially in cities.[43]

Activist entrepreneurs latched onto small businesses' almost mythical status in the United States as the "backbone of democracy" and gave this status a radical edge. Most activist enterprises of the 1960s and 1970s were small businesses with nine or fewer employees, or what the Small Business Administration refers to as "microbusinesses." Like the Populists of the late nineteenth century and the anti-chain-store movement of the 1920s and 1930s, activist entrepreneurs viewed small businesses as community institutions. But they also considered them vehicles for democratic, participatory economics, allies of a wide range of social movements, and antidotes to the alienating effects of big business and modern consumer culture. What set activist entrepreneurs apart from earlier admirers of small enterprise was their fusion of the small-business ethos with contemporary counterculture and leftist activism.[44]

As the antiwar cause, feminism, Black Power, and the counterculture faded from public awareness in the second half of the 1970s, activist businesses took on an even greater importance in representing their movements. Although most of the media lost interest in these movements, activist entrepreneurs steadily continued to operate. "It is astonishing to learn that such bursts of forward motion are happening," remarked the *New York Times* in 1977 in a profile on the continued success of the feminist publishing house Daughters, Inc., "when the regular news media are filled only with the token advances of a handful of women 'stars' in corporate jobs and politics, or else with elaborate hand-wringing over the 'movement's' death or dismemberment." Numerous observers interpreted a decline in demonstrations, antiwar activity, mass meetings, and rock festivals as signs of the death of New Left social movements and of the counterculture after the early 1970s. Activist businesses' well-being was certainly affected by the setbacks those movements faced. Nonetheless, activist entrepreneurs soldiered on throughout the decade, serving as physical and institutional reminders of those embattled movements' survival. If anything, the businesses discussed in this book demonstrate that these social movements and countercultures in fact extended deep into the 1970s and even beyond.[45]

Although activist businesses and their movements diminished by the 1980s and 1990s, their success is visible in how widespread and unremarkable many of their products and principles have become. Half a century later we can see that activist entrepreneurs' influence has extended far beyond the lives of their enterprises. Indeed, their vision has given rise to ever more widespread demands that businesses serve the goals of social justice and equality, not just financial gain. Activist businesses remain an endangered species in our contemporary marketplace, but they have left an unmistakable mark on our society's debate over businesses' responsibilities to citizens and communities.

2

Liberation Through Literacy

AFRICAN AMERICAN BOOKSTORES, BLACK POWER, AND THE MAINSTREAMING OF BLACK BOOKS

Una Mulzac wanted to make a career for herself in the literary world. It was the early 1960s, and the most common way of breaking into publishing was to secure an entry-level position at a major press in Manhattan. Mulzac found work at Random House as a secretary, but within a few years she became bored with her desk job. Instead of looking for a position with another publisher in New York, Mulzac immigrated to British Guiana in early 1963. There, she joined the People's Progressive Party, an anticolonial group pushing for Guyanese independence led by Cheddi Jagan, an American-educated, ethnic Indian Marxist who had served for three years as the colony's premier. Mulzac's move might have seemed an odd choice for an American woman with career ambitions in publishing in the early 1960s, but it reflected a family history that had long fused professional pursuits with international radicalism and pan-Africanism. Una's father, Hugh Mulzac, was a native of the British Caribbean colony of St. Vincent who had worked on Marcus Garvey's Black Star line and had served as the first African American to command a ship in the U.S. Merchant Marine.[1]

In British Guiana, the younger Mulzac quickly assumed the responsibility of operating the party's Progressive Book Store. As Jagan's supporters struggled for Guyanese independence, political strife and violence between the Progressive Party and the U.S.-backed People's National Congress marred the country. One day in July 1964 a customer left an unmarked package in the store and quickly walked away. When party member and bookstore employee Michael Forde tried to remove the package from the store, a bomb hidden inside it exploded and killed him and fellow party member Edward Griffith. Mulzac was severely wounded and hospitalized for weeks, but she stayed in the country for two more years after recovering. When the People's National Congress took power in the newly independent Guyana in 1966, it denied Mulzac a visa to stay in the country, and she returned to New York City in the spring of 1967, where she promptly opened a bookstore in Harlem.[2]

Mulzac named the shop Liberation Bookstore and operated it as an information center for the Progressive Labor Party, a Marxist–Leninist organization in which Mulzac was an active member. Soon after opening, the party praised the store in its newspaper *Challenge* for answering "a crying need for the revolutionary works from China, Asia, Africa, Latin America and on the Black Liberation struggle here in the U.S." By early 1969, however, Mulzac had veered from the party's Marxist–Leninist line and was increasingly stocking black nationalist and pan-Africanist works. Mulzac eventually seized control of Liberation Bookstore and made it her own business when she changed the locks, in turn prompting her excommunication from the Progressive Labor Party.[3]

Mulzac's bookstore stirred up near endless controversy. Concerned community members discouraged her from naming the store "Liberation," thinking it would invite trouble and confrontation with authorities. Some publishers refused to ship books to Liberation. The Federal Bureau of Investigation (FBI) developed a keen interest in the store. Unfazed, Mulzac quickly turned Liberation into one of the premier institutions for pan-Africanist and black nationalist activists in Harlem. "Have you picked up on 'Wretched of the Earth' by Fanon?" an advertisement for the store asked readers of the Brooklyn black nationalist newspaper *Black News*. A logo for Liberation that appeared in store catalogs and advertisements dramatized Mulzac's unconventional approach to entrepreneurship. It featured an upraised, shackled black hand breaking free from a chain, above which appeared the message, "If you don't know, learn. If you know, teach." As

Mulzac would later explain, the purpose behind her store was "not a matter of sales. It's not a question of bookselling. . . . It's the raising of consciousness."[4]

Mulzac was just one of a cohort of radical African American entrepreneurs in the late 1960s and the 1970s who established bookstores to advance three core principles of the Black Power movement. First and foremost, black booksellers promoted African American political reeducation and knowledge of self through books, pamphlets, and journals on black nationalism and pan-Africanism.[5] Books, activists argued, could empower black Americans to recover their lost heritage and history as proud peoples of the African diaspora. These were the products that distinguished black-owned bookstores as activist businesses. As Maulana Karenga, a leading voice of the Black Power movement and the founder of the US Organization declared, "Nationalism demands study. Show me a true Nationalist and I'll show you someone who studies." A surge of political activism and racial pride provided new opportunities for black entrepreneurs to capitalize on black consumers in search of books on these subjects. Black bookstores lured customers with the era's best-selling Black Power titles, such as *The Autobiography of Malcolm X* (1965) and Eldridge Cleaver's *Soul on Ice* (1968). The vast majority of black bookstores functioned as information centers for the Black Power movement, providing visitors with access to a growing body of writings of and about the movement as well as writings on black culture and history more generally. "To publish our own books and to disseminate them in our own communities is one road toward self determination and self definition," declared the black nationalist writer, publisher, and bookseller Don Lee (later Haki Madhubuti).[6]

Second, black booksellers positioned their stores as a new generation of black public spaces, welcoming a wide range of customers, activists, and curious community members. Like other activist businesses, black booksellers understood their shops as free spaces or sites of liberation and empowerment. At stores such as Liberation, customers talked with storeowners and each other about books, political issues, black culture, and history. Black-owned bookstores provided spaces to a wide range of African Americans, including activist groups wishing to hold meetings and distribute their own locally produced media and flyers, authors and poets who gave public readings, and reading groups that met to discuss books. In short, bookstores functioned as black community centers, not entirely unlike other cherished black businesses such as barber shops and beauty salons. With their decidedly radical and black nationalist bent, however, they represented a new generation of politically oriented public spaces available to African Americans.

Third, many African American booksellers rejected the idea that black businesses' primary goal was to accumulate capital. They argued that black entrepreneurs instead had a responsibility to affirm racial pride, celebrate black history and identity, and promote connections with Africa. These activist retailers unabashedly criticized both capitalism in general and the particular tradition of black business enterprise advocated by Booker T. Washington and the National Negro Business League (NNBL), which they viewed with some justification as an accommodationist form of economic self-help that discouraged radical activism and confrontation of white power.[7] Independent African American booksellers, like the owners of most small bookstores, earned the slimmest of margins, if they profited at all. Most of the entrepreneurs who operated black-interest bookstores were not experienced businesspeople but rather had extensive backgrounds in leftist and black nationalist politics or were teachers or writers or bibliophiles. "Our purpose is not merely to gain capital, but also to enlighten as best we can," one black bookseller in Brooklyn explained. Successful black bookstores enacted Black Power's goals for self-determination by bringing together the movement's campaigns for black politics, black arts, black studies, black community control, and black economic empowerment into the space of a single business. As such, they helped to redefine what black businesses could and should be in the late 1960s and the 1970s.[8]

As late as 1966, most American cities—including major centers of black population such as Atlanta; Washington, D.C.; Oakland, California; and New Orleans—did not have a single black-oriented bookstore. Each of the country's largest cities and centers of black population, such as New York, Philadelphia, Chicago, Detroit, and Los Angeles, could claim one or in some cases two black-interest bookstores, most of which struggled to stay in business. Just a few years later, however, black bookstores were booming. Between 1965 and 1979, the number of black-themed bookstores in the

United States skyrocketed from around a dozen to somewhere between seventy-five and one hundred. Most of these stores were owned and operated by activists with ties to a wide range of black radical groups, including the Black Panther Party, SNCC, the Congress of Afrikan Peoples, the East, the Student Organization for Black Unity, and a variety of lesser-known groups in local communities across the country. Indeed, the very idea that black people needed their own bookstores drew directly on black nationalist values of institutional and community control. Yet compared to other activist business owners, black booksellers had little interest in democratizing the workplace. Few had established their stores as cooperatives or collectives. Black bookstore owners instead focused on making their products and places radical.[9]

Most significantly, African American booksellers in the 1960s and early 1970s regarded their business as a form of black nationalist movement building. Yet as black nationalism declined in the second half of the 1970s and the early 1980s, so did black bookselling. Only at the end of the 1980s did a new wave of black radical writings help black bookstores rebound. To many observers, black-owned bookstores could not survive without the support of a strong black radical movement.

Yet black bookstores received a major boost not only from revived interest in black nationalism but also from the emergence of black-authored romance novels and best-selling love stories with female protagonists. Although these books were not apolitical, they had few direct connections to black radical movements. Not coincidentally, many of the new generation of black booksellers were far less engaged in political activism than their predecessors and favored racial pluralism over black nationalism. Most black booksellers decided they could not survive if they focused solely on texts by black activists without championing the ever-growing body of popular black fiction. Meanwhile, large chains such as Barnes & Noble and Borders became increasingly interested in selling black-authored works in the second half of the 1990s, as did new online booksellers such as Amazon. Black-authored books, once the essential product of African American bookstores, were no longer the preserve of activist businesses. And in a sad irony, white booksellers' enhanced interest in selling black-authored works combined with new structural challenges to independent booksellers to drastically reduce black bookstores' sales by the end of the twentieth century. Black-authored books had earned belated acceptance from white publishers and readers. In the process, however, black book-sellers lost their role as the leading gatekeepers to the black literary mar-ketplace, and in order to survive they found themselves forced to shift away from their tradition of activist business.

AFRICAN AMERICAN BUSINESSES AND BOOKSELLING BEFORE THE 1960s

The famed New York abolitionist David Ruggles is widely credited as the first African American to own and operate a bookstore. In the 1830s, Rug-gles's Manhattan store briefly sold works of the abolitionist movement as well as general works by black writers. A tiny handful of short-lived black-owned bookstores opened around the country in the late nineteenth and early twentieth centuries. These stores, however, struggled to stay in busi-ness, and few, if any, operated for more than several years. In fact, success-ful African American booksellers rarely operated brick-and-mortar stores but chose instead to distribute their books through churches and fraternal organizations, by mail—as both the National Association for the Advance-ment of Colored People and the historian J. A. Rogers did—or through teams of traveling salesmen, as the historian Carter G. Woodson did.[10]

The first African American to enjoy a lengthy and nationally prominent career as a bookstore owner was Lewis Michaux. When Michaux arrived in Harlem from Newport News, Virginia, in the early 1930s, he brought with him a bust of Booker T. Washington and a single copy of Washing-ton's autobiography, *Up from Slavery*. Around 1932, Michaux began to sell books out of the back of a wagon on the corner of Seventh Avenue and 125th Street in Harlem. About a year later, with a collection of five books, including Washington's autobiography, he opened the National Memorial African Bookstore on the same corner. The brother of the famous preacher Elder Lightfoot Solomon Michaux, Lewis preferred bookselling to previ-ous jobs, including serving as a deacon in his brother's church and digging ditches. As Michaux would later recall, in the early 1930s there were no black-themed or black-authored "books to be had except for old copies of

Washington, Carver, Tubman, and Truth. . . . There was no market for the books, and publishers didn't publish them and didn't accept manuscripts." Harlemites were initially skeptical of Michaux, who repeatedly recounted the story of one man who remarked with disbelief, "Your brother's in DC singing 'Happy I Am' [Elder Michaux's chart-topping religious record] and you're in Harlem trying to sell a nigger a book." The store's daily receipts often totaled only 75 cents or $1 in its early years of operation (equivalent to around $20 in 2016).[11]

Over the course of two decades, however, Michaux's store gradually began to attract black shoppers. A hodgepodge of Communists, labor activists, social democrats, and black nationalists (including Michaux himself) delivered impassioned speeches in front of the store, drawing curious onlookers and prompting Harlemites to dub it Speakers' Corner. But Michaux and his books were major draws, too. Long after Marcus Garvey had been deported from the United States, Michaux remained a United Negro Improvement Association member who helped to keep the Jamaican leader's vision alive in Harlem with unapologetic celebrations of black culture and history and full-throated denunciations of white supremacy and the white power structure. Along with his hard-to-find books on black topics, Michaux's stock in trade was an unrelenting passion for glorifying black people and denouncing white racism (figure 2.1).

By the early 1950s, the National Memorial African Bookstore had earned a reputation as the best and biggest black-interest bookstore in America. In a column for the *Chicago Defender* in 1953, Langston Hughes praised Michaux's store for having "probably the biggest stock of published materials by and about Negroes in America." Michaux had also become a local celebrity in Harlem as one of the neighborhood's most cantankerous and eccentric agitators, an inveterate storyteller with a strange, unforgettable voice. A sign on the front of Michaux's store declared it to be "The House of Common Sense and Home of Proper Propaganda." Michaux was an early proponent of African independence and led an organization called "African Nationalists in America." Although fiercely proud of his race, Michaux nonetheless commonly resorted to sarcasm and ridicule in assessing the affairs of African Americans. "If you want to hide something from a Negro," Michaux is said to have exclaimed, "put it in a book."[12]

FIGURE 2.1 Lewis Michaux in the National Memorial African Bookstore, early 1970s. Courtesy of Photographs and Prints Division, Schomburg Center for Research in Black Culture, New York Public Library, Astor, Lenox and Tilden Foundations

Beyond two more stores that operated in Harlem, few black-interest bookstores operated in the United States before the 1960s. Rare examples included one in Washington, D.C., near Howard University and two founded in Los Angeles in the 1940s.[13] As the famed black writer and historian J. A. Rogers lamented in 1961, "For a people of twenty million . . . there are pitiably few Negro bookstores." Rogers, if anyone, would have known. From 1917 to 1965, he penned nearly two dozen books on the history of people of African descent, and his fame as an African American historian in the middle of the twentieth century was matched only by that of Carter G. Woodson and W. E. B. Du Bois. With titles such as *Sex and Race, World's Greatest Men and Women of African Descent*, and *From "Superman" to Man*, Rogers's works sold briskly and made him a literary celebrity in African American communities.[14] Yet white-owned bookstores and presses virtually ignored his books and other works by black authors, save for titles by a few literary giants such as Langston Hughes, Ralph Ellison, Richard Wright, and James Baldwin. Because so few stores stocked his works, Rogers founded his own press and sold his books by mail order directly to readers.[15]

The few black bookstores in operation did not promote themselves as black radical spaces. Even booksellers such as Michaux, himself an ardent believer in black nationalism, sold few works on nationalist or radical ideology in the 1940s. Michaux instead mostly sold popular literature by black authors such as Chester Himes and Frank Yerby and titles on "negro history" and "great men of color" by historians such as Rogers and Woodson that fit into a longer tradition of black uplift. "Books on the Negro, like almost everything about him in American life, take a back seat," Rogers declared in the *Pittsburgh Courier* in 1961. "Go to almost any bookstore in any city and you will see the truth of this."[16]

Booming demand for books transformed the literary marketplace after World War II. Between 1952 and 1962, the number of printed titles in the United States nearly doubled from more than eleven thousand to almost twenty-two thousand. Purchases skyrocketed. Between 1963 and 1971 alone, national sales of books jumped from $1.7 billion to $3.1 billion, an increase of 83 percent. The massive expansion of secondary and higher education and increasing rates of student enrollment at both levels drove growing institutional purchases. African Americans' median income also dramatically increased in these years, growing by more than 140 percent between 1947 and 1960 and giving black consumers much more to spend on discretionary purchases such as books. The growing popularity of a new type of book, the paperback, also helped to drive the demand for books, too. Demand for the cheaper soft-cover editions that had debuted in the late 1930s increased dramatically. Once an afterthought to publishers, these cheaper alternatives to hard covers would represent a majority of book sales by 1971. Although bookselling never became easy, the increased demand for books as well as the growing popularity of black nationalism and a reappraisal of the purpose of African American business would make operating a bookstore more enticing to black entrepreneurs by the start of the 1960s.[17]

BLACK POWER RETHINKS BLACK BUSINESS

African Americans have long celebrated black-owned enterprises as vehicles for economic and social progress. The individual most responsible for promoting a vision of black progress through business in the first half of the twentieth century was Booker T. Washington. "No race that has anything to contribute to the markets of the world is long in any degree ostracized," Washington declared in his famous speech at the Atlanta Cotton States and International Exposition in 1895—but only if they accepted "that the agitation of questions of social equality is the extremest folly." The NNBL, which Washington founded in 1900, embraced this view of enterprise, not political agitation, as the primary tool for black progress. Washington's network of African American business owners articulated a politically and socially conservative vision of racial uplift that has profoundly influenced black entrepreneurship ever since. Although the NNBL promoted economic self-help as a vehicle for achieving racial equality, its leaders shied away from confronting white supremacy. Washington insisted that members avoid addressing politics altogether at the organization's inaugural national meeting. In another incident in 1943, the NNBL's president rejected a member resolution condemning lynching.[18]

Of course, not all entrepreneurs in black communities were politically cautious or conservative. Marcus Garvey and the United Negro Improvement Association established millinery stores, groceries, and doll factories in the 1920s, and the Nation of Islam operated restaurants, laundries, bakeries, and supermarkets from the 1940s onward. But these two organizations were uncritical toward capitalism in their strong emphasis on profit making as a key to black autonomy. They also discouraged direct confrontation with white authorities and instead emphasized racial separatism and disengagement from whites, and they even met with white-supremacist organizations. To be sure, some black entrepreneurs worked directly with the civil rights movement in the 1950s and 1960s. Yet many prominent black business leaders, including those at the helm of the NNBL, followed in Washington's footsteps by insisting that black business leaders eschew direct action and not publicly challenge white supremacy but instead quietly work with white leaders for modest concessions.[19]

By the 1950s, some black critics began to castigate black entrepreneurs for favoring political caution over public activism. The African American sociologist E. Franklin Frazier argued in his seminal work *The Black Bourgeoisie* (published in French in 1955 and in English in 1957) that black businesses represented social responsibility and status to the black middle class but did not agitate for meaningful social change. Frazier had embraced cooperatives over individual proprietorships as tools for black progress in the 1920s and had strongly criticized capitalism in the 1930s. By the 1940s, he endorsed a left-leaning social democratic politics that prized trade unions and energetic regulators that regularly intervened in the economy. With his publication of *The Black Bourgeoisie*, Frazier denounced what he called the "myth of black business" or the mistaken notion that entrepreneurship alone could secure political equality for African Americans.[20]

Frazier's arguments would deeply influence the new generation of black nationalist and radical thinkers that emerged in the 1960s and became known as the Black Power movement. Black Panther cofounder Bobby Seale recalled meeting Huey Newton for the first time when Newton was speaking to a crowd outside Merritt Community College in Oakland. When an onlooker in the crowd challenged an argument Newton was making about capitalism, Newton "whipped out a copy of *Black Bourgeoisie* by E. Franklin Frazier and showed him what page, what paragraph [the argument came from] and corrected the person." Other black radicals such as Earl Ofari Hutchinson and James Boggs penned critiques of "the myth of black capitalism" that bore Frazier's clear influence.[21]

Black Power activists charged that much of African American business culture exploited and demeaned black people. As evidence, they pointed to products that downplayed or renounced black identity, such as hair straighteners and skin bleaches—big sellers for African American cosmetic businesses prior to the 1960s. The Brooklyn-based periodical *Black News*, one of the leading black nationalist publications in America, announced in its inaugural issue in 1969 a policy of rejecting advertisements that were seen as degrading to blacks. "We're choosey about ads. If they don't satisfy Black dignity, they don't satisfy *Black News*. Therefore we forward all peddlers of bleach creams, goofy dust, and wigs to the *Amsterdam* [*News*]," New York's most widely read African American newspaper.[22]

Despite such critiques of black entrepreneurs as accommodationist and self-degrading, business carried some positive meanings for a number of Black Power activists. "The business of black power" included everything from entrepreneurial undertakings by independent black nationalist organizations to community-development corporations in black neighbor-hoods to *Essence* magazine to federally funded business initiatives aimed at African American communities. Political opportunists—most promi-nently Richard Nixon—reworked Booker T. Washington's philosophy into federal backing of "black capitalism," as seen in his establishment of the Office of Minority Business Enterprise in 1969. Floyd McKissick and Roy Innis, prominent advocates of Black Power who served as national chairmen of the Congress of Racial Equality, uncritically embraced Nixon's view that business was a critical source of political power and economic self-sufficiency for African Americans.[23]

A new generation of businesses sought to create an alternative black business and consumer culture that reflected the deep influence of the Black Power movement. "Anyone who walks along 125th Street in Harlem today may be impressed by the marked changes from the Harlem street of yester-day," a reporter wrote for the *Amsterdam News* in 1972. "Black owned clothing stores, record shops, bookstores, African bazaars, and other cul-tural happenings now indicate a new pride and self-determination in the black community. . . . These changes in the face of Harlem and other simi-lar communities are largely the result of a black revolution of the mind, begun less than a decade ago." As a member of Maulana Karenga's cultural nationalist US Organization in Los Angeles explained, "Maulana gave me an alternative to this white system. . . . Now I don't have to wear some shark skin suit I had to buy from a Jew, I can wear my Buba," a West African body wrap. Anti-Semitic sentiments notwithstanding, this US member was describing an actual exodus of white ethnic, in particular Jewish, entre-preneurs from predominantly black neighborhoods in cities across the coun-try and a concomitant growth in black, African-themed retailers in these years. *Black News* carried advertisements for numerous stores in New York specializing in black books and African goods, with names such as "Free-dom Bookstore," "Woody's Record & Variety Afro Shop," "Black Fox," "Nyabinghi's African Gift Shop," and "Liberation Bookstore."[24]

This radical vision of African American business centered on "community control," the idea that black-controlled spaces and organizations were inte-gral to African American self-determination and Black Power. Support for this idea stemmed from black communities' renewed optimism in building their own institutions as well as from growing discontent with state-sponsored integration schemes of the 1960s. Black Americans should not struggle to win whites' acceptance and admission to their institutions and their society, Black Power activists argued, but instead should focus on strengthening black communities. Support for "buying black" was quite strong among African American consumers. A fifteen-city survey in 1968 revealed that 70 percent of blacks "felt that Negroes should patronize Negro-owned stores whenever possible."[25]

Black radicals particularly valued African American parallel institutions and "dual power" as concrete forms of black self-determination. Activists saw opportunities for these institutions in predominantly black inner cities and urban neighborhoods grappling with dramatic reductions in social services and urban federal funding after the election of Richard Nixon to the White House. Black-controlled spaces offered black citizens more power over their lives in the form of intellectual and political independence from whites. For most black nationalists, the idea of an independent black nation functioned more as a metaphor than as an attainable goal. Yet constructing a network of black-controlled, radical institutions across the country—be they schools, breakfast programs, health clinics, performing-arts centers, bookstores, or other businesses—offered a tangible alternative to national sovereignty.[26]

In embracing community control and a radical black business ethos, many activists and entrepreneurs invoked the concept of *ujamaa*. Originally a Kiswahili word for extended family or kinship, *ujamaa* was rearticulated by Tanzanian president Julius Nyerere in his pioneering essay "Ujamaa—the Basis of African Socialism" (1962). For Nyerere, *ujamaa* represented a form of cooperative economics firmly based in African communal values and kinship traditions, a form of "communitarian socialism." By the late 1960s, Black Power activists were endorsing *ujamaa* as a critical strategy for liberation, and black bookstores sold works by and about Nyerere. Maulana Karenga designated *ujamaa* as one of the Nguzo Saba, or the seven key principles of the winter pan-Africanist holiday Kwanzaa. *Ujamaa*, a black bookseller in Atlanta contended, was an effort to "unite the black community and to offset the commercialization of white Christmas." In Harlem, a group of local merchants including Mulzac and Michaux organized themselves into the African Trade Show Association and organized the Ujamaa Ritual, an event to highlight black artists and to "unify and educate the untapped Black economic resources within our community." Numerous African-themed businesses named themselves some variation of *ujamaa*, including the Ujamaa Kitabu bookstore in Washington, D.C., and Nyumba ya Ujamaa, a "house of cooperative economics" in Newark, New Jersey, selling books and clothing and operated by Amiri Baraka's Committee for a Unified Newark. Taken altogether, *ujamaa* offered Black Power entrepreneurs a powerful alternative concept to traditional African American businesses' profit motives and an ideological framework for low-profit or even nonprofit business operations that provided black community members tools for collective liberation and self-determination.[27]

Black Power entrepreneurs hawked a wide array of products claiming to bolster black pride, including dashikis, Afro-Sheen, and posters and T-shirts emblazoned with slogans of black empowerment. Like activist businesses and other companies purporting to sell political products, the fledgling "black is beautiful" market faced questions from critics as to whether it was driven by a desire for social change or rather by insincere entrepreneurs eager to profit from newly popular political attitudes. White-owned cosmetic companies aggressively sought to capitalize on the growing interest in black "natural" hair products. Some black-owned companies that had long championed skin lighteners and accessories for hair processes even began to promote race-affirming beauty products by the late 1960s. A writer for the *Baltimore Afro-American* welcomed efforts such as those by the Center for Black Education, a pan-Africanist independent university in Washington, D.C., because it sought to "change the emphasis from that which is seen, such as Afros and dashikis, to that which is necessary, such as living and working with black people to achieve our goal of liberation." Such critics recognized that not all businesses claiming to advance black pride were created equal. Black Power activists remained skeptical of many efforts by companies to cash in on the growing popularity of their movement. Yet by the end of the 1960s black nationalists across the country would come to regard bookselling as a legitimate and even critical business activity for advancing their movement's goals and ideology.[28]

Black Bookstores in the Early Black Power Movement

Prior to the latter part of the 1960s, when Black Power enjoyed a high profile, Michaux's National African Memorial Bookstore was one of the few prominent retail businesses in the country to align itself with black nationalism (figure 2.2). Due to the growing visibility of the Nation of Islam and especially Malcolm X in the early 1960s, the movement was gradually rebounding from its doldrums of the previous two decades. In the journal *Freedomways* in 1961, pan-Africanist writer and black studies pioneer John Henrik Clarke described Michaux's bookstore as "the main gathering place for Harlem nationalists," and the *Baltimore Afro-American*

FIGURE 2.2 Lewis Michaux's National Memorial African Bookstore, early 1970s. Courtesy of Photographs and Prints Division, Schomburg Center for Research in Black Culture, New York Public Library, Astor, Lenox and Tilden Foundations

characterized the store's backroom as "an unofficial headquarters for Malcolm X," a close friend of the bookseller. Michaux bridged the divide between the older generation of Garveyite black nationalists who had come of age in the 1920s and 1930s and a small but growing movement of younger black nationalist activists, especially those pushing for African independence. Michaux's relationship to Malcolm, who regularly held mass rallies in front of the bookstore and was wildly popular in Harlem, was particularly important for burnishing his own credentials as a leading black nationalist in New York.[29]

Beyond Harlem, activists were just beginning to explore bookselling's power as a tool for advancing black nationalism in the mid-1960s. One such person was Edward Vaughn, an Alabama-born postal worker in Detroit. When Vaughn brought a copy of Ralph Ginzburg's book *100 Years of Lynching* to the post office where he worked and showed it to coworkers, many of them expressed interest in buying their own copies. Vaughn could not find Ginzburg's compilation of historic news reports on antiblack vigilante violence at any of Detroit's downtown bookstores, so he contacted the publisher, which gladly sold Vaughn around a dozen boxes of the title. Vaughn began selling the book to friends and colleagues out of the trunk of his car and soon added other titles. By the end of 1963, Vaughn had opened Vaughn's Book Store on Detroit's West Side (figure 2.3).[30]

Vaughn soon emerged as a leader in Detroit's small but growing black nationalist community, and radical activists began to congregate at his store. "There was sort of an awakening in the community from New York," Vaughn recalled. "We were hearing about things happening" in Harlem's black nationalist circles through publications such as *Freedomways* and *Liberator*. In 1965, Vaughn hosted an event called Forum '65 in his store, followed the next two years by Forum '66 and Forum '67. They were semiweekly gatherings where community members "would speak about the problems in the black community and what we could do to solve the problems." Speakers included Detroit black nationalists such as Garveyite and Nation of Islam apostate "Papa" Henry Wells, founding Detroit member of the African Nationalist Pioneer Movement Austin Chavou, and the pan-Africanist and later émigré to Ghana Paa Kwame (Leroy Mitchell). More and more, Vaughn's Book Store became "oriented toward the people who already

FIGURE 2.3   Edward Vaughn, early 1970s. Courtesy of Edward Vaughn

were Pan-Africanists and Nationalists or people who were on the left, in the movement." Looking back at this period years later, Detroit radical activist Grace Lee Boggs would remark that Detroit had four Black Power leaders in the 1960s: the Reverend Albert Cleage of the Shrine of the Black Madonna church; the brothers Milton Henry and Richard B. Henry (Imari Obadele), best known as the founders of the New Republik of Africa; and Vaughn.[31]

Vaughn's prominent role in Detroit's black nationalist movement put him immediately under the suspicion of white leaders when violence erupted in the city on July 23, 1967. Vaughn was at the national Black Power Conference in Newark when he heard news of the uprising (Newark itself had just seen a six-day uprising triggered by the arrest and beating of a black cab driver by police). On his drive back from Newark, Vaughn was briefly detained by law enforcement in two different states. When he finally returned to his store, he saw that it had been graffitied with the phrase "Long Live the African Revolution" but was otherwise undamaged. It wouldn't stay so for long.[32]

Vaughn viewed the rebellion as an opportunity to engage Detroit's white leaders in a discussion on how to fundamentally restructure race relations in the city. Soon after returning to Detroit, he composed a telegram on behalf of the Henry brothers' Malcolm X Society, which Reverend Cleage transmitted to Michigan governor George Romney and Detroit mayor Jerome Cavanaugh. In the telegram, Vaughn promised to persuade black citizens to halt the uprising in exchange for eight demands, including the release of all prisoners from the riots, "amnesty to all insurrectionists [and] . . . funds for community businesses." No elected officials responded, but city police visited Vaughn's store a few days later. According to Vaughn, the officers first tried to firebomb the store but failed to burn it down. The next day more officers broke into the store, where they ripped books and shelves from the wall, destroyed pictures of Stokely Carmichael, Malcolm X, and a black Christ, and flooded the business by leaving the faucet running over a clogged sink. Most of the store's inventory was ruined.

Some local whites seemed to believe that Vaughn and other radical activists had orchestrated the uprising—and at least one prominent black observer agreed. Louis Lomax, the African American journalist and strident critic of black nationalism, insinuated in a syndicated newspaper article that Vaughn and five other "members of the strangest black power amalgam in the U.S." (including Cleage, James Boggs, and Grace Lee Boggs) had instigated the riots. Black booksellers were accused of fomenting civil disobedience in other cities, too. The Communist-connected and black-owned Hugh Gordon Book Store in Los Angeles was discussed in hearings held by the House Un-American Activities Committee as a likely influence on the Watts riots of 1965. And in the same month as the Newark and Detroit uprisings, the black bookseller Martin Sostre was arrested for inciting riots in Buffalo. Yet no evidence that booksellers started uprisings in any of these cities ever emerged.[33]

Nevertheless, Black Power and black bookselling were becoming increasingly intertwined. In California, the newly founded Black Panther Party turned to bookselling for fund-raising in 1967. As Bobby Seale recalled, the Panthers bought sixty copies of Mao's so-called Red Book at 30 cents apiece from a Chinese shop in San Francisco, took them to Berkeley, and "sold them motherfuckers at Cal campus some Red Books. We sold the Red Books inside of an hour, at a dollar apiece and that shocked us." The next day they bought the Chinese store's remaining inventory of the Red Book and sold it for a two-day total of profit of $170, enough "to get some shotguns" that the Panthers vowed to defend themselves with if whites threatened their safety. Although known for attacking capitalism in party writings, the Panthers were also skilled literary entrepreneurs. Party members' sales of the *Black Panther* newspaper—which at one point totaled more than 139,000 copies a week—were the party's most important tool for recruitment and fund-raising. Local Panther headquarters sold the party newspaper as well as books and pamphlets written by party members.[34]

For many Black Power activists, reading works by black authors represented a fundamental step in political awakening, a central prerequisite of the intellectual and ideological transformation from Negro accommodationism to radical Black Power. As Maulana Karenga exclaimed, "Nationalism demands study. Show me a true Nationalist and I'll show you someone who studies." By the same token, blacks who did not read about their history or culture hindered the cause of racial progress. "The 'Negro' has more records than books and is dancing his life away," Karenga declared with deep regret. If reading provided black people a critical path to liberation, then booksellers were poised to be among African Americans' most important pathfinders.[35]

The rise of Black Power reflected African Americans' growing interest in their history and culture in the last third of the 1960s. The flowering of the Black Arts movement stands as the most prominent expression of this burgeoning demand for reviving black culture and African heritage. Black Arts activity flourished at historically black colleges and in cities all over the country through public readings, book groups, black theaters, and writers' workshops and conferences. In particular, a new generation of African American poets—including Amiri Baraka, Sonia Sanchez, Haki Madhubuti, Nikki Giovanni, and Maya Angelou (figure 2.4)—found great critical and commercial success in these years. Although many people "define

FIGURE 2.4 Maya Angelou book signing, Uhuru Bookstore, Greensboro, North Carolina, ca. late 1970s. Photographs by Lewis A. Brandon III

Black Arts as the cultural wing of the Black Power Movement," as James Smethurst argues in his groundbreaking study of the movement, "one could just as easily say that Black Power was the political wing of the Black Arts Movement."[36]

Black-owned publishing thrived in the last third of the 1960s as the demand for black arts, black poetry in particular, exploded. A range of magazines and journals celebrated the Black Arts movement, most prominent among them Johnson Publishing Company's *Negro Digest* magazine, which in May 1970 became *Black World*. Before 1960, a miniscule number of presses were owned by African Americans or published extensively on African American topics. From 1960 to 1974, however, African Americans founded twenty-three presses. From 1960 to 1964, black presses published only 51 books, but ten years later, from 1970 to 1974, they published 240 books, more than four times as many.[37]

In the Midwest, a pair of critically important black publishers emerged within two years. In Detroit, librarian and poet Dudley Randall founded Broadside Press in 1965 with the publication of "Ballad of Birmingham," a single-page poem dedicated to the young girls who died in the bombing of the Sixteenth Street Baptist Church in 1963. In 1967, Haki Madhubuti joined with Johari Amini and Carolyn Rodgers to establish Third World Press on Chicago's South Side. Both Randall and Madhubuti had studied literature and enjoyed extensive connections with black radical activists. Madhubuti also founded the journal *Black Books Bulletin* and operated a printing press and bookstore, the African American Book Center. Despite these commercial moves, Randall saw presses such as Broadside as producing books "for use instead of for profit." Like their colleagues in bookstores, black publishers prioritized political and social objectives over financial gain. Nonetheless, black-owned presses' growth in the late 1960s made it clear that the marketplace for black books was expanding amid rising interest in the Black Power and Black Arts movements.[38]

Black Bookstores at the High Tide of Black Power

"A surge of book-buying is sweeping through black communities across the country," exclaimed Earl Caldwell, the *New York Times*'s senior African American reporter, in a feature on black-owned bookstores in August 1969. By the end of the decade, roughly three dozen black-interest bookstores were operating across America, and many of the roughly dozen pioneering black bookstores that had operated at the start of the 1960s began to enjoy their first taste of sustained financial stability. Dawud Hakim, who launched a small bookstore in West Philadelphia in 1961, would recall that his store first moved out of its "lean period" around 1967 or 1968. In south-central Los Angeles, Alfred and Bernice Ligon's Aquarian Book Center became "a hub for a lot of the cultural activity in their community," a change that Alfred attributed to the Watts rebellion of 1965. "After the uprisings . . . the Negroes were gone then. Everyone turned black. The interest in the black field soared. People began to wake up." Ed Vaughn remembered that his business in Detroit "really boomed" after the riots in 1967 due both to changing political attitudes and to the countless donations of books the store received after *Publisher's Weekly* reported on how police had destroyed much of the store. "You know, times are changing," remarked Jim Gray, an African American bookseller in San Francisco's Fillmore District in 1969.

"Three years ago nobody around here would even steal a book. Now look, they buy books."[39]

In the late 1960s and early 1970s, black nationalist bookstores opened for the first time in such cities as Atlanta, Baltimore, Denver, Portland, Boston, and Kansas City, and additional stores opened in major cities such as New York, Chicago, and Los Angeles. Perhaps the most significant black bookstore to open in these years was Drum and Spear in Washington, D.C., launched by several SNCC members.

SNCC had made a name for itself as the premier student civil rights organization in the first half of the 1960s with multiracial campaigns to integrate transportation and voting rolls in the Deep South. By 1964, the organization's members were also championing black institutions such as the Mississippi Freedom Schools and the Mississippi Freedom Democratic Party during the so-called Freedom Summer of 1964. In 1966, SNCC chairman Stokely Carmichael penned "Toward Black Liberation," a treatise calling for the group to radically change both its strategies and its geographical focus. SNCC would now seek "to return to the ghetto to organize these communities to control themselves." This was a call to shift movement work from southern rural areas to cities, in particular cities outside the South with majority or near-majority black populations. Carmichael urged black activists to reorient themselves to "organizing and developing institutions of community power in the Negro community." By the end of 1966, a narrow majority of SNCC members voted to ask whites to leave the organization and work against racism in white communities, in effect making the group's transition to Black Power complete.[40]

SNCC veterans in Washington, D.C., developed a variety of programs aimed at the city's black citizens. Carmichael launched the Black United Front, an organization with the stated goal of enlisting "every black Washingtonian in one or another activist or civic organization," and SNCC's first president and future D.C. mayor Marion Barry founded Pride, Inc., a summer jobs program for D.C.'s youth. Charles Cobb, a D.C. native who proposed the idea for SNCC's Freedom Schools in Mississippi in 1964, came up with an altogether different black institution. He began by establishing a nonprofit foundation called Afro-American Resources, Inc. Grants from the Episcopal Church and the United Church of Christ's Commission for Racial Justice (which happened to be led by Cobb's father, a United Church minister) provided the start-up funds for Afro American Resources to establish the Drum and Spear Bookstore.[41]

The spring of 1968 was not the most auspicious time to open a retail business in Washington, D.C. A massive uprising had devastated the city in the wake of Martin Luther King Jr.'s assassination on April 4. Drum and Spear's planned storefront sat in the heart of the black business district in the Columbia Heights neighborhood, blocks from the epicenter of the rebellion. Police were still "lobbing tear gas up and down 14th Street" as the store's staff was preparing the location's opening only a few weeks after the uprising. One day fumes seeped into the business and soaked the books, leaving them reeking of tear gas for days. But none of this stopped a group of SNCC veterans and D.C. transplants, including Courtland Cox, Judy Richardson, Jennifer Lawson, and Curtis Hayes, from teaming up with Cobb to launch Drum and Spear. Local Washington activists such as Tony Gittens, Anne Forrester, and Daphne Muse, several of whom also had worked with SNCC, soon joined them. For these fledgling booksellers and many other black Washingtonians, the uprising had demonstrated the city's potential for rebirth and revival through increased control of community institutions. The name "Drum and Spear" invoked the bookstore founders' two primary objectives: the drum symbolized "communications within the diaspora," according to Judy Richardson, and the spear provocatively suggested "whatever else might be necessary for the liberation of the people."[42]

Drum and Spear's staffers hoped their store could bring together black Washingtonians of all educational and class backgrounds in their shared pursuit of literature on black liberation. Its staff sought to provoke "intellectual curiosity and dialogue . . . [among] regular folks . . . who might not be used to reading" about African American history and politics. Drum and Spear was located in the heart of a working-class black neighborhood to reach the broadest cross-section of African Americans possible, not in downtown D.C. or even near Howard University, a longtime bastion of the black middle class. The store's staff hoped ultimately "to get certain kinds of materials out to regular people . . . in the black community in Washington DC." Although the shop was neither a co-op nor a collective, its status as an arm of the nonprofit Afro-American Resources, Inc., made it an unconventional business. As an African American enterprise that eschewed financial gain, Drum and Spear directly contradicted the Washingtonian vision of black economic empowerment through entrepreneurship.[43]

Even though it was part of a nonprofit organization, Drum and Spear was remarkably ambitious in expanding its mission beyond storefront retail. The company also produced a mail-order catalog to sell books to customers across the country. At the time, many black booksellers had difficulties finding titles that addressed black themes because there was no go-to distributor for black books. But Drum and Spear's staff developed a close relationship with a black employee at the major book wholesaler Bookazine in Manhattan, a self-taught expert on black publications who was determined to help stores stock black-interest titles. Drum and Spear soon began its own wholesaling operation, distributing black-interest books to other stores and helping to create an informal national network of black booksellers. The number of books it stocked far outnumbered what black-interest bookstores in other cities handled. The store's catalog in 1971, for instance, numbered 233 pages, three to four times larger than other prominent black booksellers' catalogs (figure 2.5). Drum and Spear's selection of roughly ten thousand volumes, although modest compared to the selection offered by major white booksellers in Washington, D.C., was likely the largest for any black bookstore in the country.[44]

A number of African American booksellers, including Drum and Spear, published their own books and pamphlets. Drum and Spear founded its own press and reprinted the Trinidadian Marxist scholar C. L. R. James's book *A History of Negro Revolt* (1938; retitled *A History of Pan-African Revolt*) and published original works such as *The African Book of Names* and *Children of Africa: A Coloring Book*. The press had locations in Washington, D.C., and Dar-es-Salaam, Tanzania, where staffers Charlie Cobb and Courtland Cox had developed a close relationship with officials in the government of Julius Nyerere on visits to the country. Julian Richardson of Marcus Books in San Francisco republished *The Philosophy and Opinions*

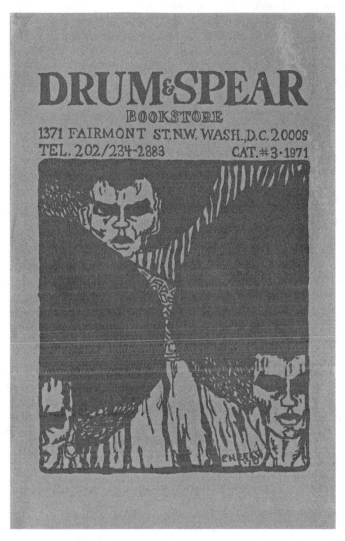

FIGURE 2.5 *Drum and Spear Bookstore* (catalog 3) (Washington, D.C.: Drum & Spear, 1971). Courtesy of Stuart A. Rose Manuscript, Archives, and Rare Book Library, Emory Library. By arrangement with Drum and Spear/Afro American Resources, INC.

of Marcus Garvey, the seminal work of black nationalism published in 1923 that had languished out of print for decades. "Blacks have to unlearn lies, grasp their roots, make informed choices," Richardson argued in an interview in 1975: "When I published an edition of *Philosophy and Opinions of Marcus Garvey* in 1967, my intention was to help speed up the process."

Prior to his death in 2000, Richardson would publish more than twenty books on a wide variety of topics pertaining to African Americans. Edward Vaughn authored and printed short books, including one titled *Red, Black, and Green: The History and Meaning of the Black Liberation Flag*.[45]

By presenting themselves as political actors first and entrepreneurs second, black booksellers embraced a vision of activist entrepreneurship that inverted the traditional operating logic of black capitalism. For years, advocates of black business had declared that the economic gains of entrepreneurship were a vital prerequisite for blacks' gaining freedom in America. Many black booksellers, by contrast, understood their retail operations as political vehicles for protesting, raising racial consciousness, and directly confronting white supremacy and institutional racism. "I'd rather rap about black roots and uprootedness," Julian Richardson explained, "than sell you a book. Of course, I'd like you to buy a few books, too. But since I decided early it wasn't worth trying to be wealthy, I can afford to be honest." Charlie Cobb explained Drum and Spear's mission in similar terms: "We don't define profit in terms of money. The profit is the patronage of the community, which allows the store to self-support . . . [and] to engage in communication and education." Drum and Spear frequently donated instead of selling books to political organizations it supported. In Baltimore, Paul Coates, the defense captain of the local chapter of the Black Panther Party (and father of writer Ta-Nehisi Coates) opened a bookstore called the Black Book in 1972. "It never occurred to me that it was a business," Coates explained years later. "I thought we were engaged in a political movement. And the books . . . were bullets that we fired at the enemy and we fired at the brains of people who needed information to liberate themselves." As Edward Vaughn and co-owner Polly Rawls declared in their store's catalog, "The Black revolution today is world wide and will continue until the dignity of Man is realized. We feel we are contributing in a small way to that revolution." The primary benefit of black bookstores, their owners insisted, was the intellectual, political, and cultural liberation they offered black citizens. As resolute activist entrepreneurs, black booksellers recognized the need to stay solvent, but they generally devoted more time and energy to their ideological efficacy than to than their financial stability.[46]

Unlike most African American business owners, black booksellers harbored considerable skepticism toward profit making. In fact, many black booksellers were quite sympathetic toward Marxist ideology. Black bookstores stocked numerous Communist and socialist texts. Vaughn's catalog devoted an entire section to "writings of Mao Tse-Tung in English." Liberation Bookstore offered a selection of Chinese "revolutionary novels." Drum and Spear organized Marxist writings into a Third World section. Black booksellers questioned the capitalist profit motive that most entrepreneurs accepted without question. In so doing, they joined a longer tradition of leftist literary entrepreneurs who embraced Marxism even as they sought to remain financially stable. These businesses did not oppose every form of profit per se but rather capitalist strategies of aggressively pursuing growth by maximizing profits. Practically speaking, black booksellers rarely found themselves forced to choose between their Marxist leanings and the lure of large profits. Most of them were small stores that struggled to make a profit. In one study done in 1966, only 37 percent of bookstores with annual sales of $50,000 or less—a category most black bookstores fell into—actually made a profit. In 1973, Bank of America estimated that stores with similarly modest sales averaged a net profit of just 1.4 percent.[47]

Burgeoning interest in black nationalism and black history greatly boosted the demand for black-themed political and historical studies in these years, and catalogs from black bookstores featured relatively few fictional works. Drum and Spear's one hundred top-recommended works included books by anticolonialist writers such as Franz Fanon and Patrice Lumumba; Black Power activists such as H. Rap Brown and Amiri Baraka; promoters of "great black men," including Lerone Bennett and J. A. Rogers; African American academics such as E. Franklin Frazier and Harold Cruse; and titans of African American political theory such as Martin Luther King Jr. and W. E. B. Du Bois.[48]

Yet the writings of Malcolm X were unrivaled in luring black readers to bookstores. Works by the former Nation of Islam minister "attracted the Afro youth more than all the rest," the Buffalo bookseller Martin Sostre explained. Malcolm's autobiography and pamphlets "would sell so fast that I had a hard time keeping my shelves stocked with his words. . . . His was the magical name that made them respond." Malcolm's writings were "introductory manuals into revolutionary thought." His remarkable sales figures lend credence to such claims. A whopping 6 million copies of *Autobiography* sold in the United States and around the world in the twelve years following its publication in 1965. As an advertisement for Liberation Bookstore asked readers of the periodical *Black News*, "Have you read the 'Autobiography of Malcolm X' for the second time?" Vaughn's Book Store catalog devoted an entire page to Malcolm and included books, vinyl records, pictures, and buttons related to his life and ideas.[49]

Black bookstores also championed pan-Africanism and anticolonial struggles. Drum and Spear's one hundred recommended books contained works by authors hailing from at least twenty different countries, and its catalog was filled with works by pioneering African heads of state. Booksellers decorated their stores with African art, which they sold alongside African music. Stores such as Timbuktu in Atlanta, Talking Drum in Portland, Sundiata in Denver, and Uhuru in Greensboro, North Carolina, invoked African imagery and words in their names (figure 2.6), and the

FIGURE 2.6 Uhuru Bookstore, Greensboro, North Carolina, c. mid-1970s. Photograph by Lewis A. Brandon III

Afro-Asia Bookstore in Buffalo and Third World Ethnic Bookshop in Los Angeles affirmed a shared struggle for liberation in the developing world. Booksellers carried magazines and journals that regularly reported on events in Africa, including *Black World*, *African World*, and *Freedomways*. The pan-Africanist journal *Présence Africaine* was a particular inspiration to African American booksellers. Founded by the Senegalese writer Alioune Diop in Paris in 1947 as the unofficial headquarters of the Negritude movement, the journal operated a publishing house and bookstore near the Sorbonne. Charlie Cobb credited the Paris bookstore—which he visited in 1967 on a layover as he was returning from a trip to Vietnam for Bertrand Russell's Vietnam War Crimes tribunal and a subsequent journey through West Africa—for giving him the idea for Drum and Spear. Indeed, books and periodicals by African writers represented black Americans' most affordable and accessible means of engaging in a transatlantic discourse with the continent in an era prior to the Internet and satellite television. By stocking African works, black bookstores had a direct hand in facilitating a pan-Africanist literary diaspora in the United States.[50]

Black booksellers' international travels, their inventory of radical texts, and of course their activism and direct involvement with Black Power organizations invited frequent persecution and harassment from law enforcement officials. In many African American communities, bookstores represented the most public manifestation of Black Power, second only to Black Panther headquarters in cities that had a local chapter. In fact, a memorandum from FBI director J. Edgar Hoover in October 1968 ordered every local bureau office "to locate and identify black extremist and/or African-type bookstores in its territory and open separate discreet investigations on each to determine if it is extremist in nature" (figure 2.7). These bookstores, Hoover contended, were "propaganda outlets for revolutionary and hate publications and cultural centers for extremism."[51]

Local and federal law enforcement officers monitored numerous black booksellers at the height of the FBI Counterintelligence Program's extensive investigation of black nationalist groups between 1968 and 1973. They included Edward Vaughn in Detroit, Lewis Michaux and Una Mulzac in New York, Paul Coates in Baltimore, Dawud Hakim and Bill Crawford in Philadelphia, Martin Sostre in Buffalo, and the owners of the Sundiata bookstore in Denver. FBI agents were ordered to identify black bookstores'

TO   :   SAC, Albany   DATE: 10/9/68

FROM: Director, FBI (157-8415)

SUBJECT: BLACK NATIONALIST MOVEMENT IN THE UNITED STATES
           RACIAL MATTERS
           BUDED: 11/8/68

> The Bureau has noted an increase in the establishment
> of black extremist bookstores which represent propaganda outlets
> for revolutionary and hate publications and cultural centers for
> extremism. Each office should locate and identify black
> extremist and/or African-type bookstores in its territory and
> open separate discreet investigations on each to determine if
> it is extremist in nature. Advise under this caption by 11/8/68
> of the investigations instituted in accordance with these
> instructions.

FIGURE 2.7 Memorandum from J. Edgar Hoover directing FBI agents to investigate black-owned bookstores, 1968. J. Edgar Hoover, "Black Nationalist Movement in the United States—Racial Matters," memo, October 9, 1968, FBI File 157-WFO-368, National Archives and Records Administration, College Park, Maryland

employees and customers, track which books they sold, scrutinize their finances, and determine any links they had to local or national Black Power or Communist organizations.[52]

Drum and Spear was an especially convenient and frequent target for federal law enforcement due to the store's location in Washington, D.C., and its ties to prominent figures in the Black Power movement. The FBI first became interested in the store within several weeks of its opening when Stokely Carmichael was sighted visiting it. About a month later, Hoover's office ordered that the investigation of the store "should be intensified" beyond occasional visits by agents to include working with undercover sources such as customers, employees, and people who attended meetings at Drum and Spear. Yet plain-clothed FBI agents who visited the store were quite conspicuous to store employees, and they aroused suspicion when they sat in their parked cars in front of the business for hours or purchased large quantities of works such as Mao's Red Book. Although these actions seemed designed to intimidate people at Drum and Spear, Judy Richardson remembers the FBI's presence as galvanizing both employees' and customers' commitment to the store.[53]

Despite experiencing pressures that were unimaginable for most businesses, the African American book trade boomed in the late 1960s and early 1970s. Around one hundred black-interest bookstores operated from 1965 through the mid-1970s, up from just about a dozen a decade earlier, and black bookselling appeared to have considerable room to grow. The Black Power and Black Arts movements were at their height. Black radical conferences flourished as part of what Komozi Woodard has dubbed the "Modern Black Convention Movement." These meetings included a series of annual black writers conferences, the inaugural meeting of the Congress of Afrikan People in Atlanta in 1970, and, most significantly, the National Black Political Assembly's convention in Gary, Indiana, in 1972, where more than ten thousand attendees devoted themselves to the question of forming an independent black political party. New journals such as Nathan Hare and Robert Chrisman's *Black Scholar* and Haki Madhubuti's *Black Books Bulletin* championed African American bookstores and offered them internationally distributed platforms through which they could communicate with black writers and publishers.[54] Newly formed black studies departments on college campuses gave black bookstores a tremendous boost, too. In the wake of student protests and a more than 50 percent increase in black college student enrollment in just a few years, institutions across the country scrambled to add courses on black topics. An estimated two hundred campuses organized search committees to hire black studies scholars in the late 1960s and early 1970s.[55] Like black booksellers, black studies scholars understood written works about African Americans and the African diaspora as vital tools for black political and intellectual liberation. Black booksellers coveted college instructors and high school teachers as institutional customers who could produce dozens or even hundreds of student course purchases. Stores such as Drum and Spear and Vaughn's found book fairs and mobile sales—many of them at public high schools and teachers' conferences—particularly lucrative. All of these developments benefitted black booksellers and helped them prosper.[56]

Black bookstores also benefited from growing interest in books aimed at black children. Activists demanded more children's books that respectfully addressed black identity, arguing that young people were particularly vulnerable to writings that rationalized racism or demeaned blacks. "Brothers and Sisters, let us give our children books . . . that mirror their lovely images," former SNCC activist Annette Jones White pleaded in a letter to the readers of *Black World* magazine in 1971. African American children needed "books that tell the facts but from a Black outlook—books that do not whiteout their heroes and ancestors—books that do not negate their very existence." At Drum and Spear, Judy Richardson organized what was likely the country's largest selection of black-oriented children's books, with more than three hundred such titles. It was never too early, advocates of black children's books argued, to expose black children to positive and empowering depictions of themselves in literary and historical works that encouraged pride, self-respect, and black unity.[57]

By the start of the 1970s, black bookselling appeared to be on the verge of achieving a level of long-term stability that had been unimaginable just a few years earlier. Black-interest bookstores had more than quadrupled in number since the middle of the 1960s. The most influential black bookstore in the country, Drum and Spear, had two stores, an international publishing arm, a distribution company, a mail-order catalog that numbered more than 250 pages, and even a radio show. Black publishers were growing rapidly, too, and were making concerted efforts to enhance their influence through trade associations such as Combined Black Publishers and magazines such as *Black Books Bulletin* and *Black World*. And beyond bookselling, highly attended events such as the National Black Political Assembly suggested that Black Power was on the rise. As the movement continued to generate enthusiasm and support in black communities across the country, black booksellers had good reason to be optimistic about their future.

Decline of a Movement and a Business

Within just a few years, however, Black Power activists would confront a drastically transformed political landscape that was much less accommodating to their movement. The National Black Political Assembly in 1972 symbolized the Black Power movement at the height of its power and organization. Just two years later, however, there were fewer than two thousand attendees at the convention in Little Rock, and in 1976 the assembly in Cincinnati drew fewer than one thousand people. The prosecution and persecution that Black Power organizations faced at the hands of federal, state, and local law enforcement severely undermined the movement. The Black Panthers in particular struggled to remain relevant in the few cities where they still operated, and many members traded their daily routines as full-time activists for the powerful lure of regular jobs and steady incomes. In addition, a number of prominent black nationalist leaders, including Owusu Sadaukai (Howard Fuller) and Amiri Baraka, renounced black nationalism in favor of Marxism in 1973–1974, helping to trigger what Manning Marable called an "increasingly fratricidal" split in the movement that dissolved organizations and split friendships, alliances, and even marriages. Black studies felt these setbacks, too, with roughly half of all departments closing between 1971 and 1976. Taken altogether, a number of rapid changes in the mid-1970s suggested the broader decline of the Black Power movement.[58]

Black nationalism's decline combined with a number of other significant threats facing black booksellers. First, tremendous financial challenges had always confronted black booksellers, even profitable ones. Many of them simply failed to remain solvent. Like many activist business owners, booksellers commonly faced conflicts with landlords and disputes over rent as they often fell behind on payments when sales were low. Even within the larger context of commonly undercapitalized black firms, black book stores stood out as particularly distressed businesses that maintained small inventories, kept irregular hours, and maintained poor financial records. Many black booksellers had limited access to capital and had difficulties obtaining credit from both banks and publishing houses. As a consequence, they often could not pay the same low bulk prices for books that larger stores could negotiate from distributors. This discrepancy proved particularly harmful to black stores' sales as better-funded white booksellers began selling black-authored books at lower prices.[59]

Black booksellers had dealt with these issues as best as they could during the years of Black Power's ascent. But the national recession that began in 1973 and continued for most of the decade hit black retailers particularly hard. By 1975, the black unemployment rate reached an astounding 13.8 percent, nearly twice the rate for whites. The most severe economic downturn since the Depression "sent the mortality rate for black businesses soaring," according to the magazine *Black Enterprise*. Black bookstores, most of them underfunded shoestring operations, were particularly vulnerable to shifts in the larger economy. For every three bookstores that opened in the boom years, about two closed in the recession-plagued second half of the 1970s. After all, there was little room for error in a business where nearly two-thirds of small retailers did not even make a profit.[60]

African American communities' decreased enthusiasm for both Black Power and written materials on black politics raised an uncomfortable question for black booksellers: Should they renounce their founding objectives as activist entrepreneurs and instead embrace nonpolitical, conventional business strategies for financial success? Such questions were more urgent for Drum and Spear than perhaps for any other black bookstore. In 1969 and 1970, although the store was still a nonprofit, it had grossed nearly $1,000 per day. Despite reincorporating as a for-profit business in 1972, that figure had sunk to a daily revenue of barely $100 by 1974. In response, the store's staff and advisory board issued a public cry for help in the newspaper the *Washington Afro American*. One of the store's board members, an accountant, blamed the store's political roots as the source of its decline. "Drum and Spear can survive if it forgoes the political aspect," she argued, "and concentrates on books and materials that are of interest to black people in light of what is happening today." Although the accountant's assessment many not have been entirely accurate, Charlie Cobb conceded that "the generally low level of activity that seems to be the case in the black community around the country" hurt Drum and Spear tremendously. Yet as Judy Richardson argued, even an unprofitable bookstore could still serve an important function in D.C.'s black communities. "It was and is important for kids to see someone who is not solely interested in pocketing money and buying a Cadillac." Bookstores could still offer black citizens an alternative vision of intellectual, cultural, and political fulfillment, she contended, something more than mere material gain.[61]

Retail businesses' declining status in black communities also hindered black bookstores. For a variety of reasons, retail ownership began to lose its appeal for many African Americans. Between just 1972 and 1977, retail's share of all African American businesses dropped from 28.4 to 23.9 percent, a decline that would continue for decades. *Black Enterprise*, founded in 1970, glorified African Americans' role in both black and white corporations but spent little time addressing black independent retailers and virtually ignored entrepreneurs involved in radical politics. Black commercial districts, where most black bookstores were located, began to falter in the 1970s amid disruptive urban-renewal projects, growing crime, and a middle-class exodus to the suburbs. Blacks' moderately increased access to corporate employment amid the implementation of affirmative action also undercut interest in retail.[62]

Some black booksellers grudgingly conceded that their activism periodically undermined their ability to operate and manage a business. Activists had opened stores in the late 1960s and early 1970s with nearly limitless passion for Black Power and community control but with little experience in business. Black-themed bookstores were so novel that simply by operating they attracted curious visitors and potential customers. Yet by the second half of the 1970s, it had become clear that black bookstores, even in hotbeds of Black Power activism such as New York and Washington, D.C., simply could not survive on mere novelty or community goodwill. In Drum and Spear's final days, Charlie Cobb conceded that the store had suffered because "those who started the store were political activists," not businesspeople. Reincorporating as a for-profit business in 1972 did not seem to help the store much at all. Judy Richardson recalled years later how one manager, a strident black nationalist with little business sense, let "politics get in the way of what could make something survive" at Maelezo, a second bookshop that Drum and Spear had established. Maelezo closed after only a few years due to poor management. Paul Coates similarly recalled that he "never thought about [the bookstore] as a business . . . [until] one day it occurred to me, 'You have people working. You have to pay those people.'" Coates's store in Baltimore, Black Book, encountered great difficulties, bouncing between four locations in six years before closing in 1978. Like many activist businesses, black radical bookstores often foundered because their owners had little experience or training in handling the complex details of inventory, accounting, and management. At the same time, many black booksellers seemed to prefer to shutter their stores rather than compromise their politics. Whether by choice or by necessity, most black bookstores ended up closing instead of shifting to a more conventional form of entrepreneurship.[63]

By the end of 1974, both Drum and Spear and the National Memorial African Bookstore—the country's two most prominent black bookstores—closed for good. Numerous stores followed, shutting their doors throughout the 1970s. New York City was home to a dozen black bookstores in 1973, but just four years later only six remained. Poetry, one of the most important genres driving the black books boom of the late 1960s and early 1970s, had "been dead since '71," the owner of the Freedom Bookstore in Brooklyn lamented. Yet the fundamental problem, he charged, was that "community values have changed. . . . It's back to Cadillacs, clothing and the glitterous [*sic*] American dream. . . . Meanwhile our own historical documents gather dust on the walls." Not even a decade removed, the 1960s and the early 1970s struck some observers in the second half of the 1970s as a distant past of political struggle that was giving way to materialism. "The urban revolutionary literature of the sixties is now historic," a writer for the *New York Amsterdam News* explained in 1977, "but also in the context of the seventies, impractical." To keep up with the changing face of racism and systematic oppression, "a new vision must be forged and . . . a sophistication in dealing with the political trends of the seventies must be recognized." As another headline in the *Amsterdam News* series somberly declared, the "prospects for black literature appear bleak." After a decade of impressive growth that paralleled the rise of the Black Power movement, black-interest bookstores now seemed to some observers out of date and too radical to sustain long-term financial stability. "Is the black bookstore an endangered species?" the *Amsterdam News* asked readers with palpable concern.[64]

Black booksellers all over the country closed in the second half of the 1970s, and no store with a national profile on the level of Drum and Spear and the National Memorial African Bookstore opened in their place. Perhaps the singular milestone for black bookselling in the late 1970s was Alex Haley's publication of *Roots: The Saga of an American Family* (1976). In contrast to *The Autobiography of Malcolm X* (1965), Haley's first best seller and the seminal text of the black bookstore boom, the theme of black nationalism was conspicuously absent from *Roots*. The book's protagonist, Kunta Kinte, is African, and his descendants make up most of its main characters, but Haley's title emphasized that *Roots* is an American story, not a black or pan-African story. The success of *Roots* raised the difficult question of how much black booksellers could rely on selling radical works if they wanted to stay in business.[65]

Although their primary goal had been to advance Black Power, black bookstores bore little responsibility for the movement's collapse. But could they still prosper if enthusiasm for black nationalism declined sharply? More generally, could activist businesses of any kind prosper if their associated movements declined? The fate of black bookstores in the 1980s and 1990s suggests not only that activist businesses struggle mightily when their movements are in remission but also that activist businesses have some capacity to help revive those movements.

BLACK BOOKSELLING WITHOUT BLACK POWER

The first half of the 1980s marked the nadir of black-owned bookstores since the 1950s. A *Los Angeles Times* article in 1982 estimated that only ten black bookstores still operated in the entire country—likely a modest underestimation but nonetheless a reflection of just how many stores had closed in recent years. The *Times* reported on Alfred and Bernice Ligon's Aquarian bookstore in south-central Los Angeles, describing it as one of the few survivors in a "starvation business" and noting that "after close to half a century in the business, [Alfred] Ligon has watched the demand for black books come almost full circle," as sales sank to their lowest point in more than two decades. Publishers' interest in black-themed books had declined significantly "now that the interest in black people has waned . . . [just like] the interest in black studies," Ligon pointed out. "Black writers just can't get published," he lamented. "It's just a vicious circle. . . . And it's all about the dollars."[66]

Black bookstores' woes also stemmed from African American communities' deeper troubles in the 1980s. The national economy for African Americans worsened dramatically at the start of the decade as the black unemployment rate rose to around 14 percent in Ronald Reagan's first term, more than twice the rate for whites. At the same time, black families' median income dropped significantly. Second, crime and violence skyrocketed in economically depressed black urban neighborhoods wracked by the crack epidemic, accelerating an ongoing exodus of black businesses and middle-class blacks to the suburbs. A rapidly expanding system of mass incarceration put ever greater numbers of young black men in prison, in turn removing countless consumers and potential entrepreneurs from black communities. To make matters much worse, the Reagan administration dramatically reduced funding for social welfare and urban development, while concurrently scaling back and in some cases refusing to enforce much of the federal civil rights legislation of the 1960s.[67]

Conservative commentators meanwhile claimed that the civil rights movement had overwhelmingly succeeded and that individual failings and even social welfare programs, not systematic racism, were responsible for any remaining racial inequalities. Yet the modest benefits of civil rights legislation and gains in racial equality had accumulated primarily to small numbers of middle-class and professional African Americans. The widely popular *Cosby Show* and its protagonists, the Huxtable family, were attractive, wholesome, highly educated, and professionally accomplished. As such, they represented to many African Americans a positive symbol of the black middle class and the possibilities of success. Many whites, however, erroneously interpreted the fictional Huxtables as proof that the civil rights movement had ensured equality of opportunity and made upward mobility possible for all African Americans. To many of these white viewers, blacks who did not achieve the Huxtables' affluence had only themselves to blame. Indeed, the show's relative reticence on matters of racial inequality helped to bolster this misperception of a postracial society.[68]

Meanwhile, the decade's most prominent black politician, Jesse Jackson, promoted his two presidential campaigns as Rainbow Coalitions, multiracial efforts to reform American society within the electoral system. "Reform," Manning Marable argues, had "supplanted rebellion" as the dominant imperative of black political activity in the late 1970s and the 1980s. If black booksellers owed much of their success to the rebellions of the 1960s and early 1970s, how could they rebound in a time marked by the decline of those struggles and the backlash against them?[69]

Surprisingly, a literary genre with no connection to the Black Power movement and with virtually no presence at black bookstores in the 1960s and 1970s would help to spark these businesses' revival. In 1980, the paperback company Dell released *Entwined Destinies*, the 575th title in its Candlelight Romance Series. The work would probably have gone largely unnoticed except for the fact that its author, Elsie B. Washington, and its characters were African American. Writing under the pseudonym "Rosalind Wells," Washington—a magazine journalist who had previously written a book on sickle cell anemia—created what was widely credited as the first black romance novel. *Entwined Destinies* was the story of an African American foreign-news correspondent who falls for a successful, handsome black executive of a multinational oil company. Vivian Stephens, the editor of the series, was also African American. Following the success of *Entwined Destinies*, Stephens was lured to the romance publisher Harlequin, where she edited the press's first novel by an African American author, Sandra Kitt's *Adam and Eva*, in 1984. By 1989, the first black-owned publisher devoted to romance novels, Odyssey Press, emerged, and a white-owned competitor, Holloway House, launched a black-authored series, Heartline Romances. By the mid-1990s, black-oriented works would account for roughly 15 percent of the $85 million in sales of romance books.[70]

The African American writer concerned with issues of love and romance who had the most profound impact on black bookselling was Terry McMillan. McMillan's first two works, *Mama* (1987) and *Disappearing Acts* (1989), centered on the professional and romantic struggles of their black female protagonists. McMillan did all of her own promotions for *Mama*, and black bookstores initially served as her only significant retail market. In 1992, McMillan followed the unexpected smash success of *Disappearing Acts* with her highly anticipated third novel, *Waiting to Exhale*, which debuted on the *New York Times* best-seller list alongside Alice Walker's *Possessing the Secret of Joy* and Toni Morrison's *Jazz*. For the first time ever, the works of three African Americans, all of them women, simultaneously appeared on the list.[71]

As romance novels and popular fiction became increasingly important for black-owned bookstores, many of the businesses moved away from the activist business vision of entrepreneurship as a vehicle for radical political change. McMillan targeted black female readers with her works, but her themes of romance and heartache did not rely on any collective black political movement. "The world of McMillan's novels is dominated by affairs of the heart that, while lived by people of color, can transcend racial barriers," remarked the journalist Nelson George. Paul Coates, former owner of the Black Book in Baltimore and founder of Black Classic Press in 1978, described *Waiting to Exhale* as "profoundly concerned with the individual," compared with the work of best-selling author Malcolm X, who "was profoundly concerned with the collective." McMillan's works, in short, were steeped in black women's culture and identity but owed little to black nationalism or other radical politics.[72]

And just as the works by McMillan and black romance writers gave a much-needed boost to black bookstores, black nationalism experienced an unexpected revival in the late 1980s. A number of high-profile cases of white-supremacist violence and police brutality spurred black protest in the second half of the 1980s and first half of the 1990s. The disproportionate impact of the spiraling rates of mass incarceration on African American men alarmed many in black communities, as did a growing conservative backlash against the civil rights gains of the 1960s and 1970s. Popular hip-hop performers such as Public Enemy, Brand Nubian, and KRS-One excoriated white Americans for turning their backs on racial equality. A deep sense of besieged retrenchment pervaded many African American communities in the 1980s, in turn helping to reawaken black nationalist movements.[73]

The demand for books on black history and radical politics rose to levels unseen since the early 1970s as a crop of new and republished works arguing for black Americans' enduring connection to African culture appeared in bookstores. In 1987 alone, Molefi Asante published his pioneering work *The Afrocentric Idea*, Martin Bernal published the academic blockbuster *Black Athena*, and a reprint of Chancellor Williams's *Destruction of Black Civilization* appeared in stores. All three works forcefully argued for Western culture's immense debt to Africa. Black booksellers took note of a new generation of teenagers and college students who frequented their stores. As Bea Dozier-Tyler, a bookseller in New Haven, quipped, "Blacks get Black every 30 years. It's a natural occurrence," citing the succession of the New

Negro movement of the 1920s and 1930s, the black power and civil rights movements of the 1960s, and the ongoing resurgence of interest in black cultural awareness of the late 1980s and early 1990s.[74]

Particularly impressive was the dramatic revival of interest in Malcolm X. Between 1989 and 1992 alone, sales of his autobiography jumped 300 percent. Malcolm's face adorned countless posters and T-shirts, and Spike Lee's biopic of the Nation of Islam minister was released to critical and commercial acclaim in 1992. As one journalist declared, "On nearly every street corner in America, vendors sell Malcolm X goods to a new generation eager for heroes," making him "the hottest selling Afrocentric symbol of the '90s." Hip-hop groups filled their lyrics and liner notes with references to Malcolm and other black nationalist thinkers, achieving a level of commercial success for black musicians who openly embraced political radicalism that surpassed even that of their predecessors in the Black Power era.[75]

After more than a decade of decline, black booksellers were once again opening more stores than they were closing. Most strikingly, black bookstores appeared not only in the large coastal and midwestern cities where the stores had thrived in the Black Power era but also in small and medium-size cities in the South and the West, such as Durham, Norfolk, Denver, Dallas, and Sacramento. Virtually every major American city and many smaller cities were now home to at least one black-interest bookstore. Black bookstores benefitted from a larger boom in bookselling in the United States, with a doubling of sales nationally between 1978 and 1988. One count of black bookstores from 1989 listed more than two hundred such retail businesses nationwide, and another from 1994 estimated there were three hundred black-themed stores—roughly three to four times as many bookstores as had operated at the height of the Black Power movement in the first half of the 1970s. The turnaround was remarkable for a business that many had considered on the verge of extinction at the start of the 1980s.[76]

Black bookstores were no longer as closely tied to radical political organizations as they had been in earlier decades. Yet they were nonetheless the primary businesses that sold a new wave of works by black nationalist thinkers such as Yosef Ben-Jochannan and Frances Cress Welsing. Few of the new black bookstores were explicitly activist businesses, but most were still eager to sell popular black radical texts side by side with less political works such as black romance novels. In addition, a handful of the older generation of activist stores such as Marcus Books in San Francisco and Oakland remained in operation. And these bookstores deserved at least part of the credit for reviving black nationalism. Few black nationalist organizations aside from the Nation of Islam had a significant profile in African American communities in the 1980s, so bookstores were some of the few public institutions that still had any affiliation with the movement. Like hip hop, black bookstores exposed younger African Americans born after the Black Power movement to black nationalism as few institutions could.

Journalists, booksellers, and publishing industry professionals declared the dawning of a new era of black bookselling, epitomized by what the journalist Nelson George called a new "literary chitlin' circuit." African Americans' book purchases jumped nearly 50 percent between 1990 and 1993, reaching $178 million, and then jumped another 68 percent from 1993 to 1996 to reach $261 million. Magazines devoted to black books proliferated, with titles such as *Blackboard*, *Your Black Book Guide*, and *American Black Book Writers' Association Journal*. "These are heady times," wrote the editor of another such new journal, *Quarterly Black Review of Books*, in early 1994. "Black writers and titles are being published in numbers unseen since the Harlem Renaissance and the 1960s and 1970s. . . . Black bookstore owners are cautiously optimistic, and mainstream publishers have 'found' a new market." Editors and publishers, many of whom had ignored black booksellers for decades, now gave them much of the credit for the black literary revival.[77]

In Denver, Clara Villarosa demonstrated the new possibilities for black booksellers. Unlike most of her predecessors, Villarosa had a background in business and corporate employment. Also a trained psychotherapist, she had once established a consulting firm to advise companies on hiring African Americans and later went to work in management for a bank, where she felt she quickly "hit the glass ceiling" of resentment from white coworkers over her rank and salary. Villarosa soon quit her bank job in search of a business opportunity that would offer the freedom and independence that eluded her in corporate work. By 1984, Villarosa had opened the Hue-Man

Experience Bookstore in Denver's historic African American neighborhood Five Points. Looking back, Villarosa described the store as "a moneymaking business run by an African-American woman selling African-American books to African-American customers." This vision, which lacked any stated connection to activist business, was a strikingly different conception of bookselling than Villarosa's predecessors had articulated in the Black Power era.[78]

Villarosa was considerably more business minded than black booksellers of just a decade earlier. Although she occasionally described her work as a community project and cultural resource for Denver's black population, she more often spoke of financial profit, not community engagement, as her primary goal. "I'm going to get a tangible product," she told herself as she opened the store, and "I'm going to the Small Business Administration to get some instruction on how to manage cash flow and marketing." By the end of the 1980s, Villarosa's keen business sense and entrepreneurial skill allowed Hue-Man to thrive financially, enough so that she could buy two Victorian-era houses in which to expand the store. Hue-Man became a national destination for African American shoppers, and Villarosa emerged as the most prominent African American bookseller in the country. She was featured in numerous national media outlets, including *Ms.*, *Emerge*, the *New York Times*, and the *Washington Post*.[79] By the early 1990s, Hue-Man was grossing well more than $300,000 annually, enough to cover the store's expenses, including staff salaries, and in some years even to make a profit.[80]

Villarosa also joined the American Booksellers Association (ABA). As the ABA's first ever black board member, Villarosa established an African American booksellers' plenary at the group's meetings as part of a larger effort to encourage black booksellers to join the historically white-dominated ABA. Whereas earlier black booksellers had networked at black writers conferences and meetings of the Association for the Study of African American Life and History, Villarosa promoted the ABA as a central meeting place for black booksellers to connect. By attending the ABA, "black booksellers put publishers on notice that Black booksellers exist and that their needs must be considered." Although she initially "questioned joining a white association," her decision to become a member of the ABA reflected a desire not for a separate African American book economy but for a caucus of black booksellers that operated within the larger white-dominated structure of the book business. These efforts contrasted sharply with black bookstores' long-standing identity as black nationalist institutions within an autonomous black literary marketplace.[81]

Indeed, Villarosa's vision of black bookselling was racially pluralist, not black nationalist. Hue-Man predominantly sold African American books, but Villarosa's concept for the store was to offer books by authors of all races. The store's name, "Hue-Man Experience," was a play on words that suggested it served a wide range of people of color. The store's slogan, "A SKU for Every Hue," articulated this vision of a bookstore that was systematically multicultural, one with a barcoded book for people of every race. In explaining her motivations for founding and operating Hue-Man, Villarosa did not recount any involvement in black political activism. The title of her how-to guide for business—*Down to Business: The First 10 Steps to Entrepreneurship for Women* (2009)—reflected a belief that her work was relevant to women of all races, not just to black women. By the end of the 1990s, Villarosa had made Hue-Man the most prominent and likely highest-earning black-owned bookstore in the country not through political work or collaboration with social movements but through dogged determination, entrepreneurial acumen, and a strong grasp of the demands of retail business.[82]

African American bookselling's transition from activist business to niche retail was virtually complete. Black bookstores had not become apolitical, but most of them relegated politics to a secondary status at best. Most booksellers simply determined that they could not survive as explicitly political enterprises, especially as the resurgence of black nationalism faded after the early 1990s. Conventional business strategy appeared to most black booksellers to be their only path to financial well-being. But as they would learn in the late 1990s and early 2000s, not even these adjustments were sufficient to secure their survival in a dramatically shifting landscape for independent booksellers.

THE SECOND DECLINE OF INDEPENDENT
BLACK BOOKSELLERS

Despite black bookstores' rapid growth in the late 1980s and early 1990s, independent booksellers of all kinds were forced to confront painful structural changes in their industry starting in the mid-1990s. A new generation of so-called megastores, most notably Borders and Barnes & Noble, captured an ever-growing portion of the market by offering customers enormous selections of books, magazines, and music, along with cafés and plentiful seating. These booksellers bought directly from publishers at prices lower than those offered to their smaller competitors, and their much larger national inventories allowed them to fill orders more quickly than independents. Most independent bookstores, meanwhile, purchased from distributors who could not offer them the same markdowns. Countless independent bookstores, both black- and white-owned, faced unprecedented levels of competition from these expansive chain stores. Many independents closed in the 1990s and 2000s as a result. Independents' share of books sold in the United States fell from about 60 percent in the mid-1970s to around 33 percent in 1991 and then to just 17 percent by 1997.[83]

In addition to the crisis facing all independent booksellers, black bookstores ironically suffered from the growing attention that the publishing industry gave to black authors, marking a stinging reversal of their gains in the late 1980s and early 1990s. One African American publisher estimated that between 1993 and 1998 as many as "one-third of independent black bookstores have closed after being shut out of their community markets by white-owned discount bookstore chains that invade our territories and sell black books by black authors at a 20%–50% discount." As chain stores coveted African Americans' rising expenditures on books and the emergence of superstar authors such as Terry McMillan as new market opportunities, they began to devote unprecedented levels of attention and shelf space to books by black authors. Black booksellers complained at annual ABA meetings and to the media that chain stores not only threatened their sales but also lured away black authors from doing signings and talks in their stores. "We had no problem getting authors like Terry McMillan and many others before 1993, when a Barnes & Noble opened twelve blocks away from us," one New York store owner explained. "We were selling their books long before Barnes & Noble saw that black people do read and buy books." In one particularly confrontational exchange in 1997, Antoine Coffer, owner of Afrocentric Books and Café in University City, Missouri, outside St. Louis, demanded a national boycott of Terry McMillan's books when Viking Penguin rebuffed his requests for an in-store signing of McMillan's novel *How Stella Got Her Groove Back* (1996). McMillan's sole promotional appearance in St. Louis was at a white-owned store called the Library. Taking his case to local media, Coffer threatened to organize a protest in front of the store. Major publishers, Coffer explained, wanted black independent stores to "make their unknown authors" famous so that white-owned stores could later profit from selling those authors' works. McMillan replied in kind: Coffer had "made money off of selling my books, and now he wants to boycott and picket my book signing. I pay his mortgage!" Sadly, the conflict between Coffer, McMillan, and Viking Penguin illustrated one of the fundamental challenges facing black booksellers from the second half of the 1990s on. In short, the more books by black authors that appeared on best-seller lists, the more white chain stores sought to compete with black bookstores to sell those books. Popular African American authors no longer depended on black bookstores as they once had.[84]

Unfortunately, black booksellers' newfound recognition from whites in the industry made them much more vulnerable to powerful competitors. Although a resurgence of black nationalist works helped to drive black bookstores' revival, works by writers such as McMillan and black romance novelists made up a bigger share of the market for black-authored books than ever before. Even *Black Enterprise*—the unofficial organ of the African American corporate elite and black bourgeoisie, which Black Power entrepreneurs had once criticized so stridently in the 1960s and 1970s—was now interested in black bookselling. But the magazine dismissed black bookselling's political imperatives out of hand. In the 1960s, "books by African-American authors had more social and political motives and were marketed to libraries and schools rather than to general readers," the magazine remarked, paraphrasing a literary agency director. Yet "once the market was flooded with books relying on the shock value of attacking white society," black bookstores declined, the magazine contended. It was only once black writers and booksellers could appeal to a "general audience," particularly with romance and less-political works, that the business recovered. "Today, the market is more consumer driven," *Black Enterprise* claimed, oddly implying that consumers had not driven the boom of Black Power booksellers decades earlier.[85]

Looking back on the 1960s and 1970s, these commentators treated black radical bookselling and activist businesses of all kinds as youthful digressions from conventional retail practices and regrettable experiments in entrepreneurial fantasy. Yet the black people who had flocked to African American bookstores in the Black Power era *were* customers shopping at real businesses, contrary to the suggestion that they were only engaged in a movement. Indeed, in the late 1960s and early 1970s, African American radical activists struggled to keep up with their customers' rapidly growing demand for works on black history, literature, and politics. Black booksellers hoped to redefine black businesses as fundamentally political operations that confronted white supremacy and even articulated an alternative, communitarian economic vision. They had designed their stores as black radical public spaces that revealed to customers an under-acknowledged world of black history and literature, which would in turn fuel black communities' pride in self and hunger for liberation. By the mid-1970s, however, Black Power's decline, a faltering economy, and the difficulties of balancing the demands of entrepreneurship with political engagement would combine to kill most black-owned bookstores. Only in the second half of the 1980s, with the rise of black romance and superstar women authors such as Terry McMillan, did black bookstores rebound. Most of the new generation of black booksellers believed their primary objective was to earn profits, not to collaborate directly with black activist movements for radical political and social change. Such a conventional approach to business represented a shift away from the tradition of black nationalist bookselling. But it was also understandable considering the greatly increased competition black booksellers now faced from white booksellers, especially from chains such as Barnes & Noble and websites such as Amazon.

Black bookstores were not alone among activist businesses in struggling to stay relevant as interest in their associated movements waxed and waned. Head shops—established by individuals engaged with the counterculture and the antiwar and marijuana-legalization movements—thrived along with those causes in the late 1960s and early 1970s. Although they continued to grow impressively, head shops failed to retain their political significance as the antiwar movement claimed victory and the counterculture and marijuana were absorbed by mainstream popular culture in the second half of the 1970s. Whereas sales at black bookstores dropped as interest in black nationalism declined, business at head shops surged even while the movements that spurred them were no longer seen as radical or even political. Yet head shops' financial success brought unwanted attention from law enforcement and concerned citizens. As it would turn out, legal and moral scrutiny threatened activist businesses just as much as the decline of movements did.

3

The Business of Getting High

HEAD SHOPS, COUNTERCULTURAL CAPITALISM, AND THE BATTLE OVER MARIJUANA

In September 1970, the *Wall Street Journal* reported with palpable suspicion on a rather unusual retailer in Lansing, Michigan, calling the Free Spirit "a highly imaginative, though not entirely problem-free, mod department store." The store was a curious oddity compared with the other businesses that the *Journal* had favorably profiled in its ongoing series on the country's "neighborhood merchant," including a Jewish deli and an African American funeral parlor. Unlike these stores, which operated in long-established markets, the Free Spirit served a young, rebellious clientele seeking unconventional products: "Stocked within its doors are the furnishings and paraphernalia of the 'turned-on, tuned-in' generation, goods that most other merchants shun as too far out." There were several different departments in this "mod boutique," but the merchandise that most caught the *Journal*'s attention were the "pet lizards on leashes, incense, Eldridge Cleaver wanted posters and even cigarette paper for wrapping marijuana"—all of which could be found in an area of the Free Spirit that customers would have called a "head shop."[1]

Jay Hanson, the Free Spirit's owner, had grown dissatisfied with the venerable department stores in downtown Lansing's retail core, such as Knapp's and Liebermann's, which were "just coming out of the 19th century." Hanson wanted to offer a more vibrant and dynamic shopping experience, one that appealed to young people in search of new freedoms and insights. "I'm a capitalist, but not in the true sense of the word. We feel a responsibility to our culture. We aren't totally profit oriented [and] our customers are our friends," Hanson argued. "The role of the Free Spirit . . . is a cultural meeting place of young and old, rich and poor," he explained. "Everything's different" at the Free Spirit, a college student browsing the store remarked. "You walk in . . . and you feel really free." The *Wall Street Journal* affirmed the store's distinctiveness in more critical terms: "Rock music pervades the store," and sales clerks were dressed "casually, even sloppily." Customers were "encouraged to come in and just 'rap' about the draft or civil-rights or anything else on their mind," even if they didn't want to make a purchase.[2]

In the late 1960s and 1970s, Hanson and countless other countercultural entrepreneurs established head shops as an alternative to America's dominant consumer culture, a culture they believed was alienating, conformist, puritanical, and "plastic." In major cities and college towns across America, head shops appealed to a new generation of cultural and political rebels eager to purchase products that were purportedly hip or psychedelic, including paraphernalia for enhancing LSD trips or for smoking marijuana. These accessories of alternative lifestyles provided so-called hippies, freaks, and heads with a totemic material culture they could call their own. Head shop owners hoped their countercultural wares and atmosphere would provide hippies with needed public spaces where they could gather without being harassed. More importantly, they believed these products allowed people to alter their minds—and even their societies—through meaningful drug use.

Some critics from within hippie and New Left circles questioned the motives of head shop owners and accused them of operating conventional proprietary businesses that sold out their cause. So-called hip capitalists were frequently accused of commercializing dissent and retreating from political involvement. To be sure, some hippie entrepreneurs valued profit as much as or more than politics and openly admitted they were capitalists striving for financial success. Yet although historians have begun to address so-called hip capitalists' pivotal role in sustaining countercultural communities, they have largely overlooked these businesses' extensive political activism.[3]

Many head shops were, in fact, engaged in political work. Head shop owners and staff actively participated in the mass movement against the Vietnam War, and they were critical supporters of the nascent movement to reform and eradicate the country's drug laws.[4] Marijuana-law reform groups such as Amorphia and the National Organization for the Reform of Marijuana Laws (NORML) spearheaded major campaigns for decriminalization with proceeds from paraphernalia that head shops sold for them on consignment. Head shop owners distributed written materials on drug legalization in their stores and donated generously to reform groups. Observers in the New Left questioned countercultural claims that getting high offered a pathway to liberation, but they nonetheless recognized drugs' political significance, especially as drug arrests skyrocketed nationally and law enforcement increasingly used possession charges as a tool to persecute people of color and activists. Head shops were at the heart of the counterculture's politics.

Head shops were admittedly less connected to radical politics than other activist businesses were. Unlike black-owned bookstores, head shops did not function as ideological clearinghouses for a radical social movement. And in contrast to feminist businesses and natural foods stores, few head shops were collectives or cooperatives that strived to make workplaces democratic through structures of shared ownership and management. Nonetheless, head shop owners embraced their products as political tools and championed their storefronts as political spaces.

Head shop owners recognized, of course, that drug legalization would likely advance their financial interests, but their activism was no mere business strategy. Head shops' blatant endorsement of illicit activity resonated deeply with young Americans, who connected what they viewed as the federal government's immoral and illegal war in Vietnam with its enforcement of unjust drug laws. Within this context, smoking pot and dropping acid represented to many activists a powerful protest and act of defiance against the American state and the country's repressive cultural norms. A number of voices in the New Left and the counterculture maintained that head shops, by selling accessories to help people get high, were key accomplices in such acts of resistance.[5] In short, head shops made a name for themselves as deeply political spaces at the forefront of the struggle against punitive drug laws and a repressive criminal justice system.

Head shops and the marijuana legalization movement helped each other achieve remarkable levels of financial and political success in the mid-1970s. These gains were seen in the increased use and acceptance of marijuana as eleven states decriminalized minor personal possession of marijuana that decade. Head shops and the legalization movement also received a significant boost from *High Times*, the popular, nationally circulated magazine "dedicated solely to getting high," which gave them unmatched positive coverage and advertising space. By the end of the decade, an estimated thirty thousand head shops operated in the United States and organized their own industry groups and trade meetings.[6]

In contrast to their predecessors of the late 1960s and early 1970s, however, many head shops of the late 1970s embraced profit and financial growth and deemphasized radical politics and counterculture, even as many people still associated the stores with vice and law breaking. Whereas early head shop owners had embraced activism and defiance as their hallmarks, by the 1980s most cast themselves as conventional, law-abiding businesses just trying to earn enough to survive. With the marijuana subculture gaining an unprecedented reach and commercial appeal by the 1970s, head shops shed most of their politics and recast themselves as purveyors of products for pleasure and recreation.

As the industry grew, so did legal and public scrutiny. From the late 1960s on, law enforcement officers monitored, investigated, and raided head shops, and private citizens subjected them to lawsuits, pickets, and even physical attacks. For most of the 1970s, uncoordinated local efforts did little to slow head shops' remarkable growth across the country. Yet by 1979 local parents' groups began to coordinate a national campaign against the so-called commercialized drug culture spawned by head shops, which these groups charged with fueling a pandemic of marijuana abuse among youth. In response to this campaign, states and cities across the country passed laws designed to severely restrict head shops and even put them out of business—one of the opening salvos in the cultural and legislative war on drugs that would unfold in the 1980s. Thousands of head shops would close over the course of the decade, and many of those that remained open survived by retreating even further from their earlier celebration of cultural rebellion and political resistance.

Indeed, as head shops came under fierce, coordinated attacks from lawmakers and antidrug advocates in the late 1970s, they positioned themselves not as agents of a political movement but as conventional small businesses unfairly targeted for social ills they did not create. They remained active in the marijuana legalization movement, but they did so not as allies of the counterculture and the New Left, as they had a decade earlier, but as a cottage industry defending its economic interests.

To prosper beyond the confines of the counterculture and the New Left, head shops found they needed to moderate their politics and tone down their open defiance of laws and mainstream cultural norms. But even as they strived to present themselves as conventional businesses, their owners failed to convince many Americans that they were not rebellious radicals running vice enterprises. Their association with social movements and the counterculture had initially brought them attention and customers, but it had also sullied their reputation in the eyes of many citizens, politicians, and law enforcement officials. Head shops struggled to adapt to the much more conservative political and cultural landscape of the late 1970s and early 1980s. Indeed, head shops' difficulties illuminate the deeper conundrum that virtually all activist businesses confronted as they navigated the treacherous cross-currents of political efficacy and financial survival.

AMERICA'S FIRST PSYCHEDELIC STOREFRONT

In 1964, Jay Thelin attended a lecture at San Francisco State University about LSD by Richard Alpert, whose experiments with acid had resulted in his and Timothy Leary's dismissal from Harvard the previous year. Alpert, Leary, and Harvard psychology graduate student Ralph Metzner had that same year coauthored *The Psychedelic Experience: A Manual Based on the Tibetan Book of the Dead*, in which they urged readers to take up psychedelics to liberate themselves "from their life-long internal bondage."[7] Jay was riveted by Alpert's talk, and in the coming months he and his brother, Ron, tried LSD for the first time. It was a revelation.

By 1965, the Thelins had tried LSD several more times and had come to believe that the drug could positively transform people's consciousness and provide the catalyst for widespread social change in America. Frustrated by the increasing U.S. military involvement in Vietnam and the growing backlash to the civil rights movement, Jay thought LSD could provide Americans with the formula for achieving true peace and equality with each other. He and his brother wanted to introduce the drug to as many people as possible, but they also recognized that anyone who was not psychologically and emotionally prepared for acid could have a terrible experience with it, a so-called bad trip that in some cases might even trigger a psychotic reaction. Yet the Thelins also believed that people could benefit enormously from LSD with the proper preparation and information, especially if they could take acid with friends in a safe, supportive environment that had the appropriate light and music. By late 1965, Ron and Jay decided they wanted to create such a space where they could advise people on how to take LSD, which was still legal in California, and sell them literature, music, lighting, and other paraphernalia that could enhance their experiences with acid.[8]

In 1964, Ron and Jay had bought a house with a friend in Haight-Ashbury, a quiet and affordable San Francisco neighborhood where blacks and whites, working-class and middle-class families lived side by side. By the next year, the neighborhood was beginning to change as more and more students from nearby San Francisco State University and San Francisco City College continued to move into the area. According to the *San Francisco Examiner*, the neighborhood was quickly becoming the city's "new bohemian quarter for serious writers, painters and musicians, civil rights workers, crusaders for all kinds of causes, homosexuals, lesbians, marijuana users, young working couples of artistic bent and the outer fringe of the bohemian fringe." These people, according to the newspaper, were "the 'hippies,' the 'heads,' the beatniks." The newcomers' presence was most visible in newly renovated, communal houses and a trio of fledgling businesses in the Haight—the Blue Unicorn coffee house and two boutiques, Mnasidika and House of Richard.[9]

On January 3, 1966, Ron and Jay Thelin opened the Psychedelic Shop at 1535 Haight Street. With $500 that Jay had earned as a parking attendant, the brothers could afford to open their store in a neighborhood with low rents and outfit it with salvaged furnishings and equipment. The Thelins' primary goal was to "provide materials necessary for a good, enlightened, and safe trip." These materials included "books on eastern religion and metaphysics . . . along with Indian records, posters, madrases, incense, bead necklaces, small pipes, and other paraphernalia," as described by the poet Allen Cohen, an early customer and later employee of the store. This wide array of seemingly incompatible goods was believed to heighten and enhance the effects of both LSD and marijuana.[10] With the opening of their store, the Thelins were the first entrepreneurs in the Haight and perhaps anywhere in America to create a business that publicly endorsed not only LSD but also marijuana.

The Psychedelic Shop quickly attracted the Haight's young rebels seeking a community space that welcomed them unconditionally. People came in to talk about politics, religion, and, of course, their experiences consuming LSD and marijuana. The shop's bulletin board featured flyers seeking and offering housing, work, band mates, or activity groups. New arrivals to the neighborhood, whose numbers were steadily increasing through 1966, could go to the Psychedelic Shop and find written instructions for meeting old friends already living in the Haight. The store was a popular message drop with customers who did not have easy access to phones. Other visitors to the Psychedelic Shop passed time by sitting on the store's floor or on the sidewalk outside.[11] Young hippies flocked to the store because it was one of the few stores to sell tickets for the Avalon Ballroom and the Fillmore Auditorium, concert venues that helped to launch the careers of such psychedelic rock bands as the Grateful Dead, Jefferson Airplane, and Big Brother and the Holding Company.[12] By the fall of 1966, the Psychedelic Shop had become one of the most important public spaces for the Haight's burgeoning countercultural scene, second only to perhaps the Golden Gate Park's Hippie Hill and

Panhandle sections. Even if the store was not earning massive profits, it had a steady stream of customers and achieved a surprising level of financial stability.

The Thelins saw themselves and their shop more and more as agents for social change. Ron believed that the Psychedelic Shop provided a direct alternative to modern capitalism, which debased and alienated the American people. "The economy, the tyranny of money, the fight for material things," he remarked, "has become the American dream—and the dream of the Declaration of Independence is completely washed up in an advertising gimmick." These developments "were not answering the promise of America," Jay and Ron insisted. "Psychedelics and getting high," they felt, "would be the catalyst that would change everything," and the Psychedelic Shop would be the primary means of spreading that message in San Francisco. The Thelins, like many people in San Francisco's countercultural community, saw the traditional tactics of political activists as having a limited impact on American social values, in contrast to the fundamental psychological and emotional transformation they believed LSD could achieve.[13]

Skeptical about traditional forms of engagement, the Thelins were deeply unconventional in their political activism. In June 1966, the California legislature voted to ban LSD, effective October 6 of that year. Ron joined forces with the Beat artist Michael Bowen and Psychedelic Shop employee Allen Cohen to organize the Love Pageant Rally on the first day of the state's LSD ban. Writing in the *San Francisco Oracle*, the Haight's underground newspaper, which Bowen and Cohen cofounded and the Thelins partly funded, the three men announced the event with a "Declaration of Independence" in a full-page notice featuring an illustration of a marijuana leaf. The three organizers urged readers "to cease to recognize the obsolete social patterns which have isolated man from his consciousness and [instead] to create with the youthful energies of the world revolutionary communities of harmonious relations." By attending the Love Pageant, people could not only protest LSD's prohibition but also affirm their "inalienable rights," which extended to "the freedom of the body, the pursuit of joy, and the expansion of consciousness." On October 6, an estimated seven to eight hundred people showed up at Golden Gate Park to translate "this prophesy into political action" and demonstrate against the new LSD ban by dropping hundreds of tabs of acid in unison. The Love Pageant marked the beginning of a long collaboration between head shop owners and the advocates of drug legalization in the years to come.[14]

That fall, city officials informed the Thelins they would need to join a merchant group to receive an overdue business license. Long-term residents and merchants in the Haight had come to view the influx of hippies, many of whom had little money and no employment, as an invading force that threatened to ruin the entire neighborhood. Panhandling had increased dramatically, and older merchants complained that the hordes of newcomers scared away customers, especially by congregating directly in front of their stores.

The Thelins applied for membership in the Haight-Ashbury Merchants Association, hoping they might be able to serve as hippie ambassadors who could bridge the gap between the older business owners and the younger new arrivals, but their application was rejected. "Are you afraid of us?" the brothers asked the association indignantly in an open letter in the *Oracle*.

> If you think that by ignoring a problem it will go away, you are going to be shocked by the vastness of this "problem" a year from now. There is a fundamental and profound change occurring in American society. Much of the focus of that change will be in the Bay Area. You have a choice: you may fight that change and end your days bitter and hateful of your own youth, or you may trust the youth of today and be influential in the quality of the change.[15]

As long as older residents shunned the Haight's hippies, the Thelins argued, the new arrivals' burden on the city would only worsen.

In response to the rejection, the Thelins also decided to form their own merchants' group, one that could represent their interests as countercultural entrepreneurs. Over the course of 1966, a number of other stores catering to the Haight's newcomers had opened for business, including Tsvi Strauch's boutique promoting psychedelics called In Gear, and "Blind Jerry" Sealund's natural grocery, Far Fetched Foods. Along with Strauch and Sealund, the Thelins formed the Haight Independent

Proprietors (HIP). Announcing their group in a press conference, the members of HIP presented themselves as good stewards of the Haight who brought business to a declining neighborhood. In response to the neighborhood's growing unemployment woes, HIP developed a "hip jobs" placement service for hippies seeking part-time work. "Anyone qualifies, no dress requirements, etc.," a HIP notice in the *Oracle* announced. "All that's necessary is an interest to work. If this job service works, it will be because it's based on trust and the mutual good will between employer and employed."[16] In a rather unexpected turn of events, the Haight's hippies, most of whom had been in the Haight for less than two years, now had their own business association.

These hippie retailers also established HIP to defend themselves against the frequent harassment they endured at the hands of the San Francisco Police Department. Jay Thelin recalls "a lot of undercover narcs that came in and tried to sell us drugs." There were nearly constant sweeps for teenagers on Haight Street, in which half-a-dozen officers would visit multiple hip businesses in succession, demand identification from everyone, and take anyone who could not prove he or she was an adult to the police station and charge all of them with vagrancy or report them to their parents as runaways. In November 1966, police officers raided both the Psychedelic Shop and Lawrence Ferlinghetti's City Lights Books in North Beach for distributing obscene materials, specifically Lenore Kandal's *The Love Book*, a volume of erotic poetry. Some suspected that the raid was a show of force intended to intimidate the growing hippie population, and the arrest of Cohen, Jay Thelin, and a City Lights employee seemed to confirm that suspicion. The three defendants faced a five-week civil trial—one of the longest in San Francisco's history—and were ultimately fined a total of $200 and convicted with suspended sentences of six months each.[17]

In an attempt to smooth over rocky relations with law enforcement, the Thelins and other merchants associated with HIP put up a sign in the Psychedelic Shop window reading "Take a Cop to Dinner." To their surprise, the San Francisco police chief Thomas Cahill accepted this overture and sat down for a summit with the HIP merchants in early 1967. Ron Thelin and Tsvi Strauch told Cahill they represented close to a hundred shopkeepers and artists in the Haight. They then proceeded to regale the police chief with tales of the supreme enlightenment they had achieved through LSD.

Yet, more than anything, Thelin and Strauch sought to assure Cahill that HIP wanted to avoid confrontations with the police at all costs. "You're sort of the Love Generation, aren't you?" Cahill purportedly asked in disbelief. Such sympathies notwithstanding, throughout 1967 the San Francisco Police Department operated a major series of narcotics sweeps, investigations by plainclothes officers, and raids on communal houses as part of an overall strategy of discouraging the massive influx of hippies into the Haight.[18]

Perhaps the greatest challenge the Psychedelic Shop and HIP faced was growing criticism from their own countercultural colleagues. The most stinging critiques came from the Diggers, the Haight's famed group of street actors, philosophers, and all-around provocateurs. The Diggers hosted daily giveaways of free food in the Panhandle section of Golden Gate Park and even opened their own retail space in the Haight. At the Diggers' Free Store, customers could take whatever they wanted at no cost, an amenity the Diggers envisioned as the ultimate freedom from materialism. With the Free Store, the Diggers sought to "liberate human nature. First free the space, goods, and services. Let theories of economics follow social facts." Customers were periodically invited to take over the store and spontaneously manage it. The Free Store was a combination of participatory economics and "social art form." Both the store and the Diggers' food giveaways were efforts to offer the Haight radical alternatives to capitalism's profit motives, and as such they implied a critique of the growing countercultural commerce in the Haight.[19]

In 1967, the Diggers started to broadcast their displeasure with the Psychedelic Shop. Chester Anderson, an outspoken member of the group, wrote a scathing broadside titled "Uncle Tim'$ Children" (a reference to both Uncle Tom in the novel *Uncle Tom's Cabin* and Timothy Leary), in which he condemned HIP as hucksters selling "our lovely little psychedelic community to the mass media, to the world," and skewered HIP's businesses for their pivotal role in drawing thousands of curious onlookers, tourists, and young people from all over the country to the neighborhood in search of the hippie experience.

The HIP Merchants have lured a million children here recklessly & irresponsibly, & now that the children are arriving, more & more every day, the HIP Merchants are maintaining their irresponsibility with an iron-clad firmness that borders on criminal insanity.... And why should they? They are what they are: businessmen, salesmen, money counters. They see what businessmen see: business. Once you don't have any more money to spend in their plastic paisley shoppes, they stop seeing you. You become invisible.... That is, they're really good people in their way, but they have their limitations. $$$$$$$$$$$. That's as far as they go.[20]

Although Anderson didn't address the Thelins by name, anyone in the Haight would know he was describing them.

In the face of both these criticisms and the growing numbers of customers flocking to their store, the Thelins used their newfound freedom from financial considerations to push their business in an even more idealistic direction. Now, more than ever, they aspired to make the Psychedelic Shop a headquarters for hippies seeking community and enlightenment as well as a refuge from the increasingly rough streets in the Haight. When a fire devastated an apartment over the store, firefighters extinguished the blaze but in the process waterlogged and ruined a significant portion of the Psychedelic Shop's merchandise, as did a subsequent rainstorm. Instead of replacing their lost merchandise, Ron and Jay set up a space for meditation in the shop, which they christened the Calm Center. In the coming months, the center would regularly host members of the nearby Hare Krishna temple, who would "come into the meditation room and chant and the kids could come in off the street and join them." The Thelins also announced plans to incorporate the store as a nonprofit and sell shares on the streets of the Haight for mere pennies. The reorientation of their store won the Thelins approval from Anderson, who reversed course just a month after accusing them of being capitalist vultures. By early May 1967, he insisted that Ron and Jay were "turned-on people, steeped in the love of love, incredibly eager to fill the world with love, genuinely good people" who recognized that "people are more important than profits."[21]

Yet the Thelins' changes to the Psychedelic Shop soon undermined the business. Fewer paying customers came to the store, so the Thelins reduced their hours. Many people took advantage of the Calm Center for meditating or coming off bad acid trips, but some used it as a place for sleeping and, against the wishes of the Thelins, for smoking marijuana and selling drugs. As one historian of the Haight declared, the Psychedelic Shop had become "essentially a bustable crash pad at the most highly publicized address on Haight Street."[22] The Thelins had sought to turn their business into a community center, but in the process they had overestimated their customers' interest in making purchases.

The Psychedelic Shop's successes and challenges anticipated many of the decisions hippie shops would be forced to make in coming years. By embracing LSD and marijuana as tools for social change, the store was not just a purveyor of rolling papers and accessories for tripping but a countercultural business that had assumed the role of the ultimate community spot for the hippies of the Haight. With its psychedelic products and atmosphere, its hippie customers and staff, and even its underdeveloped profit motive, the Psychedelic Shop's approach to business represented a deeply unconventional form of retailing. The Thelins struggled with police repression, hostility from the neighborhoods' older merchants, and, most painfully, critical voices from their own ranks accusing them of exploitation and cheap boosterism. By de-emphasizing economic exchange in favor of collaborative consciousness raising, the staff of the Psychedelic Shop had redeemed themselves in the eyes of the Haight's more radical critics by 1967. Yet in doing so they had also undermined their own financial prosperity. Like the Thelins, countless activist entrepreneurs would struggle to find the right balance between commerce, community, and political engagement.

By the middle of 1967—the so-called Summer of Love—the day-to-day pressures of running the world's leading psychedelic storefront began to wear on the Thelins. The influx of an estimated one hundred thousand young people absolutely overwhelmed the Haight, transforming the neighborhood's modest homelessness problem into an outright crisis. Violence and the use of hard drugs, including methamphetamines and heroin, rose to unprecedented levels.[23] Ron and his wife decided to move out of the city, as did many other countercultural pioneers in the Haight, who felt the media spectacle and influx of new arrivals to the neighborhood had destroyed its magic. The burdens of running the Psychedelic Shop were too much for the Thelins to bear, and they decided to close the store.

Burned out and dispirited, a group of eighty people, including staffers from the Psychedelic Shop, commemorated the "death of the hippie" on October 6, 1967. Organizers held a wake for a handcrafted mannequin of a hippie, carrying him in a cardboard coffin down Haight Street as "Taps" played. Marijuana and beads were burned in a funeral pyre. The march concluded at the Psychedelic Shop. Ron announced to the crowd that he was closing the store and giving away its entire inventory. He invited the marchers to take anything they wanted without paying a cent—a decision he made without his brother's consent.[24]

At the time of the closing, Ron and Jay had fashioned the Psychedelic Shop into one of the most idealistic and high-minded countercultural businesses of its time. "The mass media made us into hippies. We wanted to be free men and build a free community," Ron declared. "That word hippy turned everyone off. . . . Well, the hippies are dead." In the window of the Psychedelic Shop hung several handwritten signs with messages such as "Be Free," "Don't Mourn for Me, Organize," and, in an appeal to local hippies to take their message to the rest of the country, "Nebraska Needs You More Than the Haight."[25]

THE RISE OF HEAD SHOPS AND THE
LEGALIZATION MOVEMENT

Although few if any head shops would ever achieve the renown of the Psychedelic Shop, the Thelins' countercultural store nonetheless proved an alluring model for countless aspiring hippie entrepreneurs. Businesses like the Thelins' shop, in fact, were opening all over the country. "In many cities psychedelic book stores, poster shops and rug shops are sprouting," medical professor Donald Louria reported in his guide to America's "drug scene" in 1968. Countercultural businesses appeared to have a much larger commercial potential than what the Psychedelic Shop had achieved. Louria repeated a story that "astute businessmen" thought they had discovered what could "be a 25 billion-dollar-a-year market," a questionable claim lacking evidence but one that nonetheless pointed to hippie enterprises' growing visibility and commercial profile.[26] As *Time* reported in early 1967, "Psychedelic central for the U.S. right now is a half-mile stretch along San Francisco's Haight Street, which has 27 shops catering to the needs of hippies and trippies" and selling lots of "incense, cigarette papers and bells." Several similar stores opened in New York's East Village by the start of 1967, too, including one called the Psychedelicatessan and another called simply the Head Shop. Although some of these businesses in California continued to call themselves "psychedelic shops," more and more of them opted for the term *head shop*. Since at least the 1930s, avid marijuana smokers had referred to each other as "weed heads," "pot heads," or simply "heads," terms that were circulated even more widely as media showered attention on the hippie counterculture.[27]

By 1968, head shops began to open in college towns, including Eugene, Oregon; Amherst, Massachusetts; and Austin and Denton, Texas. At the end of the decade, cities such as New York, San Francisco, and Los Angeles were home to dozens of head shops each, and smaller cities such as Miami, Cleveland, Baltimore, and Atlanta could claim at least several head shops as well. Even states such as Nebraska needed the Haight's hippies less than the staff of the Psychedelic Shop believed. Omaha, for example, already had a small but burgeoning countercultural scene strong enough to support hippie enterprises by late 1967. *Buffalo Chip*, an underground newspaper in the style of the *San Francisco Oracle*, launched in Omaha that year. The town's local head shop, the Farthest Outpost, sold "posters, beads, ear things, onions, amulets, roach holders, toys & things of interest."[28] Countercultural businesses were spreading to smaller cities and towns all over the country.

Like the Thelins, many head shop owners believed their products and services could empower people to achieve liberation through higher states of consciousness. Countercultural entrepreneurs knew that customers bought pipes, papers, posters, records, candles, black-light bulbs, and even Buddhist and Hindu paraphernalia for getting high. But the experience of visiting a head shop was supposed to transport customers psychologically, to delight their senses, to take them on a proverbial trip. To set the mood for shoppers, stores often featured loud rock music, heavy incense, and even psychedelic light shows. With names such as "Inner World," "Middle

Earth," "Mind Garden," "Sidereal Time," "Third Eye," and "The First Bardo" (a reference to the Tibetan Book of the Dead), head shops implied that they could point customers to introspection and spiritual development. Some stores, including the Electric Lotus in New York and the Psychedelic Shop in the Haight, featured meditation rooms.[29] In adding these features to their stores, head shops' owners believed they offered a more humane, thoughtful, and authentic alternative to the conformity, materialism, and alienation they attributed to "plastic" American consumer culture.

The demographics of head shop ownership are difficult to gauge precisely, but a few patterns of the proprietors' background stand out. Through the 1960s and the first half of the 1970s, virtually all of the owners had close ties to the counterculture. Most of them were men, but some women, both with male partners and by themselves, ran stores, too. The large majority of head shop owners were white, but some African Americans also owned head shops or sold drug paraphernalia in record shops. Most owners were young—some of them even still in high school—but some were middle-aged, often working with a younger partner or family member.[30]

Head shop owners often invested more time and energy pursuing enlightenment and community than profits. Accounting, inventory, and margins were not particularly high priorities for most. "Yesterday I gave away more than I sold," one owner in Eugene told a reporter in 1967. "I just want to make enough money to pay the rent, and to eat." Another head shop, the Pratt Street Conspiracy in Baltimore, was a nonprofit cooperative that employed teenage residents in the Hollins Market neighborhood (figure 3.1). The co-op's revenues came from sales, memberships sold to customers, and grant funding from the Community Action Agency, an organization funded primarily by the federal Office for Economic Opportunity. Employees were paid by the Volunteers in Service to America program (best known as VISTA) and a Title I grant administered by an "urban action development committee" at the University of Baltimore. Any profits after salaries and operating costs were channeled back into two local community nonprofit organizations working with the store. As one sociologist argued in 1972, most head shops were "community-oriented shops . . . offering for

FIGURE 3.1 The Pratt Street Conspiracy Head Shop in Baltimore, a nonprofit cooperative owned by teenagers in the Hollins Market neighborhood and partially funded by the
federal Volunteers in Service to America program. From *Harry,* January 8, 1971, 9

sale 'at cost' the accouterments for community role performance—most
especially drug 'tripping.'" They "fulfilled a number of primary community functions" for hippies and "in a loosely analogous sense [were] a combination of church, community center, and public drinking place in the
straight world."[31]

Head shops' rejection of established business practices attracted countercultural customers and employees seeking free spaces that offered an
alternative to America's dominant consumer culture. Their employees
embraced the casual, "natural" hippie look of long hair, jeans, and sometimes no shirts or shoes—at a time when strict rules still governed dress
and hairstyle in many workplaces and public institutions. Customers were

also welcome to hang out and chat with clerks and other shoppers at length without necessarily making any purchases. Yippie leader and anti-war activist Abbie Hoffman praised head shops as "community-minded stores" in his paperback countercultural and New Left how-to guide *Steal This Book* (1971). Other head shops were magnets for hippies seeking band mates or places to live, which they found by talking to other customers or reading ads on message boards. "I thought we were the housing authority," one Baltimore storeowner joked after fielding countless questions about places to stay, "but it's just because we're a head shop that they came here."[32]

Head shops were among the few places where hippies could congregate publicly without encountering significant hostility or outright harassment. Many conventional business owners discouraged hippies from patronizing their stores, and some even refused to serve them. By contrast, most head shop owners—who usually identified as hippies themselves—regarded so-called heads and freaks as their most important customers. In neighborhoods where head shops clustered, police targeted hippies for loitering, disorderly conduct, and drug use. As in the Haight, law enforcement detained countless minors in these neighborhoods in response to the emerging social problem of "runaways," or teenagers who fled from their families. Yet despite such close scrutiny from police, such districts—which some sociologists and anthropologists christened "hippie ghettoes" or "youth ghettoes"—emerged all over the country. It was in these neighborhoods where most countercultural entrepreneurs opened head shops and other countercultural storefronts that doubled as unofficial community centers. "The role of psychedelic shop as social center is probably more significant" than any of the business's other features, a reporter from the *Los Angeles Times* contended. This was especially true for "sartorially advanced hippies [who] are often made to feel distinctly unwelcome in coffee shops and restaurants."[33]

But precisely because head shops identified so closely with the counterculture, they, too, drew police officers looking to make arrests and even some private citizens hoping to harass them. Head shops raised the ire of law enforcement and local governments around the country. Some of them did sell illegal drugs and allowed customers to get high on site. One of the country's biggest hashish- and LSD-smuggling rings, for instance, the Eternal Brotherhood of Love, operated the Mystic Arts World head shop in Laguna Beach, California, from around 1967 to 1970. Nevertheless, although most head shops did not sell drugs, police often thought of them as no different than dealers. In Texas City, a suburb of Houston, local police walked into the Head Garden without a warrant and demanded that the owner remove several posters they found objectionable, in turn prompting the owner to file a $50,000 civil suit against city officials with the help of the American Civil Liberties Union. In San Clemente, Orange County, California, a petition signed by seven hundred residents unsuccessfully sought to revoke the business license of the town's first head shop, the Mind Garden. One of the directors of the town's Chamber of Commerce warned ominously that if the store were allowed to remain open for long, "it'll be too late, just as it already is too late for Laguna Beach, where the hippies have been allowed to crowd together in hovels." Head shops were even subject to violence. In Los Angeles, an unknown assailant threw a brick through the front window of the California Stash the night before it opened for business. And in Fort Worth, an unknown assailant bombed the Sunshine Phluph head shop at night while it was closed.[34] To many people, head shops were illegitimate, dirty businesses that disturbed public order, bred lawlessness, drew unwanted hippies into their communities, and sold drugs.

From the other end of the political spectrum, some underground newspapers accused head shops of being "hip capitalists"—businesses that commodified the counterculture but contributed little to meaningful political or social change. Although few entrepreneurs embraced the term *hip capitalism*, debates about it appeared regularly in the pages of underground press in the late 1960s and early 1970s. "Hip capitalists remain largely apolitical," argued one writer in the cleverly titled article "Age of Acquireous" in the San Francisco paper *Good Times*. "By doing business in the system, they perpetuate it and contribute taxes." Like Chester Anderson, some activists questioned the sincerity of these businesses, too. "The hip merchants are always getting taken to task by the arch-anarchist-Marxists," remarked Tsvi Strauch, a water-pipe seller in the Haight and member of HIP. Such critiques aligned with sentiments in the New Left that the mainstreaming of pot and acid threatened to undermine the drugs' capacity for social change and the transformation of consciousness. As one reader of Atlanta's underground newspaper *Great Speckled Bird* complained in a letter, "There has been a tremendous growth of the 'hip' element in Atlanta. . . . [But] perhaps this situation exists because the sole basis for this new cult is dope, and not because of any enlightenment to the true ideology." To its critics, hip capitalism was, at best, countercultural escapism and, at worst, both a surrender to co-optation and a profitable way to dodge political responsibility.[35]

Yet head shops were by no means apolitical. Their owners vigorously promoted the antiwar movement, often providing free protest literature in their stores and selling antiwar jewelry, buttons, and posters. Some head shop owners, such as Doug Brown of Oat Willie's in Austin, were actively involved in antiwar demonstrations. Head shops also commonly distributed underground and New Left newspapers, no small feat considering the intense backlash many such publications and their sellers faced in communities across the country. They also displayed posters and announcements for marches and political rallies.[36]

By the end of the 1960s, there was a significant overlap between political protesters and members of the so-called drug culture who frequented head shops for rolling papers, pipes, and psychedelic accessories. Indeed, student protesters were considerably more likely than nonprotestors to smoke marijuana, as a Gallup Poll demonstrated in 1969. Such an overlap provided ample fodder for politicians, who blamed marijuana's popularity on student activists. Senator James Eastland of Mississippi claimed in hearings he held on the "marijuana–hashish epidemic and its impact on United States security" that the "epidemic began at Berkeley University at the time of the 1965 Berkeley Uprising . . . [when] the right to pot became an integral part of the catalogue of demands of the uprising." And as President Nixon told Elvis Presley in their famed White House meeting in 1970, "Those who use the drugs are the protestors. You know, the ones who get caught up in dissent and violence. They're the same group of young people." By 1971, Nixon would dramatically intensify federal efforts to combat drug abuse, which he declared to be "public enemy number one in the United States."[37]

Eastland's and Nixon's dubious claims notwithstanding, many people in the counterculture, such as the Thelins, did believe that LSD and marijuana were political tools they could use to free their consciousness, advance peace, and break out of the straitjacket of repressive American cultural norms. As the Michigan-based countercultural leader and antiwar activist John Sinclair argued, smoking marijuana allowed people to "see that the whole repressive political and economic and cultural machinery of the capitalist state must be dismantled and thrown on the junkheap of history," a reformulation of Leon Trotsky's oft quoted dictum. Meanwhile, the Youth International Party, whose members, Yippies, were best known for their countercultural political theater and involvement in the radical antiwar movement, made marijuana a central part of its political program. The Yippies' flag, for instance, featured a giant, green weed leaf. "We Are a People," a manifesto presented at the Second Yip Collective in 1970, attributed the American legal system, which "put 200,000 of us in jail for smoking flowers[,] . . . [to] a society based on war, racism, sexism, and the destruction of the planet." The Yippies and Sinclair had a point: between 1965 and 1971, the annual total of marijuana arrests nationwide skyrocketed from less than 19,000 to more than 225,000—an increase of more than 1,000 percent.[38]

As the counterculture and New Left began to attack the social costs of punitive drug laws, many head shops joined the small but growing movement to decriminalize and legalize marijuana. The modern marijuana legalization movement's origins can be traced to August 16, 1964, when a young man named Lowell Eggemeier walked into the San Francisco Police Department, lit up a joint, and announced he was protesting the prohibition of marijuana. Arrested immediately, Eggemeier hired an attorney, James R. White III, who in turn founded the organization Legalize Marijuana, or LeMar. Although Eggemeier and White eventually lost the case on appeal, they published a slim, seventy-three-page volume titled *Marijuana Puff In*, a reprint of their opening brief, which LeMar distributed to bookstores and activists throughout the country. Later that year in New York, several of the leading figures in New York's thriving countercultural scene in the East Village and Lower East Side—including Beat poet Allen Ginsberg, the pioneering gay rights activist Randy Wicker, and Ed Sanders of the Peace Eye Bookstore (and later of the rock group the Fugs)—started their own chapter of LeMar. Among their early activities was a small protest at the New York City Women's House of Detention in 1965, where Ginsberg was photographed holding a sign that proclaimed "Pot Is Fun." The image was reproduced on a poster that would later become a popular seller at head shops. LeMar also published the *Marijuana Newsletter* (later renamed *Marijuana Review*), a crudely designed and partly handwritten newsletter whose stated mission was "to print position papers, medical testimonies, & general information about the campaign to legalize marijuana! . . . We have the facts about marijuana, the gentle benevolent herb." Wicker, one of the *Newsletter*'s editors, operated a successful East Village head shop, the Underground Uplift Unlimited, from 1967 to 1971.[39]

Legalization advocates' critique of drug laws as tools of political repression crystallized in the campaign to release Michigan antiwar activist, countercultural pioneer, and Trans-Love Energies collective and head shop cofounder John Sinclair from prison. Detroit police—who had put Sinclair under surveillance—arrested him for marijuana possession for the third time in 1967 as he was gathering with friends to plan a benefit concert for marijuana legalization and a community fund for drug arrestees. His arrest set into motion a long series of legal maneuvers, with Sinclair and his attorney arguing that prison time for marijuana possession represented cruel and unusual punishment and was thus unconstitutional. After extensive consideration, the motion to rule on the law's constitutionality was dismissed, and in July 1969 Sinclair was convicted of possession and sentenced to nine and a half to ten years in prison. Activists around the country organized the International Committee to Free John Sinclair in response, an effort culminating in December 1971 with a rally and benefit concert "to demand freedom for John Sinclair and an end to marijuana prohibition." John Lennon and Yoko Ono headlined, drawing more than fifteen thousand attendees to Ann Arbor's Crisler Arena. Under intense political pressure, the Michigan Supreme Court granted Sinclair bond and released him just three days later. Several months later, the court released an additional 128 prisoners convicted of marijuana possession, ruling that the state's laws were indeed unconstitutional by treating marijuana as a "hard" narcotic and imposing a cruel and unusual punishment on people convicted of its possession. Sinclair's allies—in a major upset—also won seats on the Ann Arbor City Council, and within two months the town's city council voted to reduce marijuana possession to a $5 fine, making its drug laws the most liberal in the country.[40]

Marijuana convictions and imprisonment for Sinclair and other activists, such as Houston SNCC member Lee Otis Johnson, further politicized pot. To Sinclair, marijuana held promise as a powerful tool young activists could wield against the political and legal establishment. "Hippies and radicals, once wary of each other's thing, have been united by the police who are their common enemy," he declared. As a result, "our culture is bound together with marijuana, millions of young people now smoke weed regularly, and thousands of these millions have been persecuted by the state for marijuana crimes." Marijuana had become nothing less than "a political force by virtue of the opposition it encounters from the established state."[41] Head shop owners had more reason than ever to view marijuana, and by extension their own businesses, as part of a larger ideological debate and to align themselves with the growing movement to legalize pot.

In the early 1970s, activists for drug-law reform, many of them involved in efforts to free Sinclair, came to view head shops and the paraphernalia they sold as lucrative vehicles for funding the legalization movement. Originally established as a proprietary enterprise in 1969, the California-based legalization group Amorphia reincorporated itself as a nonprofit and merged with LeMar in 1972. That year, the organization employed about a dozen full-time employees, including Gordon Brownell, a onetime junior staffer in the Nixon White House who had abandoned a career in Republican politics after a powerful first experience with mescaline. By early 1973, John and Leni Sinclair joined *Marijuana Review* editor Mike Aldrich and New York attorney David Michaels as Amorphia's national chairs. The organization's fund-raising strategy was to produce its own brand of rolling papers, Acapulco Gold, and sell them for about three times as much as normal rolling papers would cost (figure 3.2). "By selling head stuff, starting with rolling papers, and donating all proceeds from such sales to this legalization campaign," Amorphia announced in *Marijuana Review*. "We will attempt to fund an all-out media assault on Middle Amerika for legalization of marijuana (and perhaps other drug law reform)."[42]

FIGURE 3.2 Advertisement for Acapulco Gold, rolling paper. The nonprofit organization Amorphia used the sales revenue from Acapulco Gold to advocate for marijuana's legalization. Courtesy of John Sinclair

Amorphia in turn appealed to legalization activists to become salespeople to hawk rolling papers. "Become an 'acapulco gold' sales representative or jobber," an advertisement in *Marijuana Review* read. "This entails going around to head shops, bookstores, hip boutiques, and anyplace else that sells cigarette rolling papers in your area, and making sure they sell 'acapulco gold' papers." Aldrich declared that Amorphia's "self-determination program" was the best strategy for legalization that he had seen in five years in the marijuana rights movement. Yet proceeds from Acapulco Gold were intended to do more than just contribute to pot's legalization. By entering the business of supplying head shops, Amorphia planned "to pour $30 million a year into underground movements, social change, and the creation of a better world. Legalization is not an end; it is a means to create social change and a new form of economic organization."[43] Paraphernalia,

Amorphia argued, was much more than accessories for getting high. It was a set of tools for political transformation.

The first major test of Amorphia's strategy was its campaign for Proposition 19, a legalization referendum in California in 1972. Amorphia provided the primary financial support for the initiative, contributing $50,000 to the campaign, almost a third of which came from Acapulco Gold proceeds. Although Amorphia greatly outspent the antilegalization groups, the referendum easily lost by a margin of almost two to one. Nevertheless, the final vote tally suggested that the marijuana rights movement had significant room to grow. More than one-third of voters in the referendum had opted for legalization, and both San Francisco County and Berkeley approved the measure. Amorphia later contributed to legalization efforts in several other states, including Michigan and Washington. And although a referendum campaign Amorphia funded to fully legalize marijuana in Oregon failed in 1972, it did spur the state's legislature to form a committee to study and ultimately recommend decriminalizing marijuana. The following year, in 1973, Oregon's legislature voted to make the state the first in the country to eliminate criminal penalties for marijuana possession. Just three years after Congress had removed mandatory federal penalties for marijuana use in 1970, Oregon had taken the much bolder step of determining marijuana possession was not a crime at all, but rather a civil violation.[44]

Other legalization groups collaborated closely with head shops, too. By 1973, the National Organization for the Reform of Marijuana Laws was vying for leadership of the movement. Founded in 1970 by Keith Stroup, a young consumer attorney and former staffer of the congressionally mandated National Committee on Product Safety, NORML had virtually no budget until Stroup successfully lobbied Hugh Hefner's philanthropic Playboy Foundation to donate $100,000 annually. Like Amorphia, NORML worked closely with activist businesses for fund-raising purposes. The group marketed its own "line of marijuana-related paraphernalia," which it distributed primarily through head shops. The items included T-shirts, posters, and buttons that employed the rhetoric of radical activism and countercultural freedom with messages such as "Liberate Marijuana." And it was no accident that the name of NORML's national newsletter—the *Leaflet*—referred both to its role as a newsletter and to head shops' biggest seller, rolling paper. By the middle of the 1970s, NORML had assumed unofficial leadership of the marijuana-reform movement and claimed a membership of around twenty thousand.[45] Decriminalization was growing into a cause with support that extended far beyond its origins in the counterculture and the radical politics of the late 1960s.

MOVING TOWARD THE MAINSTREAM

As legalization efforts proceeded, the head shop business began making deeper inroads into the American economy. Although the stores "used to be frequented mainly by hippies and drug 'freaks,'" the *Los Angeles Times* remarked in 1972, "they now attract a broader clientele." Demand for paraphernalia was booming. Tobacco companies still made most of the money producing and distributing what was likely head shops' biggest seller, rolling papers. But a new cohort of young paraphernalia producers such as the E-Z Wider Company emerged with the explicit goals of serving marijuana consumers and earning significant profits. Sales of imported rolling papers unaccompanied by tobacco—including the French brand Zig-Zag favored by pot smokers—jumped from 1 million packets in 1965 to 157 million in 1970. As one Los Angeles grocery wholesaler admitted, "Our paper sales have grown about 75% faster than our long-cut tobacco sales. We can put two and two together. We know the buyers aren't smoking corn silk."[46]

Some head shop owners began to fuse activist approaches to business with more conventional retail strategies. Dan Lackey was one such entrepreneur who wanted to open a new kind of head shop in Atlanta in 1974. While majoring in business management at the Georgia Institute of Technology in Atlanta, Lackey considered himself a "weekend hippie." He attended large rock shows, dabbled in drugs, and spent time around the Strip, the epicenter of what was arguably the Southeast's most significant hippy community, centered at the intersection of Peachtree and Fourteenth Streets in midtown Atlanta. One of the businesses near the Strip that Lackey patronized was Middle Earth, which had opened in 1967. Lackey remembers the store looking like what he "would imagine an opium den would feel like[,] [with] dim lighting, psychedelic music, black light shining here and there." The store was "run by hippies" and had lots of "hippies hanging out in there [too]. You just kind of knew they were stoned." Middle Earth was very different from other business Lackey patronized, and it seemed to have nothing to do with the management techniques he learned in his college coursework. Middle Earth felt like "another world," one that embraced "the peace and freedom theme of the counterculture."[47]

Yet Lackey also associated head shops with defiance and disobedience, qualities that appealed to him but that he nonetheless doubted were good for business. He knew that whoever bought something from Middle Earth was "going to break the law later by using [what she or he purchased there]." For Lackey, smoking pot even made a statement of rejecting the war in Vietnam, so "if you didn't want to come out as being an antiwar protestor, you were still protesting by smoking pot." Lackey enjoyed visiting head shops such as Middle Earth and recognized that they provided marijuana smokers with a critical service that had immense commercial possibilities.[48]

But Lackey felt that head shop owners' lack of business experience and knowledge undermined their operations. So did the stores' shadowy atmosphere, which seemed to discourage potential customers, who feared running afoul of the law by patronizing businesses so clearly associated with illegal activity. In addition, Lackey suspected that drug dealers operated some Atlanta-area head shops as storefronts where they could launder money as well as sell drugs. Regardless of how strongly he supported marijuana's legalization, he believed that running a criminal enterprise—or even merely giving the impression of criminal activity—was not an effective formula for business stability.

Several months after graduating from Georgia Tech in 1974, Lackey and his friend Wayne Housworth opened their own head shop, which they called Windfaire, in suburban DeKalb County outside Atlanta. The two young entrepreneurs wanted their store to be different from the traditional hippie head shop. Windfaire would be run "in a more mainstream way" than most head shops so that "people who have to work in an office all day . . . [could have] a better comfort level coming in, so they don't have to feel much like an outsider." The store was not a countercultural free space in the style of earlier head shops. Lackey instead sought to operate the store according to "the principles of retail and retail management" he had learned in college and in a previous job at a shoe store, "rather than [according to the] principles of drugs and marijuana." Lackey and Housworth still believed strongly in the legitimacy of their products and the right to consume all kinds of drugs—"to carry on any action or put anything in your body that you wanted to as long as it wasn't detrimental to others." Windfaire's customers could get stoned with their purchases *after* they left the store, but the store's employees could not get high at work. Like other head shops that opened in the mid-1970s, Windfaire retained the products of its predecessors but had little to do with the places or processes that distinguished activist businesses from conventional enterprises.[49]

Windfaire offered a high level of customer service, but, unlike its predecessors, it did not aspire to be a free space for heads or activists. The store welcomed all types of customers, ranging from the "hippie . . . [to the] housewife." And Lackey and Housworth chose the intersection of Buford Highway and Clairmont Road as their location not because of any affinity hippies had for it, like the Strip, but because traffic studies from the State of Georgia confirmed it was one of the busiest intersections in the Atlanta area and because it sat near a string of apartment complexes that earned Buford Highway the distinction of being one of the Atlanta's largest concentration of young singles.[50] Both geographically and culturally, Windfaire was far away from the world of Middle Earth and the Strip.

The biggest boost to head shops' business in the mid-1970s came from *High Times*, the self-declared "only magazine dedicated solely to getting high." The magazine was founded in 1974 by Andy Kowl, editor of Long Island's underground newspaper *Express*, and Tom Forcade, longtime head of the Underground Press Syndicate, active Yippie, and all-around countercultural dynamo who operated a marijuana café in a secret apartment in the New York's West Village, where invited guests sampled pot varieties and made purchases of a pound or more for resale. Kowl and Forcade bragged that their magazine was "where dope, sex and politics melt, mingle and fuse into ideas too hot for the official culture to handle." Issues featured centerfold spreads of exotic and expensive varieties of marijuana, advice columns on how to intensify and enhance drugs' effects, and interviews with musicians, writers, and other countercultural figures. Demand for

High Times skyrocketed quickly after its debut. By its fifth issue in August–September 1975, the magazine had a print run of 250,000.[51]

High Times provided an unprecedented communications network for head shops and their customers all over the United States. Before the magazine emerged, the marketplace for "head gear"—essentially paraphernalia for getting high—had been a small, decentralized cottage industry of highly localized retailers and a handful of producers and distributors with regional or national reach. By advertising in *High Times*, paraphernalia producers and distributors could now reach a national audience of marijuana smokers and vice versa, and local head shops could find suppliers much more easily and vice versa. As a result, the paraphernalia business became significantly more competitive because retailers could now comparison-shop much more easily. By 1977, the overwhelming majority of *High Times*'s advertising revenue came from head shops and paraphernalia producers, and around half the pages of every issue featured ads. That year, the magazine's circulation rose to 400,000, but an independent marketing firm estimated that as many as ten people borrowed each purchased copy of the magazine from friends. Per issue readership consequently was closer to 4 million. Although the magazine did feature some political reporting, it was less activist and less radical than its predecessor, *Marijuana Review*, or than the network of underground newspapers that Forcade had worked with earlier in his career.[52] The magazine examined some issues of higher consciousness and spirituality, but it was more interested in drugs and a variety of highs as sources of sensory pleasure. *High Times*, in short, signaled that drug culture was gradually growing apart from its origins in counterculture and its connections to the New Left.

Meanwhile, many of the new generation of head shop owners, such as Lackey and Housworth, strived for recognition as competent businesspeople, not stoned hippie radicals. The very term *head shop* began to fall out of favor as companies self-identified as "paraphernalia sellers." The demand for rolling papers and pipes had grown so much that many retailers other than head shops now stocked marijuana accessories, too. Paraphernalia sold briskly at record stores, tobacco shops, drug stores, convenience marts, and even general merchandisers such as K-Mart and Sears, Roebuck, & Company. At the same time, conventional retailers sought to downplay their vital role in selling paraphernalia. In 1978, one issue of a national trade newsletter for cigarette and candy distributors, for instance, carried a four-page cover story on the inventors of the E-Z Wider rolling papers, which were widely known to be designed for marijuana. The article, however, never mentioned or even alluded to marijuana.[53]

The paraphernalia trade expanded dramatically in the second half of the 1970s, growing at a rate that had been simply unimaginable just a few years earlier. Head shops were no longer limited to college towns and cities. Paraphernalia sellers had set up shop in the suburbs, rural areas, and even shopping malls (figure 3.3). One trade representative contended that only about 20 percent of paraphernalia were sold by head shops, with the rest

FIGURE 3.3 Steve Gilbert and Bruce Hoffman, owners of the Tobacco Road head shops chain in suburban Detroit, 1978. Courtesy of Nalpac and Ralph Caplan

sold by record stores, convenience marts, and drug stores. And as *High Times* announced in 1978,

> The nuts-and-bolts business of selling things to help you get stoned … [has] exploded into the most phenomenal industrial success story of the decade. As Detroit continues to recall cars and the oil companies quiver over depletion allowances, the business of getting high continues to expand, guided by sophisticated teams of international bankers, federal loan schemes, computerized data processing and 40 million marijuana smokers.

Estimates of the number of head shops operating in the United States by 1980 varied widely, ranging anywhere from fifteen thousand to thirty thousand, with annual sales ranging somewhere between $200 million and $3 billion.[54]

The head shop business, as *High Times* proudly declared, had become a "slick form of capitalism with a multi-billion-dollar potential the government and Fortune 500 have yet to decipher." Many of the first generation of politically and community-oriented head shops that emerged amid the counterculture and New Left of the late 1960s had operated for just a few years and had already closed. Stores founded in the mid- and late 1970s were responsible for much of the business's growth. The surviving members of the first generation of head shops became less politically engaged, and many of them scaled back claims that they served a countercultural customer base. Many head shops began to believe their financial success depended on avoiding the more confrontational activist and countercultural stances they had embraced in the late 1960s and early 1970s. Once a top cause for head shop owners, the movement against the Vietnam War no longer galvanized the businesses or their customers as antiwar protests ceased and virtually all U.S. personnel pulled out of South Vietnam by 1973. Perhaps most importantly, the counterculture's rebel status was gradually being eroded by, among other things, growing tolerance for long hair, rock music, and marijuana. With growing acceptance of drug culture and the counterculture, few businesses still discriminated against hippies, who in turn no longer needed head shops as safe havens. "The new marijuana ethic today is closely allied to a general consumerism," one *High Times* contributor lamented in 1979, warning that it was eventually "bound to intrude on the consciousness-altering ritual of smoking weed."[55]

Marijuana's political gains in the mid-1970s were remarkable. Support for decriminalization was spreading from state to state. After Oregon decriminalized marijuana in 1973, ten more states followed by 1978, including California, New York, Maine, Alaska, Colorado, North Carolina, Mississippi, Ohio, Minnesota, and Nebraska. In these states, possession of small amounts of marijuana was generally treated as a civil infraction. By 1978, more than 71 million Americans—nearly one-third of the country's 220 million residents—could smoke marijuana without the threat of criminal penalties. That year, a National Institute of Drug Abuse survey revealed the highest-ever reported number of young Americans consuming marijuana. More than 36 percent of young adults reported smoking monthly. About 11 percent of young adults reported smoking marijuana daily. In addition, a whopping two-thirds of all young adults replied that they had tried marijuana at least once. In a Gallup poll, a majority of Americans—53 percent—voiced support for decriminalizing marijuana possession.[56] But as marijuana use became increasingly widespread and accepted, some critics began to ask whether permissiveness had gone too far. In the years ahead, the paraphernalia business and head shops would prove easy targets as these critics sought to curb the country's burgeoning public drug culture.

THE MOVEMENT AGAINST HEAD SHOPS

Not far from Windfaire, Ron and Marsha "Keith" Schuchard threw a party for their daughter's thirteenth birthday in August 1976 in their home in suburban DeKalb County outside Atlanta. The Schuchards quickly became disturbed as they observed how many of their daughter's friends behaved at the party. Groups of kids huddled in the backyard around small flickering lights. Teenagers whom the parents had never seen before arrived unannounced. One girl had problems dialing a phone to make a call. After the party, Ron and Keith searched their backyard and found beer cans, wine bottles, and, most shocking of all, countless "roaches," or the butts from marijuana joints.

In response, the Schuchards called an emergency meeting of the teenagers' parents. Some parents defended their kids, and others questioned whether they had the power to change their children's behavior. Ron and Keith rallied some of the parents to take a firmer stand against their teenagers' behavior by helping each other track whom their children were associating with and by implementing a shared set of curfew guidelines and strict rules against drug use. These parents soon launched their own self-guided drug-education course, sought out government and medical materials on narcotics, and taught themselves drug slang. This was a "parent peer group," or what Keith, a professor of English at Emory University, described as "just old fashioned communal child raising."[57]

Yet the name that this group adopted—DeKalb Families in Action—suggested it was much more than a traditional parents' group. The Schuchards and their friends were particularly concerned about the wide availability of rolling papers, pipes, and other head shop staples, which they believed encouraged children to use drugs. Keith contacted local, state, and federal officials directly to share her concerns that government was doing far too little to stop what she saw as the interrelated crises of juvenile drug use and the wide availability of drug paraphernalia.

In 1977, DeKalb Families in Action started organizing against head shops and other local businesses selling drug paraphernalia with door-to-door leafleting and pickets, a campaign that earned the support of a local county commissioner. Keith also corresponded with Robert DuPont, the head of the federally funded National Institute on Drug Abuse. DuPont was so impressed with Keith that he commissioned her to write a drug-prevention handbook for parents, *Parents, Peers, and Pot* (1979), using the pseudonym "Marsha Manatt" (figure 3.4). The handbook would become the most requested title in the institute's history.[58]

By late 1977, DeKalb Families in Action was beginning to have a major impact on local head shops in their area. That December the group appeared to be on the verge of convincing the chairman of the DeKalb County Commission to revoke the business licenses of all the county's head shops. Immediately after attending a hearing at the County Courthouse to

Parents
Peers
and
Pot

by
Marsha Manatt, Ph.D.
for the
National Institute on Drug Abuse

FIGURE 3.4 Title page of Marsha [Schuhard] Manatt, *Parents, Peers, and Pots*, pamphlet Washington, D.C.: U.S. Department of Health, Education, and Welfare, 1979

defend their business, Windfaire, Dan Lackey and Wayne Housworth were arrested and jailed for selling nitrous oxide to a county narcotics agent earlier that day. By the following month, the county had revoked four head shops' business licenses, including Windfaire's. Along with the owners of three other shops, Lackey unsuccessfully appealed to the county commission for the return of their licenses. Lackey then filed suit in federal court against the county. Insisting that the head shop owners were "in a fight to protect [their] constitutional rights," Lackey candidly admitted to the *Atlanta Constitution* that what his customers "really wanted was drug smoking stuff. The market was there. We didn't create it."[59]

A judge agreed and issued an injunction ruling that DeKalb County could not revoke the head shops' licenses. That the judge ruled in the businesses' favor, even after one of the plaintiffs had admitted to a major newspaper that his customers consumed illegal substances with his products, suggested the remarkable openness with which many Americans were using drugs, marijuana in particular, in the late 1970s. Nonetheless, few of the county's other head shops survived the legal costs and the prolonged loss of revenue they incurred while their licenses had been suspended.[60]

Windfaire survived, but just barely. Within a few months, it was facing a much graver challenge: a statewide ban on head shops' core products. Lawrence "Bud" Stumbaugh and Cas Robinson, state legislators who represented many of Families in Action's members in DeKalb County, had sponsored a bill that would significantly restrict head shops in two major ways. First, the law would ban all sales of items purportedly used for the consumption of illegal substances. Second, it prohibited the sale to minors of any literature that promoted the consumption of illegal substances. In a clear sign of Families in Action's rapidly gained influence, both houses of the Georgia legislature quickly passed the bill. Days before the bill was set to arrive at Governor George Busbee's desk for signature, more than one thousand people gathered for a rally in downtown Atlanta to protest against the law and in favor of marijuana decriminalization. Busbee remained undeterred, however, and signed the bill into effect on April 10. It was the second statewide ban on marijuana paraphernalia in the country, following a law passed by Indiana in 1975, which a federal judge's injunction had halted in response to a petition by several head shop owners and the state's NORML chapter. Lackey and his allies responded similarly, filing a petition in federal court requesting an injunction against the law the day Busbee signed it.[61]

Over the next two years, a contentious series of court filings, police raids on stores, and arrests would make DeKalb County ground zero for an emerging national battle over not only head shops but also the broader role of marijuana in society. Indeed, the very names of the parties to the Georgia case set in sharp relief the deep cultural divide that the head shop debate embodied. Plaintiffs included Windfaire, Starship Enterprises, and High Ol' Times, and the named defendants were Governor Busbee and Attorney General Arthur Bolton. Although the new state law had not ordered head shops to close, the statue's broad definition of drug paraphernalia required head shop owners to reduce their inventory drastically, often to the point that they lost too much revenue to remain open. In DeKalb County, the number of head shops declined from fifteen to two in just a few years. Neighboring Fulton County also began to crack down on the stores with raids and seizures of inventories. An attorney for the head shops charged that local law enforcement had illegally confiscated $20,000 in merchandise from the stores, some of it without search warrants.[62]

Paraphernalia makers and sellers across the country began to view the conflict in Georgia as the vanguard of a national attack on their livelihoods, and they organized their own trade and lobbying groups in anticipation of further challenges. In 1978, around 150 head shop owners and paraphernalia producers gathered at the first meeting of the Paraphernalia Trade Association (PTA) in New York. The PTA invited activist attorney William Kunstler to their inaugural meeting in hopes of hiring him to represent the industry. Kunstler explained head shops' dilemma as "an insidious problem" that was part of "a trend to the right in this country." Former *High Times* editor Andy Kowl launched a trade magazine called *Paraphernalia & Accessories Digest* (later renamed *Accessories Digest*), which worked closely with the PTA to promote communications among paraphernalia businesses across the country and to coordinate responses to the rising tide of antiparaphernalia laws (figure 3.5). By early 1979, the PTA had hired Keith Stroup as national lobbyist and legal coordinator after he concluded his tenure with NORML.[63]

Beyond the significant debt owed to the counterculture, the new generation of head shops such as Windfaire started with little connection to the movements of the late 1960s. As the 1970s proceeded, however, the emerging legalization movement took on a greater importance for them. Head shop owners' establishment of trade associations as a defense against

FIGURE 3.5 Inaugural issue of *Paraphernalia & Accessories Digest*, June 1, 1978, trade magazine for head shop owners and distributors. Courtesy of Andy Kowl

encroaching government regulation was not entirely unlike renewed corporate efforts to lobby elected officials in the 1970s.[64] But in contrast to the regulations that conventional corporations faced, the burdensome and often unconstitutional regulations that head shops encountered in the second half of the 1970s reflected a conservative backlash against the deeper cultural and political threat they were thought to represent. Head shop owners became convinced that organizing politically was their main defense against citizens' groups, law enforcement, and politicians who charged them not only with breaking the law but with promoting a dangerous set of radical politics left over from the previous decade.

Head shops and paraphernalia entrepreneurs consolidated their longstanding alliance with drug legalization activists. Head shops commonly sold *High Times*, which featured countless endorsements of legalization and advertisements for NORML, and they distributed literature from NORML and other legalization advocates. Paraphernalia businesses were major financial supporters of NORML, raising more than $67,000 for the organization in the first quarter of 1977 alone. A speaker at NORML's national meeting that year urged the organization to formally recognize and address paraphernalia dealers. "I know a lot of you are here, and a lot of dealers are here, and [we should] address those people who are supplying marijuana items to endorse and effectively support, as businesses and trade organizations, NORML and other facilities that could move for repeal and taxation." In states such as Indiana, head shop owners worked together with NORML as co-plaintiffs in suits against regulations of the paraphernalia trade.[65] These efforts could have amounted to little more than entrepreneurs fighting for their business interests. But by casting their lot with the drug legalization movement and free-speech advocates, head shops had rediscovered activism, even if it was a much narrower form of activism that happened to serve their financial interests.

One aspect of this narrowness was head shops' and the legalization movement's tendency to focus almost exclusively on white marijuana smokers and forego discussions of racial inequality. In particular, African Americans were close to invisible in the popular marijuana culture and decriminalization discourse promoted by head shops in the 1970s. Much of this imbalance reflected the counterculture's fraught relationship with race. Although hippies had a long tradition of romanticizing people of color and especially African American culture, they were overwhelmingly white and showed far less concern about the struggle for racial equality than about other social movements. African Americans smoked marijuana, owned head shops, and sold marijuana paraphernalia through a variety of businesses. Yet *High Times* rarely featured nonwhite writers or interviewed African Americans or even acknowledged racial differences within the marijuana culture. Indeed, a perusal of a typical issue of the magazine would lead a reader to believe that the marijuana milieu of the 1970s was virtually all white.[66]

The legalization movement meanwhile championed a color-blind analysis of drug laws that rarely acknowledged how racial inequality permeated the criminal justice system. NORML's reticence on race suggested a cynical calculation that it was politically effective to celebrate marijuana and its young white users as innocent, everyday Americans instead of challenging the prevalent stereotypes of African American drug users as dangerous criminals. NORML seemed to believe that if it could convince Americans that marijuana was safe for middle-class whites, it was much more likely to advance decriminalization. The organization also shaped its strategy in recognition of the surprisingly high frequency with which whites were being arrested for pot in the 1970s. People of color bore the disproportionate brunt of drug laws overall, and nonwhites who smoked marijuana casually had much higher rates of arrest than whites. Yet studies showed that young whites were arrested for marijuana charges at the same rates as African Americans in some jurisdictions in this period. In particular, young white men who were involved with the counterculture—most of them whom police targeted due to their clothing and long hair—had arrest rates for marijuana charges comparable to and in some categories higher than nonwhite males' arrest rates for marijuana throughout much of the decade. The 1970s were thus an unusual period in which enforcement of marijuana laws became less racially discriminatory, not out of any desire for equality but simply because more whites were being arrested. In comparison to both earlier and later decades, marijuana in the 1970s became much less racialized in the public's eye. Instead of blaming communities of color, leading critics of head shops believed marijuana and head shops spread to white suburbs because "most of the counterculture was assimilated into the mainstream of American life" by the mid-1970s.[67]

Yet NORML significantly overestimated how much the perception of marijuana as a white people's drug would protect head shops from persecution and legal scrutiny. Nothing made this overestimation more clear than the tremendous boost the anti–head shop cause received when Families in Action's new president, Sue Rusche, testified before the U.S. House of Representatives Select Committee on Narcotics Abuse and Control in hearings devoted to drug paraphernalia in November 1979. Rusche was the first witness and testified far longer than any of the other eleven witnesses, easily establishing herself as the star of the hearings. Head shops were one member of an unholy trinity responsible for a national epidemic of youth drug use, Rusche argued. "We call upon

Congress to conduct a full-scale, criminal investigation of the drug-para-phernalia industry, *High Times* magazine, and the National Organization for the Reform of Marihuana [*sic*] Laws." Rusche insisted that legal, "free enterprise" was largely responsible for youth drug consumption. Mitchell Rosenthal, the president of the nation's largest in-patient drug-abuse-treatment facility, Phoenix House in New York City, offered an even more damning analysis of head shops at the hearings. "There is no accidental parallel to the spread of drug use and the movement of head shops from grungy downtown areas to new, suburban shopping centers," Rosenthal argued. "It is not simple coincidence that growth in youthful abuse has been matched by growth of a more-than-$600 million-a-year paraphernalia industry." Rosenthal doubted "anything has been a more potent factor in the proliferation of adolescent drug use than the exis-tence of little learning centers for drug abusers all over the country." The paraphernalia business, Rusche declared with equal doses of indignation and sarcasm, was "an industry that glamorizes and promotes illicit drugs . . . an industry that, in the time-honored tradition of American free enterprise, is developing a new market of illicit drug users—our 12- to 17-year-old children."[68] If anything, the fact that head shops' public profile was so white made them all the more threatening to critics such as Ruche and Rosenthal, who were outraged by how accepted the businesses had become in suburban areas.

Head shops exploited the laws and morals of legitimate capitalism, Rosenthal and Rusche contended, to facilitate illegitimate actions in the marketplace, both the purchase of drug paraphernalia and the use of drugs themselves.

> The most lethal commodity that head shops deliver . . . [is] a message that youngsters all over America are getting and believing. It says "getting high is OK." . . . It is sanctioned by publishers, businessmen, and the free enterprise system. The getting high business holds a rightful place beside the pharmacy, the bookstore, and the super-market in our shopping centers and malls. . . . I do not believe we can permit head shops to enjoy the benefits of fair trade and free enterprise without creating a nexus for drug abuse in every community.

In Rosenthal and Rusche's eyes, the free-enterprise system was ultimately culpable for encouraging young Americans to engage in illegal trade. In an era in which federal authorities were deregulating major parts of the American economy such as air travel and telecommunications, antidrug activists insisted instead that government officials increase their role in regulating the paraphernalia business.[69]

Representatives of the paraphernalia trade invoked the notion of the free market rather than political principles to defend their right to conduct business. The paraphernalia trade "grew out of the confrontation of the sixties and still smacks a bit of confrontation politics," conceded Michael Pritzker, an attorney representing the Accessory Trade Association and a former NORML activist. But Pritzker vowed the business would "rapidly become more responsible and traditional and will more aggressively weed-out those advertisers and manufactures who specifically market and advertise their products for use in conjunction with illegal drugs."[70] Even as head shop owners continued to collaborate with the legalization movement, they had also come to believe that their survival depended on publicly disavowing their activist origins and casting their shops as respectable, conventional businesses. This transformation was deeply ironic: opponents of head shops saw them as promoters of a radical politics and culture from the 1960s, but head shop owners now fully renounced any connections to radicalism.

Andy Kowl testified in his capacity as publisher of *Accessory Digest* and cleverly turned on its head the notion that drug paraphernalia encouraged drug use. "Let me admit one thing: Drugs lead to paraphernalia," Kowl told the committee members. "You can't have drug paraphernalia without drugs. To think that it works in reverse, that paraphernalia leads to drugs, is rather naïve," he argued. "Unless you stop the importation and distribution of the drugs, the demand will dictate the supply, and paraphernalia has absolutely nothing to do with it." Drug paraphernalia, according to Kowl, was simply a symptom of drug use, not a cause of it.[71]

The growing condemnation of head shops unfolded amid a broader backlash against the so-called permissive society and the harm it purportedly inflicted on children. Critics of the permissive society essentially argued that liberal politicians and producers of popular culture had worked hand in hand to loosen the country's morals since the 1960s, resulting in a wide range of social ills, in particular crime, substance abuse, and sexual immorality. Along with their campaigns against drug paraphernalia, parents were starting to organize politically against a variety of perceived threats to young people's health and moral values, including alcohol, pornography, rock music, promiscuity, and even Satanism. Such concerns gained significant political traction in the late 1970s and early 1980s. The names of the groups that Rusche and the Schuchards led—DeKalb Families in Action, the Parents' Resource Institute for Drug Education, and the National Federation of Parents for Drug-Free Youth—reflected how they understood and framed their activism as the work of protecting children, work that Rusche referred to as a "parents' movement."[72]

Families in Action had produced an effective blueprint for parents' groups throughout America to organize against head shops. Police raids on the businesses increased dramatically across the country. The federal government also changed its rhetoric and policies toward marijuana in response to the growing backlash against head shops. Jimmy Carter had claimed early in his presidential term that he wanted to "discourage the use of marijuana . . . [without] defining the smoker as criminal," an explicit gesture toward liberalizing the nation's marijuana laws. By 1979, however, the Carter administration had decided to heed the demands of parents' groups instead. That year the White House urged the Drug Enforcement Administration to draft a Model Drug Paraphernalia Act for states and municipalities to replicate in creating their own constitutional antiparaphernalia laws. When the Select Committee on Narcotics Abuse and Control concluded two sets of hearings on paraphernalia in 1980, it could not have been clearer in denouncing the burgeoning business. Head shops and the paraphernalia trade, the committee concluded, represented nothing less than a "a severe threat to the educational, social, and emotional development of our youth."[73]

By 1980, Windfaire was the only remaining head shop in the entire Atlanta metropolitan area, according to the *Atlanta Constitution*. Since the passage of head shop laws in 1978, more than thirty "paraphernalia shops" had closed in and around the city. Lackey's store paid a tremendous price for survival. In late 1979, DeKalb County police raided Windfaire, seized $13,000 in merchandise, and arrested Lackey while local news stations filmed the bust for broadcast. The store remained closed until Lackey removed all items the county deemed to violate the state law. The seizure was a terrible blow to the store in that year's critical holiday season. Lackey and his co-plaintiffs' one victory was to convince a U.S. District Court to issue an order restraining the clause in the Georgia law banning literature that promoted illegal drug use. Such a law, the court found, violated the plaintiffs' First Amendment right to freedom of speech. The court ruled in addition that Windfaire and its fellow plaintiffs had a "history of suffering harassing arrest" at the hands of police in DeKalb and neighboring counties.[74]

In 1982, however, the U.S. Supreme Court unanimously ruled that narrowly written drug paraphernalia bans could comply with the Constitution. The Court decided that antiparaphernalia laws hinged on demonstrating the seller's or the purchaser's intent for illegal substances to be consumed with said paraphernalia. Pipes and rolling papers, for instance, could theoretically be used to smoke tobacco and thus were legal, but a so-called isomerizer that was advertised to boost marijuana's cannabinoid potency could be prohibited.[75] Law enforcement officials and legislators had finally found a constitutional strategy for prosecuting head shops.

HEAD SHOPS AND THE WAR ON DRUGS

The long trend of expanding tolerance for pot and head shops in particular, which seemed inexorable to many people in the marijuana subculture as late as 1978, had definitively come to a close. Eleven states had decriminalized possession of marijuana from 1973 to 1978, and many marijuana consumers expected the federal government to decriminalize pot. The marijuana legalization movement and head shop owners, however, severely underestimated the backlash they had inspired. States and municipalities rapidly increased their efforts to criminalize head shops with the encouragement of the Model Drug Paraphernalia Act. Many jurisdictions ratified stiff penalties for selling paraphernalia to minors.[76]

These efforts became one of the first fronts in the war on drugs that Ronald Reagan would declare early in his first term. Antiparaphernalia laws devastated head shops over the course of the 1980s. In 1986, Congress passed a federal law banning sales in person and by mail of all paraphernalia "primarily intended or designed for use . . . [of] a controlled substance" as part of the larger Anti–Drug Abuse Act of 1986. By 1987, forty-four states and the District of Columbia had laws restricting paraphernalia in some manner or another. Roughly three-quarters of those states had based their laws on the federal Model Drug Paraphernalia Act. Seven states even made the selling of drug paraphernalia a felony. Just ten years earlier, there had been virtually no laws in the country that regulated head shops and the paraphernalia business. In a federal survey released by the U.S. Department of Justice in 1987, 55 percent of sheriffs and police commissioners responded that head shops had operated in their jurisdictions prior to the enactment of paraphernalia laws. After the passage of such laws, however, nearly half of these jurisdictions no longer had any head shops. The vastly increased risk of criminal penalties as well as the financial costs of hiring defense attorneys forced many smaller head shops to close permanently, which in turn fueled a wave of consolidation that favored larger retailers.[77]

In less than a decade, parents' groups inspired by Sue Rusche's and Keith Schuchard's pioneering antiparaphernalia work had convinced prosecutors and legislators that head shops were illegitimate businesses bearing much of the responsibility for youth drug use. As a researcher for the U.S. Department of Justice admitted, "The primary purpose of drug paraphernalia laws will be to symbolize society's rejection of drug culture." At the same time, the researcher conceded that "no quantifiable evidence shows that anti-paraphernalia laws reduce drug use." This rare moment of honesty in the campaign to restrict paraphernalia, buried deep within a Department of Justice manual, suggested that even federal authorities were aware that head shops resulted from, rather than caused, drug use. Yet the movement led by Schuchard and Rusche had succeeded in casting the businesses as one of the country's primary culprits in creating drug use. Head shops had become a convenient symbol not only of immorality and crime but also of 1960s radicalism. Conservatives in the 1980s accordingly condemned the counterculture and the New Left of fifteen years earlier as the main culprits of contemporary social ills. As one defender of the Reagan administration's campaign against pot contended, marijuana had "tagged along during the present young adult generation's involvement in anti-military, anti–nuclear power, anti–big business, anti-authority demonstrations." Even in the 1980s, pot still attracted radicals who refused to accept "corollary civil responsibility" for their actions.[78]

Although head shops emerged in the late 1960s as close allies of social movements, they adamantly renounced their ties to activism by the 1980s. In the late 1960s and early 1970s, head shop owners and their customers embraced head shops as free spaces where they could build countercultural communities and pursue higher states of consciousness. Enterprising visionaries such as Ron and Jay Thelin sought to offer clear alternatives to the alienation and conformity of America's dominant consumer culture with their unconventional stores. For the heads, hippies, and freaks of that era, smoking pot, dropping acid, and even just setting foot in a head shop were gateways to deeper truths and self-understanding as well as acts of political defiance and disobedience. In addition, head shop owners envisioned their stores as activist businesses that promoted the antiwar cause and advanced the movement for drug-law reform. Legalization groups such as Amorphia and NORML, in turn, considered head shop owners some of their closest allies.

Head shops' remarkable growth in the mid- and late 1970s signaled just how much social and commercial influence the counterculture enjoyed long after the legendary days of the Summer of Love. Yet as the number of head shops grew, they became much more sensitive to the demands of long-term financial stability and conventional entrepreneurship, and they lost much of their appetite for activism. Head shops remained political, but they narrowed their focus almost exclusively on the movement to legalize drugs, marijuana in particular, which not coincidentally aligned with their business interests. Head shops strived to refashion themselves not as hippie free spaces but as businesses that welcomed anyone seeking smoking accessories. Ironically, at the same time that head shops became less political, their commercial rise sparked a powerful backlash from parents' groups, police, and legislators. As fitting symbols of the larger legacies of the counterculture and radicalism of the 1960s, the sellers of bongs and rolling papers became convenient early targets in the war on drugs of the 1980s.

Head shop owners eventually came to view activism as conflicting directly with profit making. In contrast, entrepreneurs aligned with the feminist movement refused to believe that they had to choose between political engagement and financial stability. More than any other activist business, feminist entrepreneurs sought to fulfill the tripartite vision of politicized products, places, and processes. They did so with storefronts that welcomed women and militated against sexism with a range of feminist goods and democratic workplace arrangements. Yet feminists' debates over the role of entrepreneurship in their movement were more explosive and at times more divisive than any other social movements' debates on political businesses in this period. As such, feminists' trenchant analysis of business's compatibility and contradictions with social movements produced the richest body of theory exploring the goals and outcomes of activist entrepreneurship.

4

The "Feminist Economic Revolution"

BUSINESSES IN THE WOMEN'S MOVEMENT

On April 9, 1976, the Feminist Economic Network (FEN) celebrated the grand opening of the Feminist Women's City Club (FWCC) in downtown Detroit. FEN's founders sought to create an organization "where self-sustaining feminist institutions can support each other, share experiences and build a more secure and stable feminist economy." By purchasing and renovating the defunct, six-story women's club built in 1924, FEN sought to further its mission of "sowing the seeds of feminist economic revolution." Half-a-dozen businesses owned by women opened in the new club, including the Feminist Federal Credit Union (FFCU), the Women's Choice health clinic, the Art Thou Woman? Gallery, the Uppity Woman gift shop, and a bar and café where women could "go for a drink alone without being harassed by men." In addition, the FWCC housed fifty hotel rooms, conference rooms, and even a swimming pool. It strived to make itself nothing less than a national headquarters for feminist businesses.

The leaders of the FWCC were founders of some of the leading feminist enterprises in the country. These feminist entrepreneurs viewed their endeavor in Detroit as more than just an alliance of woman-owned businesses. Rather, as cofounder Laura Brown of the Oakland Feminist Women's

Health Center in California declared, "This is the biggest financial undertaking the feminist movement has ever embarked upon." FEN's leaders contended that feminists typically worked jobs in the mainstream, male-dominated economy, where they could do little to empower women. As a result, many women active in the movement ended up "working for the patriarchy in order to survive." As FEN cofounder Joanne Parrent explained, "we began to create our own self-sustaining feminist institutions where we could spend many more hours working with each other for the values we believed in" and thus make a "real breakthrough in the development and control of our lives." Keynote speaker Gloria Steinem led the celebration of feminists who had come from all over the country to attend the club's grand opening. Local newspapers and broadcasters and even a reporter from the Associated Press covered the events. Indeed, the FWCC represented not only a major milestone for the women's movement but also one of the most ambitious activist business ventures of any kind in the 1960s and 1970s.[1]

Despite such fanfare, FEN and the FWCC sparked dissension among feminists across the country. Several feminist publications charged FEN with elitism, financial improprieties, and even authoritarianism in their efforts to make themselves economic leaders of the women's movement. Another feminist asked whether the group's members had violated federal credit union regulations in obtaining a major loan from the Detroit FFCU. One activist charged "that the politics of FEN are fascist and reactionary."[2] Most damningly, critics accused FEN and the FWCC's management of exploiting their female workers—a number of them black and working class—and thus of furthering patriarchy, racism, and capitalism in their relentless pursuit of profit.

Many feminists shared the conviction that male-controlled, American corporate capitalism was one of society's most powerful perpetuators of sexism and patriarchy, a corrupt force that relegated women to subservient roles as housewives, mothers, and sexual servants. But there was no consensus as to how feminists should respond to capitalism. Journalists and historians have paid considerable attention to debates within the women's movement, at times caricaturing them as arcane, petty, and avoidable infighting.[3] But feminists' debates over business were in fact substantive and probing examinations of what role, if any, capitalism and entrepreneurship should play in the women's movement and social movements more generally. If businesses were one of men's greatest sources of power, could they be restructured to give women power? Could women create democratic, nonpatriarchal, and nonexploitative businesses within America's capitalist economy? If so, what would feminist businesses look like, and how would they operate? What kind of products and services should they sell? Were collectives feminists' only option for business ownership, or could an individual female proprietor operate a feminist business?

Some in the movement rejected feminist businesses altogether, arguing that they retreated from substantive political engagement into small worlds of self-reflexive and self-indulgent "cultural feminism." Feminist entrepreneurs, they contended, were capitalist dupes who bolstered patriarchy by replicating male norms of social and economic domination. The utopian alternatives envisioned by feminist businesses, they argued, sidestepped but did not confront the problems of gender and class inequality. These critics claimed that feminist businesses peddled a fantasy of female separatism, and some accused feminist entrepreneurs of selling out the movement. Arguments between feminist business owners and their critics usually took the form of sincere ideological debates. Yet some feminist entrepreneurs felt that such disagreements periodically descended into ad hominem attacks fueled by jealousy and exemplified what the feminist Jo Freeman famously denounced as "trashing."[4]

Feminist entrepreneurs argued that women's oppression was premised on their economic, vocational, and domestic dependence on men. One way to secure their liberation was by establishing their own businesses that provided them with income and productive livelihoods. Like the entrepreneurs who emerged out of the counterculture and the Black Power movement, some feminists contended that they needed to establish their own enterprises to further their cause within the larger society. These women sought to establish their own autonomous "free spaces" for their movement as well as for women more generally with a diverse array of businesses that included credit unions, printing presses, bookstores, craft shops, mail-order catalogs, and restaurants. They viewed their products and services as tools for raising feminist consciousness that they could deploy to promote women's liberation in the wider society. Feminist business owners also strived to democratize workplaces with collectives and other participatory forms of management organization.

Critics of feminist business were found in virtually every wing of the women's movement. But so, too, were feminist entrepreneurs. Debates on feminist enterprise thus provide a window into the ideological diversity of the women's movement in the 1970s and at the same time undermine the hard-and-fast differences some historians have drawn between the liberal, radical, and cultural wings of the movement. Some female entrepreneurs identified as radical feminists, others as liberal feminists, others as socialist feminists. Perhaps more than any other part of the movement, lesbian feminists embraced business as a means for women to control their own culture, space, and finances without the intrusion of men or heterosexual feminists. Feminists produced an extensive set of writings on business as they struggled to agree on what it meant for their movement. Numerous essays on the "feminist business ethic" and feminist entrepreneurship appeared in the women's movement press.[5] The depth of second-wave feminists' debates about business made for the richest and most deeply probing analyses of activist enterprise by any social movement in these years.

Feminists in business found reconciling their entrepreneurial practices with their fellow activists' critical views about business and capitalism a daunting task, arguably one more challenging than the ideological struggles that black booksellers, head shop owners, and natural foods sellers faced. Strong distaste for corporate capitalism served as a check on some feminist businesses' ambitions for growth, perhaps more so than on any other type of activist business. Feminist entrepreneurs' emphasis on collective management made their businesses more democratic, but their decision-making processes often demanded more time and energy than decisions in a single or dual proprietorship would. Feminist entrepreneurs' high ideological standards exceeded those of many other activist businesses, and their drive for political efficacy often conflicted with their pursuit of financial success.

As the women's movement experienced decline, resistance, and pronounced backlash in the 1980s, many businesses of the second wave could no longer survive. Ones that did survive often downplayed their associations with the women's movement or at least sought to appeal to a customer base beyond that of feminist activists. These feminist enterprises often embraced traditional organizational structures and careful financial management instead of the forms of collective ownership and radical ideology that were so popular with feminist business pioneers.

Feminist entrepreneurs discovered over time that it was possible to run a business that stayed true to feminist principles, advanced the goals of social justice, and still managed to pay the bills. But it required a tremendous amount of dedication, perseverance, experience gained on the job, and even good fortune. Meanwhile, a number of factors militated against feminist businesses' financial success. Ironically, women's increased success at starting businesses in the late twentieth century may have convinced female entrepreneurs that collaborating with the organized women's movement was unnecessary. As late as 1972, women owned less than 5 percent of all companies in the United States. Ten years later they owned a remarkable 30 percent of all business.[6] Many of the women who started new businesses did not identify as feminists, yet they had nonetheless benefitted from the hard-earned gains of feminist activists in earlier years who had founded their own businesses.

WOMEN ENTREPRENEURS AND THE FEMINIST CRITIQUE OF CORPORATE CAPITALISM

Women have owned and operated businesses in the United States since the nation's founding. Indeed, the preindustrial era was surprisingly hospitable to female business owners: an estimated 10 to 25 percent of women in North America were engaged in entrepreneurial activities in the colonial years. As late as the 1840s, the most common form of entrepreneurship by far was farming, a business in which female family members were generally allowed if not expected to participate. Women also operated businesses as the wives and daughters of artisans, shopkeepers, and landlords, and common law allowed an unmarried woman, or *feme sole*, to make contracts, own property, and obtain credit. Women lost many of the opportunities for entrepreneurship they previously enjoyed, however, with industrialization and the rise of the modern white-collar economy. The rise of bigger, more capitalized businesses in such traditionally female industries as dressmaking, prostitution, laundering, and boardinghouses generally reduced the numbers of female owners. Although hundreds of thousands of women continued to own businesses—most of them quite small—wage labor such as stenography and secretary work attracted many more women, as did largely female professions such as teaching, nursing, and librarianship. Through much of the twentieth century, male leaders in business, academia, and government generally ignored women's businesses or considered them hobbies that women pursued for pocket money—not as intentional, long-term, and legitimate firms. From the 1930s to the 1950s, many feminists gladly kept their distance from the business world, often because they were deeply involved in the trade-union movement and socialism.[7]

In the 1960s, a new generation of feminists indicted corporations and their advertising in particular for oppressing women and consigning them to roles of financial dependence.[8] In her pioneering work *The Feminine Mystique* (1963), Betty Friedan devoted an entire chapter, "The Sexual Sell," to excoriating Madison Avenue and Fortune 500 companies. "The perpetuation of housewifery, the growth of the feminine mystique makes sense (and dollars) when one realizes that women are the chief customers of American business," Friedan argued. Borrowing a phrase popularized by Vance Packard, Friedan based much of the chapter on conversations she had with one of "the most helpful of hidden persuaders," the Austrian-born, Freudian marketer and psychologist Ernst Dichter (who remained unnamed in the book). These "manipulators and their clients in American business can hardly be accused of creating the feminine mystique. But they are the most powerful of its perpetuators," Friedan charged.[9]

These criticisms of American consumer culture continued as a resurgent women's movement, a so-called second wave, emerged out of the New Left in the late 1960s. Such criticisms were central to one of the earliest feminist direct actions, the protests by the group New York Radical Women at the Miss America contest in 1968. In a press release announcing the protest, Radical Women member Robin Morgan explained that protesters would "throw bras, girdles, curlers, false eyelashes, wigs, and representative issues of *Cosmopolitan, Ladies' Home Journal, Family Circle,* etc." into a "Freedom

Trash Can." Protestors threatened to organize "a Boycott of all those commercial products related to the Pageant." The New York Radical Women's
ten points of protest railed against the pageant as a "Consumer Con-Game"
that promoted "the Degrading-Mindless-Boob-Girlie Symbol." Each year, a
newly crowned Miss America was reduced to a "shill . . . a walking commercial for the Pageant's sponsors. Wind her up and she plugs your product on
promotion tours."[10] American corporate capitalism, early second-wave
feminists argued, both manipulated women as consumers and commodified them for selling products to men.

Feminists dramatized their criticisms of corporate power and consumer
culture through a variety of means. One of the most spectacular purveyors
of such political theater was the Women's International Terrorist Conspiracy from Hell. Better known as WITCH, this New York–based feminist
group described itself as "the striking arm of the Women's Liberation
Movement, aiming mainly at financial and corporate America, at those
institutions that have the power to control and define human life." WITCH
first gained prominence when members dressed as witches and placed a
"hex" on Wall Street on Halloween in 1968. In early 1969, WITCH staged
a protest against the "Whoremakers" at New York's Bridal Fair and trade
show, charging that brides were "manipulated—by the giant corporations
who need consumers on which to unload their over-productivity, and who
have one answer for the anxious women: *buy*!" In March 1970, feminists
from several organizations staged a sit-in at the office of the *Ladies' Home
Journal* and forced the magazine's editors to negotiate with them. The
protesters ultimately triumphed in forcing the magazine to publish in its
August 1970 issue an eight-page supplement on feminism and sexism they
wrote.[11]

By the start of the 1970s, Madison Avenue and its clients began to
grudgingly heed feminists' criticisms out of fear of alienating young female
consumers, even if they did not necessarily agree with those criticisms.
Feminist organizations had put advertisers and their corporate clients on the
defensive. Women working in advertising also began to demand changes to
their industry's discriminatory hiring practices and its demeaning por-
trayal of women. At least one advertising firm organized focus groups to
test self-identifying feminists' responses to products and ads. Pepsi-Cola

even announced it would stop sponsoring the Miss America contest in 1968 due to "changing values of our society." Feminists rightly questioned, however, whether marketers' change of heart was sincere. Leo Burnett's "You've Come a Long Way, Baby" advertising campaign for Virginia Slims cigarettes, for instance, memorably invoked the women's movement, but many feminists saw these ads as a transparent attempt to exploit and co-opt the movement for profit.[12]

Regardless, by 1970 many corporations and advertisers recognized that they ignored the criticisms expressed by the women's movement at their own peril. A significant plurality of women—42 percent—had entered the American workforce by 1970, pointing to women's growing stake in public life. Yet women at this time still owned less than 5 percent of America's businesses.[13] Some feminists wondered if exacting piecemeal, grudging concessions from corporations and advertising firms was the most effective way to change American business culture, or if they could have more impact by starting their own companies.

BUILDING A FEMINIST SOCIETY
THROUGH BUSINESSES

Male-owned corporations' newfound reluctance to produce sexist advertising was a direct response to feminism's political gains and increased visibility at the start of the 1970s. In 1970, feminists published three works that would become among the movement's most influential and widely read works: Shulamith Firestone's *The Dialectic of Sex: The Case for Feminist Revolution*, Kate Millett's *Sexual Politics*, and the anthology *Sisterhood Is Powerful*, edited by Robin Morgan. In August of that year, the U.S. House of Representatives passed the Equal Rights Amendment. An estimated twenty to fifty thousand marchers participated in the Women's Strike for Equality in New York City later that month. National media, meanwhile, clamored like never before to report on the surge of feminist activity throughout the country. The diversity of feminist organizations was growing, too. New radical groups were emerging out of "consciousness-raising" (CR) sessions held by female New Left activists in cities such as New York, Boston, Chicago, Washington, D.C., and Baltimore. CR offered women the chance to share with each other their personal encounters with sexism in virtually every aspect of their lives, including employment, family, sex, housework, etiquette, and language. Women conceptualized CR groups as freeform, egalitarian settings in which they could connect such anecdotes of lived sexism to broader, collective analyses of women's oppression. As the Florida-based feminist Carol Hanisch famously wrote, CR showed that "the personal is political," a pithy turn of phrase that became one of the rallying cries of the women's movement. Indeed, CR groups implemented some of the New Left's most cherished ideals of authenticity, collaboration, and participatory democracy. As such, they exemplified the feminist Pamela Allen's concept of "free space," or places where activists and marginalized people could build liberation movements and communities to combat oppression.[14]

Despite the freedoms that CR provided, some feminists, many of them lesbians, believed that CR groups and other existing forms of organized feminism did not ensure them equal treatment within the women's movement. Indeed, prominent feminists contended that lesbians distracted from or even threatened to undermine the pursuit of full equality and liberation for women. Most famously, Betty Friedan denounced lesbians as a "lavender menace." In retaliation, a newly formed group, the Radicalesbians, organized a takeover of the Second Congress to Unite Women in May 1970, where they distributed to attendees a manifesto of lesbian feminism, *The Woman-Identified Woman*. Rather than desperately seeking to persuade established feminist organizations to accept them, more and more lesbian feminists decided to create their own groups and institutions. In 1971, a group of lesbian feminists in Washington, D.C., formed the Furies, a residential collective named after the Greek goddesses of vengeance. Members included Rita Mae Brown, one of the leading members of the Radicalesbians; Coletta Reid, who had resigned from the feminist newspaper *off our backs* in protest of its treatment of lesbians; and Charlotte Bunch, an antiwar activist and research fellow at the progressive think tank the Institute for Policy Studies. As Bunch declared in the first issue of the collective's newspaper, *The Furies*, "Lesbians must form our own movement to fight male supremacy." Reid argued that a critical task of the collective was to develop "projects that would help us see what the roots of our oppression were, what kind of new society we wanted to create, and how to get from here to there."[15] First living together in two and then four houses in D.C., the Furies shared household duties and pooled their earnings from jobs according to a sliding scale to pay for food, housing, and other necessities. The Furies believed that communal living and an egalitarian economic structure served the larger goals of women's equality by relieving its members of unequal romantic relationships and living arrangements with men.

In the less than two years the Furies lived together, the collective developed an economic ideology that would deeply influence radical feminists in the 1970s. Collective members Helaine Harris and Lee Schwing articulated this ideology in "Building Feminist Institutions," an article in the spring 1973 issue of *The Furies*. Harris and Schwing began by asking readers a difficult question: How could feminists, especially lesbian feminists, "continue developing ideology while also having to work to survive?" The two women felt that the demands of economic survival—namely, taking "straight" jobs in the mainstream economy—left too little time for members of the collective to engage in political work. Employment disparities highlighted class inequalities within the Furies. Working-class members, especially ones without college degrees, had few employment options, whereas the college-educated members could easily find office jobs. But for middle-class women to take working-class jobs in the name of solidarity only made matters worse. "Why should a middle class woman be 'poor by choice' alongside a working-class woman 'poor by caste,' when she could be working at a job that would support both of them?" asked Schwing and Harris. Middle-class members of the Furies addressed this issue by devoting a higher proportion of their earnings to the collective and by helping the group's working-class women pay for vocational training.[16]

Most importantly, feminists needed to establish their own alternative institutions, Schwing and Harris argued. Chief among these institutions would be egalitarian workplaces where feminists could do the ideological work of the movement and serve women beyond the small circles of the most devoted activists. Although Harris and Schwing may not have known it, as early as the 1910s feminist organizations such as the National American Woman Suffrage Association and the Women's Political Union had owned and operated several of their own "suffrage shops" where activists sold pro-suffrage literature and memorabilia. Schwing and Harris's vision was not entirely unlike that of such early enterprising feminists. They also drew inspiration from the many women's centers that second-wave feminists established on college campuses at the start of the 1970s. "We must continue services within our communities, services like health care, legal defense, self-defense centers and rape crisis centers," wrote Schwing and Harris. "We must have control over videotape (TV), record companies, printing presses, publishing houses."[17]

Such all-women institutions offered feminists a range of political and economic freedoms. They did not force feminists to engage in endless debates with nonfeminists over the validity of the women's movement. They welcomed lesbians, who would not have to downplay or conceal their sexuality as they did in most workplaces and even in many parts of the women's movement. Feminist institutions could provide women with the autonomy that eluded them at outside, "straight" jobs. Harris and Schwing charged that New Left and countercultural institutions of the late 1960s had avoided the issues of gender inequality and patriarchy and had relegated women to menial tasks. Male-dominated institutions such as the Free Stores created by the Diggers in San Francisco had "viewed money and survival in a classist and unrealistic way" and had survived on support from middle-class people who could afford to donate their labor for free. Employees at feminist institutions, however, would earn an equal base salary adjusted for financial need so that each woman would be compensated to the point of economic self-sufficiency. By the end of the 1973, Harris and another member of the Furies had put these ideas to practice by cofounding Olivia Records, a recording label for women's music that later launched a popular cruise-ship line for lesbians.[18]

Indeed, lesbians were emerging as leading proponents of feminist business in the 1970s. Long before second-wave feminism, lesbians had operated their own businesses, especially bars. Such establishments had long appealed most strongly to working-class lesbians. In the 1970s, lesbians launched an even wider range of all-women institutions and businesses. As the historian Heather Murray argues, "The meaning of being a lesbian took on a broader feminist significance." That meaning of lesbianism extended beyond female same-sex romantic relationships to encompass a distinctive, all-women's culture and a set of political beliefs that were strongly influenced by the women's movement.[19]

Consumer culture and businesses played a critical role in the development of lesbian identities. Lesbians increasingly sought to affirm feminism through the cultural and political spaces they established. Many of these spaces were businesses in which lesbian feminist entrepreneurs undermined normative gender and sexual roles and promoted artisanship and artistic production as alternatives to mass production and economies of scale. Some lesbians used businesses to distinguish themselves from the straight women's movement. These women regarded themselves as part of a lesbian movement in which businesses allowed them control of their own culture, space, and finances without the intrusion of men or heterosexual feminists.[20]

Yet all-women institutions' appeal extended beyond lesbians to the larger women's movement and pointed to a separatist current in feminism that grew more influential over the course of the 1970s. More and more radical feminists came to believe that only autonomous organizations led by feminist women could advance women's interests. In so doing, the predominantly white radical feminist movement demonstrated the deep influence of black nationalists' notions of power through racially separate organizations and spaces. Although some feminists insisted that separatist groups should be lesbian, others argued that their groups only needed to comprise feminists. "Our definition of the feminist organization/workplace is that it must be controlled by feminists," wrote Alexa Freeman and Jackie McMillan for *Quest: A Feminist Quarterly*, a movement publication with connections to the Furies. Women could "do feminist work in traditional workplaces . . . [but] it is much more difficult than working directly through independent feminist organizations."[21] Women thus had to take their economic fates into their own hands and stop waiting for men to accept them as equals. One way feminists could do this was to create their own workplaces.

The Rise of Feminist Entrepreneurs

Both Rose Fontanella and Stephanie Marcus were working in the male-dominated world of advertising in New York City in the late 1960s when they met through the Brooklyn chapter of the National Organization for

Women (NOW). The two women quickly bonded by sharing their frustrations over their limited advancement opportunities at work and their supervisors' unspoken but clear preference for single female employees in their early twenties. Marcus and Fontanella came to believe they would never be able to advance as middle-aged women working for male-owned advertising companies, so "we started thinking of how we could build something for ourselves." In February 1972, Marcus and Fontanella established a mail-order business called Liberation Enterprises in a loft workspace in Brooklyn (figure 4.1). The two women set about designing a variety of clothing, jewelry, and paraphernalia with feminist themes. Examples included T-shirts emblazoned with the slogan "Liberté, Égalité, Sororité"; note cards that read "Susan B. Lives!"; and earrings that featured the word *SISTER* inset in a combination flower blossom and women's symbol. In

WOMANPOWER! The feminist artists of Liberation Enterprises offer note cards, posters, cloisonne jewelry, records, sweatshirts, bags, all sorts of gifts, and a few surprises. Free catalog. Bulk rates for movement fundraising available on request. Write:

LIBERATION ENTERPRISES
Dept. NA, 131 Joralemon St.
Brooklyn, N.Y. 11201

7

FIGURE 4.1 Liberation Enterprises advertisement, 1973. Courtesy of the Arthur and Elizabeth Schlesinger Library on the History of Women in America, Radcliffe Institute for Advanced Study, Harvard University, Cambridge, Mass.

addition to their own designs, Fontanella and Marcus hoped to sell products from "all the women who were trying to support themselves by making feminist items" but did not have the means to market their products. The two women believed selling feminist items would give women a "visual voice" and "serve as consciousness-raisers, by making the feminist spirit more visible." Without saying a single word, a woman could wear feminist-themed clothing or jewelry and convey her support for the women's movement to everyone around her.[22]

Business ownership transformed Marcus and Fontanella. Starting a company "was a giant step," Marcus admitted. "Neither of us knew anything about business." Operating a business gave the women a form of confidence and independence that would be unavailable to them as employees or homemakers. As Marcus remembered, "Most women had this problem. When you're talking to a man in a suit and tie, he's looking down at you and you're looking up at him. And after the business, I looked at men in the eye. You're a businessman? I'm a businesswoman." Liberation Enterprises, she proudly recalled, "gave me a sense of myself."[23]

Yet Marcus and Fontanella also confronted numerous difficulties in their business's early days. An accountant told them they would need $10,000 to $20,000 to launch their company, but the two could put together only $5,000 in combined funds. Some of Liberation Enterprises' products were quite difficult to market, too. An apron featuring the succinct slogan "Fuck Housework" proved particularly controversial (figure 4.2). Several journalists who contacted the company to write stories on Liberation Enterprises suddenly lost interest when they saw the aprons in the company's catalogs. Even the *Village Voice*, New York's supposed champion of free speech, refused to carry an advertisement for the apron. When Liberation Enterprises submitted their design for the apron to a lawyer for review, he gave them the nearly impossible task of writing every jurisdiction to which they planned to mail the catalog and to request copies of their obscenity laws. Not until a postal official informed the women that the catalog was legal because it featured only one product with an obscenity did the two women finally feel comfortable advertising the apron.[24]

Despite these challenges, Marcus and Fontanella found great success selling their products to feminists at local meetings and national conferences. Liberation Enterprises offered design work for feminist organizations

FIGURE 4.2   Stephanie Marcus and Rose Fontanella model Liberation Enterprises' best
selling items. Courtesy of Stephanie Marcus

in exchange for access to membership rolls. By early 1973, the company had
built a mailing list of more than ten thousand feminists. That year, appear-
ances in the *Los Angeles Times* and *Ms.* brought tremendous attention to
the company. Titled "How to Start Your Own Business," the article in *Ms.*
produced "an avalanche of orders" for the company and "prompted a
flood of fan mail from women who had been inspired to start their own
businesses." Women from as far away as Mississippi and Australia wrote to
thank Marcus and Fontanella for starting a feminist mail-order catalog.
Ms. praised Liberation Enterprises for "building a distribution system for
women" and "providing a base on which other women can stand and
grow."[25]

Even NOW launched its own mail-order catalog of feminist products, *Financing the Revolution* (figure 4.3). NOW's vast national membership received the catalog, which featured advertisements for independent

FIGURE 4.3 *Financing the Revolution*, NOW's mail-order catalog for feminist businesses, 1973. Courtesy of the Arthur and Elizabeth Schlesinger Library on the History of Women in America, Radcliffe Institute for Advanced Study, Harvard University, Cambridge, Mass.

businesses that had been established by NOW members, such as Liberation Enterprises, and sold feminist-themed posters, jewelry, note cards, books, and "liberating Christmas cards." The catalog also advertised an array of goods produced by NOW, including organization publications and stationary as well as the sheet music and 45-RPM record of the

NOW-penned song "Liberation, Now."[26] Indeed, business was becoming a major part of the women's movement in the early 1970s.

Pioneers such as *Financing the Revolution* and Liberation Enterprises inspired other feminists to launch their own businesses all over the United States in the first half of the 1970s. Feminist entrepreneurs chose names for their businesses that proudly and humorously declared their connection to the women's movement: ERA Enterprises, Those Uppity Women, United Sisters, Amazon Bookstore, Feminist Forge, and It's About Time Women's Book Center. Yet some feminist entrepreneurs refused to characterize their work as capitalistic or even as business. In Oakland, ICI: A Woman's Place, the first second-wave feminist bookstore, opened with a total inventory of four shelves of books by and about women in 1970. As one collective member explained, the business "was really a Women's Center disguised as a bookstore," a free space for women "interested in mingling with other women . . . [and a] place we could go and not be interfered with by men." Amid "the rapidly growing disillusionment with big business and capitalism," staffers at A Woman's Place described their work as an experiment in creating "a more equitable form of the future, comparable to the various forms of cooperatives." Each collective member "served the needs of the community according to ability and personal interest and thereby qualified for a reasonable share, small but adequate food, shelter, clothing, but without interest in or ambition toward personal accumulation of wealth and useless possessions." The collective published its own how-to guide for bookselling with practical advice on retailing, accounting, and keeping inventory, *Starting a Bookstore: Non-capitalist Operation Within a Capitalist Economy*. A Woman's Place proudly described itself as "the largest, feminist bookstore in the United States," but as the women in the collective insisted, the store was neither a business nor capitalist (figure 4.4).[27]

The democratic and nonhierarchical features of collectives held a particular appeal for radical feminists who established business enterprises. One of the most successful of such efforts was the Boston Women's Health Course Collective, which authored a women's health guide, *Our Bodies, Ourselves*, in 1970. Initially a 130-page book printed by the New England Free Press that sold for just 75 cents, the first edition of *Our Bodies,*

FIGURE 4.4 ICI: A Woman's Place, the first second-wave feminist bookstore in the United States, Oakland, California, n.d. Courtesy of the Lesbian Herstory Archives, New York

Ourselves was republished ten times and sold 225,000 copies before it was released in a revised version by Simon & Schuster in 1973.[28] The spectacular success of the book's first edition suggested that feminist publishers had a strong potential for growth.

In Baltimore, another women's collective launched a print shop that would become one of the best-known feminist businesses in the country.

Furies cofounder Coletta Reid and Casey "KC" Czarnik, an antiwar activist who also worked as a printer at *Women: A Journal of Liberation* in Baltimore, joined several other women in establishing the printing collective in 1972. Originally the women shared an office with "a group of leftist hippy men"; the men typed and laid out the orders, and the women printed them. By October of that year, however, political infighting prompted most of the women to leave the collective. Those who stayed asked the men to leave and settled on the name "Diana Press" for their newly all-female business. The name choice represented a compromise between some collective members. Some of the women wanted to commemorate Weather Underground member Diana Oughton, who had died when a bomb she was making to detonate at an army officer's dance exploded in her hands, while others wanted to honor the Roman goddess Diana "as a symbol of ancient women's culture."[29] The business's name thus highlighted the collective's ties to the radical antiwar movement and feminists' growing interest in the cultural and spiritual dimension of women's liberation.

The newly established Diana Press set a goal of achieving financial self-sufficiency within nine months. The company did not seek profits per se but rather the financial autonomy they felt they needed to keep their feminist enterprise operating. The women of the shop started with just $400 of their own savings, a donation of another $400 to purchase a twenty-five-year old Multilith printer, and a loan of $170 to buy a plate maker. The women did not yet even know how to operate the two pieces of complex printing equipment. Undaunted, they opened their storefront on Twenty-Fifth Street near Charles Village and Waverly, two Baltimore neighborhoods with vibrant communities of radical feminists and antiwar activists in the 1970s. Each woman received a monthly salary of $100, which she then promptly reinvested in the business. All of Diana Press's workers had quit their outside jobs, so they would depend entirely on the shop to make a living. The collective initially set prices for print jobs simply by underbidding other neighboring shops. Despite this combination of high stakes and meager finances, the women of Diana Press "didn't worry about making money, or our profit margin, or whether we were underpricing." Rather, they sought to learn printing skills and survive financially, while "freeing women entirely from male printing establishments." As Reid would tell the

Wall Street Journal for a front-page story on feminist businesses, "Men don't touch any job that we do" at Diana Press. "Our goal is to help other women."[30]

In late 1972, the young lesbian author and activist Rita Mae Brown approached Diana Press with a job to produce her second book, a collection of poetry titled *Songs to a Handsome Woman*. Brown had made a name for herself in May 1970 as a leader of the Radicalesbians in the "lavender menace" action at the Second Congress to Unite Women. After unsuccessfully pitching her manuscript to established publishers, Brown offered her book to Reid, whom she had known as a fellow member of the Furies. Brown paid $300 for the paper on which to print the book, and the press donated the labor. By early 1973, the shop had printed two thousand copies of the book, each of which staffers collated and stapled by hand. The Diana Press print shop had made its first foray into literary publishing. As Reid recalled, "We got into publishing with no experience but with a strong feeling that there were women's words that could not be spoken or heard because all publishing companies were owned by men." In 1973, Diana Press published three more books and several pamphlets with titles such as *Class and Feminism* and *Heterosexuality & the Women's Movement*. Diana Press quickly became one of the premier woman-owned publishers devoted to works by feminists, joining established publishers such as the Feminist Press in New York City.[31]

At a time when many feminists still glossed over issues of labor and economic inequality, Diana Press's workers developed complex analyses of the intersection of class, political economy, and sexism. Reid and her fellow Diana Press authors Nancy Myron and Charlotte Bunch—all of them former Furies—staked out positions at the forefront of analyzing the relationship between class and feminism. The company's staffers were well aware of their entry into a business traditionally reserved for working-class men. By acquiring skills in printing, a form of manual labor that had historically excluded women, they saw themselves as overcoming a form of gender discrimination intertwined with class inequality. "We felt it was important for working-class women to own the means of production and to learn how to operate and fix machinery," Reid explained. "As working class women we wanted the movement to include the kinds of jobs that ordinarily working class men have."[32] Whereas jewelry making, fashion, and bookselling were middle-class forms of labor that women had a history of doing, women at Diana Press did dirty, physically demanding labor that directly contradicted traditional gendered expectations of work. Unlike liberal feminist groups such as NOW, the women of Diana Press did not celebrate women's increasing representation in the professions. They instead envisioned the woman-owned workplace as the most important arena in which women could combat interconnected forms of gender and class oppression. Indeed, the staff at Diana Press firmly believed that making business and manual labor more democratic and accessible to women was a critical priority for feminists.

Grappling with Growth

Despite the advances of both liberal and radical feminist businesses, some feminist entrepreneurs encountered significant resistance from other activists in the women's movement. As Susan Sojourner, an owner of the First Things First bookstore in Washington, D.C., explained, "The attitude of many movement non-businesswomen is that our businesses are 'ripping off the movement'—exploiting, leaching, profiting from the movement and its gains." Such charges echoed accusations that nearly all activist businesses faced periodically. Other feminist business owners recounted stories of angry confrontations and ad hominem attacks at meetings. "Seeing women in business stirs absolute rage," remarked Lorraine Allen, the owner of the Equation Collective, a company that strived "to become an alternative to unanimously sexist toiletries companies." As Allen explained, "Just when the movement tried to perpetuate the myth that women are somehow intrinsically, i.e. unmaterialistic, [sic] here we come along with our balance sheets and income statements."[33] Indeed, numerous feminists still believed that businesses had no role to play in their movement.

These tensions came to a head at NOW's national convention in Washington, D.C., in 1973. Feminist entrepreneurs in an exhibit hall experienced such hostility from organizers and one of the conference's committees that they "jointly protested the shoddy treatment." This confrontation, one of the entrepreneurs remarked, "raised the consciousness of many NOW women and pointed up what each businesswoman had heretofore been suffering alone: the ambivalence and frequent hostility of movement women toward feminist business."[34] Although NOW eventually refunded half the fees the businesses had paid for their tables, the conflict galvanized feminist business owners.

Several months later a group of twenty feminist businesswomen who had attended the NOW conference organized their own conference in Kerhonkson, New York, to address "common fears and doubts about ourselves [as entrepreneurs] and the attitudes of other women toward us." There the women created the Feminist Business Alliance, an organization that sought to offer professional training workshops and to pool advertising and fund-raising resources among feminist entrepreneurs. The group also published an essay collection on the immense challenges feminist businesses faced, *Dealing with the Real World: 13 Papers by Feminist Entrepreneurs*. As one feminist bookseller explained, "Feminist businesswomen see the work that we do as furthering the movement, spreading the word, servicing the needs of movement women, and changing the idea of new women who don't now identify with the movement." Yet they were still plagued with self-doubt and felt compelled to overcompensate in proving their value to other activists. "We are ridiculous in self-effacing ourselves, in denying and feeling guilty . . . [and we] have been plagued by self-destructive fear and guilt about making profits," another entrepreneur lamented.[35]

Some feminist entrepreneurs interpreted the hostility they faced as a result of years of conditioning that pressured women to depend on men and low-wage employment for economic survival. "Why should we feel guilty about struggling for economic independence through doing something we enjoy doing?" asked Marjorie Collins, owner of the feminist magazine *Prime Time*. "Is it because our entire previous work experience has been so shrouded in meaningless discipline and ideological compromise that we cannot believe in the legitimacy of making a living enjoyably?" Feminist entrepreneurs were "sick of self-sacrificing," so now they aimed "to make the capitalist system work *for* us instead of against us."[36]

The hostility notwithstanding, activists in the women's movement continued to open businesses all over the country. "The Tide of the women's movement recently seems to be drifting more toward an 'I can do that myself' posture. More and more women and women's organizations have taken to creating and selling their own products rather than buying it [*sic*] from the man," reported one writer for the Los Angeles magazine *Lesbian Tide* in 1973. "Feminists are now saying that women, even those in the movement, should be PAID for their products and services. And why not? One cannot eat rhetoric."[37] Despite some individual feminists' enthusiasm about business, entrepreneurs in the women's movement still struggled to communicate with their peers around the country.

Two feminists in New York City wanted to change that situation. In 1971, Susan Rennie and Kirsten Grimstad had produced a bibliography of women's studies for Columbia University that cited thousands of works on feminism. The guide also included a brief directory of women's centers, health clinics, and bookstores. Inspired by the countercultural *Whole Earth Catalog*, Rennie and Grimstad decided to expand their directory into a large-format guidebook to feminist institutions and businesses across the country. Released in November 1973, *The New Woman's Survival Catalog* generated considerable press, including mentions in the *New York Times*, the *Los Angeles Times*, and the *Baltimore Sun*. Rennie and Grimstad proudly summarized the state of feminist institution building in the book's introduction: "Throughout the United States women are forming their own law firms and legal clinics, establishing their own business companies, running their own printing presses, publishing their own magazines and newspapers, starting their own credit unions, banks, anti-rape squads, art galleries, and schools, hospitals, non-sexist playgrounds and child care centers, bands, theater groups, restaurants, literary magazines and scholarly journals." With rhetoric that invoked second-wave feminism, *The Whole Earth Catalog*, and Booker T. Washington, Rennie and Grimstad announced that their book was "meant, above all, to be a self-help tool for ALL women to take control of their lives." The growing number of feminist institutions expressed "a rejection of the values of the existing institutional structures and, unlike the male hip counterculture, represent an active attempt to reshape culture through changing values and consciousness."[38].

The New Woman's Survival Catalog legitimized feminist businesses as meaningful institutions of the women's movement more than any single news account or story in the feminist press. The book appeared on the *New York Times*'s best-seller list for one week and ultimately sold more than one hundred thousand copies. In 1975, Rennie and Grimstad published a substantially revised edition of the catalog, *The New Woman's Survival Sourcebook*. Looking back years later, Grimstad described the *Catalog*'s impact in dramatic terms: "It felt as though we were part of a world-changing movement, that we were ending patriarchy."[39]

An ever larger part of the women's movement now embraced business as a tool for economic and political transformation. In 1974, former Furies Charlotte Bunch and Rita Mae Brown helped to cofound *Quest: A Feminist Quarterly*, a journal with a particular interest in building feminist institutions. Diana Press printed the journal. *Quest*'s second issue was devoted to "money, fame, and power," factors that one writer argued had "significantly fragmented our power as a Movement." Coletta Reid penned "Taking Care of Business," a manifesto for feminist entrepreneurs. "In a capitalist society, women in general, and workers in particular, have never had any control over the economy," Reid argued. In the past, feminists had "too often chosen to integrate women into the economic system, rather than to integrate the economic reality of that system into our strategy for change." Small businesses, however, offered the women's movement a means to challenge men's economic dominance. Feminist enterprises could in fact contribute to a "primary aim of socialism": "put[ting] people back into control of the economy."[40] As Reid suggested, women's businesses that gave their workers real control of their operations were not capitalist.

Reid did acknowledge the considerable concerns that feminists had about business. She recognized worries that some "women who start businesses will become owner/exploiters in the way men have." She also admitted that some self-identifying feminist entrepreneurs sold "superfluous consumer goods and services based on female oppression (like *Ms.* nameplates and women symbol swizzle sticks) [that] are not helpful in gaining economic power." Reid conceded that some "female capitalists . . . accept basic structures of capitalism as good but want women to be involved at higher levels" of the corporate economy. Some feminist business owners did seem overly credulous of their powers to secure positive change. "If we intend not to exploit people along the way, we have nothing to apologize for," Lorraine Allen, owner of the Equation Collection, maintained.[41]

But for Reid and most feminists in business, good intentions were not enough. Instead, concrete structures of economic democracy and justice needed to accompany those intentions. Real feminist businesses had to give "all the people who work . . . some say over what they do and [the chance to] participate in determining the direction of the business, the organization of the work, etc." Reid insisted that legitimate feminist businesses provided "women with a good or service that is important both to their needs and to their developing consciousness." And only paid labor would allow feminists to advance beyond the self-defeating and exploitative volunteerism that undermined their movement. "Women's businesses which do not aim to pay their workers decent wages, which do not price their products and service to make a reasonable return are not contributing to women's economic independence," Reid argued. Instead of relying on grants, university connections, and underpaid workers, projects of all kinds coming out of the women's movement needed "to start thinking of themselves as businesses   as businesses which are financially independent and self-sufficient and as businesses which support their workers."[42]

Many feminists agreed. To liberate themselves from the capitalist structures that left them dependent on men, feminists believed they needed to continue to build their own economy of self-sustaining, participatory, and democratic businesses. They saw activist businesses not only as vehicles for economic self-sufficiency but also as critical goals unto themselves for the women's movement. By the mid-1970s, roughly 150 businesses in the United States aligned themselves with the organized women's movement.[43] Feminists were heartened by such growth, but some thought businesses could do more for their movement. These women looked to the financial sector as the next frontier of feminist enterprise, and they also made plans for uniting feminist businesses across the United States through national coalitions. Yet although these dreams excited some in the women's movement, others began to worry that feminists businesses might become too successful or powerful for their own good.

FINANCIAL FEMINISM AND THE DEBATE ON
ECONOMIC LEADERSHIP

Women's growing interest in economic independence from men helped to push equal access to credit to the forefront of the movement's concerns in the early 1970s. "The significance of our inability to obtain credit assumes greater dimension when we view it as a reflection of woman's insignificance in the eyes of the financial community," NOW argued. The organization established a task force on credit discrimination in 1971, and two years later it published its findings in *Women and Credit* (figure 4.5). NOW's thirty-page guide identified a wide range of types of credit discrimination women faced and offered chapters and their members concrete advice for combating such discrimination in their local areas. Although unmarried women could generally obtain retail credit, lending agencies commonly denied them mortgages and scrutinized them much more than male applicants. Single women's individual credit ratings were often cancelled if they married. Married women could rarely establish credit in their own names, even if they were employed. Creditors commonly cited pregnancy—and even the mere possibility of it—as justification for denying married women credit, presuming that mothers would automatically stop working. Divorced women generally lost any credit history they had accumulated before and during marriage. Creditors contended that women were less financially knowledgeable and less creditworthy than men. Such blatant discrimination was all the more frustrating for women in light of research that showed that they were in fact more reliable borrowers than men.[44]

Such discriminatory practices prompted Joanne Parrent and Valerie Angers to establish the Feminist Federal Credit Union in Detroit in 1973. Around the start of the decade, Parrent and Angers had been living in a cooperative residence with several other families when they left their husbands for each other. Parrent and Angers soon established a CR group, and in 1972 they founded the Women's Health Project, a workshop series with antirape education, pregnancy testing, and abortion referrals. By 1974, the women had expanded the project into the Women's Health Center, a comprehensive gynecological clinic that performed abortions.

Parrent and Angers decided to establish a credit union to raise capital for the Health Center's expansion. They initially envisioned the credit

FIGURE 4.5 NOW publication on credit discrimination, 1973. Courtesy of the Arthur and Elizabeth Schlesinger Library on the History of Women in America, Radcliffe Institute for Advanced Study, Harvard University, Cambridge, Mass.

union as nothing more than an auxiliary institution to the Health Center, but they soon began to contemplate how it might serve a larger function in Detroit's feminist community. They wondered if women's health work, by giving "us more understanding and control of our own bodies and therefore ultimately more control of our own lives as women," might serve as a model for the credit union. "How could we also have more control over our economic lives as women?" Parrent and Angers asked themselves.[45] They soon came to believe that credit unions held untapped promise for feminists by giving women economic control in a world of male-controlled banking.

Credit unions were well positioned to serve feminists and other activists who sought a modicum of stable financial growth but did not wish to invest in traditional, for-profit corporate lending institutions intent on maximizing profits. As not-for-profit financial cooperatives, credit unions were owned by their members, operated on a "one member, one vote" management system, encouraged thrift and savings, and did not issue joint stock. Credit unions grew spectacularly after World War II. Widely heralded as "people's banks," more than 8,600 credit unions boasted a total membership of 2.8 million in the United States by 1945. By 1969, those numbers had skyrocketed to more than 23,700 credit unions with 21.6 million members.[46] And, unlike banks, they required very little capital to charter—just $35 in the early 1970s.

Credit unions not only allowed but also required a higher degree of member engagement than banks, exhibiting a degree of participatory democracy that Parrent and Angers believed was "not unlike that of the women's movement." By law, only groups of people who shared a common organizational affiliation, such as state employees or members of a trade union, were permitted to establish credit unions. When Parrent and Angers first proposed the FFCU, the National Credit Union Administration (NCUA) questioned whether feminists represented an appropriate constituency for a credit union. The FFCU placated the NCUA by deciding that account holders should be dues-paying members of one of eight feminist organizations, including NOW, the National Black Feminist Organization, and the Women's Liberation Coalition of Michigan. After three months of back-and-forth negotiations, the NCUA finally agreed to charter the FFCU in August 1973. The credit union opened with just fifteen members and $1,950 in deposits.[47]

The FFCU expressly sought to provide Detroit-area feminists the financial foundation they needed for collective economic liberation from men. "We can invest our savings in loans to our sisters instead of in male-owned and controlled banking institutions with sexist lending polices and employment practices," a FFCU informational flyer explained. "Now we can borrow where we are not discriminated against because of marital status or the credit rating of husband or father." The FFCU was a female-run free space where women could obtain funding for difficult purchases they needed to make without the approval of male partners or bank employees. "With women we can be honest about why we want a loan; whether it be for a divorce, an abortion, a vacation, or a means to become a self-directing person." The FFCU viewed itself "like a woman's center . . . with bulletin boards and posters about Feminist news and activities. Women can call the credit union for information about any Feminist group or project or referral." Yet unlike "the women's centers of the old days," the FFCU kept "regular hours and it doesn't disappear in a few months," explained Beverly Buthwoman, a Michigan State University undergraduate who headed a branch the FFCU had opened in Lansing. "No matter how important individual woman's needs are, the needs of women as a class are greater," Buthwoman explained. The FFCU was not just a financial institution but also a "tool that Feminists can use to achieve change in combination with other tools" and to advance their interests collectively.[48]

From 1973 to 1975, the Detroit FFCU thrived and inspired feminists all over the country to establish their own local credit unions. In Michigan, the FFCU opened branches in Lansing, Ann Arbor, and Flint, and their collective assets rose to more than half a million dollars. The Ann Arbor branch alone grew to three hundred members. Compared to most other financial institutions, these numbers were small, but the FFCU's assets qualified it not only as one of the largest feminist businesses in the country but as one of the most highly capitalized woman-owned businesses of any kind. Meanwhile, a dozen different feminist credit unions opened for business in cities across the country, including San Diego; Dallas; Washington, D.C.; Charleston, South Carolina; and Harrisburg, Pennsylvania. By 1975, feminist credit unions' total assets reached an estimated $1.5 million (more than $6.7 million in 2016 dollars, adjusted for inflation). Feminists opened banks, too, starting in 1975 with the First Women's Bank of New York, which claimed Betty Friedan as a board member. By 1980, at least seven other women's banks had opened in the United States.[49]

In May 1975, a coalition of leaders from the Detroit FFCU and other feminist credit unions met in New Haven, Connecticut, to explore how to capitalize on their collective strength as financial institutions of the women's movement. Attendees established FEN, an organization for pooling feminist credit unions' resources and taking advantage of economies of scale in advertising and credit available to larger financial institutions. The organization's founding members nominated the Washington, D.C., and Connecticut FFCUs to draft two sets of bylaws that would be circulated before the next conference over Thanksgiving weekend later that year in Detroit, where members would merge them into a single document for ratification.[50]

Soon after FEN's inaugural meeting, two starkly different visions of the organization's mission emerged. The Connecticut contingent quickly pre-circulated a proposal for FEN to serve as a national umbrella organization through which feminist credit unions could share information and pool modest resources with each other but not do much else. The Washington FFCU unveiled a plan at the November conference that was much more ambitious: FEN was supposed to do nothing less than "accept financial leadership for the feminist movement" and head up a network that would unite the sprawling array of feminist businesses across the country. FEN also vowed to establish an educational arm that would train women in business and a lending arm that would provide capital to feminist entrepreneurs. The main supporters of the Washington group's proposal were the Detroit FFCU, Diana Press, and the Oakland Feminist Women's Health Center.[51]

Although most feminist businesses stressed collective decision making, the Washington proposal gave only some FEN members voting privileges. The women who invested the most time and energy into FEN would instead form an eight-member voting board of directors and determine most of the group's operations. The Connecticut contingent responded by accusing the Washington group of cynically attempting to seize control of the feminist business movement. FEN, they insisted, should remain true to its original vision as a coalition of feminist credit unions and not presume to serve all feminist enterprises. The differences between the two factions quickly became irreconcilable, and the Washington–Oakland–Baltimore–Detroit group walked out of the meeting, taking FEN with them. The Connecticut-led contingent, meanwhile, launched a rival organization for feminist credit unions, the Feminist Economic Alliance (FEA).

FEN was nothing if not ambitious. The organization followed through with its plans and established two nonprofit corporations: the educational FEN Institute for training women in business and a consulting and public relations group. As founders of one of the most highly capitalized feminist businesses in the country, Parrent and Angers were in a particularly strong position to shape FEN's decision making. By 1976, the FFCU's assets reached $1 million (more than $4.2 million in 2016 dollars), and its membership grew to 3,500 account holders. Parrent and Angers soon put forward another dramatic plan. In downtown Detroit, a dilapidated but still handsome building that had housed a women's civic organization since the 1920s had recently closed and was for sale. FEN member businesses could pool their resources, purchase the former meeting place of the Women's City Club, and lease out its spaces to other feminist businesses, including FFCU branches, Diana Press, and the Oakland Feminist Women's Health Center. The building in turn could serve as a national headquarters for feminist enterprise.[52]

The women behind FEN felt that feminist enterprises did not need to cling to shoestring operations as a badge of honor. Rather, they believed that activist businesses truly succeeded if they enriched thousands of women beyond their small circle of ownership. Small activist businesses could work best when they operated as a consortium of free spaces anchored by a not-for-profit financial institution such as a credit union. Yet other feminists viewed the unprecedented scale and ambition of FEN's plans for activist business with trepidation and concern. The ongoing split between FEN and the FEA threatened to overshadow any excitement generated by the City Club plans.

"The story of Detroit is the story of the growing pains of the feminist movement," wrote Jackie St. Joan, a member of the Ann Arbor FFCU who sided with the FEA, in a story for the nationally distributed Denver feminist paper *Big Mama Rag* in January 1976. These debates reflected more than differences over organizational structures or competing strategies for consolidating the power of feminist businesses. The FEN–FEA split represented something more fundamental. St. Joan conceded that money could be "a tool for liberation." But she also considered it, along with violence, "the ultimate instrument of control." How could FEN, St. Joan asked rhetorically, "'accept financial leadership for the feminist movement' when no body of feminists has, in fact, offered it to the group?" The debate over feminist businesses and FEN, she argued, was nothing less than a debate over the livelihood, leadership, and core principles of the women's movement.[53]

The FWCC prepared to open in April 1976. FEN planned a massive gala celebration for the opening and invited national media and feminist leaders, including Gloria Steinem. Yet the pressures of preparing the spacious, multistory club for the event wore heavily on the organizers. FEN hired a number of women, many of them from the Ann Arbor FFCU branch, to help complete the extensive cleaning and renovations necessary for opening the club. Crews of workers labored for up to fifteen hours a day. Days before the opening, the women from Ann Arbor contemplated striking for better working conditions. "They worked us like mules!" one woman charged. "In all of my 42 years, and in all my jobs, I have never worked for any male chauvinist pig who was as oppressive an employer as" the FEN leaders, another worker claimed. Some women even contended they were held in the club against their will at the end of their shifts. The workers eventually decided against striking but scheduled a meeting for after the opening to discuss how Michigan's FFCUs could hold FEN and the Detroit FFCU accountable.[54]

Outside observers nonetheless believed the club was off to a remarkable start when the opening festivities began on April 9. Hundreds of women attended the grand opening and keynote talk by Steinem, who cut a "ribbon of dollar bills signed by famous feminists." As Steinem dramatically announced, "The eyes of the women of the world are on Detroit tonight." Guests marveled at the club's Olympic-size swimming pool, its ornate architecture, and its seven different feminist businesses. For a $100 annual membership, women could patronize the club's bars, pool, hotel, and nightclub. "We expect to be inundated with membership applications," one club member declared. Initial coverage in the Detroit press was overwhelmingly positive. "Feminists give new life to downtown club," reported a story in the

Detroit Free Press, and the women's renovation of the old building was reminiscent of "a butterfly struggling out of a dead cocoon."[55]

Yet the founders of the FWCC quickly realized they faced immense challenges. Operational costs amounted to a whopping $22,000 per month. Women in Detroit were slow to embrace the club and its $100 membership fee, perhaps especially at a time when a national recession plagued the struggling city.[56] Criticisms of the club intensified. Disgruntled members of the Ann Arbor FFCU publicized three main objections to FEN's administration of the club. First, they saw the FWCC as undemocratic and its leadership style as autocratic. Second, they believed the Detroit FFCU's decision to fund the FEN members' purchase of the building may have violated federal rules against credit unions making loans to businesses. Third, they argued that the club was too expensive to join, too enthusiastic about profits, and simply too capitalistic to serve the women's movement. In other words, they accused FEN of being insufficiently devoted to its stated mission of activist business.

The Ann Arbor women shared these objections with writers for regional and national feminist publications such as *her-self*, *off our backs*, *Big Mama Rag*, and *Quest: A Feminist Quarterly* in the spring of 1976. A torrent of negative press soon overshadowed the early positive reports. Perhaps no one damaged FEN's reputation more than Martha Shelley, the author of a twenty-two-page screed titled simply "What Is FEN?" Shelley, a member of the Women's Print Collective in Oakland and a cofounder of the Radicalesbians, self-published the essay and circulated it among feminists in the San Francisco Bay Area and throughout the country. Shelley said the work was based on extensive research and interviews with numerous disaffected former employees of FEN, several of whom she claimed chose to remain anonymous out of fear of violent retribution. She condemned FEN in even harsher terms than most journalists. Most damningly, Shelley remarked that she could simply not "imagine how a mass movement based on a fascist variety of lesbian feminism could be successful in America." Yet the businesses in FEN did not always publicly identify themselves as lesbian companies per se but called themselves "feminist businesses" and "women's businesses." They did not, as Shelley charged, demand their allies be lesbians. Nor did they defensively play down their lesbianism in order to attract a broad female clientele, as one historian has claimed.[57]

The political and financial costs of the FWCC soon became too great for FEN. Roughly five months after the opening, several of the club's directors packed up their belongings and moved to California without any warning. FEN soon thereafter relinquished the building to the Detroit FFCU and dissolved its charter. Unable to maintain the building, the credit union soon shuttered it and two years later sold it to a developer.[58] One of the grandest experiments by any activist business since the 1960s had come to a definitive, quick, and disappointing end.

GROWING RESISTANCE

Martha Shelley's denunciation of FEN reflected growing criticisms in the women's movement that cast feminist businesses as fanciful experiments in "cultural feminism." Although very few (if any) women described themselves as "cultural feminists," some feminists employed the term as an epithet to hurl at other feminists they viewed as escapist and inconsequential. Perhaps more than anyone, Brooke Williams helped to popularize the term in her essay "The Retreat to Cultural Feminism" (1975). Another former member of the Radicalesbians, Williams published this piece in the anthology *Feminist Revolution* by the Redstockings, a radical feminist group. Williams argued that cultural feminism was the "belief that women will be freed via an alternate women's culture." By "embracing the dope and back-to-nature" ethos championed by hippies, cultural feminism was "a direct descendant of the counter culture."[59]

Williams was particularly disturbed by "women promoting the idea of small shops as the road to liberation." Feminist businesses attempted "to transform feminism from a political movement to a lifestyle movement." This distortion of feminist praxis responded to "male supremacy by withdrawing from it and pretending it isn't there." Feminist businesses "reach very few people. They have to struggle just to keep themselves afloat, much less reach out to others." Small enterprises offered no "solution to women's oppression . . . [because] setting up 'alternative' situations doesn't really work."[60]

In 1976, Williams partnered with Hannah Darby to expand this critique into a full-throated jeremiad against feminist businesses in the pages of *off our backs*. Williams and Darby charged feminist enterprises not only with "changing feminism to a commodity which business can sell at a price and for a profit" but also with perpetrating acts of "economic, social, and even sexual exploitation . . . [that were] frequently more subtle and far-reaching than in straight businesses." Unlike organizations such as NOW, feminist businesses' brand of cultural feminism was "more insidious than outright reformism" because many of them had "pretensions to radicalism." By distracting employees with "pseudo-movement busywork," feminist businesses actually "militate[d] against women participating in the women's (political) movement." Feminists should instead organize "alternate institutions" that benefited working-class women and "provided basic necessities" to the female masses. Such institutions included newspapers and mail-order distributors of movement texts, which for unstated reasons the authors did not consider businesses.[61]

Yet a number of women defended feminist businesses in *off our backs*. Janis Kelly and Wendy Stevens conceded that "capitalism has in some way succeeded in turning feminism into a commodity," but they argued nonetheless that feminist businesses' vulnerability to co-optation was actually quite limited because their products were not very profitable. Feminist enterprises were instead "non-hierarchical, anti-profit businesses [that] are basically antagonistic to" what they called "authoritarian capitalism." As such, feminist businesses had the power "both [to] add to feminist theory and to change the lives of women who encounter them" by building a "women's culture [that] is as integral to revolution as is political theory."[62]

This exchange over feminist businesses set off a fierce debate in the pages of *off our backs* and triggered an "unusually voluminous" reader response. One woman wrote that Williams and Darby articulated a "dangerously simplistic blending of Socialism 101 with Feminism 102." The writer accepted that "*feminist* and *business* are contradictions in terms. Ideally, of course. But I do not have the luxury of your purism," she wrote. "I do not believe in private property either but I need a place to sleep, unhassled, so I still pay rent." Feminist businesses' primary purpose was not to provide "an economic powerbase for making it in the system." Rather, the "spreading of feminist consciousness is the primary goal," along with providing spaces "where alienation begins to dissolve, where women have access to each other's energy/consciousness through a sharing of women's culture." Critics of feminist businesses would do best to "loosen up" and "begin to enjoy the revolution you are creating." Another reader, describing herself as a former president of a feminist talent agency, conceded that "most 'feminist businesses' exploit the people who own them and work in them." But she vowed to continue to support women-owned businesses "because there is no *immediate alternative*. . . . There is no economic system in the world today that has *proven itself any better for women* than the capitalist system."[63] Feminist businesses were far from perfect but still highly preferable to prevailing forms of male-controlled corporate capitalism.

Other readers agreed that feminist business retreated from confronting economic and gender oppression. "I would, please, like some good, solid, structural arguments that these 'alternative' businesses are revolutionary or antithetical to capitalism," wrote one reader. "The exact same cant was put forth about Black and hippy businesses." Rather, feminist businesses "actually help capitalism by absorbing prospective dissidents (even giving them a stake in the system)."[64]

Debates over what role small businesses should play in the feminist movement reached a fever pitch by 1976. They spread from the FEN–FEA split to the FWCC to the pages of the most widely read feminist publications in the country. Although a large part of the movement established and supported feminist businesses, there was little agreement as to what those businesses should look like, how they should operate, or how they should relate to other feminist organizations. Indeed, one of the defining features of feminist businesses had become feminists' lack of consensus over their impact and value.

Few businesses were more affected by the consequences of bitter debates over feminist enterprise than Diana Press. By 1976, the press had transformed from a print shop that produced a few books as a sideline to two incorporated businesses, a printing arm and a publishing arm, each with a separate bank account and bookkeeping. It had published almost thirty different titles since 1973, nearly all of which focused on feminism and women's culture and many of which were on lesbian topics. In 1975, the press printed sixty-five thousand copies of books, its most productive year ever.[65]

Diana Press had come to view its work as part of a larger movement of "women in print." In the five years following the emergence of the first second-wave periodicals in 1968, feminists launched no fewer than 560 journals, newspapers, and magazines. Feminists established their own publishing houses, including Diana Press, Daughters, Inc., the Feminist Press, and Shameless Hussy. A few feminist publishers even specialized in children's books (figure 4.6), such as Lollipop Power in Chapel Hill, North Carolina. In August 1976, Charlotte Bunch of *Quest*; June Arnold, founder of Daughters, Inc.; and Coletta Reid organized a coalition of feminist presses, bookstores, and journals for the inaugural Women in Print Conference, held in Omaha, Nebraska. Discussions at the conference centered

FIGURE 4.6 Advertisement for Sisterhood Bookstore, Los Angeles, 1972. Courtesy of the Arthur and Elizabeth Schlesinger Library on the History of Women in America, Radcliffe Institute for Advanced Study, Harvard University, Cambridge, Mass.

on how feminists could create their own national, woman-controlled communications and distribution network for publishing.[66]

Diana Press's participation in Women in Print and its membership in FEN had bolstered the company's contacts with other feminist entrepreneurs across the country. Coletta Reid and Casey Czarnik were particularly close with FWCC leaders Laura Brown and Barbara Hoke, who directed the Oakland Feminist Women's Health Center. In March 1977, Czarnik and Reid relocated Diana Press to Oakland, where they could work closely with the Feminist Women's Health Center, pay lower rent, and possibly merge with the city's Women's Press Collective. With a new headquarters in Oakland's vibrant feminist community, circumstances boded well for Diana Press's continued expansion and success in 1977. By that fall, the press had grown to employ eighteen women, many more than had worked for the company when it started in Baltimore.[67]

Yet the move to Oakland proved much more difficult than the women of Diana Press imagined. Reid and Czarnik had significantly underestimated the dissension within women's groups in the Bay Area over the issue of feminist businesses. Although primarily aimed at the FWCC, Martha Shelley's essay "What Is FEN?" also painted a very unfavorable picture of the Oakland Feminist Women's Health Center. Shelley, who worked with the Women's Press Collective in Oakland, claimed that FEN hoped to take over the collective and to acquire successful West Coast feminist media businesses such as Olivia Records, Chrysalis Magazine, and the Los Angeles Women's Building. The women of Diana Press felt that the FEN and FWCC controversies had "helped create a climate of distrust of us in the Bay Area that became virtually impossible to break through." In Oakland, the press found itself in a much worse financial position than it had been in Baltimore, owing to the move and the FWCC's collapse.[68]

Yet these challenges paled in comparison to what happened on October 26, 1977. That morning workers discovered that someone had broken into the press and vandalized it almost beyond recognition. The perpetrator had soaked in chemicals and ruined five thousand copies of the press's best seller, *Plain Brown Rapper* by Rita Mae Brown. Other titles were smeared with ink and paint. Even worse, the culprits had poured paint and chemicals on various printing machines and destroyed photo plates and negatives for producing books. The total damage was around $100,000, barely half of which insurance would reimburse. The damage was so extensive that the press could not complete any print jobs or publish any books for the foreseeable future. The press's workers could not help but think that the vandalism was "aimed at our financial ruin."[69]

Two months later a writer for *off our backs* considered a range of culprits who might have sought to destroy Diana Press. "The government" and "agents of the State" were "always suspect in cases of this kind," or perhaps the "anti-feminist, homophobic, women-fearing Right" was responsible. Someone with a personal grudge might have attacked the press—a disgruntled author or employee, for example. A "freeform crazy" could have even chosen to commit a random act of violence. The women at Diana Press offered another theory: the vandals had come from within the feminist movement. Footprints found at the scene suggested that one or more women had broken into the workspace. The press contended that the likeliest perpetrators were either "women in the movement who were opposed to Diana Press and FEN . . . [or] a combination of agent provocateurs and women who felt they were saving the movement from 'feminist capitalism.'" Either way, the company's staff believed the attack had been "made possible by the climate of gossip, trashing, back-biting and verbal violence that the movement had encouraged about Diana Press and FEN for the last 2 years." The utter failure "to deal with political differences constructively" had made the violence against the press possible.[70]

Some feminists offered another theory: that the press's staff had sabotaged their own workplace for political gain, insurance money, and even the nearly $15,000 in relief funds they received from feminists across the country by the summer of 1978.[71] Yet such an act of utter self-sabotage seems improbable, considering that the vandalism absolutely crippled the company. Eleven titles were postponed for publication for more than a year; commercial print jobs were suspended; and the press had to spend more than $50,000 of its own funds to repair and replace the print jobs and equipment it lost.

Diana Press's demise quickly followed the vandalism. Both Laura Brown and Casey Czarnik left the company in 1978. Czarnik's departure was particularly difficult because it coincided with her and Coletta Reid's decision to end their relationship of many years.[72] Although Diana Press initially vowed to continue publishing, staffers finally felt they had no choice but to close their doors for good in 1979. The company's closing was a fitting symbol for the larger decline that feminist businesses began to experience by the end of the decade.

HARD TIMES AFTER THE SECOND WAVE

The closing of Diana Press occurred amid a broader decline in feminist businesses that began at the end of the 1970s and continued into the 1980s. In an article on lesbian and feminist companies in the fall of 1979, *Lesbian Tide*, a Los Angeles newspaper, reported that "all of the women's businesses [the newspaper] surveyed . . . experienced financial difficulties in the last year." As one feminist entrepreneur regretfully admitted, "We didn't understand the capitalist system. Businesses make it through understanding tax breaks, p.r. [*sic*], efficient management, etc. We assumed we could do it our way without paying attention to any of those factors." Like many activist enterprises, feminist business owners grappled with the impossibility of operating both within *and* outside the dominant system of American capitalism. One business owner cited the pitfalls of "our movement's masturbatory emphasis on process" and frequent struggles to perfect "internal dynamics." Another argued that movement businesses often struggled financially because "many women feel it's unfeminist to charge competitive prices in terms of market value for services and products."[73] A number of feminist entrepreneurs argued that the ideological demands of running their businesses were too high.

Many prominent feminist businesses closed. Feminist credit unions folded in Colorado, Los Angeles, and Washington, D.C., by the start of the 1980s. The once mighty Detroit FFCU was absorbed by the University of Michigan Credit Union in 1982. That year an internal struggle became public at the first and one of the largest feminist bookstores, ICI: A Woman's Place in Oakland, where women of color working at the store accused some staffers of racism. One faction of the collective's employees effectively excommunicated other collective members by changing the locks on the bookstore's doors, sparking a highly publicized dispute. Although the women finally settled their dispute in arbitration in 1983, high turnover, financial woes, and a divided staff and customer base would continue to plague the store until it eventually closed in 1989.[74] All in all, the 1980s proved to be rather unkind to the pioneers of second-wave feminist business.

Feminist businesses' woes also stemmed from the declining fortunes of the broader women's movement. The failed ratification of the Equal Rights Amendment in 1982 symbolized for many people a reversal of momentum for feminists, a signal of a larger backlash against women's gains. For many women in the 1980s who were too young to have participated in second-wave feminism, the legal and institutionalized sexism that the movement had fought in the 1970s seemed abstract and part of a distant past. Second-wave veterans worried that this "postfeminist" generation failed to recognize the persistence of deep sexism and the continued need for an organized women's movement. In a poll conducted in 1983, for instance, only 25 percent of woman responded "yes" when asked if the women's movement had "achieved anything that made your life better," and in a poll taken in 1989 only 37 percent of women responded that "there is a need for a strong and organized women's movement." Anecdotal evidence suggested that a sizable proportion of young women viewed feminists as bitter, antimale lesbians fixated on inequalities of the past.[75] To be sure, these increasingly common criticisms levied at the women's movement hurt feminist businesses.

In addition, the tremendous economic, logistical, and psychological burdens of operating businesses drove many feminist entrepreneurs to shutter their enterprises. Although most companies—especially activist businesses—faced similar difficulties, feminist businesses' ideological standards, dedication to democratic workplaces, and frequent debates with fellow feminists tended to intensify such struggles. The deep recession of the late 1970s and early 1980s proved particularly treacherous for feminist businesses. Not only did potential customers have less income to spend on such discretionary purchases as feminist literature, artwork, and merchandise, but many women who worked for low wages or volunteered at feminist businesses had to leave those businesses for better-paying jobs. Of course, these challenges affected all varieties of activist enterprises, but feminist businesses, with their strong emphasis on collectivism and non-profit trade, were particularly vulnerable to these pressures. As financial difficulties mounted, so did stress and conflict. Many women at feminist bookstores identified "burnout" as a primary culprit of store closings. Some feminist entrepreneurs cited a declining number of willing volunteers among middle-aged feminists seeking greater financial stability as a major factor that undermined their ability to staff their businesses. The climate for independent bookstores was also the worst in years, particularly due to the skyrocketing prices for paper and shipping amid a larger backdrop of national inflation.[76] Feminists businesses' high standards for collective work made political and interpersonal disagreements all the more painful. For some women, the dissolution of feminist businesses was not only a financial loss but also akin to personal and ideological defeat or even a death in the family.

Some feminist enterprises downplayed their allegiance to the women's movement—and even to women more generally—as part of their survival strategy. Like many other activist businesses struggling to remain open in the 1980s, quite a few feminist entrepreneurs believed that only by distancing themselves from the movement could they stay financially viable. The Feminist Press, an esteemed movement publisher found in 1970, remained loyal to its political roots but began publishing on topics other than women and feminism. As one of the company's directors conceded, the Feminist Press could no longer limit itself to "already politicized readers." A marketing expert and cultural anthropologist told the *New York Times* in 1988 that "an overwhelming number" of women had come to "reject products with a feminist identification, just as they reject other aspects of the 1960's culture." The National Association of Women Business Owners, whose founders in 1975 included prominent New York NOW members Jacqui Ceballos and Donna Ferrante, did not even mention feminism or the women's movement by name in its bylaws in 1985, a decade later. Other feminist businesses sought to broaden their customer base by changing their names and management. In 1986, Martin Simon, a man, became the chief executive officer of the First Women's Bank in New York, an institution founded in 1975 at the height of the second wave. In 1988, the company renamed itself the First New York Bank for Business, and its new CEO declared "acceptance of women in our economic life is so complete that our [previous] name [was] almost anachronistic." Simon's rationale, of course, belied the reality that women still confronted significant economic discrimination in the 1980s.[77]

Yet the decline of businesses that aligned themselves with the women's movement coincided with an opposing trend: tremendous gains for most women entrepreneurs in the 1980s. Indeed, from 1977 to 1987 the number of women's businesses in the United States more than quintupled, from about 700,000 to more than 4.1 million. Women's increased share of American companies was remarkable. In 1977, women had owned just 7 percent of all companies. Ten years later they owned 30 percent of all firms. The proportion of women's businesses that publicly identified with feminism had always been relatively small, but that proportion shrank even further in the 1980s. Now even fewer female entrepreneurs had connections to organized feminism. At a time when many woman who benefitted from feminism did not identify as feminists, countless woman-owned businesses aided by the gains of earlier feminist enterprises chose not to associate with the women's movement. A number of male and female marketing experts argued that women's increased integration into the ranks of entrepreneurs and salaried workers gave them a preference for gender-neutral businesses. Such claims echoed conservative arguments that African Americans who benefited from civil rights legislation should prefer a "color-blind" society that acknowledged racial differences as little as possible. The term *feminist business* even seemed to go out of favor in the women's movement. A search for the term in the entire run of *off our backs* reveals that the magazine published twenty-three articles and letters about "feminist business" or "feminist businesses" between 1970 and 1984 but only six articles from 1985 to 2008.[78]

Yet some women who started businesses in these years still insisted on putting feminism at the center of their operations. In a subtle but important semantic shift, many of these companies came to identify simply as women's businesses or as lesbian businesses. Most lesbian entrepreneurs in the 1970s strongly emphasized their businesses' connections to the women's movement. In the 1980s and particularly the 1990s, more and more lesbian entrepreneurs primarily identified not as feminist but as lesbian business owners. Lesbians had been at the forefront of feminist business in the 1970s, and by the 1990s lesbian enterprises had grown to represent a much more sizable segment of the overall feminist business community. Indeed, it would seem that the gains of queer activists in the 1980s and 1990s had helped to create more space for lesbians within the larger women's movement and the overall landscape of women's institutions. Meanwhile, a fledgling, self-styled lesbian, gay, bisexual, and transgender marketplace emerged but primarily promoted gay men as business owners and consumers. Lesbian businesses were cast as auxiliaries to the gay male marketplace. And the ever more common stereotype that all feminists were lesbians further encouraged the idea that feminist businesses were lesbian businesses.[79]

Another new development was the emergence of enterprises owned by African American feminists. African Americans had played key roles in a handful of feminist companies that made antiracism a central part of their work, including Diana Press, ICI: A Woman's Place, and the Women's Press Collective. Yet black women were significantly underrepresented in feminist businesses in the 1970s. Indeed, many of them identified widespread racism in feminist presses and bookstores, which offered very few works by or about black women, as well in the women's movement more generally.[80] Black feminists formed various organizations in the early and mid-1970s and gained greater visibility in the wake of the publication of the black lesbian feminist Combahee River Collective's Statement in 1977. In 1981, one of the collective's founding members, Barbara Smith, established Kitchen Table: Women of Color Press at the suggestion of black lesbian and feminist pioneer Audre Lorde. The first nationally prominent black feminist business, Kitchen Table described itself as "an activist and literary publisher" that worked toward "the liberation of women of color and of all people" by marketing books "as thoroughly and as aggressively as possible." The press quickly made a name for itself by publishing groundbreaking anthologies such as *Home Girls: A Black Feminist Anthology* and *This Bridge Called My Back: Writings by Radical Women of Color* in 1983, the latter selling nearly fifty thousand copies in its first decade. Other black feminist businesses opened in the 1990s, including the black feminist bookstore Sisterspace in Washington, D.C. Meanwhile, white-owned feminist businesses increasingly focused on

combating racism and making space for women of color on their staffs by
the 1990s.[81]

Like black-owned bookstores and head shops, however, feminist enterprises in the 1980s and 1990s embraced conventional business practices
much more than their second-wave predecessors had. These new feminist
businesses were far less likely to be collectives. Many feminist businesses
found the financial and interpersonal costs of shared ownership too much to
bear amid a tough economy and political backlash against feminism. Loraine
Edwalds and feminist Third Side Press founder Midge Stocker captured
this shift in their essay collection *The Woman-Centered Economy* (1995).
The 1970s had been a time when feminist businesses, "like babies, grew
incredibly quickly, and one day without even knowing they had done it . . .
[and] were able to take a long breath." The 1980s, by contrast, had been
"ugly teenage years" for feminist businesses, a time "filled with self doubt
and the dreadful realization that some of the feminist sisters who shared
our experience were women we not only disagreed with but who we couldn't
trust."[82] Aware of the ideological shifts, financial struggles, and interpersonal conflicts that had destroyed many second-wave businesses, feminist
entrepreneurs in the 1980s and 1990s sought refuge in conventional business practices, especially in the form of single and dual proprietorships.

Most of the credit unions, art shops, jewelry shops, and presses that had
made up the diverse feminist economy of the 1970s had closed for good by
the end of the 1980s. Yet despite the downturn in most feminist businesses,
more than 120 feminist bookstores were operating in the United States by
1994. Most of them were newer bookstores because more than two-thirds
of the feminist bookstores operating in the late 1970s had closed by the
end of the 1980s. The new generation of feminist bookstores needed to be
much more financially ambitious than their predecessors had been. Pioneers such as A Woman's Place had opened with just $400 in 1970 and
survived for nearly twenty years. But, according to Carol Seajay, the editor
of *Feminist Bookstore News* and a former volunteer at A Woman's Place,
feminist booksellers in the 1990s needed to start with $200,000 in capital
if they wanted to survive for more than three years.[83]

Nonetheless, specialist booksellers' future seemed bright. From 1978 to
1988, the total value of book sales in the United States more than doubled.

And as late as 1991, roughly one-third of all books in the country were sold by independents. More so than chains, independent stores had the specialized knowledge and relationships needed to sell titles published by the independent presses that *Publishers Weekly* described as the "guardians of the quality, offbeat, minority and sometimes eccentric books that bigger publishers" often overlooked. Even while many other kinds of feminist businesses struggled, women's bookstores' proliferated in the 1980s and 1990s amid a larger overall growth of independent bookstores. African American booksellers similarly flourished.[84]

But as bookstore chains such as Barnes and Noble and later the online bookseller Amazon pursued ever greater growth in the second half of the 1990s and early 2000s, they stocked more women's and African American titles than ever before. Feminist bookstores took a leading role in fighting major presses' preferential treatment of chain booksellers by agitating for the ABA to bring a series of lawsuits against publishers. Even though the association prevailed in some of these cases, dramatically increased competition from chains meant that the prosperity of independent specialists such as women's bookstores and African American bookstores would prove to be short-lived.[85] Although specialized independent bookstores did not know it at the time, the 1990s would prove to be the high water mark for their business and particularly for booksellers with connections to social movements.

The full title of Loraine Edwalds and Midge Stocker's essay collection— *The Woman-Centered Economy: Ideals, Reality, and the Space in Between*— spoke directly to the central challenge that all kinds of feminist businesses had faced since the start of the 1970s. Feminist entrepreneurs invested more energy than any other social movement in creating businesses that sought to transform deep-seated social values, promote egalitarian labor relations, and render capitalism more humane. Yet in setting the bar for their companies so high, most feminist entrepreneurs struggled to reconcile these ideals with the daily realities of business operation. Such exuberant idealism may have made the failure to sustain most feminist businesses in the long term all the more painful and disheartening. But even if second-wave feminists fell short at times, they came closer than any other activists in the 1960s and 1970s to fulfilling a vision of nonhierarchical, nonsexist, and partici-patory business. And scores of new businesses established in the 1980s and 1990s suggested the resilience of feminism's entrepreneurial vision through the end of the twentieth century. Perhaps most significantly, millions more American women started their own businesses for the first time. Even if most second-wave feminist businesses ultimately failed, they still played a meaningful role in helping to bring about the extraordinary rise of women entrepreneurs.[86]

Like feminists who established businesses, environmentalists and anti-war activists launched natural food stores in the 1960s and 1970s to trans-form Americans' social, political, and economic values. These small retailers sold organic and vegetarian foods with the goals of promoting pacifism, spirituality, democratic workplaces, and ecological sustainability. They also hoped to provide alternatives to chain grocery stores. Yet unlike femi-nist businesses, some natural food stores proved to be financially successful far beyond their owners' expectations. By the late 1970s, natural foods would attract much more ambitious entrepreneurs who sought to create their own chains. In so doing, these retailers would make the natural foods business the most profitable activist enterprise by the end of the twentieth century.

5

Natural Foods Stores

ENVIRONMENTAL ENTREPRENEURS AND THE PERILS OF GROWTH

One day in June 1966, federal agents from the U.S. Food and Drug Administration (FDA) made a surprise visit to a grocery store called Erewhon in Boston. There agents found a tiny converted shop in a basement tended by Keizo Kushi, an elderly Japanese man who was nearly deaf and spoke little English. The agents demanded to view copies of *Zen Macrobiotics*, a book written by the Japanese author, spiritual leader, and pacifist George Ohsawa, whose acolytes had founded Erewhon. *Zen Macrobiotics* urged readers to avoid "industrialized food and drink," including sugar, canned goods, and produce grown with pesticides and nonorganic fertilizers, as well as virtually all animal products. Erewhon stocked items that complied with Ohsawa's prescribed diet, which he claimed could alleviate or even cure a wide range of disease, including colds, fevers, whooping cough, leprosy, leukemia, gonorrhea, and meningitis. The FDA, whose agents had just days earlier raided another macrobiotic store run by an Ohsawa follower in New York City, believed that Erewhon's distribution of literature claiming certain foods cured disease was a violation of the Food, Drug, and Cosmetic Act of 1938. As one FDA administrator remarked in response to Ohsawa's claims, "Quackery is the lowest form of thievery."[1]

Keizo Kushi's son, Michio, and his daughter-in-law, Aveline, who managed the store as two of Ohsawa's key followers in America, instructed

Erewhon's staff to hide *Zen Macrobiotics* and sell it only to sympathetic customers. When Aveline arrived at the store, she swore to the FDA agents that Erewhon did not sell *Zen Macrobiotics*. They nonetheless insisted on searching the store. As they went to their car to retrieve flashlights to inspect Erewhon's stockroom, Aveline gathered the store's copies of the book and hid them in a dumpster. The FDA agents eventually left empty-handed after searching in vain for the book.[2]

At the time of the raid, Erewhon had been open for just a few months. The store measured a mere ten by twenty feet. It started with $500 in cash, and initial sales totaled roughly $20 to $30 a day. Most of the store's employees, including its managers, were macrobiotic followers of the Kushis and Ohsawa in their early twenties with virtually no background in business. Most of Erewhon's shoppers came from Boston's tiny macrobiotic community, too.[3] The embattled storefront, with few customers and miniscule sales, seemed the unlikely target of a federal investigation. To most Americans who had even heard of macrobiotics, the idea that Erewhon's employees favored the dietary advice of a charismatic Japanese spiritual leader over that of the U.S. federal government was simply absurd. The people behind Erewhon might have seemed crazy, but they hardly fit the profile of dangerous hucksters threatening to upend established American medical and dietary opinion.

Yet Erewhon would transform America's grocery business by the early 1970s. Just a few years after being raided by the FDA, the besieged hole-in-the-wall selling brown rice, adzuki beans, and obscure diet books had become the national leader of a $200 million retail sector offering alternatives to the processed foods sold by America's supermarket chains. By 1971, Erewhon's annual sales had grown to $1.8 million. The store had moved to a larger location in Boston, opened additional stores in Los Angeles and Seattle (figures 5.1 and 5.2), and would soon open a fourth location in Toronto. Erewhon began sourcing pesticide-free products directly from farmers and distributing them to a growing network of self-styled "natural foods" stores that specialized in vegetarian, unprocessed, and especially organic foods. That year, a somewhat incredulous but nonetheless positive story highlighting Erewhon's success and the business of "food faddism" appeared on the front page of the *Wall Street Journal*.[4]

Natural foods sellers made surprising financial gains in the early 1970s. But many of them participated in the era's counterculture and movements

FIGURE 5.1 Erewhon, Boston, c. early 1970s. Courtesy of Paul Hawken

FIGURE 5.2 Erewhon, Los Angeles, c. early 1970s. Courtesy of Paul Hawken

for environmentalism, animal rights, and peace more eagerly than they pursued profits. They understood natural foods not just as a business but also as a larger crusade for sustainability, health, and harmony. They believed that processed food and an overabundance of animal products had made Americans sick in every sense of the word, that the modern diet represented a form of "food pollution." Natural foods entrepreneurs saw their stores as providing the means to physical, environmental, and even spiritual rejuvenation. They believed that natural foods offered an ethical alternative to corporate agribusinesses and supermarkets that relentlessly pursued profits through exploitative labor and environmentally destructive systems of production and distribution. Natural foods sellers and shoppers proudly embraced their small retail spaces and bypassed America's chain supermarkets, which they considered promoters of poor health and a stultifying, "plastic" consumer culture.[5] And like many activist retailers, natural foods sellers saw their stores as laboratories for making work more democratic through consensus decision making, open records, hiring by vote, and other collectivist management practices. Natural foods, in short, were more than a different diet—they were also a different way of doing business.

Yet the two primary sellers of natural foods—independent proprietors and cooperative storefronts—diverged on the question of what ownership model was most appropriate for their business. Co-op members insisted that consumers or workers should own their natural foods stores and that such shared ownership was as important as the pursuit of environmental sustainability and improved health. Independent retailers, meanwhile, invoked humanistic psychology and "right livelihood," a Buddhist concept of ethically and spiritually informed labor, to articulate a vision of principled but proprietary pursuit of profit.[6] The question of worker representation vexed the natural foods community, too. Some of the most successful businesses resisted efforts by employees or activists to organize unions, rejecting the idea that organized labor should play a role in securing workplace democracy.

Natural foods stores experienced more financial success and made deeper inroads into the American marketplace than any other retailers discussed in this book. Yet despite—or perhaps because of—their considerable success, these businesses faced an array of criticisms, including charges of cliquish dogmatism, excessive prices for questionable products, and hostility toward people of color, the poor, and organized labor. These criticisms highlighted fundamental questions that nagged most activist entrepreneurs but were particularly urgent for natural foods sellers. Critics questioned whether natural foods sellers promoted radical, collective transformation, or simply individual lifestyle change. Natural foods sellers' fraught relationship with the federal government also raised difficult questions. Retailers characterized government investigations into how they marketed products as heavy-handed, intrusive, and corrupt, and they denounced federal agricultural subsidies for enabling an unhealthy, unsustainable, and monopolistic industrial agricultural system. To be sure, both libertarian and anarchist varieties of antigovernment sentiment thrived among natural foods sellers. At the same time, however, natural foods businesses appealed to federal and state governments to create systems of organic food certification. Some critics of government in the natural foods business even took advantage of government financial assistance. In short, natural foods businesses treated the government as friend or foe depending on the circumstances.

More than any other activist entrepreneurs, natural foods sellers debated if they could advance meaningful change by serving a subculture of principled devotees or if they should transform the larger conventional marketplace by enticing ever greater numbers of less-politicized consumers into their stores. Natural foods entrepreneurs in the late 1960s and early 1970s initially embraced the heterodox economist E. F. Schumacher's mantra of "economics as if people mattered" and "small is beautiful," while objecting to the prevailing capitalist logic of economies of scale and constant growth.[7] Many natural foods sellers believed that operating on a small scale would allow them to serve progressive social movements, democratize the workplace, and offer customers a humane and authentic shopping experience. Yet these beliefs increasingly came into question as demand for natural foods continued to increase. Entrepreneurs launched chains such as Bread & Circus and Whole Foods Market, which sold natural foods in supermarket settings in the late 1970s and early 1980s. Natural foods pioneers now struggled with the question of whether big retail chains and even bigger systems of organic foods production and distribution could continue to advance their ideals.

Natural foods businesses have failed to replace conventional supermarkets or to seriously challenge the reigning capitalist approach to producing and distributing food. But a small number of independent natural foods stores have shown it is possible, albeit difficult, to attain modest, long-term financial success without abandoning the goals of environmental sustainability and democratic workplaces. By the end of the 1980s, however, the number of politically oriented, small natural foods stores dwindled, squeezed out by corporate organic supermarket chains such as Whole Foods Market. Co-ops have survived but have declined in number and influence. The mission of most natural foods businesses has shifted away from collective political change through small storefronts in favor of chain stores that offer individuals the chance to improve their health and diet but not much more. Taken altogether, these transformations have indelibly shaped not only the natural foods business but also the broader project of activist enterprise in the United States.

THE EARLY YEARS OF THE ORGANIC FOOD BUSINESS

The origins of the food-reform business in the United States extend at least as far back as the 1820s, when the Presbyterian minister and temperance activist Sylvester Graham began to market "health foods" and vegetarian cookbooks as tools for physical and spiritual rejuvenation. Another religiously inspired entrepreneur who followed in Graham's wake was the pacifist and Seventh Day Adventist John Harvey Kellogg, who launched several highly successful health food and cereal businesses in the late nineteenth century. For much of the twentieth century, self-described health food businesses sold mostly vitamins and whole-grain foods. The largest concentration of these businesses was in southern California, where natural foods sellers enjoyed close ties to fitness, dieting, and bodybuilding communities.[8]

The market for "organic" foods produced without chemicals and pesticides first emerged during the middle of the twentieth century. In 1942, Jerome Irving "J. I." Rodale launched the magazine *Organic Gardening* (later *Organic Gardening and Farming*) in Emmaus, Pennsylvania. Three years later, Rodale published a primer on organic agriculture, *Pay Dirt: Farming and Gardening with Composts*, which sold more than fifty thousand copies. In 1946, the pacifist couple Paul and Betty Keene began selling organic produce at their Walnut Acres farm in Penn's Creek, Pennsylvania. In 1958, the Keenes opened a store on their property—possibly the first business in the country explicitly devoted to selling organic produce.[9]

Yet the larger transformations of American agricultural production far overshadowed the efforts of organic farmers. Purchases of agricultural fertilizers increased 800 percent between 1940 and 1970, and farmers' expenditures on pesticides grew from around $1 per acre to more than $6 per acre between 1950 and 1975. Among the most widely bought pesticides was DDT. The U.S. Department of Agriculture and the U.S. Army approved the synthetic chemical developed originally for military use for civil applications in 1945, in turn allowing DuPont to sell its extensive stockpiles of the chemical as a pesticide in the commercial marketplace. Grocery stores, meanwhile, sold virtually no organic food.[10]

At the end of the 1950s, Rodale's magazine enjoyed a monthly circulation of 135,000. Thousands of Americans grew organic produce, but virtually all of them did so for their private consumption, not to sell to others. Organic farms that sold directly to customers, such as the Keenes' farm, Walnut Acres, were modest, isolated operations far from major cities. Organic enthusiasts included immigrants or children of immigrants, like Rodale; bodybuilders, dieters, and fitness enthusiasts; and middle-aged and older customers looking for health benefits.[11] Young people showed very little interest in organic food. At the start of the 1960s, virtually no one imagined that a significant retail marketplace for organic foods might emerge in the United States.

ORGANIC FOODS, MACROBIOTICS, AND THE COUNTERCULTURE

At the same time that Rodale's publication was gaining a significant audience in the United States, several of George Ohsawa's most loyal disciples moved from Japan to New York City in the early 1950s with the goal of disseminating his teachings. Ohsawa's followers believed that the macrobiotic diet of soy products, brown rice, and organic vegetables was the key to achieving optimal health and the spiritual and physical balance known in Chinese philosophy as yin yang. They contended further that macrobiotics provided a path to a "peaceful revolution," a deeper physical and psychological transformation that could cure industrialized societies' widespread health problems, curb their citizens' growing sense of alienation, and even bring about world peace and solve social problems such as violent crime and drug addiction.[12]

Macrobiotic followers started their own small stores, restaurants, and buying clubs for sourcing organic foods and Japanese staples such as tamari and miso that were scarce outside Asia. In New York City, Ohsawa's followers opened the Zen Teahouse in Greenwich Village and the Musubi Restaurant in Midtown, and the actress Irma Paule sold Ohsawa's books and a few groceries out of the Nature's Cupboard shop at the George Ohsawa Foundation office. Serious macrobiotic followers went to great lengths to obtain staples and even drove hundreds of miles from Boston to central Pennsylvania to buy organic food directly from the Keenes' Walnut Acres store.[13] Despite these occasional interactions, macrobiotics followers and the readers of Rodale's publications represented two separate camps of organic enthusiasts.

By the mid-1960s, the United States was home to an estimated two thousand macrobiotic followers, most of whom were concentrated in California and the Northeast. In 1964, Michio and Aveline Kushi moved to Brookline, Massachusetts, outside Boston, where they held macrobiotic gatherings and established several residential "study houses" where followers took meals, meditated, and attended talks together. Ohsawa was gaining stature as a charismatic spiritual leader in countercultural circles. Scores of young people, many of them from San Francisco, began arriving in Boston and asked to join the community. In 1965, *Newsweek* published a short, incredulous piece depicting macrobiotic followers as a "bizarre" group seeking "beyond-the-fringe benefits." The author compared macrobiotics' appeal to that of LSD, citing aficionados who claimed that the diet elevated consciousness and could "trigger hallucinations." As one eighteen-year-old macrobiotic follower claimed, the diet "helps you leave the Great American deception . . . which is a self-deluding stimulus that makes you content in a kind of fat, disgusting way."[14] Another macrobiotic adherent was the psychologist Richard Alpert, whom Harvard had fired for taking LSD with Timothy Leary and who later became the countercultural spiritual leader Ram Dass. Macrobiotics, it seemed, offered the young and curious not only a new dietary regime but also an alternative form of consciousness and a critique of the dangers of American consumer culture.

The year 1965 also marked a moment of crisis for the macrobiotic movement, however. That November, a woman named Beth Ann Simon died in New Jersey after following one of the strictest macrobiotic diets for nine months, much longer than Ohsawa recommended. Media quickly condemned macrobiotics as a dangerous "cult diet." Simon's death also brought considerable scrutiny from a local county prosecutor, the New Jersey Health Department, and the FDA. Federal authorities eventually ordered the closing of the Ohsawa Foundation in Manhattan.[15] Macrobiotic followers meanwhile pointed to Simon's long history of heroin use as the decisive factor in her death.

Undaunted, macrobiotic adherents continued to establish small businesses. Macrobiotic followers in Boston converted a private buying club into Erewhon in April 1966. The store's name, "Erewhon," paid homage to Samuel Butler's novel of the same title, published in 1872, about an imaginary country with no machines. At first, Erewhon was "never seen as a business or money-making venture," according to one of its managers. It was instead essentially an effort by macrobiotic followers in Boston to create a self-sustaining buyers club for themselves at a time when they struggled to find the Japanese and organic food they craved. Even though the store was public, it initially served a very small number of customers and made just $150 to $300 a week.[16]

Most of Erewhon's staffers were young, white, highly educated, and from middle- and upper-class backgrounds. Several employees had been involved in the counterculture as well as the civil rights and student movements before embracing macrobiotics. Early manager Paul Hawken had worked for the Southern Christian Leadership Conference and Congress of Racial

Equality as a photographer documenting voter registration campaigns in Mississippi and Louisiana in the summer of 1965 at the age of eighteen. He later studied with the anarchist Paul Goodman at San Francisco State University and helped found the Calliope Company, which produced some of the first psychedelic light shows for rock concerts. Around 1967, Hawken discovered the book *The Order of the Universe*, a small collection of writings by Michio Kushi that was gaining a devoted readership in countercultural circles. In later years, Hawken would maintain that the macrobiotic diet had cured his asthma and gave him drug-free highs. Deeply moved by these experiences and seeking refuge from growing violence and turmoil in San Francisco's countercultural scene, Hawken and his friend Bill Tara left the city to join one of the Kushis' macrobiotic study houses in Boston. They quickly became involved in Erewhon's operations.[17]

Erewhon had started as a tiny store serving a minuscule market, but within a year of opening it struggled to meet the growing demand for its products. Some customers drove from hundreds of miles away to buy groceries and trade ideas about macrobiotics with Erewhon staffers. The store began to fill mail orders from individual customers, shipping food around the country. An early catalog from the store featured fewer than forty vegetarian items for mail order, including brown rice, beans, sea vegetables such as nori, and soy bean products such as *seitan*. Mail order was good for business, but it pointed to deeper problems in American society. "It is a pretty ridiculous country that has to send rice and beans around by parcel post," noted Paul Hawken with regret.[18]

With very little competition on the East Coast, Erewhon grew dramatically. By the end of its first year, monthly sales had grown ninefold. By the end of 1968, Erewhon moved into a larger storefront. The store began directly importing macrobiotic foods from Japan, and it soon was selling to wholesale buyers out of the back of its store. By the fall of 1969, the store netted $1,000 on some days and started shipping wholesale orders to natural foods stores throughout New England.[19] Erewhon's impressive growth in just three years since its founding suggested that the market for vegetarian and organic foods had grown far beyond the small numbers of macrobiotic devotees.

RIGHT LIVELIHOOD AND SOCIAL MOVEMENTS

Demand for natural foods exploded at the end of the 1960s. Stores specializing in vegetarian and organic products opened in major cities and college
towns across the country. Customers and former employees from Erewhon
began to establish their own macrobiotic stores, including Essene Macrobiotic Supply in Philadelphia, Eden Foods in Ann Arbor, and Food for Life
in Chicago. These new businesses joined a few existing organic foods stores
founded around the time of Erewhon, including Fred Rohe's New Age
Natural Foods and "Blind Jerry" Sealund's Far Fetched Foods, both in San
Francisco.[20]

Yet a growing demand for vegetarian and chemical-free foods was not
the only factor responsible for these businesses' growth. America's burgeoning environmental movement also encouraged interest in organic agriculture and natural foods. In the twenty years following World War II,
environmental activism had expanded beyond its conservationist roots as
pacifist and antinuclear groups undertook protests against the environmental dangers of atomic energy. Growing concerns about the dangers of
chemicals brought further attention to environmentalism. In 1962, the
marine biologist Rachel Carson published *Silent Spring*, catapulting the
relatively small environmental movement into the public limelight and
giving it an unprecedented boost of momentum. The book was a damning
indictment of the environmental and health risks posed by chemical companies, especially makers of DDT, and it firmly established poison and pollution as two concerns at the center of the environmental movement. By
the late 1960s, growing concerns about air and water pollution would fuel
further environmental activism and spur calls for federal environmental
legislation.[21]

Although environmentalism is often remembered as a liberal reformist
movement, it also attracted more radical activists on the left who viewed
environmental degradation not solely as a matter of pollution and waste
but also as the product of political oppression and capitalist exploitation.
One of the most influential leftist thinkers on the environment was the
Marxist-turned-anarchist Murray Bookchin, a strident critic of capitalism.
Bookchin's pioneering article "The Problem of Chemicals in Food" (1952)

in the leftist journal *Contemporary Issues* highlighted the dangers of chemical fertilizers, growth hormones, and pesticides, including DDT, years before *Silent Spring* was published. Bookchin would expand this argument in his book *Our Synthetic Environment* (1962) and further articulate his leftist vision of environmentalism in such works as *Post-scarcity Anarchism* (1971).[22] Bookchin's work played a key role in promoting the idea among left activists that industrial production of food and pesticides was a form of capitalist exploitation.

By the end of the 1960s, Carson, Bookchin, and others' concerns had given rise to a new generation of environmental activists that drew heavily on social movement strategy and countercultural values. More than any single event, the celebration of Earth Day signaled the insurgent ecology movement's newfound strength in the United States. Billed by organizers as the "first national environmental teach-in," the inaugural Earth Day on April 22, 1970, drew an estimated 20 million participants across America, roughly one-tenth of the country's population. Another popular expression of countercultural environmentalism was the publishing sensation *The Whole Earth Catalog*. Originally designed to offer hippie communes much needed information and products, the large-format catalog also disseminated ideas on ecology, organic agriculture, and vegetarianism to millions of readers in more than a dozen editions between 1968 and 1972. Meanwhile, the radical group Greenpeace emerged out of the counterculture and antiwar movement and popularized a new form of environmental direct action.[23]

Environmentalism provided the natural foods business with a political framework for analyzing America's industrialized, chemical-reliant agricultural and food system as a direct product of the excesses of corporate power. Environmentalists challenged the widespread belief that the tremendous economic and scientific advances of the postwar years were unqualified victories for the human race. The natural foods business similarly aimed to undermine Americans' unquestioning embrace of technology, big business, and uninterrupted economic growth. Natural foods entrepreneurs contended that pesticides and mechanized agriculture had severed the connection to nature Americans had once enjoyed as a nation of farmers. Culinary innovations such as TV dinners, preservatives, and synthetic flavors and colorings made matters worse. As Murray Bookchin argued, modern "industrial agriculture" was responsible for a "regressive simplification of the environment." In the eyes of natural foods enthusiasts, both the means and the ends of the American food system were dangerously unnatural.[24]

Organic and natural foods were heralded as powerful tools against environmental degradation. The term *food pollution* enjoyed wide circulation as a description of agribusinesses' processed and chemically enhanced products. Natural foods enthusiasts understood organic produce as a means of minimizing their intake of chemicals and pesticides and easing the problems of pollution. In a chapter on "ecotactics," the official Earth Day "environmental handbook" encouraged readers to patronize their local "ecologically sound alternative to the supermarket" that sold organic food, which the handbook called an "ecology food store." Murray Bookchin endorsed organic methods of agriculture because they "defer to the dictates of ecology rather than those of economics." Store names such as "Good Earth," "Brookwood Ecology Center," "Friends of the Earth," "Eco-Symbio Coop," "Green Revolution," "Living Earth," and "Back to Earth" reflected natural foods entrepreneurs' embrace of environmental stewardship and sustainability.[25]

Activists viewed natural foods and especially vegetarianism as pathways to nonviolence and peaceful coexistence. Organic enthusiasts drew direct parallels between the dangers of chemical-laden food and the war in Vietnam by citing such companies as Dow that produced pesticides for agricultural use as well as chemicals for military applications in Southeast Asia. Many people with backgrounds in the antiwar movement embraced vegetarianism as a radical personal choice, and countless antiwar activists shopped at and worked in natural foods stores and cooperatives. Vegetarians had long enjoyed a strong affinity with the peace movement. Famous pacifists such as Mohandas Gandhi, Albert Schweitzer, George Bernard Shaw, and John Harvey Kellogg as well as pacifist Quakers had embraced vegetarianism as a deeply meaningful form of nonviolence. Before developing his macrobiotic teachings, George Ohsawa had been actively involved in the World Federalist Movement, an international organization that sought to secure peace through the establishment of a global body stronger than the United Nations. Fierce opposition to the Vietnam War sparked a broader skepticism of established authority that vegetarians believed strengthened their cause. As H. Jay Dinshah, the president of the North American Vegetarian Society, argued, "People started thinking for themselves" by opposing the war in Vietnam. "They figured out that if the government could lie to them, then the supermarkets could lie to them and the nutritionists could lie to them." Frances Moore Lappé's best-selling book *Diet for a Small Planet* (1971) promoted vegetarianism as a humanitarian act. If people from wealthy countries could reduce their environmental burden by forgoing meat, Lappé argued, they would free up more of the world's arable land for feeding the swelling population in developing countries.[26]

Natural foods stores also drew support from the animal rights movement that emerged in the first half of the 1970s. In the movement's seminal text, *Animal Liberation* (1975), Peter Singer denounced "factory farming," where "animals are treated like machines that convert low-priced fodder into high-priced flesh . . . [and live] miserable lives from birth to slaughter." Vegetarianism was not only a dietary choice but also a principled rejection of "factory farming and all the other cruel practices used in rearing animals for food."[27] Natural foods stores appealed to people concerned with animal rights not only because they usually did not sell meat but also because they sourced much of their foods from small organic farms and had few dealings with industrial-scale agricultural companies. In short, natural foods stores benefited from a reputation as retailers that were kinder to animals than conventional supermarkets were.

Some natural foods entrepreneurs celebrated their business as a spiritual activity that embodied the best values of Asian religions and philosophy. The Buddhist concept of "right livelihood" appealed to natural foods sellers because of its vision of spiritual and humane labor and particularly because of its explicit prohibition of selling meat and poisons. One natural foods seller in Boston urged aspiring natural foods entrepreneurs to seek enlightenment "in order to make yourself more effective in changing the world and bringing on the new age through righteous distribution." Zen Buddhism in general captivated many different people involved in the counterculture in the 1960s and 1970s, as did Hinduism and Taoism. Erewhon's staff saw their work in natural foods as a key aspect of devoting themselves to the macrobiotic interpretation of Zen Buddhism. Natural foods store names such as "Food Chakra," "Naturally High," "Natural Universe," and "Ombillical Chord" reflected this emphasis on non-Western spiritual consciousness. As Paul Hawken explained, Erewhon's staff strived "to reflect the common will of those who seek physical and spiritual regeneration through the biological transformation of their bodies." Although he conceded that "business is not the sage's path," he contended that "it does have one redeeming factor in that it is a way to serve people while working out one's material karma. All who have worked at Erewhon for any length of time have been grateful for at least one thing, and that is that we have been able to have this fantastic medium through which to channel our energy."[28]

Natural foods businesses cast their pursuit of a spiritual right livelihood as a means of maximizing workers' freedoms. Erewhon discouraged formal hierarchies within the organization and instead promoted a form of collective management. "Decisions at Erewhon are almost always the consensus if not the unanimous wish of those people who have been there for a while," Hawken explained. Problematic employees were rarely fired but instead asked to take a sabbatical in which they could contemplate their role in the company and return at a later date if they wished. In fact, at Erewhon there was "no structure . . . , no rules, no by-laws or regulations," Hawken declared.[29]

Hawken's claims of a structureless, unregulated workplace hinted at a deeply skeptical attitude toward government that pervaded the natural foods business. Natural foods enthusiasts criticized federal food and agriculture policies, arguing that the government neglected its duty to feed its citizens by treating farms not as a source of health and nourishment but as a form of capitalist profit making. The macrobiotic *East–West Journal* accordingly decried "the conspiracy of agri-business and the Federal Government," which prioritized profit over "the real needs of man." The U.S. government endangered the food supply by subsidizing pesticide use and actively spraying the chemicals on millions of acres of public and private lands. The U.S. Department of Agriculture's hugely influential nutritional dietary guidelines, the so-called "Basic Four," drew widespread criticism from the natural foods community for promoting an excess of animal products at the expense of fruits and vegetables. "The enemies of health are the government agencies," declared one natural foods seller.[30]

The federal government's scrutiny of natural foods advocates further exacerbated such tensions. In 1964, the Federal Trade Commission issued a cease-and-desist order to Rodale Press for its advertisements for J. I. Rodale's book *The Health Finder* on the grounds that they contained false medical and dietary claims. Rodale Press responded with a lawsuit against the Federal Trade Commission, and in 1968 a federal appeals court vacated the agency's order. State and federal investigations of macrobiotic businesses and raids of stores in New York and Boston also made natural foods businesses more hostile toward the state. As Paul Hawken would argue, "The best government is no government although few can see that or believe it.... I think we are working towards that."[31] Such antigovernment sentiment in the natural foods community were predominantly anarchist in nature because they were coupled with strong criticisms of capitalism. Nonetheless, these attitudes planted the seeds for a more conservative libertarianism that would take root in later years among some natural foods sellers who embraced capitalism.

Environmentalism, pacifism, animal rights, anarchism, and the counterculture—all contributed to natural foods' ideological profile in the early 1970s. By embracing various social movements, natural foods retailers recast their business as a form of political resistance against powerful corporations, environmental degradation, and even war and animal cruelty. Meanwhile, the Buddhist concept of right livelihood provided them with a set of spiritual objectives they could deploy against a so-called plastic, spiritless American consumer culture. Most activist businesses aligned themselves with a single movement; natural foods businesses aligned themselves with many. These varied connections gave natural foods retailers a broad ideological appeal that few other activist enterprises had. But natural foods sellers' ties to activist networks were not as strong as those enjoyed by activist businesses that emerged directly out of movements. For all of these reasons, each natural foods business would face a dilemma regarding which, if any, movements it should associate with in the years ahead. In any case, a new generation of entrepreneurs had succeeded in making natural foods radical, rebellious, and even hip.

GROWTH AND ITS CHALLENGES

By 1972, roughly four hundred natural foods retail storefronts were operating in the United States. Almost all of them had opened since the mid-1960s. In addition, several hundred old-line health food stores, nutrition centers, and organic farms sold produce. Natural foods sellers operated in almost every state, and they flourished especially on the West Coast. California alone was home to around one hundred natural foods stores. The earnings of one California distributor of organic produce doubled from $6 million to $12 million in just two years, from 1969 to 1971. Erewhon was the most successful natural foods seller in the country. For fiscal year 1970, Erewhon reported sales of nearly $500,000 and net profits above 6 percent, considerably higher than grocery stores' typical margin of 1 to 2 percent. By 1972, the company's sales totaled more than $3 million. The market for natural foods had grown exponentially in the five years since 1967.[32]

Natural foods' appeal was strongest among young, educated, middle-class, and affluent whites. Yet some African Americans also embraced natural foods. On Chicago's Southside, the influential black doctor Alvenia Fulton promoted natural foods and vegetarianism through her naturopathic medical practice. Fulton's most famous patient was the comedian Dick Gregory, who enthusiastically promoted natural foods and published a popular book on the topic. Many black natural foods advocates had ties to black nationalism and the Black Power movement. Nation of Islam leader Elijah Muhammad encouraged his followers to eat fruit, vegetables, and whole-wheat bread and urged them to minimize their meat intake and to avoid foods made with chemical fertilizers, preservatives, and pesticides. In 1967, Muhammad published his dietary beliefs in *How to Eat to Live*, a primer on "pure food." Members of the Nation of Islam opened grocery stores in several cities based on these teachings. A number of other black nationalists endorsed natural foods and vegetarianism as tools for black liberation. Prominent examples include the Brooklyn-based black nationalist organization The East, which operated the co-op store Kununuana, and the Chicago black poet, publisher, and bookseller Don Lee (later Haki Madhubuti). In the preface to the black nationalist book *A Food Guide for Afrikan People* (1973), Lee lamented that most African

Americans "eat anything as long as it has been sanctioned by ABC, CBS, and NBC or some black entertainer with a crown on his head." By eating natural foods, African American activists argued, black people could reduce their dependence on the industrial agricultural system and the white-controlled consumer culture that promoted it.[33]

Despite their growing numbers, natural foods stores remained small independent storefronts with little buying power and little contact with wholesalers and farmers. They had a remarkably difficult and labor-intensive process for sourcing organic produce. Demand far outstripped supply, and the prices of organic produce were much higher than prices of produce grown with pesticides. Erewhon sought to address this dilemma by organizing its own distribution arm. Without help from an intermediate buying agent, Erewhon painstakingly procured its products from more than fifty different farms and spent $10,000 annually to have a third party certify that the farms' foods were organic. Erewhon had almost singlehandedly created its own national distribution network for organic food from scratch. In 1970, it opened a twenty-thousand-square-foot distribution warehouse in south Boston. In fewer than four years, the company had become the country's biggest wholesale purchaser of organic produce and grains.[34]

Paul Hawken and Fred Rohe launched Organic Merchants (OM), a countercultural trade association for organic foods retailers, in response to their distribution challenges. Rohe and Hawken envisioned OM—a convenient acronym that referenced the pair's interest in Hinduism and mediation—as a natural foods communications and distribution network that could also establish industry standards for certifying organic produce. At an OM retreat in 1969 at Mt. Shasta in California, thirty-five representatives from West Coast natural foods stores discussed the intricacies of their business while they did yoga and joined hands around a campfire. OM's members intended to make cooperative purchases from distributors and organic farmers, to supervise suppliers, and to "eventually assure the availability of the highest quality natural foods in every part the nation." OM also published free educational materials on natural foods. Yet OM's goals were loftier than merely improving a burgeoning cottage industry. As one OM member stated dramatically,

"Our purpose is to save the planet."[35] The natural foods business, OM contended, combined in equal parts philanthropy, public education, and environmentalism.

The natural foods retailers began to attract considerable attention from major corporations and national media. "Organic Food: New and Natural," the cover of *Life* announced to readers in December 1970 above a photograph of model Gunilla Knutson, owner of a natural foods store in New York City. "A dedicated and growing band of people—most of them young—has taken to cooking and serving no-nonsense natural foods," particularly at "small country-style stores," the magazine told readers. The natural foods business was still far from mainstream. Members of what *Life* called the "organic food movement" worried about "the fanatic fad image that health foods used to have ... [and that] a large part of the public still believe that it's just wheat germ and molasses all over again, ingested chiefly by body builders and other exotics." Yet the *Life* story confirmed that natural foods were clearly making inroads into the conventional marketplace, as did a front-page story in the *Wall Street Journal* a month later in January 1971. The article repeated the common criticism of natural foods as "food faddism," and it quoted a medical writer's claim that "never before in history have absurd notions regarding nutrition enjoyed such widespread popularity." Yet the *Journal* marveled at the explosive growth of natural foods companies such as Erewhon. Shortly after the article appeared, a representative from Merrill Lynch approached Erewhon's staff and offered to assist them in making an initial public offering. Erewhon turned down the offer.[36]

Another sign of natural foods' growing popularity came in 1972 when Bank of America published a guide to natural and health foods stores for aspiring entrepreneurs in its *Small Business Reporter* series. "Health foods have come into their own," the bank declared. "Once considered an insignificant segment of the grocery field, the health food industry has racked up impressive market gains in record time." Natural foods businesses were no longer attracting only "aging arthritics, would-be Tarzans, and all manner of food faddists" but had expanded their customer base to include "anyone and everyone—from counterculture youths to young matrons and corporate executives." The bank predicted national sales of health foods would double from $200 million in 1971 to $400 million in

1972 and that the business would soon "attract aggressive competitors," including supermarkets.[37]

Nevertheless, both natural foods entrepreneurs and outside observers doubted that major corporations were fit to sell natural foods. "I don't know [if] big business can sell organic foods to the people," Paul Hawken wondered. "Small family distributors and small family stores" were best prepared to support "a marketing system that is going to be very direct and have the highest standards possible." Yet Hawken insisted that "big businesses violate these standards." Even *Life* argued that "organic foods and the supermarket economy are incompatible." Natural foods entrepreneurs contended they had to develop their own environmentally sustainable distribution network separate from the established grocery business as well as promote a new set of just and enlightened business values different from those espoused by corporations. Erewhon, for instance, did not charge commissions when it distributed organic food to other distributors or co-ops. "Some think this is bad business, and I suppose it is in the conventional sense," Hawken said. "But it seems to me that what has been 'good' business for so long has been bad for the people." Another macrobiotic retailer in Chicago claimed that "just by eating the food you become less materialistic."[38]

Natural foods sellers also believed that their business's transparency and lack of artificiality would make it difficult for corporations to use traditional advertising strategies to sell their products. "If you are in a truly meaningful business, there is no need to promote yourself other than being open, honest, and communicative to your customers," Hawken argued. By contrast, "there is nothing truthful about advertising," he argued. Indeed, natural foods businesses rarely employed the polished graphic design and emotional appeals of modern advertising but instead used subdued photographs of organic produce, hand-drawn scenes of nature, and lengthy narratives that sought to explain a product's real value in earnest and authentic terms (figures 5.3 and 5.4).[39]

Yet with increased popularity came increased scrutiny. The American Medical Association declared in 1971 that organic and natural foods were "unusual diets" in need of research studies to confirm their safety. It also condemned macrobiotics as a "major public health problem" due to Ohsawa's insistence that his teachings could cure numerous diseases. The most vocal

FIGURE 5.3 Erewhon advertisement, 1971. Courtesy of the National Museum of American History, Smithsonian Institute, Washington, D.C.

critic of natural foods was Frederick Stare. A professor of nutrition at Harvard University, Stare enjoyed a national reputation for questioning claims regarding the benefits of natural and macrobiotic foods. In 1967, he told *Vogue* magazine that he did "not know of one single documented case of ill health, not even of stomachache, that has been caused by the residue of insecticides, pesticides, or chemicals on food." In an essay published in *Ladies' Home Journal* in October 1971, "The Diet That's Killing Our Kids," Stare denounced "macrobiotic eating [as] no more than an excursion into make-believe Oriental cultism . . . [and] the most dangerous fad diet around." He found it sadly ironic that affluent, educated young people at the country's top universities embraced diets he believed to be poor in protein while scientists struggled to solve the developing world's malnourishment crisis. In a college nutrition textbook he coauthored in 1973, Stare denounced "food quackery" and mocked "food faddists [who]

Rice Flour Pickles

This is the time of year to put up pickles and one of the most popular kinds is the bran pickle. These are made from roots such as bur-
dock, carrot and daikon radish which have been dried and placed in wood-
en kegs with a mixture of salt, water and rice bran. By mid-winter the
pickles should be ready for eating. Not only are they tasty but they are
also rich in lactic acid and B vitamins. There is one problem in making
bran pickles, however; namely, the bran.

Organic rice growers never polish their rice. They always sell it whole,
with only the outer husk removed. Therefore the bran that is available
on the market is from rice that has been sprayed. Nothing at all is known
about the effects of the sprays, such as Dioxin and other growth-stim-
ulating hormones. When they are applied in the Spring, these chemicals
force the weeds to flourish, mature and die within days or weeks. Of
course a small amount falls on the rice. The concentration of chemicals
in the rice grain at maturity is around two parts per million. The concentration in the bran, however, is around twenty parts per million.
White rice which you can buy in the supermarket has, ironically enough,
almost no trace of the chemical sprays.

At any rate, rice bran is not the best thing to use. A good substitute
is finely-ground brown rice flour. You can use it, in your recipe, in the
same proportion as bran. The pickles may turn out sweeter. That's
about the only difference.

If you have any questions please write to us at 33 Farnsworth St.,
Boston, Massachusetts 02120

Erewhon Inc.

FIGURE 5.4 Erewhon advertisement, 1972. Courtesy of the National Museum of American History, Smithsonian Institute, Washington, D.C.

have described the loss of nutrients when wheat is refined." Yet critics
questioned Stare's impartiality in light of his deep ties to industrial agriculture, the sugar industry in particular, which gave Stare generous funding for research. Not coincidentally, Stare frequently defended sugar and
other food industries in the media. In later decades, clinical researchers

would confirm some of the very claims about natural foods that Stare ridiculed.[40]

In spite of such criticisms and growing corporate interest in their business, independent natural foods stores flourished through the first half of the 1970s. But inspired by E. F. Schumacher's mantra "small is beautiful," they also embraced limits to their growth. Small independents continued to enjoy a strong hold on the natural foods market. The number of retailers had exploded nationally, but the average natural foods store ranged in size between just 1,500 and 2,400 square feet in 1972. New supermarkets built that year by contrast averaged 25,000 square feet. Even as natural foods sellers became more popular, they considered their smallness an advantage, not a deficiency, and they believed that their modest size and independence gave them a political and moral advantage over supermarkets.[41]

COOPERATIVES, DEMOCRACY, AND INCLUSION

By the mid-1970s, some activists began to question whether small spaces and good intentions were enough to ensure that natural foods sellers fulfilled their lofty mission. Such critics argued that any business striving to be inclusive and democratic needed formal cooperative structures for sharing ownership and management responsibilities. For these people, cooperative ownership held the most promise for the natural foods business.

Cooperative stores date to the 1820s in the United States. Owned by their workers or customers, co-ops pursued profits in conjunction with stated goals of social and mutual benefit. At many co-ops, owners also had to work as part of their membership requirements. In return, the businesses generally distributed at least some profits back to their member-owners. They also granted considerable decision-making power to their member-owners, who usually elected a board of directors from their ranks. Co-ops also appealed to consumers by offering savings through near-wholesale prices and annual refunds tied to membership. As a consequence, they experienced particular popularity during periods of economic downturn. Members of radical organizations such as the Grange movement and the Farmers' Alliance founded their own co-ops during the depressions of the late nineteenth century. Co-ops proliferated in the 1930s and early 1940s, when the New Deal established the Division of Self-Help Cooperatives within the Federal Emergency Relief Administration and made grant funds available to the businesses. Labor unions established numerous co-ops, too.[42]

Groceries were among the most common cooperatively owned retail businesses. Although co-op groceries used an unconventional ownership and management model, for most of their history they offered the same foods as conventional grocery stores. In the 1950s and 1960s, many co-ops believed they could compete with ever-expanding supermarkets by emulating their size, standardization, and products. Co-ops embraced frozen and convenience foods just as supermarkets did, for instance, and they rarely if ever sold natural or organic foods.[43]

Co-ops abandoned many of their connections to radical political organizations in the decades following World War II. The situation began to change in the late 1960s, however. At the Consumers' Cooperative of Berkeley—a New Deal–era co-op that had grown to be the largest in the country—young insurgents pushed the store to join the United Farm Workers (UFW) grape boycott, to withdraw from the local Chamber of Commerce, and to endorse cherished causes of the consumers' movement, such as legislation for fair labeling. As natural foods became more popular in the San Francisco Bay Area, the younger and increasingly countercultural members of the Consumers' Co-op forced the organization to change the foods it stocked, too. The Co-op responded by adding organic produce to its stores in 1970, and the next year it opened a new store devoted to natural foods.[44]

By fueling a major revival for co-ops, natural foods stores revitalized an older form of democratic ownership that had existed for more than a century. An estimated five to ten thousand food co-ops opened for business between 1969 and 1979 in what one journalist called "the most important surge of food co-ops since Franklin Roosevelt's New Deal." Organic produce and whole grains drove much of this growth, as natural food staples found their way into the inventories of both brick-and-mortar co-op storefronts and cooperative consumer collectives known as "food conspiracies," which bought directly from farmers. Shoppers were also drawn to co-ops in search of lower prices amid the rapid inflation in food costs—a rise of nearly 50 percent—triggered by the severe economic downturn from 1972 to 1976. Others consumers joined co-ops because they viewed them as alternatives to alienating and environmentally destructive chain grocery stores. In Austin, Texas, for instance, an umbrella organization of that city's co-ops vowed to be "ecologically sound in its policies and operating practices[,] . . . [to] re-create a consciousness of common needs, interest and cultural values," and "never [to] sacrifice human relationships to efficiency."[45] Yet by adding environmental sustainability and humanistic social relations to co-ops' already ambitious mission, the new generation of co-op members sparked fierce debate among their colleagues, who had traditionally focused on the economic benefits of shared ownership.

Nowhere was this debate fiercer than in the Twin Cities, Minneapolis and St. Paul, where a series of conflicts that became known as the Co-op Wars wracked local cooperatives in the mid-1970s. As Minnesota's largest city and the home of the state's flagship university, Minneapolis in particular thrived as a center of counterculture and activism in the upper Midwest. During the Vietnam War, the city was home to a vibrant antiwar movement that revolved around the Twin Cities Draft Information Center. At the end of the 1960s, some Information Center members and other activists began to establish their own co-ops. By 1972, the city had become a national leader in cooperative business and was home to no fewer than ten co-op storefronts, including a bakery, a clothing store, a bookstore, and seven groceries.[46]

The Twin Cities co-op grocery stores eagerly promoted natural foods as a means for countering corporate power. The People's Pantry co-op proudly sold "good food for strong, revolutionary bodies," especially for the "brothers and sisters who are tired of eating plastic shit." The Mill City co-op meanwhile vowed that "the less money we give to [supermarket chains such as] Red Owl, Super Valu, etc., the more we recycle funds in our own community projects, and the less dependent we become on corporate capitalism."[47] At least one area co-op periodically allowed customers to operate cash registers and to pay for their purchases on an honor system, although it purportedly lost several hundred dollars through such an experiment in democratization.[48] Perhaps more than in any region in the country, activists in the Twin Cities made cooperative enterprise a central part of their organizing work.

Yet some local activists felt that the Twin Cities' co-ops were still not radical or inclusive enough. In 1975, a secretive Marxist group calling itself the Co-op Organization (CO) formed to wage a public campaign against what it saw as elitist, classist co-ops in Minneapolis and St. Paul. The CO denounced the overwhelmingly white antiwar activists who had founded most of the area's co-ops as "college graduates, college students, and college drop-outs which composed the hippie cult." Some community members claimed middle-aged and elderly customers were made to feel "confused and unwelcomed" at Twin Cities co-ops. Others contended that poor and working-class shoppers and people of color were unwanted at local co-ops. At least a few co-op workers conceded that some of their colleagues often displayed a "careless and flippant attitude" toward customers.[49]

Criticisms of snobbery and dogmatism plagued natural foods sellers of all kinds, not just co-ops. As Paul Hawken admitted about Erewhon in its early years, "One got the feeling that the customers were there to serve the store instead of the opposite." Natural foods sellers were also accused of abstemious moralism. An Organic Merchants publication from 1971, *The NOT List*, exemplified such rarefied asceticism by discouraging organic retailers from selling a long list of items, including bleached flour, artificial flavors and colors, hydrogenated fat, monosodium glutamate, and all kinds of sugar. Members of the CO found co-ops' similar dietary directives to be elitist and politically ineffective. "Changing diet is an escape route that few can afford . . . [and it] diverts fire from attacks on the economic system," one CO member argued. "If your aim is community control of the storefront, then in most cases you'd be hypocritical not to sell shit foods." Many co-ops refused to stock items such as canned goods and white sugar, but "that's what most of America eats." If co-ops wanted to effect real change, the CO argued, they would have to change their practices to appeal to normal working people, not just to idealistic hippies. In a sense, the CO was attacking the co-ops for being insufficiently activist and too invested in matters of lifestyle.[50]

The CO soon set about refashioning the area's co-ops in its own ideological vision. It began by having its members infiltrate a struggling co-op, the Beanery, and seize control of its management and operations. Then, at a meeting of the People's Warehouse, the distributor that served most co-ops in the area, CO members purportedly brandished lead pipes, assaulted attendees, ripped phones out of the walls, and forced everyone but CO members to leave. The CO promptly took control of the Warehouse's operations and financial records. Yet the founders of the Warehouse had no legal recourse for regaining possession of the building. In the anarchist spirit of avoiding contact with the state, they had never filed for incorporation and thus did not legally own the Warehouse.[51]

For more than a year, the conflict divided the Twin Cities co-ops into two camps: the supporters of the CO-controlled People's Warehouse and the allies of a new warehouse called the Distributing Alliance of the Northcountry Cooperatives, or DANCe, which was founded by the original activist co-ops. Co-ops and natural foods stores all over the country had done business with the original People's Warehouse before the conflict. Now they were expected to pick sides and align themselves with one or the other Twin Cities distributors. The CO gained control of several more co-ops, often by physically attacking its rivals. In one instance, it was thought to have been responsible for the firebombing of a co-op leader's car. In another instance, CO members marched en masse to the Mill City Co-Op to take it over, but more than two hundred Mill City members gathered outside the co-op and successfully blocked the CO members from entering it.[52] Only by mid-1976 did the original directors of the People's Warehouse successfully petition for a restraining order that forced the CO to abandon the distribution facility.

Many people in the Twin Cities' co-op community denounced the CO's tactics, but some conceded that the organization raised urgent questions about natural foods and co-ops' political mission. Some believed the CO had been justified in asking if organic products were just "for those with lots of money in their pockets, etc., or [are they] available for everyone?" To be sure, organic foods bought at natural foods stores typically cost between one-third and two times as much as nonorganic food bought at conventional supermarkets.[53] Yet the CO had argued that it was more than the high price of organic foods that kept working-class shoppers out of co-ops. It maintained that co-ops and natural foods stores promoted a form of elite class identity that allowed educated middle- and upper-class shoppers to distinguish themselves from working-class people and mainstream consumer culture. Buying and appreciating natural foods required considerable education and complicated knowledge that working-class people usually lacked. Did natural foods stores and co-ops have a responsibility to serve poor and working-class customers, as the CO insisted? If so, how could they attract people with unhealthy eating habits—those who ate what the CO called "shit foods"—without compromising their staffs' own values?

Co-ops were also supposed to maximize workers' power through shared ownership and management structures. But did they actually achieve that goal? How could workers protect their interests at co-ops and natural foods stores? Did organized labor have a role to play? Unions were integral in establishing co-ops in the late nineteenth century and early twentieth century, but by the middle of the twentieth century they operated few cooperatives. Many union members belonged to co-ops, but most unions themselves did little more than lend co-ops promotional support. By the mid-1970s, one observer remarked that the new generation of co-op stores "relate[d] not at all to established unions but rather to small work collectives."[54] Indeed, natural foods workers continued to debate among themselves what best served their interests in the workplace: the cooperative model of shared ownership, the spiritually informed and consensus-driven management model of companies such as Erewhon, or labor unions?

ORGANIZING LABOR IN THE ORGANIC WORKPLACE

By contrast, the management of some of the larger natural foods stores seemed intent on avoiding the question of workers' representation within their operations. Activist entrepreneurs in the 1960s and 1970s were deeply suspicious of large institutions. Many New Left activists, in a manner not unlike how they viewed government and corporate businesses, regarded labor unions as materialist, alienating institutions that stymied meaningful political change and radical social movements, especially the antiwar and black freedom movements. "Labor has succumbed to institutionalization, its social idealism waning under the tendencies of bureaucracy, materialism, [and] business ethics," the SDS contended in its Port Huron Statement in 1962. Many people behind co-ops, natural foods stores, and other activist businesses believed that organizational structures such as collective management and shared ownership made unions unnecessary. Worker collectives could proudly claim to have "no bosses here," as the title of a popular "manual on working collectively" by the organization Vocations for Social Change suggested in 1976. Indeed, workers at activist enterprises gave much more thought to the possibilities of collectives and employee-owned co-ops than to unions. The disinterest was mutual. Unions such as the Retail Clerks International Association focused on organizing the employees of chain businesses, not workers at the small storefronts operated by activists or any other entrepreneurs.[55]

Yet some natural foods workers began to reconsider their aversion to organized labor by the mid-1970s. At Berkeley's Westbrae Foods, one of the premier natural foods stores and distributors in the San Francisco Bay Area, workers sought to turn their workplace into a collective. After the store's management opted instead to incorporate, however, the workers decided to unionize. In response to management's objections to the union, the workers issued a biting critique of natural foods businesses' hostility toward organized labor: "Ours is an industry in which companies have capitalized their fantastic growth rates with substandard wages, wooing workers' loyalties with a hypocritical anti-establishment or alternative image or, even worse, with a quasi-spiritual view of the right livelihood that seems to create the feeling, with no substantial basis in reality, of a family business."[56] Natural foods businesses' high-minded idealism disguised their indifference to positive working conditions and workers' right to representation, Westbrae's workers contended.

By the end of 1975, Westbrae workers secured certification from the National Labor Relations Board as the Alternative Food Workers Alliance (AFWA). Employees of at least three other natural foods stores and restaurants soon joined the AFWA. As a flyer for the union announced, AFWA sought to "make this industry truly an alternative . . . so as to empower workers to make decisions affecting their livelihood and to optimize individual creativity in the workplace." Spiritual, ecological, and emotional empowerment, the workers argued, were no substitutes for a democratic workplace. Although members decertified the unaffiliated union in 1982, AFWA nonetheless represented a milestone for workers in the natural foods business.[57]

At almost the same time AFWA was formed, employees at Erewhon began to challenge their management's contention that the company's decentralized structure and Buddhist ideals maximized workers' freedom. By 1975, relations between Erewhon's management and its growing workforce at the company's stores, distribution warehouse, and production facility had frayed. Compared to Erewhon's early years, fewer and fewer employees were macrobiotic adherents who held to the company's original philosophical and spiritual tenets. "Serious problems of morale and loyalty were developing" within the company, according to one of the company's most veteran employees. Even in a company with a "grand, altruistic design," many workers now considered tasks such as "roasting granola and loading rice on trucks" as "dull work for a large, impersonal company."[58]

In December 1976, workers at Erewhon's production facility formed a caucus to discuss their grievances about pay and the inadequate input they had in the company's decision making. The company's recently appointed president, Jeff Flasher, agreed to meet with the caucus, only to tell them that any workers who wanted to discuss grievances should instead meet with him individually. Erewhon denied the caucus's request to send a representative to meetings where Michio Kushi and managers made key decisions. In response, the caucus formed a workers' council, which promptly published a searing indictment of Erewhon's labor policies, which contradicted its lofty ideals. The company no longer deserved the "family image" it once enjoyed as a small collaborative business. Its positive reputation had instead "become little more than a façade and sort of idealistic blanket that can be pulled over our dissatisfaction with questionable policy." Erewhon's workers needed real policy changes if the company still wanted to achieve its larger mission.

Erewhon's management responded to the caucus by proposing a series of new employee benefits that included improved medical insurance plans, an employee credit union, and even profit sharing. Flasher pleaded with employees to settle their disputes in-house. "If we have disagreements, misunderstandings, and miscommunications from time to time, let's take them into account as growing pains, the natural eruptions any family is likely to have, and as opportunities to understand one another more deeply." A union would only create an adversarial relationship between workers and management, the company insisted. Management claimed the company had a right to prohibit any supervisors from working with the union. The announcement effectively banned any efforts at unionization because most of the leaders in the caucus were the lower-level supervisors.

The caucus promptly defied management's orders and asked workers to sign cards authorizing the Service Employees International Union to represent them. "We wish to remain true to the principles on which Erewhon was founded . . . [and to] maintain . . . the individual's responsibility for health and happiness. . . . [We] want the hours we devote to Erewhon not to become drudgery but to be a vital and worthy part of our lives." As the caucus argued, formal worker representation would preserve the company's mission of creating an enlightened, humane, and fulfilling workplace. In an election conducted by the National Labor Relations Board in April 1979, Erewhon's workers voted to affiliate with the Service Employees International Union.

Michio Kushi responded in a letter to employees with a heavy dose of macrobiotic idealism about the company's need for harmonious human relations. Kushi insisted that employees' problems could "be solved only through our own self-reflection and our own improvements of spirit and daily operations as well." Workers who collaborated with an "outside organization" to address the company's problems would trigger a "loss of unity" and potentially even "the total collapse of our past efforts and future dream for the reconstruction of humanity." Longtime manager Evan Root contended meanwhile that employees expected too much of Erewhon. "Our main intention has been to get good food out. Basically, we're just a grocery business." Of course, such modest claims contradicted Erewhon's long-standing argument that its business was a positive force for peace, environmental healing, and human progress.[59]

Erewhon's management admitted that transformations in the natural foods business were forcing the company to change its operations on the cusp of the 1980s. "The natural food industry is growing . . . [and] it's melding with the mainstream," Root conceded. Erewhon was still the national leader in natural foods, what one storeowner called "the General Motors of macrobiotics." But most of the company's revenues now came from distribution. Other companies had launched larger natural foods stores in Boston and Los Angeles to compete with Erewhon's storefronts in the second half of the 1970s. Natural foods retail was becoming a "competitive big business with slick enterprises." Root was justified in arguing that competition among natural foods companies was devolving into the "survival of the fittest." In contrast to the start of the 1970s, natural foods were now no longer a small cottage industry in which virtually all the major players knew and depended on each other. By 1979, the business had grown more than fivefold since the decade's start and had transformed into a major specialty segment of the grocery trade, with nearly $750 million in sales. In a business that had long proclaimed that "small is beautiful," competition between natural foods retailers was poised to become increasingly cut-throat as companies experimented with unprecedented economies of scale at the start of the 1980s.[60]

WHOLE FOODS MARKET AND THE RISE OF THE ORGANIC CHAIN

In 1980, a new store called Whole Foods Market opened its doors in Austin, Texas, and forever changed the natural foods business. Home to the state's capital and its flagship university, Austin had carried the unofficial title of countercultural and progressive capital of Texas for decades. In the 1960s, the University of Texas had been home to one of SDS's largest chapters. From 1966 to 1977, local activists published one of the country's premier underground newspapers, the *Rag*. Music venues such as the Vulcan Gas Company and Armadillo World Headquarters as well as thriving head shops such as Oat Willie's counted among the city's most cherished hippie institutions. Like other major college towns such as Berkeley and Ann Arbor, Austin was a place where the New Left and counterculture had a deep and lasting influence that extended far beyond the early 1970s.[61]

The city was also home to one of the most vibrant natural foods communities in the country. The Good Food Store opened in 1971 as the city's first major natural foods seller (figure 5.5). By 1976, it had five locations in Texas, a 14,000-square-foot warehouse, and almost eighty employees.

Another dozen or so independent natural foods stores operated in the vicinity of campus and the adjacent Clarksville neighborhood. Small single- and dual-proprietorships such as Craig Weller and Mark Skiles's store the Hobbit Hole reflected the strong influence of the counterculture (figure 5.6). Austin was also home to exceptionally strong natural co-ops. In the mid-1970s, it had four natural foods co-ops, ten co-op houses, three co-op farms, and a variety of worker collectives that included a bakery and a vegetarian restaurant. The Austin Community Project, an umbrella organization for the city's co-ops, claimed nearly one thousand members. The city's co-op stores grossed a combined $25,000 a month (well more than $100,000 in 2016 dollars).[62]

One person in Austin deeply impressed by both natural foods and co-ops was John Mackey. A native of Houston, Mackey had attended Trinity University and then the University of Texas for several years before dropping out in the mid-1970s. Lacking a clear sense of his life's direction, Mackey felt "alienated from society, and . . . wanted there to be a deeper meaning to my

FIGURE 5.5 Good Food Store, Austin, Texas, 1970s. Courtesy of the Austin History Center, Austin Public Library

FIGURE 5.6 Hobbit Hole natural foods store, Austin, Texas, 1970s. Courtesy of the Austin History Center, Austin Public Library

life." As he would explain years later, "Food is what I got into." Mackey moved into a vegetarian co-op residence in search of deeper meaning as well as "attractive, interesting women." He soon began dating Renee Lawson, another resident. Mackey got a job working at one of the Good Food stores, where he learned about the business side of natural foods. Yet he also joined three different co-op groceries and came to believe that "business and corporations were essentially evil because they selfishly sought only profits." As he saw it, "the co-op movement was the best way to reform capitalism because it was based on cooperation instead of competition." Along the way, Mackey "studied ecology" and embraced "social democratic philosophy," and his "search for meaning and purpose led [him] into the counterculture movement."[63]

In 1978, Mackey and Lawson started their own natural foods store, which they called SaferWay. The store's name reflected Mackey and Lawson's desire to offer an alternative both to corporate supermarket chains and to industrial agriculture produced with chemical pesticides. The business was nothing less than an attempt "to make our country and world a better place to live." The name was a swipe at Safeway, not only America's largest grocer and one of the biggest sellers of food produced with preservatives and pesticides but also the second-largest retail chain of any kind in the country. Safeway made for an especially easy target in Austin. Just two years earlier, sustained community protests had forced the company to scrap plans to tear down a beloved two-hundred-year-old pecan tree on the University of Texas's campus and instead build a glass-encircled atrium around the tree in the middle of the store.[64]

Although Mackey was only twenty-five and Lawson just twenty-one, the couple started SaferWay with $45,000 in capital (more that $165,000 in 2016 dollars), much of which came from Mackey's father and family friends. This amount was about forty times Erewhon's initial capital in 1966. It was four times what Craig Weller and Mark Skiles had initially invested in SaferWay's main competitor, the Clarksville Natural Grocery. At 3,000 square feet, SaferWay was considerably larger than most independent natural foods stores, and it even had a restaurant on the second floor of the house it occupied. But the store had too few parking spaces and too many rodents. SaferWay had so little space for inventory that Mackey and Lawson's apartment doubled as a warehouse until their landlords caught them storing groceries at home and evicted them. The young couple had to move into their store and sleep there after hours. In its first year, SaferWay lost $23,000, more than half of its original capital.[65]

In 1979, Mackey traveled the country in search of a new business model. In Brookline, Massachusetts, outside Boston, he visited Bread & Circus, a large store founded by a former Erewhon clerk and described by one journalist as "a cross between supermarket and traditional health food store." In Los Angeles, Mackey visited Mrs. Gooch's Ranch Market, a store similar to Bread & Circus.[66] Both stores were much larger than any natural foods store Mackey had ever visited. Bread & Circus and Mrs. Gooch's also had plans to open additional stores and to create their own natural foods supermarket chains.

Inspired by these stores' success, Mackey returned home and decided that opening a high-volume natural foods supermarket was the only way to make a profit and gain a competitive edge in Austin's crowded market.

Mackey and Lawson approached Weller and Skiles about merging Safer-Way and Clarksville Natural Grocery and opening a new store. Weller and Skiles agreed, and in September 1980 the four of them opened Whole Foods Market on Lamar Boulevard in Austin. At more than 10,000 square feet, the store was much larger than the typical natural foods store and had nineteen employees. The trio's initial capital investment of around $100,000 was virtually unheard of for a natural foods store.[67]

Whole Foods combined elements from natural foods stores and conventional supermarkets while distancing itself from both retail models. "What do you get when you cross a supermarket with a health food store?" *Texas Monthly* asked readers in January 1981. "You get the Whole Foods Market in Austin—an honorable truce between two old enemies. On the one hand, you can find plenty of soy products and sprouts," the magazine explained. "On the other hand the store takes orders from customers for fresh, hormone-free turkeys. . . . What you won't find are white flour, refined white sugar, and interminable aisles of junk breakfast cereals." An advertisement in the *Austin American-Statesman* in 1982 celebrated the store's "chemical free food" and condemned the "chemical feast" found in "commercial grocery products." As Mackey explained,

> The typical health foods store has either an announced or implicit philosophy about what is good for people and those things are all it offers to shoppers. The supermarkets are the exact opposite; they carry only what the customers demand, a demand which is often manipulated by mass marketing and advertising. What we try to do is forge a dialogue between us and our customers. . . . Our beliefs are changed by this process and it results in changes in our product mix. At the same time, we are changing—for the better—the way a lot of people eat.

Mackey believed that by avoiding natural foods sellers' didactic tendencies and the deceptions of conventional supermarkets, Whole Foods could transcend the shortcomings of both approaches to groceries.[68]

The future looked bright for Whole Foods and the new generation of natural foods supermarkets, but organic pioneer Erewhon confronted a diverse set of difficulties by the start of the 1980s. To some observers, Erewhon might have seemed to be at the height of its powers. In September 1977, a group of advisers to President Jimmy Carter invited company owner Michio Kushi and a cadre of employees from his East West Foundation to Washington, D.C., to share their recommendations on rewriting federal food policy. But a boycott that year by fifteen New England natural foods stores against Erewhon for wholesaling to co-op stores had weakened the company and highlighted a growing divergence between for-profit retailers and co-ops. The stores claimed that the low prices Erewhon offered the co-ops unfairly undercut competition. Erewhon sued the stores, and although a federal judge ruled in its favor, the company did not recoup an estimated $250,000 in legal expenditures. In addition, management's costly efforts to block its workers from unionizing divided the company. Many of Erewhon's newer employees had little interest in Ohsawa's spiritual teachings. More and more Erewhon customers began shopping at Bread & Circus's supermarket stores. The ongoing national recession compounded the company's problems. In 1981, Erewhon recorded $15 million in sales but a loss of $2 million, and the natural foods pioneer was forced to file for Chapter 11 bankruptcy.[69]

That same year Whole Foods faced a crisis of its own. On Memorial Day, massive flooding hit Austin and devastated the store's inventory and equipment. The company suffered roughly $400,000 in losses but had no insurance. According to the company's official history, "customers and neighbors voluntarily joined the staff to repair and clean up the damage" in a remarkable show of support for the store. Meanwhile, "creditors, vendors and investors all provided breathing room for the store to get back on its feet." With the help of volunteers and loyal customers, Whole Foods miraculously managed to reopen in less than a month.

Whole Foods' and John Mackey's subsequent retellings of these events only partly explain the company's recovery, however. In October 1981, Whole Foods secured an emergency disaster loan of more than $200,000 from the Small Business Administration. In 1989, Whole Foods cofounder Craig Weller acknowledged the loan in an interview for a newspaper story and admitted that "the amount of the money was critical. Whether we could have raised it somewhere else, I'm not sure." Yet in virtually every account of its history, Whole Foods failed to acknowledge that federal assistance likely saved it from collapse. Although it is not entirely clear why Whole Foods insisted on omitting this critical detail from its company's history, transformations in John Mackey's political philosophy, which became public by the start of the 1990s, were the most likely reason.[70]

Whole Foods embodied an unusual, if not contradictory, set of characteristics. It had begun as SaferWay, a store whose very name criticized big business. But Whole Foods represented one of the most ambitious attempts at natural foods retail in the country. Mackey had discovered natural foods as a devoted member of Austin's co-op community, but he and three other people had cofounded Whole Foods as a conventional for-profit proprietorship. The company praised its customers as its most loyal allies, but the federal government was really its most important supporter. In the years ahead, such tensions between Whole Foods' day-to-day operations and its stated ideals would only sharpen further.

WHOLE FOODS AND THE ETHICAL PERILS OF EXPANSION

Some longtime champions of natural foods began to worry that organic entrepreneurs risked abandoning their core values in the quest for greater riches in the 1980s. Natural foods had become a "commodity in crisis," declared one writer for *New Age*, a magazine founded by two former Erewhon employees. "Now that natural foods have become big business, will there still be room in the industry for ethics?" the magazine asked with concern. Or had the "natural foods movement . . . become irrevocably co-opted?" *New Age* decried natural foods supermarkets that pursued rapid growth with questionable principles, flashy marketing, "expensive body care products . . . candy bars, frozen yogurt, potato chips, [and] even tobacco-free cigarettes." As the magazine asked in exasperation, "Where has all the *food* gone?"[71] Tensions between natural foods' dual roles as a movement and as an industry were nothing new. But *New Age* worried that business considerations were now threatening to extinguish natural foods sellers' interest in environmentalism, cooperative economics, and other social movements.

Whole Foods, however, had few of these concerns and declared its foray into the broader economy and culture as an unmitigated victory for the organic movement. "The natural foods business is no longer a weird little counterculture business," cofounder Mark Skiles proudly declared in 1984. "It's mainstream now." As Mackey would explain, the store's employees also "weren't nearly as weird as they might look." Whole Foods told employees the company was "proud to be participating in the transformation of our culture towards greater health and well being" by making natural and organic foods "widely available for the first time on a mass scale."[72]

Whole Foods embraced expansion more enthusiastically than any natural foods business before it, both through starting new stores and by acquiring competitors. Alternately described by colleagues as "immensely competitive" and "pathologically competitive," Mackey was determined to make Whole Foods the undisputed king of the natural foods business. By 1984, Whole Foods had opened stores in Austin and Houston, making it "a $16 million business." In 1986, it acquired a store in Dallas, and in 1988 it purchased a store established in New Orleans in 1974 and coincidentally named Whole Foods Company.[73]

Prior to Whole Foods, natural foods stores rarely acquired their competitors. Net profits for supermarkets typically hovered around 1 percent, but Whole Foods aimed for much higher margins of between 3 and 6 percent. By 1988, the company earned the second-highest sales of any natural foods retailer in the country. The next year, Whole Foods made its first move toward national, not just regional, retailing when it opened a store in Palo Alto, California. The company's stores measured around 20,000 square feet, much larger than other natural foods sellers. By the start of the 1990s, Whole Foods' annual sales were higher than $45 million, and the company declared that it was the biggest seller of organic food in the country.[74]

Even as Whole Foods aspired to grow into a major national retailer, it selectively retained some of the democratic and humanistic aspirations of activist business. The company offered profit sharing to employees in its first few years. Although it discontinued the policy by 1988, it continued to supplement workers' wages with a system of bonuses based on team productivity and profitability, which it called "gainsharing." The company issued a mission statement called the "Declaration of Interdependence" in which it celebrated "decentralized and horizontal management structures that promote face to face communication" and "open book, open door, open people practices." Newly hired employees served in a probationary phase for several months, and at the end of that period they could stay only if two-thirds of their coworkers approved them in a vote. Each Whole Foods store was divided into teams of six to thirty employees, and each team made many of its own decisions regarding purchasing and other aspects of the store's operations. Whole Foods pitched its offer of B-class stock to staff members as a program of "employee ownership," echoing the language of cooperative principles. The company had very few rules for dress and appearance. In the name of transparency, the company published the salaries of its entire staff and allowed any employee to view another's pay.[75]

Whole Foods also periodically encouraged its staff and customers to collaborate with environmental and animal rights organizations. In 1989 and 1990, the company's stores participated in a national boycott of companies whose fishing practices injured or killed dolphins. Some stores held rallies to promote the cause and offered customers store credits for boycotted tuna they returned. The company even organized a letter-writing campaign in which two thousand customers wrote tuna companies and President George H. W. Bush to decry commercial fishing practices. Whole Foods directly appealed to customers to donate to a range of environmental, animal rights, and consumer rights organizations, including Greenpeace, the Center for Science in the Public Interest, and People for the Ethical Treatment of Animals.[76]

Yet despite embracing some progressive causes and democratic workplace policies, Whole Foods actively opposed organized labor. The company's first conflict with unions came in 1988, when fifteen protesters from the Texas United Farm Workers launched a picketing campaign to raise awareness about pesticides' harmful effects on farmworkers. Early protests at Safeway's and the Texas grocery chain H.E.B.'s supermarkets occurred without incident, but staff at Whole Foods' Lamar Boulevard location in Austin called the police on UFW picketers. Police arrested four picketers for blocking the entrance to the store, although a manager later admitted that "they weren't trying to purposely block the entrance to the store, but it was [just] so congested." The UFW sued the city of Austin and Whole Foods for damages, and Whole Foods countersued the UFW for libel. After almost a year of court hearings and negotiations, all parties reached an undisclosed agreement. Charges were dropped against all protesters, and Whole Foods vowed to "remain committed to pesticide-free grapes."[77] But the company's conflicts with unions would not end there.

Whole Foods' antagonism toward organized labor was not unusual in the fiercely antiunion climate of its home state, Texas. Yet by expanding into California, Whole Foods had entered a state that was much friendlier to labor. In 1989, the company announced it would open its second California store in Berkeley, a city where every grocery store's workforce was unionized. For decades, the Berkeley Consumers' Cooperative had been one of the city's most pro-union businesses. Yet the Co-op's sales had declined significantly in recent years, and in 1988 it announced it was forced to close all its locations. Soon after the Co-op shuttered its flagship store on Telegraph Avenue, Whole Foods announced it would be moving into the space. By now the country's largest organic foods retail chain, Whole Foods developed plans to take over what had been the country's largest co-op grocery.[78]

Whole Foods virtually ensured a conflict over labor at its new store by strongly discouraging its Berkeley employees from affiliating with a union. Roughly forty former employees of the Co-op applied to work at Whole Foods. All of them had been unionized at the Co-op, but none of them was hired by Whole Foods. There were other major differences between the Co-op's and Whole Foods' workforce. Only about one-quarter of the Co-op's workforce had been white, compared with roughly 70 percent of Whole Foods' hires. The Co-op's nonmanagerial employees were forty years old on average, but Whole Foods' hires were on average twenty-eight.[79] Even before the store opened, dissatisfied former Co-op employees spread the word that Berkeley's incoming Whole Foods business discriminated against union members, middle-aged employees, and people of color.

As soon as Whole Foods opened in Berkeley, members of the Butchers Local 120 and United Food and Commercial Workers Local 870, many of whom were Latino and African American, picketed the store. "They were the first ones to greet us at the door," Whole Food's California executive Peter Roy recalled. This was the start of a bitter, months-long standoff between union members and Whole Foods in Berkeley. "It's like we've opened the store on a sacred burial ground," one Whole Foods staffer complained. Co-op loyalists avoided the store, but many Berkeley residents—most of them white—crossed the picket line. As one Whole Foods shopper told *The Nation*, protesters didn't "know anything about the whole good-food movement and yet they're picketing for an old form that really supports [stores like] Safeway." Michael Anderson, the union's young, Harvard-trained attorney argued that Whole Foods shoppers were ignoring bad labor politics in pursuit of health food. "The trouble with Berkeley . . . is that people's politics are ten miles wide and one inch deep. In some ways, that makes Berkeley the exact opposite of the more working-class communities in the Bay Area. . . . In working-class communities, people . . . aren't quite as advanced about buying hormone-free chicken, but they know exploitation when they see it." The faceoff with picketers continued for months.[80]

Complaints from union members and community members about the new store prompted the City of Berkeley's Commission of Labor to hold two meetings about Whole Foods. In late 1990, the commission published its findings in a highly critical report that reprimanded the company for paying low wages without offering a retirement plan, dependent health care, or any guarantee to new mothers that they could return to their jobs after maternity leave. The report also rebuked Whole Foods for failing to "demonstrate that it has not discriminated against older workers and minorities in its hiring practices." The report did acknowledge the company's donations to environmental groups and its use of some democratic management policies. Yet in the final analysis, the report declared that Whole Foods nonetheless "closely resembles a traditional corporation with the usual employee/management relationship."[81]

The commission argued that Whole Foods worked hard to obfuscate the hierarchical nature of its management practices and its conventional corporate ownership structure. The company's insistence on using the terms *team managers* and *team leaders* was really just an attempt "to disguise the employee/management relationship." Whole Foods equivocated further about the composition of its ownership by claiming that 40 percent of the company was owned by employees. Such calculation counted both Mackey and his father as employees. Together they owned a combined 26 percent share of the company. The commission also accused Whole Foods of misleadingly trumpeting its worker's compensation insurance as a company benefit, even though the state required it by law. Most disingenuous was Whole Foods' proud proclamations in press releases and advertisements that employees had rejected a union in an official election. As a banner on the facade of the Berkeley store announced, "We, the team members of Whole Foods Market, cast our ballots, 91.5% voted 'no representation' by a union." Such statements implied that a legal union election had taken place, but as the commission's report revealed, the company was actually referring to an in-house, nonpublic "plebiscite" of employees in which management tallied the final vote.[82]

Times had certainly changed in Berkeley since the first wave of natural foods business in the 1960s and 1970s. "Fifteen years ago, Berkeley would have shut Whole Foods down," the secretary of the city's Labor Commission remarked. Whole Foods' close ties to venture capital would have particularly dismayed Berkeley's activists two decades earlier. Although the company told customers and media that "team members and their families" owned a majority of Whole Foods, three venture-capital firms owned one-third of the company. The same firms had several major military contracts, including one for the Strategic Defense Initiative, or "Star Wars" program. Along with the loan made by the Small Business Administration, those companies' investments had made Whole Foods' California expansion possible. The three venture-capital firms, John Mackey, and his father owned a combined 61 percent of the company, a figure that Whole Foods admitted only reluctantly.[83]

By selling to venture-capital companies, Whole Foods had made a decisive break from the tradition of independent activist businesses seeking to democratize ownership through their companies. By the end of the 1980s, Whole Foods had announced plans to break with activist enterprises in another critical regard. The company now hoped to make a public offering to investors if it could achieve a target of $175 million in annual sales. No natural foods retailer had ever made a public offering. As the United Food and Commercial Workers' lawyer Michael Anderson quipped without any apparent knowledge of Whole Foods' original name, a publicly traded Whole Foods would just "be Safeway without a union."[84]

In the aftermath of the conflict at the Berkeley store, John Mackey published a series of editorials defending Whole Foods' antiunion policy in the company's newsletter, *The Whole Story: A Marketplace of Ideas*. He also authored a thin pamphlet titled *Beyond Unions*. Both publications were distributed for free in stores to employees and customers and provided a clear view of Mackey's unusual fusion of environmentalism, New Age cultural philosophy, and ardent antiunion attitudes. In later years, Mackey and Whole Foods would articulate these sentiments in much more diplomatic and judiciously edited statements as the company became more sensitive about its image. Like earlier retailers with activist aspirations, Mackey insisted that Whole Foods was more concerned with making the world a happier and better place than in making profits. "Business must have social consciousness," he insisted. Although some companies exploited workers and customers, most simply wanted to allow people to "voluntarily exchange for their own mutual benefit." Mackey proudly declared that a philosophy of "Reciprocal Altruism"provided the basis for Whole Foods' "company-wide consciousness of Unity and Shared Fate to unite the self-interest of the Team Members as closely as possible to the self-interest of the customers and the stakeholders." The company had "always believed that our mission of providing natural and organically grown food for people is a noble enterprise and one where we experience 'right livelihood' daily." In later years, Mackey would articulate such sentiments as part of a business philosophy he christened "conscious capitalism."[85]

By emphasizing emotional fulfillment, Mackey drew on activist entrepreneurs' long tradition of celebrating their stores as humanistic, participatory "free spaces." The section of Whole Foods' Declaration of Interdependence devoted to staff was titled simply "Team Member Happiness." At store meetings, employees were encouraged to "express their positive feelings toward one another . . . [in] a heart opening exercise [that] enhances self-esteem and allows the extension of love to flow throughout the teams and store." The stated objective of such exercises was to "help create the context of happiness, joy, and love for everyone who works at Whole Foods Market."[86]

Yet unlike most activist businesses, Mackey emphasized individual fulfillment at the expense of social equality and workplace democracy. As the company's official handbook cautioned employees in 1988, "We must make sure that we do not become so involved in social/environmental/global issues that it negatively affects our ability to serve our stakeholders."[87] Although Whole Foods selectively borrowed practices from activist enterprises, it dismissed their idea that businesses were political participants that should collaborate with social movements. Indeed, the company rejected most tenets of activist business by the end of the 1980s.

Mackey adamantly objected to efforts to redress structural inequalities. "Why do so many people believe it is wrong for there to be inequalities in wealth among people? Should the more talented be handicapped so that no one will feel inferior or envious of them?" he asked. Mackey attributed struggles for equality to selfish covetousness. As he explained, "Resentment provides the ideology to justify stealing under the guises of 'equality,' 'social justice,' or the class struggle." One Whole Foods customer objected to these views in a letter that the company published in *The Whole Story*. "I don't understand your recent propagandizing concerning 'free market' capitalism,'" wrote the customer. "No educated person could really agree that opposition to this system emanates primarily from envy and greed. As an African-American it is difficult for me to stomach the flag waving and jingoism intrinsic in espousing 'democracy' and capitalism." In response, Mackey published a lengthy statement that opened, "Thank you for taking the time to express your viewpoint. It just so happens that your accusations against free market capitalism reflect the same issues of envy and resentment that I addressed in my previous editorial." In another instance, a Whole Foods employee and self-described "inspired feminist" penned a column in the company's employee newsletter, arguing that the "Austin store blatantly lacks the influences of blacks, hispanics, orientals [*sic*] and other minorities. . . . What are we doing to encourage their application?" Mackey responded defensively in the newsletter's next issue two weeks later: Whole Foods "strives to be race and color blind. . . . However, to give minorities special treatment is to discriminate against whites. To give women special treatment is to discriminate against men. . . . Each of us is ultimately responsible for our own success."[88]

Mackey had come to fully embrace libertarianism. By the late 1980s, the Whole Foods founder's public comments on free-market fundamentalism far exceeded the criticisms of government that had long circulated in the natural foods community. Earlier natural foods enthusiasts had expressed anarchist sympathies by combining their deep distrust of the state with a significant skepticism about the virtues of capitalism. Mackey by contrast described capitalism as inherently virtuous, even "fundamentally good and ethical." As he recounted in later years, his "worldview underwent a massive shift" as he read writings by such free-market fundamentalists as Milton Friedman, Thomas Sowell, Ludwig von Mises, and Friedrich Hayek.[89]

Mackey regularly promoted libertarian ideas to customers and staff through Whole Foods' in-store newsletter in the early 1990s. He was particularly fond of quoting from Milton and Rose Friedman's work *Free to Choose* (1980). In one issue, Mackey argued that businesses, not government, should provide education and mail service for citizens. "Unfortunately many of our country's most influential figures in government, in our universities, and the media still believe Marx's basic teaching that profit comes only from coercive exploitation of labor," he lamented. Because the federal "government produces no capital [and] . . . merely expropriates it from businesses and individuals through taxes," he argued, "all economic progress and prosperity rests on the foundation of profits from business individuals." Some Whole Foods employees appeared to share such sentiments, including one who blasted the federal Nutrition, Labeling, and Education Act of 1990 as "threaten[ing] our business and the natural foods industry, as well as our right to freedom to pursue personal health and happiness."[90] Mackey, with his shift to ardent libertarianism, had dispensed with any earlier concerns he had about the dangers of expansive, profit-driven corporations.

Mackey's criticism of government's regulatory role in the American economy was especially surprising. After all, Whole Foods probably would have never recovered from the flood in 1981 without the federal loan it had received from the Small Business Administration. For whatever reason,

Mackey appears to have never publicly disclosed that loan. As the chief executive officer of a company that might not have survived its second year without federal assistance, he displayed an extraordinary antagonism toward government. Mackey oddly combined this conservative libertarianism with Whole Foods' selective application of collective practices, participatory economics, and countercultural spirituality. The biggest organic retailer in the country emerged out of Austin's hippie and activist small-business milieu in the 1970s with a vow to offer customers a "Safer Way" of buying groceries. Yet by the start of the 1990s Whole Foods sounded much more like major American corporations that funded antiregulatory lobbying organizations such as the Business Roundtable and the U.S. Chamber of Commerce.[91] Whole Foods descended from the family of activist business, but it was now barely recognizable as one of its offspring.

Mackey's increased libertarianism coincided with a remarkable period of growth for Whole Foods in the early 1990s. In January 1992, the company made an initial public offering of its stock on the NASDAQ exchange, becoming the first ever publicly traded natural foods retailer. The sale raised more than $23 million, and a second sale of stock the following year raised an additional $35 million. This infusion of capital allowed the company to embark on an aggressive growth strategy and a buying spree to acquire its competitors. Over the course of the 1990s, Whole Foods purchased the pioneering natural foods supermarkets Bread & Circus and Mrs. Gooch's Natural Foods Market as well as the North Carolina chain Wellspring. It also opened scores of new locations. By 1998, Whole Foods operated more than seventy-five stores in eighteen states and the District of Columbia.[92]

For decades, tensions between dietary, political, economic, and social imperatives wracked the natural foods business. Of course, organic retailers sought profits or at least to cover their costs. But they also aimed to advance the goals of the environmental, animal rights, and antiwar movements, to help people improve their health, to advance cooperative enterprise, and to make employer–employee relations emotionally and spiritually fulfilling and even democratic. These entrepreneurs viewed natural foods not only as a better way of eating but also as a better way of doing business. Leading pioneers in the business, such as Erewhon, had combined various elements of nearly all these motivations in their operations. Yet in the second half of the 1970s, employee union drives and accusations of dogmatic elitism directly challenged natural foods sellers' claims of creating democratic workplaces that welcomed a diverse range of customers.

Yet more than anything, the emergence of a new generation of natural foods supermarket chains transformed the natural foods business. With its roots in co-ops and the counterculture, Whole Foods selectively retained some language and management practices from activist business. For the most part, however, John Mackey embraced individual, libertarian change in the marketplace, not the collective political actions of his natural foods predecessors. By the start of the 1990s, Whole Foods became the nation's largest organic foods seller. The company's further expansion over the course of the decade and its rejection of the progressive and even radical potential of activist enterprise dramatically altered the natural foods marketplace. Although some of the small activist storefronts from the 1970s survived, Whole Foods effectively had become the public face of the natural foods business. Once an upstart natural retailer rooted in Austin's left-leaning counterculture, Whole Foods had remade itself into a publicly traded, libertarian corporation that was now the country's largest seller of organic food. This extraordinary transformation would have profound implications not only for natural foods companies, but for businesses of all kinds that professed to work toward political and social change.

6

Perseverance and Appropriation

ACTIVIST BUSINESS IN THE
TWENTY-FIRST CENTURY

How do we assess the legacy of activist businesses in the twenty-first century? On the one hand, a small number of companies have kept alive the activist business ethos of the 1960s and 1970s. Entrepreneurs have created innovative forms of corporations whose charters require their owners to fulfill social and environmental obligations. A new generation of activists is busy creating and operating a "solidarity economy." Progressive-minded small-business owners have launched national organizations to counter major corporations' growing power in local communities. A few activist businesses from the 1960s and 1970s even continue to operate today.

On the other hand, major corporations with little interest in working toward collective political change have appropriated the language of conscious capitalism, social enterprise, and mission-driven business but promote a rhetoric of benevolent business without questioning or challenging established economic, social, and racial power relations. Meanwhile, the number of entrepreneurs who work with social movements has declined significantly. African American booksellers, feminist businesses, and cooperative storefronts have struggled, even as the products they pioneered have become more popular. Natural foods stores, in contrast, have experienced significant success—none more so than Whole Foods Market, which epitomizes many of the contradictions of activist businesses' contemporary legacy.

Whole Foods Market still considers itself an activist company. On its website and store displays, the company presents itself as an heir to Rachel Carson's *Silent Spring*, early organic pioneers such as the radical pacifist Paul Keene, and the environmental movement writ large. John Mackey proudly advocates "conscious capitalism" in a popular book he published in 2013 and in a series of CEO summits he organizes. Whole Foods' first ever national advertising campaign in 2014 centered on the theme "values matter." The company remains one of the most environmentally conscious chain retailers in the country, ranking highly on a variety of sustainability metrics and participating in a wide range of energy- and waste-reduction initiatives. In-store "Take Action Centers" offer shoppers information on issues such as genetic engineering and pesticides. Whole Foods still deploys some collective-management practices such as employee votes to approve or reject new hires after their trial period.[1]

Yet although the company continues to selectively use the language and practices of activist enterprise, it does not collaborate with social movements as activist businesses do. Customers are instructed to take responsibility for these issues as individuals outside the store, not in conjunction with Whole Foods or its staff. The company's message for environmental and social transformation is essentially a philosophy of self-reform, a prescription of individual health and wellness that avoids making any demands for systemic change. As such, it rejects the vision of activist businesses of the 1960s and 1970s. And Mackey's embrace of conservative libertarianism and the company's dogged insistence on having a nonunion workforce have put it at odds with many social movements' vision of economic justice and environmental sustainability, as does Mackey's denunciation of the Affordable Care Act as "like fascism" and his claim that global warming is not "that big a deal."[2]

When convenient, Whole Foods vows that it seeks to "co-create a world where each of us, our communities and our planet can flourish" and "to fulfill a higher purpose: helping to make the world a better place." Yet such claims that Whole Foods serves the greater good are dubious for a number of reasons. Most significantly, the company's high prices keep their products out of reach of many consumers. Despite the company's ongoing efforts to counter the widespread epithets "Whole Wallet" and "Whole Paycheck," independent price comparisons have repeatedly shown that Whole Foods' prices are significantly higher than those of its competitors. For years, Whole Food's single most important criterion for locating its stores was to find sites that had a high proportion of college graduates living within a sixteen-minute drive's radius. As a result, the company located its stores far from working-class and lower-income neighborhoods. Whole Foods has recently begun to open locations in more financially distressed and less-educated cities such as Detroit and Newark. Yet there is little evidence to suggest that these stores have achieved their stated goals of making healthy and organic food more accessible to poor people and people of color.[3]

Indeed, when activists and journalists criticize the gap between Whole Foods' ideals and its practices, the company often restates its utopian aspirations in much more modest terms. "We're not miracle workers," one Whole Foods executive explains. Or as John Mackey has insisted, "Gosh, we're just a grocery store! We're not going to save the world!" In these instances, the contradiction between Whole Foods' utopian rhetoric of altruism for the collective good and its claims of being "just a grocery store" is striking.[4]

Ironically, some of Whole Foods' larger, more conventional corporate competitors are friendlier to workers and more philanthropic than the organic foods chain. America's two largest supermarket chains—Kroger and Safeway, Mackey's one-time bête noir—are certainly much more hospitable to unions than Whole Foods. More than 60 percent of the two companies' hundreds of thousands of employees belong to the United Food and Commercial Workers International Union. These companies also far exceed Whole Foods in their charitable giving. Whole Foods proudly proclaims its philanthropy with announcements on store bulletin boards and check-out clerks' frequent requests for charitable donations. The company donates 5 percent of its after-tax profits to nonprofit organizations, but Kroger and Safeway dwarf that amount by regularly giving away between 7 and 10 percent of their *pretax* profits.[5]

Whole Foods' meteoric rise took place amid the nearly uninterrupted growth of the natural foods market since the early 1980s. In 2002, natural foods received a major boost of legitimacy when a legally binding certification program for foods labeled as organic went into effect, as required by the federal Organic Foods Production Act of 1990. In the twenty-first century, the organic foods business stands out as the most lucrative descendent of activist business of the 1960s and 1970s. Decades of annual double-digit growth have produced a natural and organic foods marketplace with sales greater than $130 billion. Yet although natural foods stores pioneered the organic marketplace, today they account for a little more than 40 percent of that market's revenue. Conventional grocery chains and big-box retailers such as Walmart have come to embrace organic foods. In 2015, Whole Foods earned $15.3 billion in revenue and $536 million in net profits, and by late 2016 it operated more than 450 stores. The company has continued to regularly earn a profit margin of 3 to 4 percent, considerably higher than conventional grocery stores' typical margin of 1 to 2 percent. As the seventh-largest grocery chain and the twenty-fourth-largest retailer of any kind in the United States, Whole Foods has risen to the ranks of the supermarket chains that it originally chastised.[6]

SUCCESS AND SETBACKS

Whole Foods' tremendous financial success raises the question of why some activist businesses thrived more than others. Natural foods stores have flourished, and head shops (now better known as "smoke shops" or "vape shops") have survived despite significant legal challenges. But enterprises such as black-owned bookstores and feminist companies—in which there was virtually no line between movement and business—have dwindled nearly to the point of extinction. These struggling stores make significant demands of their customers in terms of ideological commitment and political engagement. Yet as the organized movements that gave rise to these businesses have waned in power and influence, so have their associated storefronts. The activist businesses that collaborated less with social movements over time and became less political since the 1970s appear to have had greater financial success. Although organic foods stores still promote environmental causes and head shops still promote marijuana legalization, many of these businesses have shifted away from collective political action in favor of emphasizing individualized change and self-transformation. Decreased politicization, in turn, has allowed natural foods stores and head shops to appeal to a much larger proportion of the population than they did in the 1960s and 1970s.

Head shops may not be as widespread and accepted as natural foods stores, but they continue to flourish despite legal challenges and the stigma they still carry, even as more and more states decriminalize marijuana. Like natural foods, marijuana has lost much, if not all, of the radial political significance it held at the height of the counterculture and New Left, especially as legal pot businesses seek to recast their products as legitimate consumer goods. Although some head shop owners still champion nonviolence and gesture to the antiwar movement of the Vietnam era with their store names and generous use of peace symbols, the promoters of marijuana culture are far less politically engaged than they were in the 1960s and 1970s. *High Times* examined a range of political topics in its early years, for example, but a survey of the magazine today shows that its focus is limited almost exclusively to marijuana.[7] Head shops may still advocate for marijuana's legalization, but they have little to say about developing new consciousness or undertaking political action.

Since 2012, several states have decriminalized and even legalized marijuana, ushering in a new chapter in the history of marijuana-related businesses. National media outlets are awash with profiles of entrepreneurs in Colorado and Washington State eager to recast the marijuana business as a clean-cut, reputable, and legitimate line of work. "We're weeding out the stoners," explained Olivia Mannix, cofounder of Cannabrand, a Colorado advertising agency seeking to promote a more positive image for marijuana businesses. Marijuana retailers have their own trade group, the National Cannabis Industry Association, which advocates for reforming the laws regulating both marijuana businesses and their customers. There is even a marijuana retail trade school in Oakland, California, called Oaksterdam, which one writer for *The Atlantic* has described as having an "atmosphere of purposeful endeavor [that] was like what you might find at a night-school business class of aspiring franchisees."[8] These advances by well-funded and highly organized legal marijuana businesses contrast sharply with many early head shop owners' haphazard approach to the shoestring operations they established in the 1960s and 1970s.

Although natural foods stores and head shops have reoriented themselves politically and flourished, most African American bookstores and feminist businesses have stayed true to their political objectives but have struggled. The number of African American bookstores peaked in the mid-1990s. In the second half of the decade, they increasingly had to compete with neighboring chain megastores such as Barnes & Noble, which added extensive selections of black-authored books. Independents and chain stores alike faced the rise of online booksellers, Amazon in particular, which cut even further into sales. An overall decline in reading has hurt black bookstores, too. A study by the National Endowment for the Arts showed that the proportion of all Americans who read books declined by 7 percent between 1992 and 2002, with even larger declines in literary reading across all demographic groups, including a decrease of more than 18 percent of African Americans who read literature. The African American Literary Book Club website lists other factors among its top ten reasons for the decline of black bookstores, including storeowners' failure to diversify their product selection, the popularization of tablets such as the iPad and Kindle, as well as, most troublingly, a perceived decline in African American customers' loyalty to black bookstores and a "lack of commitment from owners." Although intended as a criticism of weak-willed owners, such an explanation highlights how the deeply discouraging landscape for independent bookselling since the 1990s has undermined black bookstore owners' resolve to stay open. Between 1999 and 2012, roughly two of every three African American bookstores—more than one hundred stores—closed. As of May 2016, only about seventy black-owned bookstores operated in the entire United States.[9]

Even some of the country's most beloved black bookstores have closed their doors. Harlem's Hue-Man Experience Bookstore, arguably the most successful African American bookstore in the country since the late 1980s, closed in July 2012 with virtually no warning or fanfare. Although the store's sales had reportedly increased 37 percent since the previous year, Hue-Man's manager and CEO Marva Allen said the store's investors did not feel that current sales justified signing a new ten-year lease for the store. In a pointed rejection of the political and social imperatives that had traditionally motivated black bookselling, Allen explained, "If you're making money, it's a business; if you're not, it's social work. I'm not interested in social work."[10] Black bookstore owners of the 1960s and 1970s made the exact opposite claim, declaring that selling books by African Americans was in fact a form of social work and community development. Allen's rationale suggested that political motivations may have lost some of their appeal for black booksellers by the twenty-first century.

The next year, 2013, Marcus Books—the country's longest-operating black-owned bookstore, which was also devoted to political engagement—closed its oldest location in San Francisco, leaving its Oakland branch as its only remaining store. In San Francisco, Marcus Books' landlord evicted it for missing several rent payments and then quickly sold the building for $1.6 million to real estate investors. Several months later, Marcus Books raised enough capital to offer $1.8 million to the speculators who had just bought the property, but the offer was rejected. In a letter to supporters, store owner Karen Johnson rued the chain of events as the outcome of financial predation. "The 'bottom line' is the only line worth respecting, though it respects no one. This is a common conception, but not right," she lamented. "Millions of people have been put out of their homes by bottom-line-feeders. It's common, but it's not okay, now or at any other time." Echoing black booksellers' long-standing tradition of criticizing corporate capitalism, Johnson forcefully questioned the commercial imperatives that prompted the closing of the country's oldest black-owned bookstore.[11]

Businesses aligned with the feminist movement have fared just as badly, if not worse. The number of feminist credit unions, nearly 20 of which operated in the late 1970s, declined through the 1980s and 1990s. In 2012, the Women's Southwest Federal Credit Union of Dallas—believed to be the last feminist credit union in the country—closed its doors for good. Feminist and women's bookstores, although not extinct, have also suffered a dramatic decline. After the number of stores in the United States and Canada peaked at around 120 in the mid-1990s, it fell to about 70 by the mid-2000s. As a feminist bookseller in Toledo, Ohio, told the journal *off our backs* in 2007, "Feminist bookstores are a part of our endangered and crumbling infrastructure . . . [of] feminist businesses and culture." Indeed, by 2014, only a dozen feminist bookstores remained in the entire United States, a shocking reversal from two decades earlier.[12]

Businesses that collaborate with feminist activists have become rare. But feminist enterprises nonetheless were forerunners of the huge wave of companies of all kinds that women have established since the 1970s. Millions of women have started their own businesses in recent decades. As of 2014, women owned nearly half—47 percent—of all businesses in the United States, a remarkable increase from the start of the 1970s, when the portion was less than 5 percent.[13] One of feminist businesses' main objectives in the 1970s was to defeat sexist notions that business ownership was limited to men. In this regard, the feminist businesses in this book succeeded by creating models of female entrepreneurship for future generations to emulate.

At the same time, shifting notions of feminism have redefined the meaning of feminist business. As some feminists have argued, a shifting interpretation of feminism that privileges individual women's career achievements and commodifies the movement into "marketplace feminism" now overshadows the collective, organized work of the women's movement for gender equality. As a consequence, prevailing interpretations of feminism's relationship to business also tend to minimize the role of organized political movements. Facebook CEO Sheryl Sandberg's mantra "lean in," made famous by the title of her best-selling book in 2013, has become one of the dominant narratives for explaining women's success (or lack thereof) in achieving equality in American business. Sandberg measures gender equality in the workplace primarily in terms of whether individual women effectively advocate for promotions and higher pay, and she largely refrains from structural critiques of business or capitalism.[14]

Such an approach offers a very different interpretation of feminist business than the one that prevailed in the women's movement in the 1970s. Writer and early Facebook employee Kate Losse describes *Lean In* as "not so much a new *Feminine Mystique* as an updated *Protestant Ethic and the Spirit of Capitalism.*" Losse argues that Sandberg effectively recasts the relationship between feminism and business as a recipe for making women more productive workers. The prominent feminist theorist bell hooks meanwhile excoriates Sandberg's "trickle-down theory . . . that having more women at the top of corporate hierarchies would make the work world better for all women, including women on the bottom." The historian Linda Gordon interprets Sandberg's mission as a symptom of the growing influence of "very individualist" contemporary approaches to feminism.[15] Sandberg's emphasis on individual career success and her uncritical approach to capitalism, even if articulated in a language of feminism, have little in common with feminist entrepreneurs' collective struggles for gender and economic equality in the 1970s.

Overall, the subset of activist businesses that implement shared ownership and democratic management structures have not fared well since the 1970s. It is impossible to accurately count the number of activist businesses or calculate their revenues, either in the 1960s and 1970s or today. Nonetheless, statistics on the number of cooperative grocery stores in the United States in this period suggest a large decline in activist business. In the late 1970s, more than 725 food cooperative storefronts operated in the United States. By early 2016, that number had fallen to fewer than 450. In 1970, retail co-ops of all kinds in the United States had 515,000 members. By 2009, the number of members had shrunk to 487,000—despite the 50 percent increase in the country's population, an additional 100 million people. These numbers appear even worse in international comparison. As of 2009, the United States was home to 29,322 co-ops, or one for about every 10,460 residents. In Italy, by contrast, 70,000 co-ops operated, or roughly one per every 850 residents. Cooperatives account for around 20 percent of the gross national product in Sweden and Switzerland. In the United States, that figure hovers lower than 2 percent. Major corporations in the United States gladly sell products pioneered by activist businesses but have no interest in cooperative or collective workplaces. A company such as the Mondragon Corporation, a federation of cooperatives with a total membership of more than 30,000 worker-owners in the Basque region of Spain, dwarfs its counterparts in the United States.[16]

One reason for co-ops' decline may be the impoverished economic discourse among American media, corporate businesses, and academics. This discourse rarely acknowledges cooperatives' success—or even their mere existence. In the early twentieth century, American economic textbooks examined co-ops at length. Contemporary textbooks, by contrast, do so only in passing and sometimes misleadingly.[17] The notion that business success is limited to sole proprietorships and limited-liability companies that maximize profits is so widespread that cooperatives likely strike many Americans as farfetched and destined for failure. Indeed, one of the major questions left unanswered by this work is why there aren't more cooperatives in the United States.

Activist businesses have failed for a number of other reasons. To be sure, the quest for equality and justice does not easily map onto traditional business structures. In many ways, the very notion of sole proprietorship and the inherent individualism of business contradict movement goals of achieving political and social change through collective action. In many instances, entrepreneurs failed to reconcile their individual ambitions and interests with their movements' collective objectives. Even some of the most ideologically committed activists found themselves motivated by the income, attention, and power they could accrue as individuals operating a business. Political and personal conflicts, burnout, career changes, and of course the failure to stay solvent destroyed countless activist businesses. The small number that endured for decades, however, showed that the fusion of political progress and financial survival is possible. Activist entrepreneurs never eliminated capitalism. But they have succeeded in demonstrating alternatives to the rapacious and exploitative approach to business that many conservatives champion as the natural form of economic activity.

Activist enterprises illuminate the path not taken by business leaders and policy makers who embraced neoliberal ideology and market fundamentalism. In 1970, the economist Milton Friedman ascended to the presidency of the influential Mont Pelerin Society and made the widely quoted claim that the "social responsibility of business is to increase its profits." Since the 1970s, numerous world leaders and state economists have enacted policies reflecting this view that businesses are economic actors with few obligations to workers and citizens and little need for regulation.[18] In sharp contrast to this rising tide of neoliberal thought, activist entrepreneurs have rejected the idea that unfettered markets, minimally regulated businesses, and corporate takeover of many of the state's social duties make for a better economy and society. Although neoliberalism has sought to make society more business oriented, activist entrepreneurs have sought to make business more socially oriented and attuned to social justice.

Despite long odds, a few activist entrepreneurs of the 1960s and 1970s continue to thrive today and have retained community involvement and progressive political action as central features of their operations. They include Yes! Organic Foods in Washington, D.C. (founded in 1970); the Sevananda Natural Foods Market co-op in Atlanta (founded in 1974); Marcus Books, whose Oakland branch, opened in 1976, is still operating; and the vegetarian feminist restaurant collective Bloodroot in Bridgeport, Connecticut (founded in 1977). Simply by surviving for four decades, these activist enterprises have achieved a legitimate form of business success. This is especially true in light of the fact that less than 25 percent of all small businesses survive for fifteen years or longer.[19]

Meanwhile, other entrepreneurs who worked with pioneering but defunct activist businesses have popularized some of the ideas they learned earlier in their careers. Most significantly, Paul Hawken, who helped transform Erewhon into a national leader in the organic food business, wrote some of the most influential books advocating environmentally sustainable business after he left the company. They include the best-selling works *The Next Economy* (1983), *The Ecology of Commerce* (1993), and *Natural Capitalism* (1999) as well as a popular television series aired on PBS in 1988. Similarly, Stewart Brand, the editor of *The Whole Earth Catalog* and cofounder of the Whole Earth Truck Store in Menlo Park, California, helped to launch the consulting firm Global Business Network in 1987. Although most activist enterprises did not survive the 1970s, many of their ideas did.[20]

Along these lines, a new generation of activist businesses that embrace leftist movement work has arisen as part of the so-called solidarity economy. Many of these businesses emerged in the early twenty-first century in conjunction with the rise of anti-globalization movements. Solidarity enterprises include worker cooperatives, community-development credit unions, consumer cooperatives, and fair-trade initiatives. According to one conservative estimate, nearly seven hundred solidarity businesses operated in the United States as of late 2016. "We do not need to wait for a revolution or for 'capitalism to hit the fan,'" one advocate of the solidarity economy insists. Solidarity businesses have instead already started to "build a coherent and powerful social movement for another economy . . . [and to] integrate economic alternatives into social movements and social movements into economic alternatives." Businesses such as the bookstore and café Red Emma's in Baltimore and Treasure City Thrift in Austin emphasize worker ownership, environmental sustainability, racial justice, close collaboration with social movements, and minimal hierarchy in the workplace. In so doing, they reflect the broader legacy of activist business as well as the more specific influence of anarchism, in particular the tradition of anarchist bookstores and political action centers known as "infoshops." Meanwhile, nonprofit organizations such as the Democracy Collaborative work closely with solidarity businesses as part of its larger mission of "building community wealth" and making local economies more inclusive through shared ownership and democratic workplaces. [21]

The emergence of "benefit corporations" represents another promising but less political development in socially oriented business. In 2010, Maryland became the first state to enact legislation recognizing this unconventional form of incorporation, and thirty more states have followed as of the summer of 2016. Conventional C-corporations are legally obligated by their charters to prioritize financial benefit to their stockholders above all else. By contrast, benefit corporations must demonstrate that they have a measurable positive social, environmental, or workplace impact. Benefit corporations are required by law to meet certain levels of public transparency—for instance, by issuing annual assessments of their positive public impact for a wide range of stakeholders, including workers and local communities. The nonprofit organization B-Lab has created a closely related certification program for "B-corporations"—akin to the LEED (Leadership in Energy and Environmental Design) certification program for energy-efficient building—that can demonstrate measurable positive public impact. As of May 2016, nearly nine hundred companies in the United States have completed their certification as B-corporations, and many of them have also incorporated as benefit corporations. Many are small businesses, but prominent examples of companies that are both B-corporations and benefit corporations include the baking-product company King Arthur Flour and the outdoor apparel and gear producer Patagonia. A similar development has been the emergence of low-profit limited-liability companies, or L3Cs. As of publication, eight states allow this form of incorporation in which companies are governed by the same federal tax laws as those that govern socially beneficial foundations.[22]

Independent businesses informed by progressive politics have also launched two new national organizations to promote their work: the American Independent Business Alliance (AMIBA), founded in Boulder, Colorado, in 1997, and the Business Alliance for Local Living Economies (BALLE), established in New York City in 2001. By emphasizing themes of community empowerment and social engagement that sound strikingly similar to the goals of activist businesses, these organizations contrast with the older and more conservative National Federation of Independent Businesses. BALLE seeks to promote "human-scale, interconnected local economies that function in harmony with local ecosystems to meet the basic needs of all people, support just and democratic societies, and foster joyful community life." The organization's founding members include Judy Wicks, a self-proclaimed "activist entrepreneur" who cofounded the nonprofit, antiwar Free People's Store in Philadelphia in 1970 that later became Urban Outfitters, and Laury Hammel, founder of the national organization Business for Social Responsibility. AMIBA similarly strives to "advance not solely economic democracy and entrepreneurship but to shift the balance of power between giant corporations and communities . . . [and] to stop corporate chains from driving out local businesses." The organization works with local governments and citizens to promote small retail as a form of community investment, an argument bolstered by its research showing that independent businesses return between 75 and 350 percent more revenue to local communities than do their chain competitors. In addition, AMIBA sponsors nearly seventy-five local independent business alliances across the country that coordinate "buy local" campaigns in their communities.[23] Although most of the businesses associated with AMIBA or BALLE promote progressive politics and community investment, they generally do so without participating directly in social movements.

These legacies of activist business force us to rethink the contours of America's capitalist economy in the neoliberal era. This is especially true as dominant interpretations of capitalism privilege large corporations and understand challenges to market norms—what popularly passes as "disruption" today—in terms of innovation and technological change, not political resistance or social experimentation. With their sustained emphasis on cooperation and collective ownership, activist businesses show that neoliberal economics, for all its power, has not conquered all. In so doing, they demonstrate that businesses are not limited to conventional forms of growth-oriented, profit-driven capitalism.

USES AND ABUSES OF ACTIVIST BUSINESS IDEALS

The emerging solidarity economy, benefit corporations, and organizations of progressive-minded independent businesses all reflect the influence of activist business. But activist entrepreneurs' most far-reaching legacy may be the language of liberation and social change they have bequeathed to contemporary companies, both big and small. Countless corporations have come to embrace activists' idea that business is a means to a better world, not an end unto itself. Yet many of these companies are unwilling to work in earnest for the goals of social justice and equality. The result is a depoliticized, opportunistic, and individualistic reinterpretation of the activist business vision. Such a change reflects the deep influence of neoliberal market fundamentalism. Like Whole Foods, most contemporary corporations believe their work empowers individual consumers to bring about social change in the marketplace, but these companies have little interest in collaborating with social movements to challenge and dismantle economic, racial, or gender power structures.

The term *social enterprise* represents a particularly popular appropriation of activist business ideals. In the late 1990s and early 2000s, the business scholar Greg Dees helped to popularize the term to describe companies whose central mission is not just to build wealth but also to "create and sustain social value." One of the most impressive social enterprises has been Nobel Peace Laureate Muhammad Yunus's microcredit initiative with Grameen Bank. Another key social enterprise is the Vermont-based company Ben & Jerry's Ice Cream, which offers its workers a living wage and has long partnered with environmental, antipoverty, and social justice organizations. Ben & Jerry's was also one of the first corporations to contract a third party to conduct annual assessments of its environmental and social impact.[24]

Yet for every honorable and effective social enterprise, just as many businesses have co-opted the concept to glorify even the most modest forms of corporate philanthropy. These businesses include massive for-profit multinational corporations such as Walmart and Citi-Bank as well as countless "greenwashing" companies that claim to provide a "green" product or service without making any real commitment to environmental sustainability. Indeed, companies have embraced social enterprise to justify virtually every form of business activity imaginable, regardless of their intended and measurable social impact. One writer for *Entrepreneur* magazine has dubiously claimed that "all entrepreneurship is 'social' entrepreneurship" because "all business helps provide a social good." Based on this all-encompassing definition, the writer holds up Uber as a social enterprise because it can "save a customer time" and Exxon as another because it is "among the largest sources of government tax revenue."[25]

The exploitation of activist businesses' ideals may be most evident in the technology sector centered in northern California's Silicon Valley. In the late 1960s, Stewart Brand and the Portola Institute's countercultural sourcebook *The Whole Earth Catalog* anticipated the World Wide Web and forged a virtual network of commune residents across the United States by pointing readers to a vast array of mail-order suppliers' products for back-to-the-land living. Brand and his colleagues popularized what one scholar has described as "a free-wheeling, interdisciplinary, and highly entrepreneurial style of work" as part of a vision of "bohemian technocracy" that has influenced tech entrepreneurs ever since. Brand also cofounded the Whole Earth 'Lectronic Link (abbreviated WELL) in 1985, one of the earliest influential online communities. This connection between tech and activist businesses goes far beyond hippies who were skilled with computers. Tech companies have enthusiastically adopted the language of activist businesses as they proudly declare their efforts to build a kinder, gentler capitalism and a more flexible workplace culture. A wide variety of tech business trends draw on activist businesses' rhetoric of democracy, transparency, and cooperation, from "bossless offices" to the "sharing economy" to open office floor plans. Tech leaders' embrace of New Age spirituality and meditation as well as the surprisingly common view of technology work as a sacred undertaking are all legacies of activist entrepreneurs' fascination with Asian religions and especially the Buddhist idea of "right livelihood."[26]

Perhaps no tech company has embraced the language and imagery of activist business more than Apple. In the 1970s, Apple cofounder Steve Jobs absorbed many of the same notions of liberated, countercultural business that inspired natural foods stores and head shops. As a teenager and young adult, Jobs avidly smoked marijuana and took LSD, embraced vegetarianism, shopped at food co-ops, started following Zen Buddhism, and decorated his own personal meditation room with head shop staples such as Indian prints, candles, and incense. Among Jobs's favorite books was Baba Ram Dass's *Be Here Now* (1971), one of the earliest American writings to advocate "right livelihood." Years later Jobs described his own business philosophy in terms that were strikingly similar to the humanistic, ethical vision of Buddhist economics endorsed by Ram Dass and E. F. Schumacher and embraced by activist businesses: "creating great things instead of making money, [and] putting things back into the stream of history and of human consciousness as much as I could."[27]

Jobs also eagerly incorporated leftist iconography into Apple's marketing when it served the company's purposes. Shortly after rejoining the company in 1997, he worked closely with an advertising agency to develop Think Different, a print and television campaign that celebrated a series of the "crazy ones, the misfits, the rebels . . . [who] push the human race forward." Among the figures the ads featured were Mahatma Gandhi, Martin Luther King Jr., and César Chavez. Although left unstated, the ads' message was clear: like the social movement leaders whom Think Different championed, Apple purported to play a decisive role in bringing freedom, democracy, and social justice to the world.[28]

Yet, like Whole Foods and many other self-styled conscious capitalists, Apple and other companies in Silicon Valley have shown little interest in working toward substantive political and social change. Under Jobs's leadership, Apple was notorious for its virtually nonexistent record of philanthropic giving, leading one writer for Stanford University's Center for Social Innovation to suggest the company was among "America's least philanthropic companies." Tech companies' founders have traditionally shown much less interest in political engagement than leaders in other major industries. Those who have taken an interest in politics, such as Peter Thiel, often advance a libertarian ideology like that of Whole Foods' cofounder John Mackey and strongly criticize government regulation of business. An abiding faith in technology's power to solve social problems verging on utopianism underlies many tech companies' claims of producing change, and technological advances are frequently treated as their owns forms of political and cultural progress. Facebook founder Mark Zuckerberg, for instance, proudly declared to investors in 2012 that his company's social media platform created "a more open and connected world … with more authentic businesses" that could "bring a more honest and transparent dialogue around government that could lead to more direct empowerment of people." The Burning Man festival, long celebrated by tech companies, exemplifies this utopian vision of liberation by celebrating shared participation, technology, and a cashless sharing economy. Critics meanwhile contend that Burning Man offers an escapist and libertarian vision devoid of any meaningful effort to question capitalism or build enduring forms of equality, democracy, and inclusion.[29]

In the prevailing corporate culture of the twenty-first century, the rhetoric of activist business has become largely divorced from its political origins and reduced to advances in individual freedom, self-therapy, and wellness. Activist entrepreneurs in the 1960s and 1970s, by contrast, conceived their enterprises as part of a larger leftist critique of American society and politics. Tech leaders have adopted activist businesses' language of change and liberation for their own purposes, but they remain largely indifferent toward direct political engagement due to their mistaken belief that their products and workplace culture produce meaningful social and political progress.

Finally, activist businesses have suffered in large part due to broad declines in Americans' political participation, community engagement, and social connectedness in the past fifty years. Americans have become more individualistic, and activist businesses have as well.[30] Amid this shift, social enterprises and tech companies that have adopted the language of activist enterprise have found great financial success in dressing up individual buying decisions as acts of social and political change. More than ever before, corporate businesses deploy messages of activism and consciousness to serve their own narrow financial interests.

Conclusion

Despite its many misappropriations of activist enterprise, America's business culture in the twenty-first century is more inclusive than the Consumers' Republic of the mid–twentieth century in several key regards. Through the hard work of advocacy and operating their own companies, activist entrepreneurs proved that business was not the sole preserve of straight white men. Activist businesses have helped to make the country's business culture more pluralistic in terms of race, gender, sexuality, and lifestyle. They have long welcomed and often been operated by women, people of color, and queer people. Major corporations have taken notice, and, today, retailers pay much more careful attention to the millions of Americans whom they overlooked, ignored, and demeaned in the middle of the twentieth century. The white, male-led, middle-income family is no longer retailers' only target consumer. Although American corporations have fallen far short of eliminating inequality in their operations, they have made measurable gains in diversifying their staff, management, and advertising since the 1960s, particularly in the areas of racial and gender representation.[1]

Activist businesses have also played a critical supporting role in advancing the goals and spreading the messages of their movements. Black nationalism, feminism, environmentalism, and the drug legalization movement were buoyed by activist entrepreneurs who worked hard to promote their causes to the wider public. Books written by African Americans are now quite easy to find; pesticide-free and vegetarian food is widely available; feminist texts such as *Our Bodies, Our Selves* have sold in the millions; and nearly twenty states have removed criminal penalties for marijuana possession. These results are all forms of political progress that activist businesses helped to bring about through years of hard work in the marketplace of ideas. Activist businesses achieved these gains by popularizing and disseminating niche, political products that were hard to find in the 1960s and 1970s, in turn paving the way for larger, more conventional retailers to pick up those items in later decades. Although some may see these changes as a form of co-optation, the diffusion of these products and ideas instead represent a victory for marginal activist businesses over the economy of the middle.

Yet activist businesses of the 1960s and 1970s have also become victims of their own success. As their products have spread to conventional retailers, they have struggled to stay relevant and attractive to customers, even those who are sympathetic to their politics. Although many consumers may still identify these products with progressive politics or social movements, most of the corporations that sell them have little interest in activist businesses' political goals. Countless businesses gesture toward equality and the goals of social justice, but few establish meaningful structures of shared ownership and participatory management. Many contemporary entrepreneurs who champion small businesses as community spaces are more interested in attracting an affluent customer base than in creating political change, and their businesses are often economically and culturally inaccessible to lower-income consumers. Today, few customers are willing to track down an independent natural foods store when they can get tofu and organic produce at most grocery chains. Nor are many willing to locate a black-owned bookstore to find a black-authored book or a feminist bookstore for a book on feminism when either can be bought more easily and less expensively at chains or online. Similarly, feminist credit unions declined and eventually closed as gender-based credit discrimination became much less common by the 1990s.[2] Even if consumers are enthusiastic about the products that were once activist entrepreneurs' stock in trade, they now seem largely indifferent about what kind of companies they purchase them from.

In short, activist businesses' products have prospered much more than their processes and places.

Activist storefronts have also lost much of their currency as the Internet has increasingly become a home for political organizing and retail. Both activism and commerce depend much less on face-to-face interactions than they did just twenty years ago. Although the growth of competing brick-and-mortar chain stores undermined independent retailers in the 1980s and early 1990s, the rise of Internet retailers emerged as an even greater threat in the late 1990s. These changes hit black-owned bookstores and feminist businesses particularly hard. As Internet retailers drove many independent storefronts out of business, they severely curtailed shoppers' opportunities for browsing, seeking advice from knowledgeable clerks, and interacting with like-minded customers. And it remains to be seen whether any online platform can actually replace the hard work of face-to-face organizing that occurs in the protests, demonstrations, and meetings that grow out of activist storefronts' free spaces.[3] As organizing and retail continue to shift from physical to virtual spaces, activist entrepreneurs face unprecedented challenges in maintaining the free spaces that they have long depended on to attract customers and comrades.

Even as more and more Americans question how traditional forms of corporate capitalism serve the country's common good, independent businesses that advance progressive political action, democratize their workplaces, and welcome a diverse range of consumers remain rare. Many independent businesses do make positive contributions to their communities, but the alternative they offer to chain retail does not in and of itself represent meaningful political or social progress. The new freedoms of the twenty-first-century workplace—more flexible hours, telecommuting, relaxed norms for interpersonal office relations and workplace dress—accrue predominantly to the salaried workforce in financial, technical, and professional services, not to hourly wage earners in retail or other low-paying sectors.[4] The current impulse to reflexively champion small business is not a meaningful counter to corporate power. Neither are attempts at "green business," "social entrepreneurship," or "buying local" if they fail to make political demands for structural change. The businesses most effective at counterbalancing concentrated corporate power are still those that seek to advance collective political transformation in conjunction with organized social movements.

Yet the worker-owned businesses, collectives, and stores aligned with social movements are often the hardest to keep alive. They are difficult to staff, demand a high level of ethics and dedication from their workers, and are challenging to sustain financially. Democracy requires tremendous work, in both the political realm and the economic realm. In addition to these challenges, competition from chains since the 1980s and the generally high failure rate of small businesses of all kinds—not just of activist businesses—combine to explain the low survival rate of activist enterprises.

Activist entrepreneurs have rejected the idea that survival without significant financial growth is a form of business failure. Some might argue that if a company such as Whole Foods Market wanted to prosper, it had no choice but to renounce the activist leanings and skepticism of corporate power it originally articulated as SaferWay. A similar argument would be that Whole Foods owes its very success to its willingness to take over its competitors, relentlessly expand, and forgo its original ideals. Such arguments rest on the idea that a business must net millions in profits and gain significant market share in order to truly succeed. Yet as activist entrepreneurs have shown, business success has no fixed meaning in America's economy. Numerous cooperatives, collectives, and other activist businesses have managed to survive while staying true to their radical origins, sometimes even for decades.

Activist businesses of the 1960s and 1970s certainly did not dislodge capitalism or systematically reform it, as their owners might once have hoped. Powerful corporations eventually understood the challenge posed by businesses aligned with social movements. They responded by skillfully diffusing the threat of activist businesses—not by attacking them but by co-opting their popular products and successful management strategies while dispensing with their radical politics. Corporate proponents of neoliberal capitalism have been quite agile in disabling challenges to their existence. But activist businesses' continued existence demonstrates that companies can survive with different financial goals and different approaches to management than those promoted by corporations intent on maximizing profits above all else.

Activist businesses have created political and social change, but on a modest scale. Systematic change has proven elusive for them. They have not defeated white supremacy, patriarchy, homophobia, a repressive war on drugs, or environmental degradation. But they have given consumers meaningful alternatives to capitalism's most exploitative forms and have provided options for investing in enterprises that work against those forces. Moreover, activist entrepreneurs have not surrendered in their quest to create alternatives to the profits-at-all-costs model of corporate capitalism that so many people wrongly believe is our only option for economic activity. Half a century after the 1960s, activists from multiple generations continue to struggle in the face of ever-growing corporate power to sustain businesses that are more inclusive, more democratic, and more just.

Notes

INTRODUCTION

1. *Psychedelic Generation Gap*, KRON-TV, c. 1967, San Francisco Bay Area Television Archive, https://diva.sfsu.edu/collections/sfbatv/bundles/189594; Jay Thelin, interviewed by the author, Skype, September 11, 2014; Allen Cohen, *The San Francisco Oracle, Facsimile Edition: The Psychedelic Newspaper of the Haight-Ashbury* (Berkeley, Calif.: Regent Press, 1991), xxv; "A Prophesy of a Declaration of Independence," *San Francisco Oracle*, September 20, 1966, 12; Charles Perry, *The Haight-Ashbury: A History* (New York: Rolling Stone Press, 1984), 97; Martin A. Lee and Bruce Shlain, *Acid Dreams: The Complete Social History of LSD: The CIA, the Sixties, and Beyond* (New York: Grove Press, 1992), 149.

2. Joe Elam, "Drum and Spear: When the Smoke Cleared on 14th St., a Bookstore Came," *Washington Afro American*, February 15, 1969.

3. Kirsten Grimstad and Susan Rennie, eds., *The New Woman's Survival Catalog: A Woman-Made Book* (New York: Coward, McCann & Geoghegan, 1973), 9; "Est. Your Printshop," p. 2, Diana Press Records, Collection 2135, Box 13, Folder 10, University of California at Los Angeles Library Special Collections; *Diana Press*, catalog, c. 1978, Atlanta Lesbian Feminist Alliance Collection, Box 11, Folder 24, Sallie Bingham Center for Women's History and Culture, Duke University, Durham, N.C.

4. Sam Gwynne, "Born Green: Behind Whole Foods Empire Is a Texan Tale of Gastronomic Gumption," *Saveur*, May 26, 2009, 27–28; John Mackey, "Introduction: Awakenings," in John Mackey and Raj Sisodia, *Conscious Capitalism: Liberating the Heroic Spirit of Business* (Boston: Harvard Business Review Press, 2013), 2–4; John Mackey, "The Accidental Grocer," *The Whole Story: A Marketplace of Ideas*, September–October 1989, 7.

5. Francesca Polletta, *Freedom Is an Endless Meeting: Democracy in American Social Movements* (Chicago: University of Chicago Press, 2002); James Miller, *Democracy Is*

in the Streets: From Port Huron to the Siege of Chicago (New York: Simon and Schuster, 1987), 141–156; Richard Flacks and Nelson Lichtenstein, eds., *The Port Huron Statement: Sources and Legacies of the New Left's Founding Manifesto* (Philadelphia: University of Pennsylvania Press, 2015); Doug Rossinow, *The Politics of Authenticity: Liberalism, Christianity, and the New Left in America* (New York: Columbia University Press, 1998), 10–11, 17–18. The term *entrepreneurs* was relatively uncommon in the 1960s and 1970s compared to the late twentieth and early twenty-first centuries, as demonstrated by database searches of *Harvard Business Review*, the *Wall Street Journal*, and Google Ngram Viewer.

6. Van Gosse, "A Movement of Movements: The Definition and Periodization of the New Left," in *A Companion to Post-1945 America*, ed. Roy Rosenzweig and Jean-Christophe Agnew (London: Blackwell, 2002), 277–302. On the counterculture as a New Left social movement, see Van Gosse, *Rethinking the New Left: An Interpretive History* (New York: Palgrave Macmillan, 2005), 201–208; Terry H. Anderson, *The Movement and the Sixties* (New York: Oxford University Press, 1995), 241–291; and Rossinow, *Politics of Authenticity*, 16, 247–295.

7. See, for instance, Anderson, *The Movement and the Sixties*, 257; Theodore Roszak, *The Making of a Counter Culture: Reflections on the Technocratic Society and Its Youthful Opposition* (Garden City, N.Y.: Anchor Books, 1969), 16; Charles Reich, *The Greening of America* (New York: Random House, 1970), 257; Todd Gitlin, *The Sixties: Years of Hope, Days of Rage* (New York: Bantam Books, 1987), 421; Rossinow, *Politics of Authenticity*, 252.

8. On the counterculture and the New Left as separate phenomena, see Maurice Isserman and Michael Kazin, *America Divided: The Civil War of the 1960s*, 4th ed. (New York: Oxford University Press, 2012), 138–178; Gitlin, *The Sixties,* 427; Timothy Miller, *The Hippies and American Values* (Knoxville: University of Tennessee Press, 1991), xix–xx; Fred Turner, *From Counterculture to Cyberculture: Stewart Brand, the Whole Earth Network, and the Rise of Digital Utopianism* (Chicago: University of Chicago Press, 2006), 4–5, 31–32. On business and conservatism, see Bethany Moreton, *To Serve God and Wal-Mart: The Making of Christian Free Enterprise* (Cambridge, Mass.: Harvard University Press, 2009); Kevin Kruse, *One Nation Under God: How Corporate America Invented Christian America* (New York: Basic Books, 2015); Benjamin Waterhouse, *Lobbying America: The Politics of Business from Nixon to NAFTA* (Princeton, N.J.: Princeton University Press, 2014); Kim Phillips-Fein, *Invisible Hands: The Making of the Conservative Movement from the New Deal to Reagan* (New York: Norton, 2009); Kim Phillips-Fein and Julian E. Zelizer, "Introduction: What's Good for Business?" in *What's Good for Business: Business and American Politics Since World War II*, ed. Kim Phillips-Fein and Julian E. Zelizer (Oxford: Oxford University Press, 2012), 3–15.

9. Paul Dean, "Flat and Egalitarian? Evaluating Worker Hierarchies in Software Companies," M.A. thesis, University of Maryland, College Park, 2007; Michelle Goldberg, "The Long Marriage of Mindfulness and Money," *New Yorker*, April 18, 2015, http://www.newyorker.com/business/currency/the-long-marriage-of-mindfulness-and-money.

10. Other works that focus on countercultural and activist businesses in this era include Michael Kramer, *Republic of Rock: Music and Citizenship in the Sixties Counterculture* (Oxford: Oxford University Press, 2013); Junko R. Onosaka, *Feminist Revolution in*

Literacy: Women's Bookstores in the United States (New York: Routledge, 2006); Kristen Hogan, *The Feminist Bookstore Movement: Lesbian Antiracism and Feminist Accountability* (Durham, N.C.: Duke University Press, 2016); Craig Cox, *Storefront Revolution: Food Co-ops and the Counterculture* (New Brunswick, N.J.: Rutgers University Press, 1994); Anne Enke, *Finding the Movement: Sexuality, Contested Space, and Feminist Activism* (Durham, N.C.: Duke University Press, 2007); Susan Krieger, *Hip Capitalism* (Beverly Hills, Calif.: Sage, 1979); Amy L. Scott, "Remaking Urban in the American West: Lifestyle Politics, Micropolitan Urbanism, and Hip Capitalism in Boulder, Colorado, 1958–1978," Ph.D. diss., University of New Mexico, 2007; Michael Doyle, *Radical Chapters: Pacifist Bookseller Roy Kepler and the Paperback Revolution* (Syracuse, N.Y.: Syracuse University Press, 2012). Figures on the number of activist businesses compiled by the author and discussed further in chapters 2–6 and the conclusion.

11. Marc Simon Rodriguez, *Rethinking the Chicano Movement* (New York: Routledge, 2014), 64–65; "Amerasia Bookstore," in *Japanese American History: An A-to-Z Reference from 1868 to the Present*, ed. Brian Niiya (New York: Facts on File, 1993), 100; Christopher Adam Mitchell, "The Transformation of Gay Life from the Closet to Liberation, 1948–1980: New York City's Gay Markets as a Study in Late Capitalism," Ph.D. diss., Rutgers University, 2015; Helene Slessarev-Jamir, *Prophetic Activism: Progressive Religious Justice Movements in Contemporary America* (New York: New York University Press, 2011), 105–106; Mary A. Littrell and Marsha A. Dickson, *Social Responsibility in the Global Market: Fair Trade of Cultural Products* (Thousand Oaks, Calif.: Sage, 1999), 61–88; William Sturkey, "Crafts of Freedom: The Poor People's Corporation and Working-Class Activism for Black Power," *Journal of Mississippi History* 74, no. 1 (2012): 25–60; Jack Barnes, *The Changing Face of U.S. Politics: Working-Class Politics and the Trade Unions* (New York: Pathfinder, 1994), 354–355.

1. ACTIVIST BUSINESS

1. Regina Lee Blaszczyk, *American Consumer Society, 1865–2005: From Hearth to HDTV* (Wheeling, Ill.: Harlan Davidson, 2009), 180–182; Lawrence R. Samuel, *Brought to You By: Postwar Television Advertising and the American Dream* (Austin: University of Texas Press, 2001), xiv–xvi; Lizabeth Cohen, *A Consumers' Republic: The Politics of Mass Consumption in Postwar America* (New York: Vintage Books, 2003), 302, 257–290; *1971 Business Statistics—18th Biennial Edition* (Washington, D.C.: U.S. Department of Commerce, 1971), 55, 58–59, 64.

2. Cohen, *Consumers' Republic*, 13; Stanley Buder, *Capitalizing on Change: A Social History of American Business* (Chapel Hill: University of North Carolina Press, 2009), 421–423; John Kenneth Galbraith, *The New Industrial State* (Boston: Houghton Mifflin, 1967); Lawrence Glickman, *Buying Power: A History of Consumer Activism in America* (Chicago: University of Chicago Press, 2009), 189–254. See also Charles S. Maier, "The Politics of Productivity: Foundations of American International Economic Policy After World War II," in *Between Power and Plenty: Foreign Economic Policies of Advanced Industrial States*, ed. Peter J. Katzenstein (Madison: University of Wisconsin Press, 1977), 23–49.

3. Sloan Wilson, *The Man in the Gray Flannel Suit* (New York: Simon and Schuster, 1955); William Hollingsworth Whyte, *The Organization Man* (New York: Simon and

Schuster, 1956); Vance Packard, *The Hidden Persuaders* (New York: McKay, 1957); Karl Marx, "Estranged Labor," in *Economic and Philosophic Manuscripts of 1844* (New York: International, 1964), 106–119. On the publication history of *Economic and Philosophic Manuscripts of 1844*, see Gary Tedman, "Marx's 1844 Manuscripts as a Work of Art: A Hypertextual Reinterpretation," *Rethinking Marxism* 16, no. 4 (2004): 427–428.

4. C. Wright Mills, *White Collar: The American Middle Classes* (New York: Oxford University Press, 1951), 283; Herbert Marcuse, *One-Dimensional Man: Studies in the Ideology of Advanced Industrial Society* (1964; reprint, Boston: Beacon Press, 1991), 8.

5. Paul Goodman, *Growing Up Absurd: Problems of Youth in the Organized System* (1956; reprint, New York: Random House, 1960); Murray Bookchin, *Our Synthetic Environment* (New York: Knopf, 1962); E. Franklin Frazier, *Black Bourgeoisie* (Glencoe, Ill.: Free Press, 1957); Betty Friedan, *The Feminine Mystique* (1963; reprint, New York: Norton, 1997), 245, 270.

6. Scott Ward and Greg Reale, *Student Attitudes Toward Business and Marketing Institutions and Practices*, working paper (Cambridge, Mass.: Marketing Science Institute, 1972), 3; *Youth in Turmoil: Adapted from a Special Issue of* Fortune (New York: Time-Life Books, 1969), back cover, 8, 11–12, 17–19, 29–30.

7. Joshua Clark Davis, "For the Records: How African American Consumers and Music Retailers Created Commercial Public Space in the 1960s and 1970s South," *Southern Cultures*, Winter 2011, 81–82; Paul Kramer, "White Sales: The Racial Politics of Baltimore's Jewish-Owned Department Stores, 1935–1965," *Enterprising Emporiums: The Jewish Department Stores of Downtown Baltimore* (Baltimore: Jewish Museum of Maryland, 2001), 37–65; Shaun L. Gabbidon, "Racial Profiling by Store Clerks and Security Personnel in Retail Establishments: An Exploration of 'Shopping While Black,'" *Journal of Contemporary Criminal Justice* 19, no. 3 (2003): 353–356.

    On advertising, see Marilyn Kern-Foxworth, *Aunt Jemima, Uncle Ben, and Rastus: Blacks in Advertising, Yesterday, Today, and Tomorrow* (Westport, Conn.: Greenwood Press, 1994), xvii–xx, 115–118; Carol M. Motley, Geraldine R. Henderson, and Stacey Menzel Baker, "Exploring Collective Memories Associated with African-American Advertising Memorabilia—the Good, the Bad, and the Ugly," *Journal of Advertising* 32, no. 1 (2003): 47–57; Elspeth H. Brown, "Black Models and the Invention of the U.S. Negro Market," in *Inside Marketing: Practices, Ideologies, Devices*, ed. Detlev Zwick and Julien Cayla (Oxford: Oxford University Press, 2011), 189–194; Don Lee, *From Plan to Planet—Life Studies: The Need for Afrikan Minds and Institutions* (Detroit: Broadside Press, 1973), 95.

8. Louis Hyman, *Debtor Nation: The History of America in Red Ink* (Princeton, N.J.: Princeton University Press, 2011), 192–202; Steven Lysonski and Richard W. Pollay, "Advertising Sexism Is Forgiven, but Not Forgotten: Historical, Cross-Cultural, and Individual Differences in Criticism and Purchase Boycott Intentions," *International Journal of Advertising* 9, no. 4 (1990): 318–319; Katherine J. Parkin, *Food Is Love: Food Advertising and Gender Roles in Modern America* (Philadelphia: University of Pennsylvania Press, 2006); Daniel Delis Hill, *Advertising to the American Woman, 1900–1999* (Columbus: Ohio State University Press, 2002); Friedan, *Feminine Mystique*, 270; Katherine Sender, *Business, Not Politics: The Making of the Gay Market* (New York: Columbia University Press, 2004), 24–28; Arlene Dávila, *Latinos, Inc.: The Marketing and Making of a People* (Berkeley: University of California Press, 2012),

24–26; Minjeong Kim and Angie Y. Chung, "Consuming Orientalism: Images of Asian/American Women in Multicultural Advertising," *Qualitative Sociology* 28, no. 1 (2005): 73–75; Stephanie Molholt, "A Buck Well Spent: Representations of American Indians in Print Advertising Since 1890," Ph.D. diss., Arizona State University, 2008; Lori Rotskoff, *Love on the Rocks: Men, Women, and Alcohol in Post–World War II America* (Chapel Hill: University of North Carolina Press, 2002,) 202–204; Allan M. Brandt, *The Cigarette Century: The Rise, Fall, and Deadly Persistence of the Product That Defined America* (New York: Basic Books, 2007), 105–106, 167–210; Warren James Belasco, *Appetite for Change: How the Counterculture Took on the Food Industry* (Ithaca, N.Y.: Cornell University Press, 2007), 113–115, 127–131; *Small Business Reporter—Health Food Stores* (San Francisco: Bank of America, 1973), 1; "For the People—Nutrition, a Final Revolution," *East–West Journal*, March 31, 1972, 7.

9. Charles Reich, *The Greening of America* (New York: Random House, 1970), 221; see also Timothy Miller, *The Hippies and American Values* (Knoxville: University of Tennessee Press, 1991), 102.

10. Van Gosse, *Rethinking the New Left: An Interpretive History* (New York: Palgrave Macmillan, 2005), 1–8, 200–201.

11. Kirkpatrick Sale, *SDS: The Rise and Development of the Students for a Democratic Society* (New York: Random House, 1973), 69; Students for a Democratic Society, *The Port Huron Statement*, drafted 1962 (New York: Students for a Democratic Society, 1964), 15, 8; James Miller, *Democracy Is in the Streets: From Port Huron to the Siege of Chicago* (New York: Simon and Schuster, 1987), 332–334, 78–79, 84–85. See also Richard Flacks and Nelson Lichtenstein, eds., *The Port Huron Statement: Sources and Legacies of the New Left's Founding Manifesto* (Philadelphia: University of Pennsylvania, 2015).

12. Carol Hanisch, "The Personal Is Political," in *Notes from the Second Year: Women's Liberation, Major Writings of the Radical Feminists* (New York: Radical Feminism, 1970); Wini Breines, *Community and Organization in the New Left: 1962–1968* (New York: Praeger, 1982), 15; Howard Brick, *Transcending Capitalism: Visions of a New Society in Modern American Thought* (Ithaca, N.Y.: Cornell University Press, 2006), 202–212; Maurice Isserman, *If I Had a Hammer: The Death of the Old Left and the Birth of the New Left* (New York: Basic Books, 1987).

13. "No More Miss America!" (August 1968), reprinted in *Sisterhood Is Powerful: An Anthology of Writings from the Women's Liberation Movement*, ed. Robin Morgan (New York: Random House, 1970), 521–524; William Cronon, "*Silent Spring* and the Birth of Modern Environmentalism," in *DDT, Silent Spring, and the Rise of Modern Environmentalism: Classic Texts*, ed. Thomas R. Dunlop (Seattle: University of Washington Press, 2015), ix–xii; Leonard Silk and David Vogel, *Ethics and Profits: The Crisis of Confidence in American Business* (New York: Simon and Schuster, 1976), 7.

14. Andrew Cornell, *Unruly Equality: U.S. Anarchism in the Twentieth Century* (Berkeley: University of California Press, 2016), 1–2, 242, 256, 276–277.

15. On countercultural institution building through business, see David Farber, "Building the Counterculture: The Counterculture at Work," *The Sixties* 6, no. 1 (2013): 1–24; Fred Turner, *From Counterculture to Cyberculture: Stewart Brand, the Whole Earth Network, and the Rise of Digital Utopianism* (Chicago: University of Chicago Press, 2006); John McMillian, *Smoking Typewriters: The Sixties Underground Press and the Rise of Alternative Media in America* (Oxford: Oxford University Press, 2011); Andrew Kirk, *Counterculture Green: The Whole Earth Catalog and American*

Environmentalism (Lawrence: University of Kansas Press, 2007); Michael Kramer, *Republic of Rock: Music and Citizenship in the Sixties Counterculture* (Oxford: Oxford University Press, 2013); Belasco, *Appetite for Change*; Sam Binkley, *Getting Loose: Lifestyle Consumption in the 1970s* (Durham, N.C.: Duke University Press, 2007).

16. On Christianity and corporatism, see Bethany Moreton, *To Serve God and Wal-Mart: The Making of Christian Free Enterprise* (Cambridge, Mass.: Harvard University Press, 2009), and Kevin Kruse, *One Nation Under God: How Corporate America Invented Christian America* (New York: Basic Books, 2015).

17. Michael Bennett, *Democratic Discourses: The Radical Abolition Movement and Antebellum American Literature* (New Brunswick, N.J.: Rutgers University Press, 2005), 18–54; Lawrence Glickman, "'Buy for the Sake of the Slave': Abolitionism and the Origins of American Consumer Activism," *American Quarterly* 56, no. 4 (2004): 889–912; John Curl, *For All the People: Uncovering the Hidden History of Co-operation, Cooperative Movements, and Communalism in America* (Oakland, Calif.: PM Books, 2009), 37, 90–102, 111–114, 164–191; Matthew Hild, *Greenbackers, Knights of Labor, and Populists: Farmer–Labor Insurgency in the Late-Nineteenth-Century South* (Athens: University of Georgia Press, 2010), 16, 61, 207; Dana Frank, *Purchasing Power: Consumer Organizing, Gender, and the Seattle Labor Movement, 1919–1929* (Cambridge: Cambridge University Press, 1994), 40–65; Florence E. Parker, "Labor Unions and Nonfarm Cooperatives," *Monthly Labor Review*, October 1948, 389–390; Margaret Mary Finnegan, *Selling Suffrage: Consumer Culture & Votes for Women* (New York: Columbia University Press, 1999), 2, 123–124, 199 n. 39; Colin Grant, *Negro with a Hat: The Rise and Fall of Marcus Garvey* (Oxford: Oxford University Press, 2008), 137–156; Jessica Nembhard, *Collective Courage: A History of African American Cooperative Economic Thought and Practice* (University Park: Pennsylvania State University Press, 2014); Stephen J. Stein, *The Shaker Experience in America: A History of the United Society of Believers* (New Haven, Conn.: Yale University Press, 1992), 134–142, 269–281; Edward E. Curtis, *Black Muslim Religion in the Nation of Islam, 1960–1975* (Chapel Hill: University of North Carolina Press, 2006), 41–43, 106–110.

18. Karl Marx, "Inaugural Address of the Working Men's International Association" (October 21–27, 1864), in *Karl Marx, Friedrich Engels: Collected Works*, vol. 20 (New York: International, 1985), 11; Bruno Jossa, "Marx, Marxism, and the Cooperative Movement," *Cambridge Journal of Economics* 29, no. 1 (2005): 3–18; V. I. Lenin, "On Cooperation" (January 4–6, 1923), in *Collected Works*, vol. 33, 2nd English ed. (Moscow: Progress, 1965), 467–471; Natalya Chernyshova, *Soviet Consumer Culture in the Brezhnev Era* (New York: Routledge, 2013); Judd Stitziel, *Fashioning Socialism: Clothing, Politics, and Consumer Culture in East Germany* (Oxford: Berg, 2005); Dorothy J. Solinger, "The Private Sector: The Regulation of Small Rural Traders," in *Chinese Business Under Socialism: The Politics of Domestic Commerce, 1949–1980* (Berkeley: University of California Press, 1987), 157–205.

On Marxist small businesses, see "How to Start a Socialist Bookshop," *International Socialist Review*, April 1910, 954; David A. Lincove, "Publishing to 'Reach the Million Masses': Alexander L. Trachtenberg and International Publishers, 1906–1966," *Left History* 10, no. 1 (2004): 97, 120 n. 55; Ellen Graff, *Stepping Left: Dance and Politics in New York City, 1928–1942* (Durham, N.C.: Duke University Press, 1997), 5–6; Robert Minor, "A Yankee Convention," *Liberator*, April 1920, 28.

19. Daniel Gross, "Capitalism Is Saving the Climate, You Hippies," *Daily Beast*, October 24, 2014, http://www.thedailybeast.com/articles/2014/09/24/capitalism-is-saving

-the-climate-you-hippies.html; "Anti-capitalist Protestors Occupy Wrong Building," *Spectator*, March 16, 2015, http://blogs.new.spectator.co.uk/2015/03/anti-capitalist-protesters-occupy-wrong-building/; Lincoln Mitchell, "Occupy Wall Street and the Dirty Hippie Narrative," *Huffington Post*, November 1, 2011, http://www.huffington post.com/lincoln-mitchell/occupy-wall-street-and-th_b_1069490.html.

On the counterculture, New Left, and business, see Doug Rossinow, *The Politics of Authenticity Liberalism, Christianity, and the New Left in America* (New York: Columbia University Press, 1998), 252; Terry H. Anderson, *The Movement and the Sixties* (New York: Oxford University Press, 1995), 257; Todd Gitlin, *The Sixties: Years of Hope, Days of Rage* (New York: Bantam Books, 1987), 421; Theodore Roszak, *The Making of a Counter Culture: Reflections on the Technocratic Society and Its Youthful Opposition* (Garden City, N.Y.: Anchor Books, 1969), 16; Reich, *The Greening of America*, 257; Thomas Frank, *Conquest of Cool: Business Culture, Counter Culture, and the Rise of Hip Consumerism* (Chicago: University of Chicago Press, 1997); Binkley, *Getting Loose*; Turner, *From Counterculture to Cyberculture*; Joseph Heath and Andrew Potter, *Nation of Rebels: Why Counterculture Became Consumer Culture* (Toronto: Collins, 2005); Art Kleiner, *The Age of Heretics: Heroes, Outlaws, and the Forerunners of Corporate Change* (New York: Doubleday, 1996); Louis Hyman, *Borrow: The America Way of Debt* (New York: Vintage Books, 2012), 135–137.

20. Frank, *Conquest of Cool*; Paul White, "Time Has Come," *Big US*, October 28, 1969, 7; Ralph J. Gleason, "Columbia Records . . . Home of the Revolution," *Dallas Notes*, January 8–21, 1969, 13.

21. "Note on Import Export," in *Drum and Spear Bookstore* (catalog 3) (Washington, D.C.: Drum and Spear, 1971), 1; Paul Hawken, "Developing a Conspicuous Alternative," *East–West Journal*, October 30, 1972, 6; Kirsten Grimstad and Susan Rennie, eds., *The New Woman's Survival Catalog: A Woman-Made Book* (New York: Coward, McCann & Geoghegan, 1973), 182.

22. Sara Evans and Harry Boyte, *Free Spaces: The Sources of Democratic Change in America* (Chicago: University of Chicago Press, 1992); Francesca Polletta, "'Free Spaces' in Collective Action," *Theory and Society* 28 (1999): 1–8; Darcy K. Leach, "Scenes and Social Movements," in *Culture, Social Movements, and Protest*, ed. Hank Johnston (Aldershot, U.K.: Ashgate, 2009), 255–261.

23. Beverly Buthwoman, FFCU Lansing office, memo, June 14, 1975, 1, Feminist Federal Credit Union Papers, MSS 251, Box 1, Folder 1, Special Collections Manuscripts and Archives, Michigan State University, Ann Arbor; Judy Richardson, interviewed by the author, Skype, October 11, 2012, digital recording; "Life in a Hash Pipe Factory," *Rags*, September 1970, 26.

24. On "movement culture," see Verta Taylor and Nancy Whittier, "Analytical Approaches to Social Movement Culture: The Culture of the Women's Movement," in *Social Movements and Culture*, ed. Hank Johnston and Bert Klandermans (Minneapolis: University of Minnesota Press, 1995), 163–187, and Doug McAdam, "Culture and Social Movements," in *New Social Movements: From Ideology to Identity*, ed. Enrique Laraña, Hank Johnston, and Joseph R. Gusfield (Philadelphia: Temple University Press, 1994), 37–57. On activists' challenges in finding work and enduring harassment in the workplace, see Lee Schwing and Helaine Harris, "Building Feminist Institutions," *The Furies*, May–June 1973, 2–3; Carrie N. Baker, *Women's Movement Against Sexual Harassment* (Cambridge: Cambridge University Press, 2008), 129; Kenneth J. Heineman, *Campus Wars: The Peace Movement at American State*

Universities in the Vietnam Era (New York: New York University Press, 1992), 74; Jennifer Jensen Wallach and John A. Kirk, *Arsnick: The Student Nonviolent Coordinating Committee in Arkansas* (Fayetteville: University of Arkansas Press, 2012), 67.

On the harassment hippies faced, see Michael E. Brown, "The Condemnation and Persecution of Hippies," *Trans-Action*, September 1969, 33–46; Mark Naison, *White Boy: A Memoir* (Philadelphia: Temple University Press, 2002), 124; Marshall Chapman, "Keeping Secrets: Why You Should Never Tell a Soul About Your Favorite Hangout," *Garden & Gun*, August–September 2009.

25. Patrizia Battilani and Harm G. Schröter, "Introduction: Principle Problems and General Development of Cooperative Enterprise," in *The Cooperative Business Movement, 1950 to the Present*, ed. Patrizia Battilani and Harm G. Schröter (Cambridge: Cambridge University Press, 2012), 2–3; Vocations for Social Change, *No Bosses Here: A Manual on Working Collectively* (Cambridge, Mass.: Vocations for Social Change, 1976), 2; Joyce Rothschild-Whitt, "The Collectivist Organization: An Alternative to Rational-Bureaucratic Models," *American Sociological Review* 44 (August 1979): 511–518; Rossinow, *Politics of Authenticity*; Cornell, *Unruly Equality*, 1–3, 242, 284; Breines, *Community and Organization in the New Left*, 6–7; Staughton Lynd, "The New Radicals and Participatory Democracy," *Dissent*, Summer 1965, 327–329; Russell Rickford, *We Are an African People: Independent Education, Black Power, and the Radical Imagination* (Oxford: Oxford University Press, 2016), 13–15; *The Catalog of the Women's Graphics Collective*, Fall 1971, 5, Special Collections, Deering Library, Northwestern University, Evanston, Ill.

26. Rothschild-Whitt, "The Collectivist Organization," 511–518; Suzanne Staggenborg, "Can Feminist Organizations Be Effective?" in *Feminist Organizations: Harvest of the New Women's Movement*, ed. Myra M. Ferree and Patricia Y. Martin (Philadelphia: Temple University Press, 1995), 343–344; Economic Research and Action Project, *A Movement of Many Voices* (Ann Arbor, Mich.: Students for a Democratic Society, 1965), 10. See also Francesca Polletta, *Freedom Is an Endless Meeting: Democracy in American Social Movements* (Chicago: University of Chicago Press, 2002).

27. Cornell, *Unruly Equality*, 1–2, 11–12, 171–182, 242, 256, 276–277; Marina Sitrin, "The Anarchist Spirit," *Dissent*, Fall 2015, 84–86. See also Brian Doherty, *Radicals for Capitalism: A Freewheeling History of the Modern American Libertarian Movement* (New York: PublicAffairs, 2007).

28. Benjamin Waterhouse, *Lobbying America: The Politics of Business from Nixon to NAFTA* (Princeton, N.J.: Princeton University Press, 2014); Kruse, *One Nation Under God*; Lawrence B. Glickman, "Free Enterprise versus Socialism," *Dissent*, March 25, 2016, https://www.dissentmagazine.org/online_articles/free-enterprise-vs-socialism-brief-history-bernie-sanders-chamber-commerce.

On harassment of activist businesses, see Wallace Author, "Head Shop Harassed," *Space City*, August 3, 1971, 3; "Phluph Bombed," *Dallas Notes*, September 2, 1970, 5; J. Edgar Hoover, "Black Nationalist Movement in the United States—Racial Matters," memo, October 9, 1968, FBI File 157-WFO-368, National Archives and Records Administration, Washington, D.C.; Edward Vaughn, interviewed by the author, Dothan, Ala., June 5, 2013; "Cult Foods Seized in U.S. Raid Here—Linked to Diets Said to Have Caused Deaths," *New York Times*, June 3, 1966, 40.

29. On new religious groups and non-Western religions in the 1960s and 1970s, see Philip Jenkins, *Mystics and Messiahs: Cults and New Religions in American History* (Oxford:

Oxford University Press, 2000), 165–186; Wouter J. Hanegraaff, *New Age Religion and Western Culture: Esotericism in the Mirror of Secular Thought* (Albany: State University of New York Press, 1997), 10–12; Maurice Isserman and Michael Kazin, *America Divided: The Civil War of the 1960s*, 4th ed. (New York: Oxford University Press, 2012), 229–246.

30. E. F. Schumacher, *Small Is Beautiful: A Study of Economics as If People Mattered* (New York: Harper and Row, 1973); Michael Phillips, *The Seven Laws of Money* (Menlo Park, Calif.: Word Wheel, 1974); Baba Ram Dass, *Be Here Now* (San Cristobal, N.Mex.: Lama Foundation, 1971), 63–64; "Austin Community Project—Building a Cooperative Community," *Communities: A Journal of Cooperative Living*, March–April 1976, 44–47, Clipping File AF GROCERIES G4200 (65), Austin History Center, Austin Public Library.

31. "The Age of Acquireous," *Good Times*, September 11, 1970, 10; "Money vs. People," *Georgia Straight*, September 10–17, 1969, 6; Earl Ofari, *The Myth of Black Capitalism* (New York: Monthly Review Press, 1970); James Boggs, *Racism and Class Struggle: Further Pages from a Black Worker's Notebook* (New York: Monthly Review Press, 1970), 133–145; Dick Roberts, *The Fraud of Black Capitalism* (New York: Pathfinder Press, 1970); Brooke L. Williams and Hannah Darby, "God, Mom & Apple Pie: 'Feminist' Businesses as an Extension of the American Dream," *off our backs*, January–February 1976, 18–20; Elinor Lerner, "Basic Change," *off our backs*, March 1976, 26–27.

32. "The Age of Acquireous," 10.

33. Hawken, "Developing a Conspicuous Alternative," 6.

34. Marcus Garvey, *Philosophy and Opinions of Marcus Garvey, or Africa for the Africans*, vols. 1 and 2, comp. Amy Jacques Garvey (San Francisco: Julian Richardson Associates, 1967); *Our Bodies, Ourselves* (Boston: Boston Women's Health Book Collective, 1971). On the history of the fair-trade movement's political and anticolonial roots, see Mary A. Littrell and Marsha A. Dickson, *Social Responsibility in the Global Market: Fair Trade of Cultural Products* (Thousand Oaks, Calif.: Sage, 1999), 61–88, and Peter van Dam, "Moralizing Postcolonial Consumer Society: Fair Trade in the Netherlands, 1964–1997," *International Review of Social History* 61 (2016): 223–250.

35. Buck Mcloy, "This Is a Capitalist Society, so We're Capitalists . . . ," *Northwest Passage* 6, no. 8 (1972): 10. On consumer activism, see Glickman, *Buying Power*; Meg Jacobs, *Pocketbook Politics: Economic Citizenship in Twentieth Century America* (Princeton, N.J.: Princeton University Press, 2005); Matthew Hilton, *Prosperity for All: Consumer Activism in an Era of Globalization* (Ithaca, N.Y.: Cornell University Press, 2009).

36. For a similar argument on economic activity prior to the rise of modern capitalism, see Karl Polanyi, *The Great Transformation* (New York: Farrar and Rinehart, 1944). On the central features of capitalism, see Jürgen Kocka, *Capitalism: A Short History* (Princeton, N.J.: Princeton University Press, 2016), 7–9, 21; James Fulcher, *Capitalism: A Very Short Introduction* (Oxford: Oxford University Press, 2004), 13–18; and Luc Boltanski and Eve Chiapello, *The New Spirit of Capitalism* (London: Verso, 2005), 4–7. See also Karl Marx, *Wage-Labor and Capital* (1849), trans. Harriet E. Lothrop (New York: New York Labor News, 1902), and "Part VII: The Accumulation of Capital" (1867), in *Capital: A Critique of Political Economy*, vol. 1: *The Process of Capitalist Production* (New York: International Publishers, 1967), 564–565.

37. Small businesses of all kinds, not just activist businesses, also tend to be more skeptical of capitalist notions of profit maximization above all else. See Paul Greenbank,

"Objective Setting in the Micro-business," *International Journal of Entrepreneurial Behaviour and Research* 7, no. 3 (2001): 108–127; Elizabeth Walker and Alan Brown, "What Success Factors Are Important to Small Business Owners?" *International Small Business Journal* 22, no. 6 (2004): 577–594; Michael Morris, Minet Schindehutte, and Jeffrey Allen, "The Entrepreneur's Business Model: Toward a Unified Perspective," *Journal of Business History* 58 (2005): 730–731; Kate Lewis, "Small Firm Owners in New Zealand: In It for the 'Good Life' or Growth?" *Small Enterprise Research* 16, no. 1 (2008): 61–69; H. Jeff Smith, "The Shareholders vs. Stakeholders Debate," *MIT Sloan Management Review*, Summer 2003, 85; R. Edward Freeman, Jeffrey S. Harrison, Andrew C. Wicks, Bidhan L. Parmar, and Simone De Colle, "Stakeholder Theory: The State of the Art," *Academy of Management Annals* 4, no. 1 (2010): 403–445.

38. Erik Olin Wright, "Eroding Capitalism: A Comment on Stuart White's 'Basic Capital in the Egalitarian Toolkit,'" *Journal of Applied Philosophy* 32, no. 4 (2015): 432–439. On the related concept of the "politics of economic possibility," see Julie Katherine Gibson-Graham, *A Postcapitalist Politics* (Minneapolis: University of Minnesota Press, 2006), and "Diverse Economics: Performative Practices for Other Worlds," *Progress in Human Geography* 32, no. 5 (2008): 616.

39. Henry B. Hansmann, "The Role of Nonprofit Enterprise," *Yale Law Journal* 89, no. 5 (1980): 835–902; Burton A. Weisbrod, "The Nonprofit Mission and Its Financing: Growing Links Between Nonprofits and the Rest of the Economy," in *To Profit or Not to Profit: The Commercial Transformation of the Nonprofit Sector*, ed. Burton A. Weisbrod (Cambridge: Cambridge University Press, 1998), 1–19, and *The Nonprofit Economy* (Cambridge, Mass.: Harvard University Press, 1988), 1–5; Philip Scranton and Patrick Fridenson, "Non-profits and Quasi Enterprises," in *Reimagining Business History* (Baltimore: Johns Hopkins University Press, 2013), 87–91.

40. Battilani and Schröter, "Introduction," 2–3; Vocations for Social Change, *No Bosses Here*; Grimstad and Rennie, *New Woman's Survival Catalog*, 23 (quoting ICI, *Starting a Bookstore*).

41. Susan Sojourner, "Profit—That Nasty, Ugly Word," in *Dealing with the Real World: 13 Papers by Feminist Entrepreneurs* (New York City: Feminist Business Association, 1973), 4; William A. Gamson, *The Strategy of Social Protest* (Homewood, Ill.: Dorsey Press, 1975); Marco G. Giugni, "Was It Worth the Effort? The Outcomes and Consequences of Social Movements," *Annual Review of Sociology* 24, no. 1 (1998): 371–393; Paul Burstein, Rachel L. Einwohner, and Jocelyn A. Hollander, "The Success of Political Movements: A Bargaining Perspective," in *The Politics of Social Protest: Comparative Perspectives on States and Social Movements*, ed. J. Craig Jenkins and Bert Klandermans (Minneapolis: University of Minnesota Press, 1995), 275–295.

42. Scott A. Sandage, *Born Losers: A History of Failure in America* (Cambridge, Mass.: Harvard University Press, 2005); A. B. Cochran, "Small Business Mortality Rates: A Review of the Literature," *Journal of Small Business Management*, October 1981, 57–58; Small Business Administration, Office of Advocacy, "Frequently Asked Questions," March 2014, p. 2, https://www.sba.gov/sites/default/files/FAQ_March_2014_0.pdf.

43. Galbraith, *New Industrial State*; Buder, *Capitalizing on Change*, 421–423. On the decline of independent retail, see , and *1971 Business Statistics*, 58–59, 64, and Shelley M. Rinehart and Deborah Zizzo, "The Canadian and U.S. Retail Sectors: Important Changes Over the Past 60 Years," *Journal of Retailing and Consumer Services* 2, no. 1

(1995): 44. On reactions to this decline, see Mills, *White Collar*, 3, xii, and Jane Jacobs, *The Death and Life of American Cities*, fiftieth anniversary ed. (New York: Modern Library, 2011), 6, 65–71, 191.

44. On small business as the "backbone of democracy," see Jonathan J. Bean, *Beyond the Broker State: Federal Policies Toward Small Business, 1936–1961* (Chapel Hill: University of North Carolina Press, 1996), 2. See also Mansel Blackford, *A History of Small Business in America* (Chapel Hill: University of North Carolina Press, 2003), and "Small Business in America: A Historiographic Survey," *Business History Review* 65 (Spring 1991): 1–26; Philip Scranton and Patrick Fridenson, "Microbusiness," in *Reimagining Business History*, 77–82; Brian Headd, "The Role of Microbusiness in the Economy," *Small Business Facts*, February 2015, https://www.sba.gov/sites/default/files/Microbusinesses_in_the_Economy.pdf.

45. Lois Gould, "Creating a Women's World: The Feminists Behind Daughters Inc.," *New York Times Sunday Magazine*, January 2, 1977, 34; Anderson, *The Movement and the Sixties*, 408–410; Bruce Schulman, *The Seventies: The Great Shift in American Culture, Society, and Politics* (New York: De Capo Press, 2001), 19–20; Gitlin, *The Sixties*; Edward B. Fiske, "Campus Mood Focuses on Grades as Protests Wane," *New York Times*, November 23, 1977, 21; Paul Delaney, "Civil Rights Unity Gone in Redirected Movement," *New York Times*, August 29, 1973, 1.

2. LIBERATION THROUGH LITERACY

1. "Re: Una Godfrey Mulzac," memo, December 13, 1963, FBI File 100-HQ-400520, sec. 1, 181, National Archives and Records Administration, College Park, Maryland; Hugh Mulzac, *A Star to Steer By* (New York: International, 1963).

2. "Personality of the Week: Woman Among the Books," *Mirror* (Georgetown, Guyana), May 28, 1967; "Remembering Michael Forde," *Guyana Chronicle*, July 17, 2010, http://guyanachronicle.com/2010/07/17/remembering-michael-forde/; Herb Boyd, "Books Are in Her Blood," *New York Amsterdam News*, September 26, 2002, 28.

3. "Harlem's New Liberation Bookstore," *Challenge: The Revolutionary Communist Paper*, October 1967, 5; "Progressive Labor Party," memo, March 17, 1969, 1–8, FBI File 100-HQ-400520, part II, 55–62, National Archives and Records Administration. On Progressive Labor, see Max Elbaum, *Revolution in the Air: Sixties Radicals Turn to Lenin, Mao, and Che* (New York: Verso Books, 2002), 63–72.

4. Abiola Sinclair, "Liberation Bookstore—15th Anniversary," *New York Amsterdam News*, 48, 60; "Re: Una Godfrey Mulzac"; Colin Anthony Beckles, "PanAfrican Sites of Resistance: Black Bookstores and the Struggle to Re-present Black Identity," Ph.D. diss., University of California at Los Angeles, 1995, 204; "Liberation Book Store" (advertisement), *Black News*, October 1969, 14; Herb Boyd, "We Are Liberated at Liberation," *New York Amsterdam News*, July 12, 2001, 3; *Liberation Book Store Catalogue*, c. 1968, Clipping File 1925–1974, BOOKSTORES, SCF Micro F-1, FSn Sc 000, 614-1, Schomburg Center for Research in Black Culture, New York Public Library; Carolyn A. Butts, "Black Community Viewing Books as Tools of Liberation," *New York Amsterdam News*, November 23, 1991, 4.

5. I use the terms *Black Power* and *black nationalism* interchangeably, although I recognize that whereas black nationalism has a centuries-old history, Black Power was a movement primarily of the 1960s and 1970s. Key works on the Black Power

movement include Donna Murch, *Living for the City: Migration, Education, and the Rise of the Black Panther Party in Oakland, California* (Chapel Hill: University of North Carolina Press, 2010); Manning Marable, *Malcolm X: A Life of Reinvention* (New York: Viking Press, 2011); Russell Rickford, *We Are an African People: Independent Education, Black Power, and the Radical Imagination* (Oxford: Oxford University Press, 2016); Rhonda Y. Williams, *Concrete Demands: The Search for Black Power in the 20th Century* (New York: Routledge, 2015); Dan Berger, *Captive Nation: Black Prison Organizing in the Civil Rights Era* (Chapel Hill: University of North Carolina Press, 2014); Komozi Woodard, *A Nation Within a Nation: Amiri Baraka (LeRoi Jones) and Black Power Politics* (Chapel Hill: University of North Carolina Press, 1999); James Smethurst, *The Black Arts Movement: Literary Nationalism in the 1960s and 1970s* (Chapel Hill: University of North Carolina Press, 2005); Yohuru Williams, *In Search of the Black Panther Party: New Perspectives on a Revolutionary Movement* (Durham, N.C.: Duke University Press, 2006); Timothy B. Tyson, *Radio Free Dixie: Robert F. Williams and the Roots of Black Power* (Chapel Hill: University of North Carolina Press, 1999); William Van Deburg, *New Day in Babylon: The Black Power Movement and American Culture, 1965–1975* (Chicago: University of Chicago Press, 1992); Peniel Joseph, ed., *The Black Power Movement: Rethinking the Civil Rights–Black Power Era* (New York: Routledge, 2006) and *Waiting 'til the Midnight Hour: A Narrative History of Black Power in America* (New York: Henry Holt, 2006); Scot Brown, *Fighting for US: Maulana Karenga, the US Organization, and Black Cultural Nationalism* (New York: New York University Press, 2003).

6. Maulana Karenga, *The Quotable Karenga*, ed. Clyde Halisi and James Mtume (Los Angeles: US Organization, 1967), 1–3; Malcolm X, *The Autobiography of Malcolm X* (New York: Grove Press, 1965); Eldridge Cleaver, *Soul on Ice* (San Francisco: Ramparts Press, 1968); Don Lee, "The Necessity of Control: Publishing to Distribution—a Short Proposal for Black Distributors," in *From Plan to Planet—Life Studies: The Need for Afrikan Minds and Institutions* (Detroit: Broadside Press; Chicago: Institute of Positive Education, 1973), 115.

7. Booker T. Washington, *The Negro in Business* (Chicago: Hertel, Jenkins, 1907); John Howard Burrows, "The Necessity of Myth: A History of the National Negro Business League, 1900–1945," Ph.D. diss., Auburn University, 1977; Michael B. Boston, *The Business Strategy of Booker T. Washington: Its Development and Implementation* (Gainesville: University Press of Florida, 2010), 95. On the broader history of African American business and consumers in the twentieth century, see also Juliet E. K. Walker, *The Encyclopedia of African American Business* (Westport, Conn.: Greenwood Press, 1999), and *The History of Black Business in America: Capitalism, Race, Entrepreneurship* (New York: Macmillan Library Reference, 1998); Robert E. Weems, *Desegregating the Dollar: African American Consumerism in the Twentieth Century* (New York: New York University Press, 1998), and *Business in Black and White: American Presidents and Black Entrepreneurs in the Twentieth Century* (New York: New York University Press, 2009); N. D. B. Connolly, *A World More Concrete: Real Estate and the Remaking of Jim Crow South Florida* (Chicago: University of Chicago Press, 2015); Tiffany M. Gill, *Beauty Shop Politics: African American Women's Activism in the Beauty Industry* (Urbana: University of Illinois Press, 2010); Suzanne Smith, *Dancing in the Street: Motown and the Cultural Politics of Detroit* (Cambridge, Mass.: Harvard University Press, 1999) and *To Serve the Living: Funeral Directors and the African American Way of Death* (Cambridge, Mass.: Harvard University Press,

2010); Laura Warren Hill and Julia Rabig, eds., *The Business of Black Power: Community Development, Capitalism, and Corporate Responsibility in Postwar America* (Rochester, N.Y.: University of Rochester Press, 2012); Susannah Walker, "Black Dollar Power: Assessing African American Consumerism Since 1945," in *African American Urban History Since World War II*, ed. Kenneth L. Kusmer and Joe W. Trotter (Chicago: University of Chicago Press, 2009), 376–403; LaShawn Harris, *Sex Workers, Psychics, and Numbers Runners: Black Women in New York City's Underground Economy* (Champaign: University of Illinois Press, 2016).

8. "Profit Factors in Successful Bookselling," *Publisher's Weekly*, June 27, 1966, 53–55; *Small Business Reporter: Bookstores* (San Francisco: Bank of America, 1973), 15; Dawad Wayne Philip, "Is the Black Bookstore an Endangered Species? Prospects for Black Literature Appear Bleak," *New York Amsterdam News*, January 8, 1977, B2.

9. List of black-owned bookstores in the 1960s and 1970s compiled by the author, updated January 12, 2016.

10. Graham Russell Gao Hodges, *David Ruggles: A Radical Black Abolitionist and the Underground Railroad in New York City* (Chapel Hill: University of North Carolina Press, 2010), 60. On other early African American booksellers, see Booker T. Washington, *The Story of the Negro: The Rise of the Race from Slavery* (New York: Doubleday, 1909), 202; *The Twentieth Century Union League Directory: A Compilation of the Efforts of the Colored People of Washington for Social Betterment* (Washington, D.C.: Union League, 1901), 25; Alisha R. Knight, "'To Have the Benefit of Some Special Machinery': African American Book Publishing and Bookselling, 1900–1920," in *U.S. Popular Print Culture, 1860–1920*, ed. Christine Bold (Oxford: Oxford University Press, 2012), 437–456; "A Selected List of Books," *The Crisis*, March 1914, 260; "Books by J. A. Rogers, World Traveler and Historian," *Pittsburgh Courier*, December 12, 1942, 18; Lorenzo J. Greene, *Selling Black History for Carter G. Woodson: A Diary, 1930–1933*, ed. Avarah E. Strickland (Columbia: University of Missouri Press, 1996), 1–5.

11. Lewis Michaux, interviewed by James Vernon Hatch, 1974, Hatch-Billops Collection, Schomburg Center for Research in Black Culture, New York Public Library; C. Gerald Fraser, "Lewis Michaux, 92, Dies; Ran Bookstore in Harlem," *New York Times*, August 27, 1976, 34.

12. Langston Hughes, "Harlem's Bookshops Have a Wealth of Material by and About Negroes," *Chicago Defender*, February 14, 1953, 10; Charlayne Hunter, "The Professor," *New Yorker*, September 3, 1966, 28–29; Charles Baillou, "Booksellers Note Growing Number of Black Families Reading," *New York Amsterdam News*, January 2, 1993, 24.

13. Juana E. Duty, "Age of Aquarian Book Shop: Bookstore Still Surviving in 'Starvation Business,'" *Los Angeles Times*, March 24, 1982, F1; "Joe Maxwell Is Heart Victim," *Baltimore Afro-American*, June 3, 1939, 1; Helen Whitley, "Hugh Gordon Book Store: Ghetto's Cultural Center," *Baltimore Afro-American*, September 10, 1966, A5.

14. J. A. Rogers, "History Shows . . . ," *Pittsburgh Courier*, December 30, 1961, A26. See also J. A. Rogers, *From "Superman" to Man* (Chicago: Goodspeed Books, 1917), *World's Greatest Men and Women of African Descent* (New York: J. A. Rogers, 1931), and *Sex and Race: Negro–Caucasian Mixing in All Ages and All Lands*, vol. 1: *The Old World* (New York: J. A. Rogers, 1941).

15. "Books by J. A. Rogers, World Traveler and Historian."

16. "National Memorial Book Store," *New York Amsterdam News*, May 4, 1946, 11; "World's History Book Outlet on 600 Million Colored People," National Memorial Book Store catalog, c. 1942, in Clipping File 1925–1974, BOOKSTORES, SCF Micro

F-1, FSn Sc 000, 614-1, Schomburg Center; Pero Gaglo Dagbovie, *The Early Black History Movement, Carter G. Woodson, and Lorenzo Johnston Greene* (Urbana: University of Illinois Press, 2007); Thabiti Asukile, "J. A. Rogers: The Scholarship of an Organic Intellectual," *Black Scholar* 36, nos. 2–3 (2006): 35–50; Rogers, "History Shows . . . ," A26.

17. Weems, *Desegregating the Dollar*, 72; *Small Business Reporter*; Laura J. Miller, *Reluctant Capitalists: Bookselling and the Culture of Consumption* (Chicago: University of Chicago Press, 2006), 38–44, 245–246 n. 46.

18. Booker T. Washington, "The Atlanta Exposition Address," in *Up from Slavery: An Autobiography* (New York: Doubleday, Page, 2007), 223; Boston, *The Business Strategy of Booker T. Washington*, 95; Walker, *History of Black Business in America*, 240. See also Washington, *The Negro in Business*, and Burrows, "The Necessity of Myth."

19. Colin Grant, *Negro with a Hat: The Rise and Fall of Marcus Garvey* (Oxford: Oxford University Press, 2008), 137–156, 320–321, 333–334; Edward E. Curtis, *Black Muslim Religion in the Nation of Islam, 1960–1975* (Chapel Hill: University of North Carolina Press, 2006), 31, 41–43, 92, 106–110; Claude Clegg, *An Original Man: The Life and Times of Elijah Muhammad* (New York: St. Martin's Press, 1996), 152–154; Adam Ewing, *The Age of Garvey: How a Jamaican Activist Created a Mass Movement and Changed Global Black Politics* (Princeton, N.J.: Princeton University Press, 2014), 117–118.

Black business owners who participated actively in the civil rights movement included the serial entrepreneur T. R. M. Howard in Mississippi, restaurant owners such as James and Robert Paschal in Atlanta, and countless beauty-salon owners across the South. Yet other nationally prominent black business owners such as A. G. Gaston in Birmingham and Samuel Fuller in Chicago, both of whom served as presidents of the National Negro Business League, regularly discouraged public protest against white supremacy. See David T. Beito and Linda Royster Beito, *Black Maverick TRM Howard's Fight for Civil Rights and Economic Power* (Urbana: University of Illinois Press, 2009); Dave Hoekstra, *The People's Place: Soul Food Restaurants and Reminiscences from the Civil Rights Era to Today* (Chicago: Chicago Review Press, 2015); Gill, *Beauty Shop Politics*; Walker, *History of Black Business in America*, 298–299.

20. Dale R. Vlasek, "Economics and Integration: The Economic Thought of E. Franklin Frazier," *American Studies* 20, no. 2 (1979): 27–35; E. Franklin Frazier, *The Black Bourgeoisie* (Glencoe, Ill.: Free Press, 1957).

21. Bobby Seale, *Seize the Time: The Story of the Black Panther Party and Huey P. Newton* (New York: Random House, 1970), 13; Earl Ofari [Hutchinson], *The Myth of Black Capitalism* (New York: Monthly Review Press, 1970); James Boggs, *Racism and Class Struggle: Further Pages from a Black Worker's Notebook* (New York: Monthly Review Press, 1970), 133–145. See also Dick Roberts, *The Fraud of Black Capitalism* (New York: Pathfinder Press, 1970).

22. On African American hair- and beauty-product distributors, including manufacturers of wigs, weaves, and skin lighteners, see Walker, *History of Black Business in America*, 302–311; *Black News*, advertisement, October 1969, 1.

23. Dean Kotlowski, "Black Power—Nixon Style: The Nixon Administration and Minority Business Enterprise," *Business History Review* 72, no. 3 (1998): 409–445; Michael O. West, "Conclusion: Whose Black Power? The Business of Black Power and Black Power's Business," in Hill and Rabig, *Business of Black Power*, 283–291;

Weems, *Business in Black and White*, 110–126; Hill and Rabig, *Business of Black Power.*

24. V. Thomas, "Move to Rediscover Black Heroes Gaining," *New York Amsterdam News*, March 18, 1972, A5; Karenga, *The Quotable Karenga*, 1; Steven J. Gold, *The Store in the Hood: A Century of Ethnic Business and Conflict* (Lanham, Md.: Rowman and Littlefield, 2010), 110–111. See the advertisements in *Black News*, April 10, 1970, 18, 25, 39; May 29, 1970, 14; June 12, 1970, 10; and September 10, 1971, 9.

25. Angus Campbell and Howard Schuman, "Racial Attitudes in Fifteen American Cities," in *Supplemental Studies for the National Advisory Commission on Civil Disorders* (New York: Praeger, 1970), 20.

26. Michael Katz, *In the Shadow of the Poorhouse: A Social History of Welfare in America* (New York: Basic Books, 1996), 272–277; Thomas J. Sugrue, *Sweet Land of Liberty: The Forgotten Struggle for Civil Rights in the North* (New York: Random House, 2008), 521–522; Rickford, *We Are an African People*, 13–16, 41–45; Michael C. Dawson, *Black Visions: The Roots of Contemporary African-American Political Ideologies* (Chicago: University of Chicago Press, 2003), 91–93, 97–100.

27. Julius K. Nyerere, "Communitarian Socialism," *Liberation*, Summer 1962, 13–15; *Drum and Spear Bookstore* (catalog 3) (Washington, D.C.: Drum and Spear, 1971); Edward Vaughn, interviewed by the author, Dothan, Ala., June 5, 2013; Maulana Karenga, *Kwanzaa: Origin, Concepts, Practice* (Inglewood, Calif.: Kawaida, 1977), 42–43; Greg Huskisson, "Kwanza Seen as Substitute For 'Commercial' Christmas," *Atlanta Daily World*, December 24, 1978, 7; "Black Shops Will Hold Ujamaa Ritual," *New York Amsterdam News*, January 17, 1970, 21; "Nyumba Ya Ujamaa—'House of Cooperative Economics,'" *New York Amsterdam News*, September 4, 1971, B6; "African Bazaar Opens," *New York Amsterdam News*, August 7, 1971, C1; "Places Where You Can Buy BBB," *Black Books Bulletin* 6, no. 2 (1978): 67.

28. Tanisha Ford, *Liberated Threads: Black Women, Style, and the Global Politics of Soul* (Chapel Hill: University of North Carolina Press, 2015); Walker, *Encyclopedia of African American Business* and *History of Black Business in America*; Deburg, *New Day in Babylon*; John Lewis, "Black Voices," *Afro-American*, August 9, 1969, 5.

29. Joseph, *Waiting 'til the Midnight Hour*, 11–15, 68; John Henrik Clark, "The New Afro-American Nationalism," *Freedomways* 1, no. 3 (1961): 288; Frank Hunt, "Malcolm X Still Lives," *Baltimore Afro-American*, February 19, 1966, A4; Lewis H. Michaux, "Cooperation and Unity: A Way Out," *New York Amsterdam News*, July 28, 1962, 1; Williams, *Concrete Demands*, 70–71; Peter Goldman, *The Death and Life of Malcolm X*, 2nd ed. (Urbana: University of Illinois Press, 1979), 51–54.

30. Vaughn interview by the author, June 5, 2013; Ralph Ginzburg, *100 Years of Lynching* (New York: Lancer Books, 1962).

31. Godfrey Mwakikagile, *Africans and African Americans: Complex Relations—Prospects and Challenges* (Dar es Salaam, Tanzania: New Africa Press, 2009), 157; "Leading Pan-Africanism in Detroit, Austin Chavou Joins the Ancestors," *Michigan Citizen*, January 15 2005, B4; Ahmad Rahman, *The Regime Change of Kwame Nkrumah: Epic Heroism in Africa and the Diaspora* (New York: Routledge, 2007), xii; Ed Vaughn, interviewed by Sam Pollard, June 6, 1989, in interviews for *Eyes on the Prize II*, Washington University Digital Gateways Texts, http://digital.wustl.edu/e/eii/eiiweb/vau5427.0309.166edvaughn.html; Grace Lee Boggs, *Living for Change: An Autobiography* (Minneapolis: University of Minnesota Press, 1998), 118–120.

32. Vaughn interview by Pollard, June 6, 1989; Kim D. Hunter, "1967: Detroiters Remember," interview with Edward Vaughn, *Against the Current*, September–October 1997, 20–21.

33. Vaughn interview by Pollard, June 6, 1989; Hunter, "1967," 20–21; Louis E. Lomax, "Bookstore Pros Mapped Detroit Riot," *Vancouver Sun*, August 8, 1967, 11; "Testimony of James C. Harris," U.S. Congress, House of Representatives, *Subversive Influences in Riots, Looting, and Burning, Part 1—Hearing Before the Committee on Un-American Activities*, 90th Cong., 1st sess., October 25, 26, 31, and November 28, 1967, 1211; Martin Sostre, *Letters from Prison: A Compilation of Martin Sostre's Correspondence from Erie County Jail, Buffalo, New York, and Green Haven Prison, Stormville, New York*, 2nd printing (Buffalo: Philosophical Society, 1969); Vincent Copeland, *The Crime of Martin Sostre* (New York: McGraw-Hill, 1970); Malcolm McLaughlin, "Storefront Revolutionary: Martin Sostre's Afro-Asian Bookshop, Black Liberation Culture, and the New Left, 1964–75," *The Sixties* 7, no. 1 (2014): 1–27.

34. Seale, *Seize the Time*, 80–81; Black Panther Party, *Black Panther Party Platform and Program: What We Want, What We Believe* (Oakland, Calif.: Black Panther Party, 1966); Murch, *Living for the City*, 155; Paul Coates, interviewed by the author, Baltimore, June 13, 2012, digital recording.

35. Karenga, *The Quotable Karenga*, 1–3.

36. Smethurst, *Black Arts Movement*, 14. See also Lisa Gail Collins and Margo Natalie Crawford, *New Thoughts on the Black Arts Movement* (New Brunswick, N.J.: Rutgers University Press, 2006); Cheryl Clarke, *After Mecca: Women Poets and the Black Arts Movement* (New Brunswick, N.J.: Rutgers University Press, 2005); Daniel Widener, *Black Arts West: Culture and Struggle in Postwar Los Angeles* (Durham, N.C.: Duke University Press, 2009).

37. Donald Franklin Joyce, *Gatekeepers of Black Culture: Black-Owned Publishing in the United States, 1817–1981* (Westport, Conn.: Greenwood Press, 1983), 1–3, 100–102.

38. Dudley Randall, *Roses and Revolutions: The Selected Writings of Dudley Randall*, ed. Melba Joyce Boyd (Detroit: Wayne State University Press, 2009), and *Broadside Memories: Poets I Have Known* (Detroit: Broadside Press, 1975), 31; Melba Joyce Boyd, *Wrestling with the Muse: Dudley Randall and the Broadside Press* (New York: Columbia University Press, 2003), 161–162; Salim Muwakkil, "Indigenous Wealth on the South Side: Haki Madhubuti," *Chicago Tribune*, October 29, 2001, sec. 1, 17.

39. Earl Caldwell, "Black Bookstores Creating New Best-Seller List," *New York Times*, August 20, 1969, 39; list of black-owned bookstores compiled by the author; Barnett Wright, "Books Promote Pride in Black Heritage," *Philadelphia Tribune*, April 21, 1992, A1; Duty, "Age of Aquarian Book Shop," F1; Vaughn interview by the author, June 5, 2013; "Detroit: A Riot-Torn City Survives and Bounces Back," *Publisher's Weekly*, August 28, 1967, 267.

40. Stokely Carmichael, "Towards Black Liberation," *Massachusetts Review* 7, no. 4 (1966): 646–651.

41. Stokely Carmichael, with Ekwueme Michael Thelwell, *Ready for the Revolution: The Life and Struggles of Stokely Carmichael (Kwame Ture)* (New York: Scribner, 2003), 571, 643.

42. Judy Richardson, interviewed by the author, Skype, October 11, 2012, digital recording; Charles Cobb, interviewed by the author, Tampa, Fla., October 16, 2015.

43. Richardson interview, October 11, 2012.

44. Ibid.; Cobb interview, October 16, 2015; *Drum and Spear Bookstore* (catalog 3); *Liberation Book Store Catalogue*; *Vaughn's Book Store: 1969–1970 Catalogue of Books* (Detroit: Vaughn's Book Store, 1969), copy in author's files; Carol Eron, "All Booked Up: Bookstores," *Washington Post*, January 27, 1974, BW2.

45. C. L. R. James, *A History of Pan-African Revolt* (Washington, D.C.: Drum and Spear Press, 1971); Seth Markle, "Book Publishers for a Pan-African World: Drum and Spear Press and Tanzania's 'Ujamaa' Ideology," *Black Scholar*, Winter 2008, 16–26; Gene Ulansky, "Marcus Garvey's Man in San Francisco," interview with Julian Richardson, *Encore American & Worldwide News*, May 19, 1975, 36; Marcus Garvey, *Philosophy and Opinions of Marcus Garvey, or Africa for the Africans*, vols. 1 and 2, comp. Amy Jacques Garvey (San Francisco: Julian Richardson Associates, 1967); Edward Vaughn, *Red, Black, and Green: The History and Meaning of the Black Liberation Flag* (Detroit: E. Vaughn and Associates, 1975).

46. Ulansky, "Marcus Garvey's Man," 36; Joe Elam, "Drum and Spear: When the Smoke Cleared on 14th St., a Bookstore Came," *Washington Afro American*, February 15, 1969; Gerard Burke, "Hard Times for Drum and Spear," *Washington Afro American*, March 23, 1974, 11; Coates interview, June 13, 2012; *Vaughn's Book Store*.

47. *Drum and Spear Bookstore* (catalog 3), 9; *Liberation Book Store Catalogue*; *Vaughn's Book Store*; Allan Ruff, *"We Called Each Other Comrade": Charles H. Kerr & Company, Radical Publishers* (Urbana: University of Illinois Press, 1997); "Profit Factors in Successful Bookselling," 53–55; *Small Business Reporter*, 15.

48. For titles and authors sold, see *Drum and Spear Bookstore* (catalog 3), 4–9; *Liberation Book Store Catalogue*; *Vaughn's Book Store*.

49. Sostre, *Letters from Prison*, 26; McLaughlin, "Storefront Revolutionary," 9; Eric Pace, "Alex Haley, 70, Author of 'Roots,' Dies," *New York Times*, February 11, 1992, B8; "Liberation Book Store" (advertisement), *Black News*, October 1969, 14; *Vaughn's Book Store*.

50. *Drum and Spear Bookstore* (catalog 3); Ovid Adams, *Adventures of Black Eldridge* (San Francisco: Marcus Books, 1970), 24; *Vaughn's Book Store*, 44–47; Sostre, *Letters from Prison*, 26; *Presence Africaine* to Richard B. Moore, c. 1968, Manuscripts, Archives, and Rare Books Collection, Box 5, Folder 4, Schomburg Center; Cobb interview, October 16, 2015; Elam, "Drum and Spear."

51. J. Edgar Hoover, "Black Nationalist Movement in the United States—Racial Matters," memo, October 9, 1968, FBI File 157-WFO-368, National Archives and Records Administration, College Park, Maryland.

52. See the following FBI memos and files in the National Archives and Records Administration: "Re: George Jackson Prison Movement aka Black Book Store," memo, November 7, 1973, FBI File 157-HQ-26110; Special Agent in Charge (157-4981) to Special Agent, "Memorandum: David Hakim aka RM-RNA," December 16, 1970, FBI File 100-PH-47598; "Miriam W. Crawford," February 18, 1971, FBI File HQ 100-366614; Special Agent to Special Agent in Charge, Denver, to Director, FBI, "Sundiata," memo, December 12, 1968, FBI File 105-HQ-173904; "Re: Una Godfrey Mulzac," FBI File 100-HQ-400520; "Lewis Michaux," FBI File 105-HQ-150242. See also Edward Roeder, "Police Filed Data on Black Politicians," *Baltimore Sun*, December 29, 1974, A16; McLaughlin, "Storefront Revolutionary," 13–14; Vaughn interview by the author, June 5, 2013; Hoover, "Black Nationalist Movement in the United States"; Richardson interview, October 11, 2012. On the FBI's Counterintelligence Program,

see Nelson Blackstock, *Cointelpro: The FBI's Secret War on Political Freedom* (New York: Vintage Books, 1976), and Joseph, *Waiting 'til the Midnight Hour*, 187–189.

53. Director, FBI, to Special Agent in Charge, Washington Field Office, "Drum and Spear Bookstore; Racial Matters," memo, June 13, 1968, National Archives and Records Administration. Freedom of Information Act requests by the author to the FBI produced nearly four hundred pages of documents concerning Drum and Spear Bookstore; see FBI File 157-HQ-9594. See also Colin A. Beckles, "Black Bookstores, Black Power, and the F.B.I.: The Case of Drum and Spear," *Western Journal of Black Studies* 20, no. 2 (1996): 68; Richardson interview, October 11, 2012.

54. List of black-owned bookstores compiled by the author; Woodard, *A Nation Within a Nation*, 1–48.

55. Fabio Rojas, *From Black Power to Black Studies: How a Radical Social Movement Became an Academic Discipline* (Baltimore: Johns Hopkins University Press, 2007); Martha Biondi, *The Black Revolution on Campus* (Berkeley: University of California Press, 2012), 4, 188; Ibram Rogers, *The Black Campus Movement: Black Students and the Racial Reconstitution of Higher Education, 1965–1972* (New York: Palgrave Macmillan, 2012).

56. Richardson interview, October 11, 2012; Vaughn interview by the author, June 5, 2013.

57. Annette Jones White, "An Open Letter—a Need for Books," *Black World*, November 1971, 73–74; "Preface," in *Drum and Spear Bookstore* (catalog 3), unpaginated.

58. Joseph, *Waiting 'til the Midnight Hour*, 275–283; Woodard, *A Nation Within a Nation*, 3, 206; Harold Cruse, "The Little Rock National Black Political Convention," *Black World*, November 1974, 4; Dean E. Robinson, *Black Nationalism in American Politics and Thought* (Cambridge: Cambridge University Press, 2001), 99; Manning Marable, *Race, Reform, and Rebellion: The Second Reconstruction and Beyond in Black America, 1945–2006*, 3rd ed. (Jackson: University of Mississippi Press, 2007), 134–135; Imamu Amiri Baraka, "Toward Ideological Clarity," *Black World*, November 1974, 24–33, 84–95.

59. Trans-Urban Staff Reporter, "Tree of Life Vows Not to Be Uprooted," *New York Amsterdam News*, June 23, 1979, 2; Ted Watson, "Bookseller Hits CCC with $500,000 Lawsuit," *Chicago Defender*, June 7, 1975, 3; "Michaux Fights for Bookstore," *New York Amsterdam News*, February 9, 1974, B3; Dawad Wayne Philip, "Is the Black Bookstore an Endangered Species? First of a Series," *New York Amsterdam News*, January 1, 1977, B2.

60. William Julius Wilson, *The Truly Disadvantaged: The Inner City, the Underclass, and Public Policy* (Chicago: University of Chicago Press, 1987, 2012), 31; "Growing with the Economy: Black Business—1977," *Black Enterprise*, June 1978, 66; "Profit Factors in Successful Bookselling," 53–55.

61. Burke, "Hard Times for Drum and Spear," 11, including quote from Richardson.

62. *1977 Survey of Minority-Owned Business Enterprises—Black* (Washington, D.C.: U.S. Department of Commerce, Bureau of the Census, 1979), 10–11. See also *1992 Economic Census—Survey of Minority-Owned Business Enterprises: Black* (Washington, D.C.: U.S. Department of Commerce, Bureau of the Census, 1992), 9; *1997 Economic Census—Survey of Minority-Owned Business Enterprises: Black* (Washington, D.C.: U.S. Department of Commerce, Bureau of the Census, 1997), 17; *Black-Owned Firms: 2002* (Washington, D.C.: U.S. Department of Commerce, Bureau of the Census, 2002), 1. On *Black Enterprise*, see Earl G. Graves, *How to Succeed in Business Without Being White: Straight Talk on Making It in America* (New York: Harper Business, 1997); Joshua Clark Davis, "For the Records: How African American Consumers and

Music Retailers Created Commercial Public Space in the 1960s and 1970s South," *Southern Cultures*, Winter 2011, 84–85.

63. Burke, "Hard Times for Drum and Spear"; business filings search, U.S. Department of Consumer and Regulatory Affairs, https://corp.dcra.dc.gov/BizEntity.aspx/View EntityData?entityId=2738798; Richardson interview, October 11, 2012; Coates interview, June 13, 2012.

64. Philip, "Is the Black Bookstore an Endangered Species? First of a Series," B2, and "Is the Black Bookstore an Endangered Species? Prospects," B2.

65. Alex Haley, *Roots: The Saga of an American Family* (Garden City, N.Y.: Doubleday, 1976). See also Matthew Delmont, *Making* Roots: *A Nation Captivated* (Berkeley: University of California Press, 2016).

66. Duty, "Age of Aquarian Book Shop," F1.

67. Wilson, *The Truly Disadvantaged*, 31; Marable, *Race, Reform, and Rebellion*, 183, 188–205; Andrew Wiese, *Places of Their Own: African American Suburbanization in the Twentieth Century* (Chicago: University of Chicago Press, 2005), 265–267; Elizabeth Kai Hinton, *From the War on Poverty to the War on Crime: The Making of Mass Incarceration in America* (Cambridge, Mass.: Harvard University Press, 2016); Heather Ann Thompson, "Why Mass Incarceration Matters: Rethinking Crisis, Decline, and Transformation in Postwar American History," *Journal of American History* 97, no. 3 (2010): 703–734; Bradford Martin, *The Other Eighties: A Secret History of America in the Age of Reagan* (New York: Macmillan, 2011), 119–143.

68. On conservative commentaries on the impact of the civil rights movement, see Thomas Sowell, *Civil Rights: Rhetoric or Reality?* (New York: Morrow, 1984); Charles Murray, *Losing Ground: American Social Policy, 1950–1980* (New York: Basic Books, 1984). For contrasting interpretations of African Americans' status in these years, see William Julius Wilson, *The Declining Significance of Race: Blacks and Changing American Institutions* (Chicago: University of Chicago Press, 1978), 21–22, 99–103; Leslie B. Inniss and Joe R. Feagin, "*The Cosby Show*: The View from the Black Middle Class," *Journal of Black Studies* 25, no. 6 (1995): 692–711; Sut Jhally and Justin Lewis, *Enlightened Racism:* The Cosby Show, *Audiences, and the Myth of the American Dream* (Boulder, Colo.: Westview Press, 1992).

69. Marable, *Race, Reform, and Rebellion*, 145.

70. Rosalind Wells, *Entwined Destinies* (New York: Dell, 1980); Sandra Kitt, *Adam and Eva* (New York: Harlequin, 1984); Ray Walters, "Paperback Talk," *New York Times*, July 13, 1980, BR36; Gwendolyn Osborne, "How Black Romance—Novels, That Is—Came to Be," *Black Issues Book Review*, January–February 2002, 50; Ann Yvonne White, "Genesis Press: Cultural Representation and the Production of African American Romance Novels," Ph.D. diss., University of Iowa, 2008, 25–26.

71. "Writing a New Chapter in Book Publishing," *Black Enterprise*, February 1995, 110; Terry McMillan, *Mama* (New York: Houghton Mifflin Harcourt, 1987), *Disappearing Acts* (New York: Penguin, 1989), and *Waiting to Exhale* (New York: Viking, 1992); Alice Walker, *Possessing the Secret to Joy* (New York: Washington Square Press, 1992); Toni Morrison, *Jazz* (New York: Knopf, 1992).

72. Nelson George, "Black Books, Black Souls: The Literary Chitlin' Circuit from McMillan to Asante," *Village Voice*, July 12, 1994, 21–24.

73. Marable, *Race, Reform, and Rebellion*, 188–205; Marilyn S. Johnson, *Street Justice: A History of Street Violence in New York City* (Boston: Beacon Press, 2003), 282–294; Martin, *The Other Eighties*, 119–143.

74. Barnett Wright, "Books Promote Pride in Black Heritage," *Philadelphia Tribune*, April 21, 1992, A1; Butts, "Black Community Viewing Books as Tools of Liberation," 4; Molefi Asante, *The Afrocentric Idea: The Theory of Social Change* (Philadelphia: Temple University Press, 1987); Martin Bernal, *Black Athena: The Afroasiatic Roots of Civilization* (London: Free Association Books, 1987); Chancellor Williams, *Destruction of Black Civilization: Great Issues of a Race from 4500 B.C. to A.D. 2000* (1974; reprint, Chicago: Third World Press, 1987).

75. Lewis Lord, Jeannye Thornton, and Alejandro Bodip-Memba, "The Legacy of Malcolm X," *U.S. News and World Report*, November 15, 1992, 76; Allison Samuels, "Malcolm for Sale," *Los Angeles Sentinel*, December 26, 1991, A6; Baillou, "Booksellers Note Growing Number of Black Families Reading," 24.

76. John Baker, "The '80s: Reaching New Heights, It Was a Decade of Sometimes Reckless Growth," *Publishers Weekly*, January 5, 1990, 19; list of black-owned bookstores compiled by the author; Mwalimu I. Mwadilifu, *Who's Who in African Heritage Book Publishing, 1989–90*, 2nd ed. (New York: E.C.A. Associates, 1989), 133–168; Brenda Mitchell-Powell, "The Trouble with Success," *Publishers Weekly*, December 12, 1994, 33.

77. George, "Black Books, Black Souls," 21–24; Tananarive Due, "Black Literary Movement Flourishing," *Denver Post*, September 11, 1995, G10; Karen Angel, "Black Booksellers Aim to Get Their Groove Back," *Publishers Weekly*, September 15, 1997, 20; Max Rodriguez, "Publisher's Statement," *Quarterly Black Review of Books*, February 28, 1994, 3; "Black Book Sales in the 1990s: Will This Be the Decade for Black Books and Black Writers?" *ABBWA Journal*, Spring 1993, 10–11.

78. Nicholas Siropolis, "Case 3A: The Hue-Man Experience Bookstore," in *Small Business Management*, 6th ed. (Boston: Houghton Mifflin, 1996), 79–80; Clara Villarosa, with Alicia Villarosa, *Down to Business: The First 10 Steps to Entrepreneurship for Women* (New York: Avery, 2009), 1–2, 83–84.

79. "Book Biz: A Community Bestseller," *Ms.*, September 1989, 85; Stuart Leuthner, "Buy the Book: Confounding Racial and Retail Stereotypes," *Emerge*, November 1990, 19; "Minority Book Fairs Fill Retailing's Cultural Gap," *New York Times*, March 13, 1994, 42; Jacqueline Trescott, "Essay: The Stories That Cry to Be Read Caught in the Truths of 3 Unconventional Bestsellers," *Washington Post*, July 2, 1992, C1.

80. Siropolis, "Case 3A," 80.

81. "Villarosa's Ten Reason Why Black Booksellers Should Attend the ABA," *ABBWA Journal*, Fall–Winter 1989, 28.

82. Villarosa, *Down to Business*, 1–2, 83–84, 155.

83. Shawn E. Rhea, "Buy the Book," *Black Enterprise*, February 1999, 175–177.

84. Shahrazad Ali, "Buying Books," *Black Enterprise*, October 1998, 13; Angel, "Black Booksellers Aim to Get Their Groove Back," 20; Terry McMillan, *How Stella Got Her Groove Back* (New York: Viking Penguin, 1996).

85. Carolyn M. Brown, "Writing a New Chapter in Book Publishing," *Black Enterprise*, February 1995, 108.

3. THE BUSINESS OF GETTING HIGH

1. James S. Kaplan, "The Corner Store: A Bronx Deli Mixes Food and Friendliness for Profit, but the Times Are Changing," *Wall Street Journal*, September 4, 1970, 20; Bill Paul, "The Corner Store: A Philadelphia Ghetto and Its Problems Are a Way of Life

for a Busy Undertaker," *Wall Street Journal*, September 2, 1970, 26; Art Glickman, "The Corner Store: Mod Boutique in Lansing Turns Tidy Profit by Offering Clients a Feeling of Freedom," *Wall Street Journal*, September 17, 1970, 34.

2. Glickman, "The Corner Store: Mod Boutique," 34.

3. "Pot Counter-Revolutionary," *Eyewitness*, June 1970, 5; Matthew Levin, *Cold War University: Madison and the New Left in the Sixties* (Madison: University of Wisconsin Press, 2013), 142–143; Jack Newfield, "One Cheer for Hippies," *The Nation*, June 26, 1967, 809; Todd Gitlin, *The Sixties: Years of Hope, Days of Rage* (New York: Bantam Books, 1987), 427. On hippie businesses and profit, see "The Age of Acquireous," *Good Times*, December 11, 1970, 10; J. Kaye Faulkner, "A Rose by Any Other Name . . . ," *Northwest Passage*, February 7, 1972, 8; "Money vs. People," *Georgia Straight*, September 10–17, 1969, 6; Jane Wilson, "Commerce in Hippieland," *Los Angeles Times*, January 28, 1968, B16, B21; Gordon Grant, "Girl's Small Psychedelic Shop Stirs Furor in San Clemente," *Los Angeles Times*, July 18, 1968, B10; Buck Meloy, "This Is a Capitalist Society, so We're Capitalists . . . ," *Northwest Passage*, February 7, 1972, 10. On the broader history of the counterculture, see Timothy Miller, *The Hippies and American Values* (Knoxville: University of Tennessee Press, 1991); Peter Braunstein and Michael William Doyle, eds., *Imagine Nation: The American Counterculture of the 1960s and '70s* (New York: Routledge, 2002); Charles A. Reich, *The Greening of America* (New York: Random House, 1970); Theodore Roszak, *The Making of a Counter Culture: Reflections on the Technocratic Society and Its Youthful Opposition* (Garden City, N.Y.: Doubleday, 1969); W. J. Rorabaugh, *American Hippies* (New York: Cambridge University Press, 2015). On countercultural businesses' role as community institutions, see Michael Kramer, *Republic of Rock: Music and Citizenship in the Sixties Counterculture* (Oxford: Oxford University Press, 2013); John McMillian, *Smoking Typewriters: The Sixties Underground Press and the Rise of Alternative Media in America* (Oxford: Oxford University Press, 2011); David Farber, "Building the Counterculture, Creating Right Livelihoods: The Counterculture at Work," *The Sixties* 6, no. 1 (2013): 1–24; Nicholas G. Meriwether, "The Counterculture as Local Culture in Columbia, South Carolina," in *Rebellion in Black and White: Southern Student Activism in the 1960s*, ed. Robert Cohen and David J. Snyder (Baltimore: Johns Hopkins University Press, 2013), 218–234.

4. On the history of marijuana in the United States, see Richard J. Bonnie and Charles H. Whitebread, *The Marijuana Conviction: A History of Marijuana Prohibition in the United States* (Charlottesville: University Press of Virginia, 1974); Jerome L. Himmelstein, *The Strange Career of Marihuana: Politics and Ideology of Drug Control in America* (Westport, Conn.: Greenwood Press, 1983); Adam Rathge, "Pondering Pot: Marijuana's History and the Future of the War on Drugs," *American Historian*, August 2015, 30–36; Jordan Goodman, Paul E. Lovejoy, and Andrew Sherratt, eds., *Consuming Habits: Drugs in History and Anthropology* (London: Routledge, 1995); Martin Booth, *Cannabis: A History* (London: Doubleday, 2003); Martin Lee, *Smoke Signals: A Social History of Marijuana, Medical, Recreational, and Scientific* (New York: Scribner's, 2012); David Farber, "The Intoxicated State/Illegal Nation," in Braunstein and Doyle, *Imagine Nation*, 17–40; Eric Schlosser, *Reefer Madness: Sex, Drugs, and Cheap Labor in the American Black Market* (Boston: Houghton Mifflin, 2003); Larry Sloman, *Reefer Madness: The History of Marijuana in America* (Indianapolis, Ind.: Bobbs-Merrill, 1979); Peter Maguire and Mike Ritter, *Thai Stick:*

Surfers, Scammers, and the Untold Story of the Marijuana Trade (New York: Columbia University Press, 2014).

5. "Life Drugs, Death Drugs" (c. 1973), in *Blacklisted News, Secret History: From Chicago, '68, to 1984: The New Yippie! Book*, ed. Steve Conliff and Grace Nichols (New York: Bleecker, 1983), 672; John Sinclair, *Marijuana Revolution* (Ann Arbor, Mich.: Rainbow People's Party, 1971), 16–18; Mike Minnich, "Prisoners Freed—Free Weed!" *Ann Arbor Sun*, April 13–27, 1972, 5.

6. "Introducing . . . *High Times*," *High Times*, Fall 1974, 10; U.S. Congress, House of Representatives, *Drug Paraphernalia: Hearing Before the Select Committee on Narcotics Abuse and Control*, 96th Cong., 1st sess., November 1, 1979 (Washington, D.C.: U.S. Government Printing Office, 1980), 5, 87; "11 States Decriminalize Marijuana Possession," *Los Angeles Times*, September 30, 1981, H22. Decriminalization of marijuana reduced individual possession for nonmedical minor possession to a civil penalty without legalizing it outright.

7. Jay Thelin, interviewed by the author, Skype, September 11, 2014; Timothy Leary, Richard Alpert, and Ralph Metzner, *The Psychedelic Experience: A Manual Based on the Tibetan Book of the Dead* (New York: University Books, 1964), 9, 68.

8. Thelin interview by the author, September 11, 2014.

9. Michael Fallon, "A New Paradise for Beatniks," *San Francisco Examiner*, September 5, 1965, 5.

10. Thelin interview by the author, September 11, 2014; Allen Cohen, "The *San Francisco Oracle*: A Brief History," in *The* San Francisco Oracle, *Facsimile Edition: The Psychedelic Newspaper of the Haight-Ashbury, 1966–1968* (Berkeley, Calif.: Regent Press, 1991), xxv; Jay Thelin, interviewed by Michael Klassen, August 1, 2011, http://www .billiondollarhippie.com/interviews/jay-thelin/; Charles Perry, *The Haight-Ashbury: A History* (New York: Rolling Stone Press, 1984), 76.

11. Cohen, "The *San Francisco Oracle*," xxx; *The Maze: Haight/Ashbury*, KPIX-TV, 1967, San Francisco Bay Area Television Archive, https://diva.sfsu.edu/collections/sfbatv/ bundles/189371.

12. Thelin interview by the author, September 11, 2014.

13. Leonard Wolf, *Voices from the Love Generation* (Boston: Little, Brown, 1968), 217; Thelin interview by the author, September 11, 2014.

14. "A Prophesy of a Declaration of Independence," *San Francisco Oracle*, September 20, 1966, 12; Thelin interview by the author, September 11, 2014; Cohen, "The *San Francisco Oracle*," xxv; Perry, *Haight-Ashbury*, 97; Martin A. Lee and Bruce Shlain, *Acid Dreams: The Complete Social History of LSD: The CIA, the Sixties, and Beyond* (New York: Grove Press, 1992),149.

15. Ron Thelin and Jay Thelin, "Open Letter to the Haight Street Merchants Association," *San Francisco Oracle*, November 1966, 14.

16. Perry, *Haight-Ashbury*, 108; "Hip Jobs," *San Francisco Oracle*, December 16, 1966, 23.

17. On teenage hippies as runaways and vagrants, see Karen M. Staller, *Runaways: How the Sixties Counterculture Shaped Today's Practices and Policies* (New York: Columbia University Press, 2006), and Risa Goluboff, *Vagrant Nation: Police Power, Constitutional Change, and the Making of the 1960s* (Oxford: Oxford University Press, 2016), 221–257; on the arrest and trial, see Thelin interview by the author, September 11, 2014, and "Appeals Planned—Vendors Fined in 'Love Book' Case," *San Francisco Chronicle*, June 24, 1967, 2.

18. Perry, *Haight-Ashbury*, 106–108, 195, 91, 131; Christopher Lowen Agee, *The Streets of San Francisco: Policing and the Creation of a Cosmopolitan Liberal Politics, 1950–1972* (Chicago: University of Chicago Press, 2014), 220–222.

19. "free store/property of the possessed," in *The Digger Papers* (San Francisco: The Diggers, 1968), 3; Staller, *Runaways*, 82–84.

20. Chester Anderson, "Uncle Tim'$ Children," broadside printed by the Communication Company, April 4, 1967, http://www.diggers.org/bibcit_fulltext_SQL.asp?bib2=33.

21. Thelin interview by the author, September 11, 2014; Perry, *Haight-Ashbury*, 132; Chester Anderson, "Street News for the Tenth of May—Public Acts Are Public Knowledge. Love Is What You Do[,] Not What You Say," broadside printed by the Communication Company, 1967, http://www.diggers.org/bibcit_fulltext_SQL.asp?bib2=41.

22. *The Maze*; Perry, *Haight-Ashbury*, 189.

23. Alice Echols, *Shaky Ground: The '60s and Its Aftershocks* (New York: Columbia University Press, 2002), 44–46; Kramer, *Republic of Rock*, 98; Staller, *Runaways,* 36–41, 71–99.

24. Thelin interview by Klassen, August 1, 2011.

25. Nicholas Von Hoffman, *We Are the People Our Parents Warned Us Against* (Chicago: Quadrangle Books, 1968), 261; Perry, *Haight-Ashbury*, 244.

26. Donald B. Louria, *The Drug Scene* (New York: McGraw-Hill, 1968), 42–43.

27. "The Psychedelicatessan," *Time*, February 24, 1967, 96; Ernest L. Abel, *A Marihuana Dictionary: Words, Terms, Events, and Persons Relating to Cannabis* (Westport, Conn.: Greenwood Press, 1982),49. See also Jesse Jarnow, *Heads: A Biography of Psychedelic America* (Boston: Da Capo Press, 2016).

28. John Kifner, "The Drug Scene: Many Students Now Regard Marijuana as a Part of Growing Up," *New York Times*, January 11, 1968, 18; Wilson, "Commerce in Hippieland," B16; *Buffalo Chip* 1, no. 2 (1967): 3.

29. Angela Taylor, "Bells, Books, and Candles: Psychedelia on Sale," *New York Times*, August 16, 1967, 44; Dan Lackey, interviewed by the author, Atlanta, Ga., August 15, 2013; Grant, "Girl's Small Psychedelic Shop," B2; Wilson, "Commerce in Hippieland," B16, B21; "Head Shop Busted," *Los Angeles Free Press*, December 26, 1969, 6; Mike Goodman, "Youngsters of All Ages Free to Browse Among Hashish Pipes, Obscene Comic Books and Posters," *Los Angeles Times*, April 9, 1972, Special Feature, C1.

30. On female owners, see Grant, "Girl's Small Psychedelic Shop"; Judy Hippler, "'Head Shop' for Hippies Lures the Squares, Too," *Atlanta Constitution*, July 27, 1968, L6; and Taylor, "Bells, Books, and Candles." On African American owners, see Wilson, "Commerce in Hippieland"; Randi Henderson, "Where There's Smoke There's Profit in Legit Paraphernalia Racket," *Baltimore Sun*, November 7, 1978, B1; and George Bishop, interviewed by the author, Greensboro, N.C., August 12, 2007. On teenage owners, see Grant, "Girl's Small Psychedelic Shop," and Jo Ann Harris, "The Pratt Street Conspiracy Is a Boutique," *Baltimore Sun*, February 7, 1971, FA15; and on middle-aged owners, see Wilson, "Commerce in Hippieland."

31. Harris, "Pratt Street Conspiracy Is a Boutique"; Clementine Flatbush, "S.W. Baltimore Conspiracy," *Harry*, January 8, 1971, 9; "Pratt Street Conspiracy," *Harry*, April 24–May 7, 1971, 16; George H. Lewis, "Capitalism, Contra-culture, and the Head Shop: Explorations in Structural Change," *Youth & Society*, September 1972, 88–89.

32. Bob Cooley, "Psychedelic Shop New Eugene 'Happening,'" *Eugene Register-Guard*, February 19, 1967, A3; "Grove's Head Shop—Another World," *Miami News*, October

10, 1967, C8; Hippler, "'Head Shop' for Hippies Lures the Squares, Too," L6; *The Maze*; Wilson, "Commerce in Hippieland," B16; Michael Lang, with Holly George-Warren, *The Road to Woodstock: A Definitive Look Back* (New York: Ecco, 2009), 20–25; Paul Wilkes, "Baltimore's Disconnecteds: One Can't Remember His Last Address . . . ," *Baltimore Sun Magazine*, December 17, 1967, 8; Clarence Newman, "Call It Psychedelic and It Will Sell Fast, Some Merchants Say . . . ," *Wall Street Journal*, February 9, 1967, 1; Lewis, "Capitalism, Contra-culture, and the Head Shop," 92; Abbie Hoffman, *Steal This Book* (New York: Pirate Editions, 1971), 32; Taylor, "Bells, Books, and Candles," 44.

33. Marshall Chapman, "Keeping Secrets: Why You Should Never Tell a Soul About Your Favorite Hangout," *Garden & Gun*, August–September 2009; Mark Naison, *White Boy: A Memoir* (Philadelphia: Temple University Press, 2002), 124; Staller, *Runaways*; Goluboff, *Vagrant Nation*, 221–257; William L. Partridge, *The Hippie Ghetto: The Natural History of a Subculture* (New York: Holt, Rinehart and Winston, 1973); John Lofland, "The Youth Ghetto," *Journal of Higher Education* 39, no. 3 (1968): 121–143; Christopher Mele, *Selling the Lower East Side: Culture, Real Estate, and Resistance in New York City* (Minneapolis: University of Minnesota Press, 2000), 153–179; Andrew E. Ligeti, "Spatial Empowerment and the Los Angeles Counterculture, 1965–1967: The Search for Hallowed Ground in the City of Angels," Ph.D. diss., California State University, Northridge, 2012; Amy L. Scott, "Remaking Urban in the American West: Lifestyle Politics, Micropolitan Urbanism, and Hip Capitalism in Boulder, Colorado, 1958–1978," Ph.D. diss., University of New Mexico, 2007. On street harassment of hippies and activists, see Michael E. Brown, "The Condemnation and Persecution of Hippies," *Trans-Action*, September 1969, 33–46, and Wilson, "Commerce in Hippieland," B20.

34. Nick Schou, *Orange Sunshine: The Brotherhood of Eternal Love and Its Quest to Spread Peace, Love, and Acid to the World* (New York: Thomas Dunne Books, 2010), 66–68, 71–72. See also Ray Ripton, "Head Shops Find Better Business in Diversifying," *Los Angeles Times*, May 7, 1972, CS1; "Youth Admits Selling Dope," *Miami News*, July 24, 1968, C6; Wallace Author, "Head Shop Harassed," *Space City*, August 3, 1971, 3; Grant, "Girl's Small Psychedelic Shop," B10; Wilson, "Commerce in Hippieland," B16; "Phluph Bombed," *Dallas Notes*, September 2, 1970, 5.

35. "The Age of Acquireous," 10; Faulkner, "A Rose by Any Other Name"; "Money vs. People"; Meloy, "This Is a Capitalist Society, so We're Capitalists"; Wolf, *Voices from the Love Generation*, 186; "Five Decades of Haight Memories with Gallery 683's Harry Strauch," *Hoodline*, November 19, 2014, http://hoodline.com/2014/11/five-decades-of-memories-with-gallery-683-s-harry-strauch; S. Cheer, "(II) Boston to Atlanta," *Great Speckled Bird*, March 17, 1969, 5. See also "Pot Counter-Revolutionary," 5; Levin, *Cold War University*, 142–143.

36. Wilson, "Commerce in Hippieland," B16, B17; Hippler, "'Head Shop' for Hippies Lures the Squares, Too," L6; Ripton, "Head Shops Find Better Business," CS1; Doug Brown, interviewed by the author, Austin, Tex., June 2, 2014; Lackey interview, August 15, 2013; McMillian, *Smoking Typewriters*, 124; Ron Jacobs, *Daydream Sunset: The Sixties Counterculture in the Seventies* (Petrolia, Calif.: CounterPunch Books, 2015), 117.

37. "Why Students Act That Way—a Gallup Study," *U.S. News & World Report*, June 2, 1969, 35; Senator James O. Eastland, introduction to U.S. Congress, Senate, *Marihuana–Hashish Epidemic and Its Impact on United States Security: Hearings Before the Subcommittee to Investigate the Administration of the Internal Security Act and*

Other Internal Security Laws of the Committee on the Judiciary, United States Senate (Washington, D.C.: U.S. Government Printing Office, 1974), v; Egil Krogh, *The Day Elvis Met Nixon* (Bellevue, Wash.: Pejama Press, 1994), 36; Lee, *Smoke Signals*, 119–120; Robert Young, "Nixon Declares War on Narcotics Use in U.S.," *Chicago Tribune*, June 18, 1971, 19.

38. Sinclair, *Marijuana Revolution*, 8; "We Are a People," in Conliff and Nichols, *Blacklisted News, Secret History*, 514; "1973 Marijuana Arrests Approach One-Half Million Mark," *Leaflet: The Publication of the National Organization for the Reform of Marijuana Laws*, July–August–September 1974, 1.

39. Dan Baum, *Smoke and Mirrors: The War on Drugs and the Politics of Failure* (Boston: Little, Brown, 1996); Kathleen Frydl, *The Drug Wars in America, 1940–1973* (Cambridge: Cambridge University Press, 2013); Rathge, "Pondering Pot," 30–36; Bonnie and Whitebread, *Marijuana Conviction*; Himmelstein, *Strange Career of Marihuana*; Michael Massing, *The Fix* (New York: Simon and Schuster, 1998); James R. White III, *Marijuana Puff In* (San Francisco: LeMar, 1965); Jack Nichols, "Randolfe Wicker (1928–)," in *Before Stonewall: Activists for Gay and Lesbian Rights in Historical Context*, ed. Vern L. Bullough (London: Routledge, 2002), 273–281; Lee, *Smoke Signals*, 97–102; "The *Marijuana Newsletter*," *Marijuana Newsletter*, no. 2 (March 15, 1965), 1.

40. On the Trans-Love Energies head shop, see Pun Plamondon, *Lost from the Ottawa: The Story of the Journey Back* (Victoria, Canada: Trafford, 2004), 64, 92, 96–97; "John Sinclair: Introducing a Counter-Culture Legend," *Sensi Seeds*, September 19, 2013, http://sensiseeds.com/en/blog/john-sinclair-introducing-a-counter-culture-legend/; John Sinclair, *10 Years for 2 Joints: Free John Sinclair* (N.p.: International Committee to Free John Sinclair, 1969), 3–5; "Dec. 1971–Dec. 1972—Year of Historic Accomplishments," *Ann Arbor Sun*, December 1–15, 1972, 2; "Michigan to Free Inmates," *New York Times*, April 8, 1972, 32; *People v. Lorentzen*, 387 Mich. 167, 194 N.W.2d 827 (Mich. 1972); "We Won!!" *Ann Arbor Sun*, April 13–27, 1972, 2; "Ann Arbor Eases Marijuana Curbs: Maximum Penalty Is Fine of $5—Tickets Issued," *New York Times*, September 24, 1972, 42.

41. "Free Lee Otis Johnson: Houston's Black Political Prisoner," 1969, SNCC, Lee Otis Johnson Defense Committee, 1970–1972, Social Protest Collection, 1943–1982, Carton 6, Reel 21, Folder 23, Bancroft Library, University of California, Berkeley; Sinclair, *Marijuana Revolution*, 8–19.

42. "Are You Ready for . . . Amorphia," *Marijuana Review*, October–December 1969, 16; Everett R. Holles, "Drive to Legalize Marijuana Is Funded by Nonprofit Company in California," *New York Times*, October 10, 1972, 19; "When Reformers Fall Out," *New York Times Magazine*, March 11, 1973, 25, 98; Mike Aldrich, "Acapulco Gold," *Marijuana Review*, January–June 1971, 11.

43. "What You Can Do to Help Legalization," *Marijuana Review*, July–September 1971, 12; Blair Newman, Michael Aldrich, and Frank Richards, "Amorphia," *Ann Arbor Sun*, May 28–June 3, 1971, 15; Aldrich, "Acapulco Gold," 11.

44. Holles, "Drive to Legalize Marijuana," 19; William Endicott, "Death Penalty Approved; Coast Environmental Plan Winning," *Los Angeles Times*, November 8, 1972, A17; Baum, *Smoke and Mirrors*, 73; "Oregonians Take Law Easing Marijuana Penalties in Stride," *Los Angeles Times*, September 9, 1973, 1, 8; Rathge, "Pondering Pot," 35.

45. Patrick Anderson, "The Pot Lobby," *New York Times*, January 21, 1973, E8, E9; Patrick Anderson, *High in America: The True Story Behind NORML and the Politics of*

Marijuana (New York: Viking Press, 1981), 58; *Leaflet*, advertisement, July–August–September 1973, 6; Paul Hentrickson, "He's the Top 'Pot' Pusher in Washington: Ex-bureaucrat Turned Lobbyist Is Known as 'Mr. Marijuana,'" *Los Angeles Times*, May 7, 1978, S2.

46. Goodman, "Youngsters of All Ages," Special Features, C1; "Giving Consumer Easy-to-Use Product Is the Basis of Robert Burton Success," *United States Tobacco Journal*, October 5, 1978, 1; Mike Aldrich, "The Most Accurate Gauge Available of the Extent of Marijuana Smoking in the U.S.," *Marijuana Review*, July–September 1971, 16–17; David Lamb, "400% Jump: Roll-Your-Own Boom Clue to Marijuana Use," *Los Angeles Times*, February 12, 1971, A1.

47. Lackey interview, August 15, 2013.

48. Ibid.

49. Ibid.

50. Ibid.; Art Harris, "Singles Revisited: Grounded Jet-Setters?" *Atlanta Constitution*, March 19, 1974, B5.

51. "Introducing . . . *High Times*," 10; McMillian, *Smoking Typewriters*, 115–139; Andy Kowl, interviewed by the author, Rockville, Md., August 2–3, 2013; John Grissim, *We Have Come for Your Daughters: What Went Down on the Medicine Ball Caravan* (New York: Morrow, 1972), 111; Thomas K. Forcade, *Underground Press Anthology* (New York: Ace Books, 1972), title page. For more on Forcade, see Sean Howe's forthcoming biography *Agents of Chaos*; "The Most Dangerous Magazine in America," *High Times*, November 1977, 29.

52. See, for example, *High Times* issues from January and July 1977; Kowl interview, August 2–3, 2013; Daniel Machalaba, "The Pot Trade," *Wall Street Journal*, July 29, 1980, 1; "It's Official: 4 Million People Read *High Times*," *High Times*, September 1978, DK10. For political reporting in *High Times*, see, for example, Glenn O'Brien, "I Remember Civil Defense: How We Survived the Apocalypse," *High Times*, May 1977, 62–66, 75–78, 90–92; Robert Singer, "The Rise of the Dope Dictators: How the Dope War Replaced the Cold War—a Study in U.S. Foreign Policy," *High Times*, March 1977, 52–58, 84–90, 108–114; and Douglas Kelley, "The $350-Billion Arms Trade," *High Times*, November 1978, 65–69.

53. "Giving Consumer Easy-to-Use Product," 1.

54. James Barron, "Issue and Debate: Can Drug Paraphernalia Be Banned?" *New York Times*, May 26, 1980, B19; "Legal Debate Grows with Drug Paraphernalia Laws," *New York Times*, August 10, 1980, 38; U.S. Congress, *Drug Paraphernalia*, 5, 40, 55–56, 87; A. Craig Copetas, "Paraphernalia '78," *High Times*, October 1978, 54.

55. Copetas, "Paraphernalia '78," 54; see also Sloman, *Reefer Madness*, 128.

56. "11 States Decriminalize Marijuana Possession," H22. In 1979, according to the National Institute on Drug Abuse, 35 percent of young adults reported they had used marijuana in the previous month. After those numbers declined in the 1980s and 1990s, they began to rebound in the twenty-first century, but in 2014 still only 19 percent of young adults reported marijuana use in the previous month (Patricia M. Fishburne, Herbert Irving Abelson, and Ira H Cisin, *National Survey on Drug Abuse: Main Findings 1979* [Rockville, Md.: National Institute on Drug Abuse, 1979], 23). See also Substance Abuse and Mental Health Services Administration, *Behavioral Health Trends in the United States: Results from the 2014 National Survey on Drug Use and Health* (Washington, D.C.: U.S. Department of Health and Human Services, 2015), 6; Renee M. Johnson, Brian Fairman, Tamika Gilreath, Ziming Xuan, Emily F. Rothman, Taylor

Parnham, and C. Debra M. Furr-Holden, "Past 15-Year Trends in Adolescent Marijuana Use: Differences by Race/Ethnicity and Sex," *Drug and Alcohol Dependence* 155
(2015): 9; David E. Newton, *Marijuana* (Santa Barbara, Calif.: ABC-Clio, 2013),
229–230; U.S. Bureau of the Census, *Statistical Abstracts of the United States: 1980*,
101st ed. (Washington, D.C.: U.S. Department of Commerce, 1980), 129; Robert E.
Schell and Elizabeth Hall, *Developmental Psychology Today* (New York: CRM/Ran-
dom House, 1979), 389. On public opinion, see Gallup, "Do You Think the Possession
of Small Amounts of Marijuana Should or Should Not Be Treated as a Criminal
Offense?" poll, April 1977, iPoll Databank at the Roper Center for Public Opinion
Research, http://roperweb.ropercenter.uconn.edu.

57. Marsha (Schuchard) Manatt, *Parents, Peers, and Pot* (Rockville, Md.: Alcohol, Drug
Abuse, and Mental Health Administration, National Institute on Drug Abuse, U.S.
Department of Health, Education, and Welfare, 1979), 1–9; Barbara Laker, "PRIDE's
War on Drugs Is Getting Results," *Atlanta Constitution*, March 21, 1984, B1.

58. "Parents Criticize 9 Stores," *Atlanta Constitution*, November 23, 1977, A8; Lucius
Lomax, "DeKalb Drug Fighter Urges Parents to Search Their Children's Bedrooms,"
Atlanta Constitution, May 28, 1978, B4; Tom Crawford, "Head Shops on Down Trip
in DeKalb," *Atlanta Constitution*, April 23, 1978, B5; Baum, *Smoke and Mirrors*, 123;
Manatt, *Parents, Peers, and Pot*.

59. Crawford, "Head Shops on Down Trip in DeKalb," B5; Barry King, "Police Jail Owners of Head Shop," *Atlanta Constitution*, December 30, 1977, A13; Mindy Fetterman,
"'Head Shops' Seek Return of Licenses," *Atlanta Constitution*, January 24, 1978, A11.

60. *J. Wayne Housworth et al. v. Patrick C. Glisson*, 485 F. Supp. 29 (N.D. Ga. 1978); Fred
Hiatt, "Parents Fight to Close Head Shops in DeKalb," *Atlanta Constitution*, October
28, 1979, B1.

61. *Code of Georgia Annotated Including Code of 1981*, Book 10, Title 26, §26-9913, 1983,
581–584; Lyn Martin, "Pot March May Lead Into Jail," *Atlanta Constitution,* April 6,
1978, C2; Jerry Schwartz, "Police Pinch Pro-pot Protesters in Park," *Atlanta Constitution*, April 8, 1978, A1; "The Anti-paraphernalia Laws," *Baltimore Sun*, November 7,
1978, B2; Barry Henderson, "Head Shop Owners Sue State Over New Statute," *Atlanta
Constitution*, April 11, 1978, C2.

62. George Rodrigue, "'Head Shops' Sue Hinson McAuliffe," *Atlanta Constitution*,
April 6, 1979, C4; Hiatt, "Parents Fight to Close Head Shops in DeKalb," B6.

63. Copetas, "Paraphernalia '78," 55; *Paraphernalia & Accessories Digest*, June 1, 1978; *Paraphernalia Digest: Newsmagazine of the Industry*, October 1979, copy in author's files;
Kowl interview, August 2, 2013; "Paraphernalia Trade Assoc. Hires Stroup to Lobby,"
Paraphernalia Digest—Newsmagazine of the Industry, January 1979, 1, copy in author's
files.

64. Benjamin C. Waterhouse, *Lobbying America: The Politics of Business from Nixon to
NAFTA* (Princeton, N.J.: Princeton University Press, 2013).

65. Brown interview, June 2, 2014; Goodman, "Youngsters of All Ages Free," Special Fea-
ture, C1; U.S. Congress, *Drug Paraphernalia*, 9; "NORML FORML: S-1437 Meets
Smoke-In," *Yipster Times*, March 1, 1978, 14; *Indiana Chapter, NORML v. Sendak*,
Th 75–142-C (S.D. Ind. 1980).

66. Laura Onkey, "Voodoo Child: Jimi Hendrix and the Politics of Race in the Sixties,"
in Braunstein and Doyle, *Imagine Nation*, 192–193, 199–201; Howard Brick, *The Age
of Contradiction: American Thought and Culture in the 1960s* (New York: Twayne,
1998), 114; Kramer, *Republic of Rock*, 10. On African American head shop owners, see

Wilson, "Commerce in Hippieland"; Henderson, "Where There's Smoke There's Profit"; Bishop interview, August 12, 2007.

67. National Organization for the Reform of Marijuana Laws, "Miscellaneous Publications, 1975–1996," Pamphlet Collection, File 74-1345, Wisconsin Historical Society Library, Madison. See also the National Organization for the Reform of Marijuana Laws organ *Leaflet*, issues for July, August, September 1973; July, August, September 1974; September, October, November, December 1975; January, February, March, April 1976; September, October, November, December 1976; and July, August, September 1977. On the racial demographics of marijuana arrests, see Weldon T. Johnson, Robert E. Petersen, and L. Edward Wells, "Arrest Probabilities for Marijuana Users as Indicators of Selective Law Enforcement," *American Journal of Sociology* 83, no. 3 (1977): 681–691; James F. Mosher, "Discriminatory Practices in Marijuana Arrests: Results from a National Survey of Young Men," *Contemporary Drug Problems* 9 (Spring 1980): 93–94, 98–99. The 1970s thus represent an unusual period in which enforcement of marijuana laws became less racially discriminatory, if only because more whites were arrested. Such narrowing of marijuana-arrest disparities was short-lived, however, and reversed with the reinvigoration of a racialized war on drugs from the early 1980s onward, as shown in Baum, *Smoke and Mirrors*, 137–250; Doris Marie Provine, *Unequal Under Law: Race in the War on Drugs* (Chicago: University of Chicago Press, 2008), 103–139; and Donna Murch, "Crack in Los Angeles: Crisis, Militarization, and Black Response to the Late Twentieth-Century War on Drugs," *Journal of American History* 102, no. 1 (2015): 162–173. On the specific patterns of racial discrimination in marijuana arrests that emerged after 1980, see Jerry Mandel, "Is Marijuana Law Enforcement Racist?" *Journal of Psychoactive Drugs* 20, no. 1 (1988): 83–84; Rajeev Ramchand, Rosalie Liccardo Pacula, and Martin Y. Iguchi, "Racial Differences in Marijuana-Users' Risk of Arrest in the United States," *Drug and Alcohol Dependence* 84 (2006): 264–272. On an alternative argument that unequal marijuana enforcement in the 1970s was designed to protect white suburban drug users and treat them as "impossible criminals," see Matthew D. Lassiter, "Impossible Criminals: The Suburban Imperatives of America's War on Drugs," *Journal of American History* 102, no. 1 (2015): 126–140. For an interpretation that blames marijuana use in the late 1970s on the counterculture, see Manatt, *Parents, Peers, and Pot*, 22–23.

68. Testimony, U.S. Congress, *Drug Paraphernalia*, 5.

69. Ibid., 14–16; Stanley Buder, *Capitalizing on Change: A Social History of American Business* (Chapel Hill: University of North Carolina Press, 2009), 332–333, 352–357; Judith Stein, *Pivotal Decade: How the United States Traded Factories for Finance in the Seventies* (New Haven, Conn.: Yale University Press, 2010), 250–251.

70. Testimony, U.S. Congress, *Drug Paraphernalia*, 56.

71. Ibid., 52–53.

72. Gary Cross, *The Cute and the Cool: Wondrous Innocence and Modern American Children's Culture* (Oxford: Oxford University Press, 2004), 182–183; Steven Mintz, *Huck's Raft: A History of American Childhood* (Cambridge, Mass.: Belknap Press of Harvard University Press, 2004), 336; Philip J. Jenkins, *Decade of Nightmares: The End of the Sixties and the Making of Eighties America* (Oxford: Oxford University Press, 2006), 256–272; Ellen Hume, "Network of Parent Groups Formed to Combat 'Massive Drug Epidemic,'" *Los Angeles Times*, May 9, 1980, B19; Massing, *The Fix*, 153; Sue Rusche, "Striking Back," *Atlanta Constitution*, April 19, 1984, H27.

73. "Carter's 1-Ounce 'Pot' Plan," *Los Angeles Times*, August 2, 1977, A1; James T. Wooten, "Carter Seeks to End Marijuana Penalty for Small Amounts," *New York Times*, August 3, 1977, 37; U.S. Congress, *Drug Paraphernalia*, 17.

74. Robert Coram, "Showdown Looms in the Head Shop War," *Atlanta Constitution*, September 10, 1980, C1 ; *High Ol' Times, Inc. v. Busbee*, 449 F. Supp. 364 (N.D. Ga. 1978); *Code of Georgia*, Book 10, Title 26, §26-9913, 584.

75. Greg Witcher, "Ruling's Effect Locally Is Debatable," *Atlanta Constitution*, March 4, 1982, A1, A11; *Hoffman Estates v. Flipside, Hoffman Estates*, 455 U.S. 489 (1982); Kerry Murphy Healey, "Controlling Drug Paraphernalia," in *Handbook of Drug Control in the United States*, ed. James Inciardi (New York: Greenwood Press, 1990), 318.

76. Healey, "Controlling Drug Paraphernalia," 319–320.

77. On the war on drugs in the 1980s, see Baum, *Smoke and Mirrors*, 137–250; Provine, *Unequal Under Law*, 103–139; Murch, "Crack in Los Angeles"; James E. Hawdon, "The Role of Presidential Rhetoric in the Creation of a Moral Panic: Reagan, Bush, and the War on Drugs," *Deviant Behavior* 22, no. 5 (2001): 419–445. On paraphernalia laws, see Mail Order Drug Paraphernalia Control Act, Anti-Drug Abuse Act of 1986, P.L. 99-570, Title I, Subtitle O, §§1821–1823; Healey, "Controlling Drug Paraphernalia," 317–320, 322–324.

78. Healey, "Controlling Drug Paraphernalia," 325. On conservative critiques, see Allan D. Bloom, *The Closing of the American Mind: How Higher Education Has Failed Democracy and Impoverished the Souls of Today's Students* (New York: Simon and Schuster, 1987); Dinesh D'Souza, *Illiberal Education: The Politics of Race and Sex on Campus* (New York: Free Press, 1991); "White House Stop-Drug-Use Program—Why the Emphasis Is on Marijuana," *Government Executive*, October 1982, 22.

4. THE "FEMINIST ECONOMIC REVOLUTION"

1. Joanne Parrent, with the cooperation of Connye Harper, *Sowing the Seeds of Feminist Economic Revolution—the Feminist Economic Network Association* (Baltimore: Diana Press, 1976), 1, 8–9, Kinsey Institute Library and Special Collections, Indiana University, Bloomington; Feminist Economic Network, "Feminist Women's City Club," Feminist Federal Credit Union, Special Collections, Manuscripts and Archives, MSS 251, Box 1, Folder 1, Michigan State University, East Lansing; John Askins, "Old Lady, New Life: A Club for 'Today's Woman,'" *Detroit Free Press*, April 9, 1976, B1, B4; "Feminists Open Club in Detroit," *Baltimore Sun*, April 10, 1976, A3.

2. Jackie St. Joan, "Feminist Economic Seeds Split—Two Groups Sprout in Detroit," *Big Mama Rag*, January 1, 1976, 1; Belita Cowan and Cheryl Peek, "Special Report: The Controversy at FEN, the City Club, and the Credit Union," *her-self*, May 1976, 10–11; Martha Shelley, "What Is FEN? I Do Not Support the Women of FEN," self-published, 1976, Diana Press Records, Collection 2135, Box 14, Folder 12, June L. Mazer Lesbian Archive, University of California at Los Angeles.

3. Nancy Levit, *The Gender Line: Men, Women, and the Law* (New York: New York University Press, 1998), 150–158; Suzanne Staggenborg, "Can Feminist Organizations Be Effective?" in *Feminist Organizations: Harvest of the New Women's Movement*, ed. Myra M. Ferree and Patricia Y. Martin (Philadelphia: Temple University Press, 1995), 339; Francine Du Plessix Gray, "That Women Know Themselves: Gornick," *New York Times*, February 4, 1979, BR3; "Divisions Among Women Held Political Hindrance," *New York Times*, July 17, 1977, 24.

4. Joreen (Jo Freeman), "Trashing: The Dark Side of Sisterhood," *Ms.*, April 1976, 49–51, 92–98.

5. On differences among radical, "politico," liberal, and cultural feminists as well as the mistaken idea that cultural feminists had a monopoly on feminist businesses, see Alice Echols, *Daring to Be Bad: Radical Feminism in America, 1967–1975* (Minneapolis: University of Minnesota Press, 1989), 3–5, 51–101, 269–281. On a lesbian-feminist movement or political lesbian movement distinct from both the male gay liberation movement and the heterosexual feminist movement, see Jill Johnston, *Lesbian Nation* (New York: Simon and Schuster, 1973), 275–279; *The Furies: Lesbian/Feminist Monthly*, 1, no. 1 (January 1972), to 2, no. 3 (May–June 1973); "Chronicle—the Lesbian Movement 1970–1976," *Lesbian Tide*, July 1, 1976, 24–25, 35; Charlotte Bunche, "Learning from Lesbian Separatism," *Ms.*, November 1976, 60–61, 99; Nancy Myron and Charlotte Bunch, "Introduction," in *Lesbianism and the Women's Movement*, ed. Nancy Myron and Charlotte Bunch (Baltimore: Diana Press, 1976), 9–13; Lillian Faderman, *The Gay Revolution: The Story of the Struggle* (New York: Simon and Schuster, 2015), 227–246; Robert O. Self, *All in the Family: The Realignment of American Democracy Since the 1960s* (New York: Hill and Wang, 2012), 179–180, 224–225. On feminist writings on business, see Toni Carabillo and Judith Meuli, "Another View: Toward a Feminist Business Ethic," *Ms.*, April 1976, 70; Coletta Reid, "Taking Care of Business," *Quest: A Feminist Quarterly* 1, no. 2 (1974): 6–24; Barbara McLean, "So You Want to Start a Business," *Lesbian Tide*, December 1973, 13–14; Susan Davis, "How to Start Your Own Business," *Ms.*, June 1973, 55–79.

6. *Selected Characteristics of Women-Owned Businesses 1977* (Washington, D.C.: U.S. Department of Commerce, Bureau of the Census, 1980), 1; *1982 Economic Census: Woman-Owned Businesses* (Washington, D.C.: U.S. Department of Commerce, Bureau of the Census, 1986), 4; *1987 Economic Censuses: Woman-Owned Businesses* (Washington, D.C.: U.S. Department of Commerce, Bureau of the Census, 1990), 6–7.

7. Angel Kwolek-Folland, *Incorporating Women: A History of Women and Business in the United States* (New York: Twayne, 1998), 9, 14–16, 45, 48, 87, 113–116, 126–129. On women business owners in the United States, see also Angel Kwollek-Folland, *Engendering Business: Men and Women in the Corporate Office, 1870–1930* (Baltimore: Johns Hopkins University Press, 1994); Mary Yeager, *Women in Business*, 3 vols. (Cheltenham, U.K.: Edward Elgar, 1999), and "Will There Ever Be a Feminist Business History?" *International Library of Critical Writings in Business History* 17 (1999): 3–44; Debra A. Michals, "Beyond Pin Money: The Rise of Women's Small Business Ownership, 1945–1980," Ph.D. diss., New York University, 2002; Caroline Bird, *Enterprising Women* (New York: Norton, 1976); Edith Sparks, *Capital Intentions: Female Proprietors in San Francisco, 1850–1920* (Chapel Hill: University of North Carolina Press, 2006); Wendy Gamber, *The Female Economy: The Millinery and Dressmaking Trades, 1860–1930* (Champaign: University of Illinois Press, 1997); Sarah Deutsch, *Women and the City: Gender, Space, and Power in Boston, 1870–1940* (Oxford: Oxford University Press, 2000). On female labor activists who criticized business, see Dorothy Sue Cobble, *The Other Women's Movement: Workplace Justice and Social Rights in Modern America* (Princeton, N.J.: Princeton University Press, 2005); Dorothy Sue Cobble, Linda Gordon, and Astrid Henry, *Feminism Unfinished: A Short, Surprising History of American Women's Movements* (New York: Norton, 2014), 1–68.

8. Key historical works on second-wave feminism include Sara Evans, *Personal Politics: The Roots of Women's Liberation in the Civil Rights Movement and the New Left* (New York: Knopf, 1979), and *Tidal Wave: How Women Changed America at Century's End* (New York: Free Press, 2003); Echols, *Daring to Be Bad*; Nancy Hewitt, ed., *No Permanent Waves: Recasting Histories of U.S. Feminism* (New Brunswick, N.J.: Rutgers University Press, 2010); Ruth Rosen, *The World Split Open: How the Modern Women's Movement Changed America* (New York: Viking, 2000); Stephanie Gilmore, ed., *Feminist Coalitions: Historical Perspectives on Second-Wave Feminism in the United States* (Urbana: University of Illinois Press, 2008); Cobble, *The Other Women's Movement;* Cobble, Gordon, and Henry, *Feminism Unfinished*; Christine Stansell, *The Feminist Promise: 1792 to the Present* (New York: Modern Library, 2010); Patricia Bradley, *Mass Media and the Shaping of American Feminism, 1963–1975* (Jackson: University Press of Mississippi, 2003); Barbara A. Crow, ed., *Radical Feminism: A Documentary Reader* (New York: New York University Press, 2000); Anne Enke, *Finding the Movement: Sexuality, Contested Space, and Feminist Activism* (Durham, N.C.: Duke University Press, 2007); Anne M. Valk, *Radical Sisters: Second-Wave Feminism and Black Liberation in Washington* (Champaign: University of Illinois Press, 2008); Melissa Estes Blair, *Revolutionizing Expectations: Women's Organizations, Feminism, and American Politics, 1965–1980* (Athens: University of Georgia Press, 2014); Barbara Love, ed., *Feminists Who Changed America, 1963–1975* (Urbana: University of Illinois Press, 2006); Stephanie Gilmore, *Groundswell: Grassroots Feminist Activism in Postwar America* (New York: Routledge, 2013); Katherine Turk, *Equality on Trial: Gender and Rights in the Modern American Workplace* (Philadelphia: University of Pennsylvania Press, 2016).
9. Betty Friedan, *The Feminine Mystique* (1963; reprint, New York: Norton, 1997), 245, 270.
10. New York Radical Women, "No More Miss America!" (August 1968), reprinted in *Sisterhood Is Powerful: An Anthology of Writings from the Women's Liberation Movement*, ed. Robin Morgan (New York: Random House, 1970), 521–524.
11. WITCH, "Confront the Whoremakers at the Bridal Fair," February 1969, in Morgan, *Sisterhood Is Powerful*, 538, 544–546; Echols, *Daring to Be Bad*, 97; Bonnie J. Dow, *Watching Women's Liberation, 1970: Feminism's Pivotal Year on the Network News* (Urbana: University of Illinois Press, 2014), 67; Jean E. Hunter, "A Daring New Concept: *The Ladies' Home Journal* and Modern Feminism," *NWSA Journal* 2, no. 4 (1990): 583–602.
12. Steve Craig, "Madison Avenue Versus *The Feminine Mystique*: The Advertising Industry's Response to the Women's Movement," in *Disco Divas: Women and Popular Culture in the 1970s*, ed. Sherrie A. Inness (Philadelphia: University of Pennsylvania Press, 2003), 13–23; Hunter, "A Daring New Concept"; Mary Bralove, "Mi$$ America: How a Beauty Spends Her Year-Long Reign Pushing Sponsors' Fare," *Wall Street Journal*, January 21, 1970, 1.
13. *Women-Owned Businesses 1972* (Washington, D.C.: U.S. Department of Commerce, Bureau of the Census, March 1976), 1; Michals, "Beyond Pin Money," 12–15, 33, 186, 253.
14. Shulamith Firestone, *The Dialectic of Sex: The Case for Feminist Revolution* (New York: Morrow, 1974); Kate Millett, *Sexual Politics* (New York: Columbia University Press, 1969); Morgan, *Sisterhood Is Powerful*; Evans, *Tidal Wave*, 26–30, 39–46, 59; Dow, *Watching Women's Liberation, 1970*; Echols, *Daring to Be Bad*, 3–22, 83–92; Carol Hanisch, "The Personal Is Political," in *Notes from the Second Year: Women's*

Liberation. Major Writings of the Radical Feminists (New York: Radical Feminism, 1970), 76–77; Pamela Allen, *Free Space: A Perspective on the Small Group in Women's Liberation*, 2nd ed. (Washington, N.J.: Times Change Press, 1970), 6; Kathie Sarachild, "A Program for Feminist Consciousness-Raising," in Crow, *Radical Feminism*, 273–276; Pamela Allen, "The Small Group Process," in Crow, *Radical Feminism*, 277–281; June Arnold, "Consciousness-Raising," in Crow, *Radical Feminism*, 282–286; Vivian Gornick, "Consciousness," in Crow, *Radical Feminism*, 287–300. On a related concept of "feminist places," see Daphne Spain, *Constructive Feminism: Women's Spaces and Women's Rights in the American City* (Ithaca, N.Y.: Cornell University Press, 2016).

15. Karla Jay, *Tales of the Lavender Menace: A Memoir of Liberation* (New York: Basic Books, 2000), 137–146; Echols, *Daring to Be Bad*, 214–217, 220–230; Radicalesbians, *The Woman Identified Woman* (Pittsburgh: Know, 1970); Valk, *Radical Sisters*, 135–157; "Lesbians in Revolt," *The Furies*, January 1972, 9; Coletta Reid, "Details . . . ," *The Furies*, June–July 1972, 7.

16. Lee Schwing and Helaine Harris, "Building Feminist Institutions," *The Furies*, May–June 1973, 2–3; Reid, "Details . . . ," 7.

17. Margaret Mary Finnegan, *Selling Suffrage: Consumer Culture & Votes for Women* (New York: Columbia University Press, 1999), 2, 123–124, 199 n. 39; Joanne Horn Rettke, "A Study of Women's Centers in Selected Institutions of Higher Education: The Relationship of Institutional and Non-institutional Funding Sources to the Center's Organizational Structure, Operational Budget, and Programmatic Thrust," Ph.D. diss., Michigan State University, 1979, 25–30; Spain, *Constructive Feminism*, 50–83; Schwing and Harris, "Building Feminist Institutions," 2–3.

18. Ginny Berson, Meg Christian, Judy Dlugacz, Cyndi Gair, and Helaine Harris, "the muses of olivia: our own economy, our own song," *off our backs* 4, no. 9 (1974): 2–3; Schwing and Harris, "Building Feminist Institutions," 2–3; Reid, "Details . . . ," 7.

19. Kelly Hankin, *The Girls in the Back Room: Looking at the Lesbian Bar* (Minneapolis: University of Minnesota Press, 2002); Maxine Wolf, "Bars," in *Encyclopedia of Lesbian Histories and Cultures*, ed. Bonnie Zimmerman (New York: Routledge, 2013), 95–96; Katie Gilmartin, " 'We Weren't Bar People': Middle-Class Lesbian Identities and Cultural Spaces," *GLQ: A Journal of Lesbian and Gay Studies* 3, no. 1 (1996): 1–51; Heather Murray, "Free for All Lesbians: Lesbian Cultural Production and Consumption in the United States during the 1970s," *Journal of the History of Sexuality* 16, no. 2 (2007): 251.

20. On a lesbian-feminist movement or political lesbian movement as a separate movement, see the sources cited in note 5.

21. Becky W. Thompson, *A Promise and a Way of Life: White Antiracist Activism* (Minneapolis: University of Minnesota Press, 2001), 140–142; Sherie M. Randolph, *Florynce "Flo" Kennedy: The Life of a Black Feminist Radical* (Chapel Hill: University of North Carolina Press, 2015), 101–102; Alexa Freeman and Jackie McMillan, "Building Feminist Organizations," *Quest: A Feminist Quarterly* 3, no. 3 (1976–77): 74; Karen Kollias, "Spiral of Change: An Introduction to *Quest*," *Quest: A Feminist Quarterly* 1, no. 1 (1974): 5, 9. On lesbian-feminist separatism during the second wave, see Verta Taylor and Leila J. Rupp, "Women's Culture and Lesbian Feminist Activism: A Reconsideration of Cultural Feminism," *Signs: Journal of Women in Culture and Society* 19, no. 1 (1993): 32–61; Bunch, "Learning from Lesbian Separatism,"

60–61, 99; Ariel Levy, "Lesbian Nation: When Gay Women Took to the Road," *New Yorker*, March 2, 2009, 30–35.

22. Davis, "How to Start Your Own Business," 70; Kirsten Grimstad and Susan Rennie, eds., *The New Woman's Survival Catalog: A Woman-Made Book* (New York: Coward, McCann & Geoghegan, 1973), 182; Stephanie Marcus, interviewed by the author, Skype, December 17, 2014.

23. Davis, "How to Start Your Own Business," 70; "Feminists in Business for Libbers," *Los Angeles Times*, January 11, 1973, H9; Marcus interview, December 17, 2014.

24. Marcus interview, December 17, 2014; Davis, "How to Start Your Own Business," 71; Grimstad and Rennie, *New Woman's Survival Catalog*, 182.

25. Davis, "How to Start Your Own Business," 70; "Feminists in Business for Libbers," H9; Bill Hieronymus, "For Some Feminists, Owning a Business Is Real Liberation," *Wall Street Journal*, April 15, 1974, 1; Marcus interview, December 17, 2014.

26. *Financing the Revolution: The NOW Catalog of Feminist Products* 2, no. 1 (1973), and *Financing the Revolution: The NOW Catalog of Feminist Products* 2, no. 2 (1973), both in Toni Carabillo and Judith Meuli Papers, MC725, Folder 29.9, Schlesinger Library, Radcliffe Institute for Advanced Study, Harvard University, Cambridge, Mass.

27. *Starting a Bookstore: Non-capitalist Operation Within a Capitalist Economy* (Oakland, Calif.: ICI: A Woman's Place, [c. 1973]), cited in Grimstad and Rennie, *New Woman's Survival Catalog*, 23. List of feminist businesses compiled by the author from various sources, including Grimstad and Rennie, *New Woman's Survival Catalog*; Kirsten Grimstad and Susan Rennie, *The New Woman's Survival Sourcebook* (New York: Knopf, 1975); *Women's Work and Women's Studies* (New York: Women's Center, Barnard College, 1972); Deena Peterson, *A Practical Guide to the Women's Movement* (New York: Women's Action Alliance, 1975); Myra E. Barrer, *Women's Organizations and Leaders Directory, 1975–1976* (Washington, D.C.: Today Publications and News Service, 1975); Cynthia E. Harrison, *Women's Movement Media: A Source Guide* (New York: Bowker, 1975); Trysh Travis, "The Women in Print Movement: History and Implications," *Book History* 11 (2008): 278–280. On feminist bookstores, see also Kristen Hogan, *The Feminist Bookstore Movement: Lesbian Antiracism and Feminist Accountability* (Durham, N.C.: Duke University Press, 2016), and "Women's Studies in Feminist Bookstores: 'All the Women's Studies Women Would Come In,'" *Signs: Journal of Women in Culture and Society* 33, no. 3 (2008): 595–621; Junko R. Onosaka, *Feminist Revolution in Literacy: Women's Bookstores in the United States* (New York: Routledge, 2006); Kathleen Liddle, "A Shop of One's Own: The Culture and Contradictions of Feminist Bookstores," Ph.D. diss., Emory University, 2006; Saralyn Chesnut and Amanda C. Gable, "'Women Ran It': Charis Books and More and Atlanta's Lesbian-Feminist Community, 1971–1981," in *Carryin' On in the Lesbian and Gay South*, ed. John Howard (New York: New York University Press, 1997), 241–284.

28. On feminist organizational models, see Ferree and Martin, *Feminist Organizations*; Lois Ahrens, "Battered Women's Refuges: Feminist Cooperatives vs. Social Service Institutions," *Radical America* 14, no. 3 (1980): 41–47; and Diana Metzendorf, *The Evolution of Feminist Organizations: An Organizational Study* (Lanham, Md.: University Press of America, 2005). On *Our Bodies, Ourselves* (Boston: New England Free Press, 1971), see Wendy Kline, "The Making of *Our Bodies, Ourselves*: Rethinking

Women's Health and Second-Wave Feminism," in Gilmore, *Feminist Coalitions*, 66–70, and Kathy Davis, *The Making of* Our Bodies, Ourselves: *How Feminism Travels Across Borders* (Durham, N.C.: Duke University Press, 2007).

29. Casey Czarnik, interviewed by the author, Skype, May 12, 2015, audio recording; Margaret Blanchard, "Speaking the Plural: The Example of *Women: A Journal of Liberation*," *NWSA Journal* 4, no. 1 (Spring 1992): 84–97; Grimstad and Rennie, *New Woman's Survival Catalog*, 9.

30. Grimstad and Rennie, *New Woman's Survival Catalog*, 9; Blanchard, "Speaking the Plural"; Laurel A. Clark, "Beyond the Gay/Straight Split: Socialist Feminists in Baltimore," *NWSA Journal* 19, no. 2 (2007): 1–31; "Est. Your Own Printshop," 1979, handwritten manuscript, Diana Press Records, Collection 2135, Box 13, Folder 10, June L. Mazer Lesbian Archive, University of California at Los Angeles; Hieronymus, "For Some Feminists," 1.

31. Coletta Reid and Kathy Tomyris, "Diana Press: An Overview," March 9, 1979, 1, Atlanta Lesbian Feminist Alliance (ALFA) Collection, Box 11, Folder 24, Sally Bingham Center for Women's History and Culture, Duke University; Grimstad and Rennie, *New Woman's Survival Catalog*, 9; Nancy Myron and Charlotte Bunch, eds., *Class and Feminism: A Collection of Essays from the Furies* (Baltimore: Diana Press, 1974); *Heterosexuality & the Women's Movement* (Baltimore: Diana Press, [c. 1973]).

32. Nancy Myron, "Class Beginnings," *The Furies*, March–April 1972, 2–3; Myron and Bunch, *Class and Feminism*; Reid and Tomyris, "Diana Press," 1. On second-wave feminists' "equal rights teleology" that elided economic and labor issues as well as on the lesser-known, labor-oriented "other women's movement," see Cobble, *The Other Women's Movement*, 7–8. Other early second-wave writings on the economic and class dimensions of feminism include Margaret Bentson, "The Political Economy of Women's Liberation," *Monthly Review* 24, no. 1 (1969): 2–13; Barbara Mehrhof, "On Class Structure Within the Women's Movement," in *Notes from the Second Year*, 103–104, 107–108; and Schwing and Harris, "Building Feminist Institutions."

33. Susan Sojourner, "Profit—That Nasty, Ugly Word," 4–5; Lorraine Allen, "The Necessity for an Ethical Veneer," 7–8, both in *Dealing with the Real World: 13 Papers by Feminist Entrepreneurs* (New York City: Feminist Business Association, 1973), 7–8; Cynthia Ellen Harris, "Products by Feminists for Feminists," in *Women's Movement Media: A Source Guide* (New York: Bowker, 1975), 47.

34. Sojourner, "Profit," 4; Marjorie Collins, "Why Do We Feel Guilty Doing Work We Enjoy? Why Do Other Women Resent or Envy Us?" in *Dealing with the Real World*, 5; Allen, "Necessity for an Ethical Veneer," 7–8.

35. *Dealing with the Real World*; Sojourner, "Profit," 4.

36. Allen, "Necessity for an Ethical Veneer," 7–8.

37. McLean, "So You Want to Start a Business," 13.

38. *Women's Work and Women's Studies*; "Woman's Building History: Kirsten Grimstad, Susan Rennie (Otis College)," interview, n.d., http://www.youtube.com/watch?v=hDQrJOIYJ_4, uploaded June 15, 2010; Christopher Lehmann-Haupt, "Books: Unusual Volumes for Gift Giving," *Baltimore Sun*, December 10, 1973, B2; Alix Nelson, "*The New Woman's Survival Catalog*," *New York Times*, January 6, 1974, F2; "Selections for the Holiday Season," *Los Angeles Times*, December 16, 1973, N84; Grimstad and Rennie, *New Woman's Survival Catalog*, 8–9.

39. Grimstad and Rennie, *New Woman's Survival Sourcebook*; "Woman's Building History."

40. Emily Medvec, "Quest Perspective on Money, Fame, and Power," *Quest: A Feminist Quarterly* 1, no. 2 (1974): 2–4; Coletta Reid, "Taking Care of Business," *Quest: A Feminist Quarterly* 1, no. 2 (1974): 9, 14.

41. Reid, "Taking Care of Business," 15, 21, 16; Allen, "Necessity for an Ethical Veneer," 7–8.

42. Reid, "Taking Care of Business," 15–16, 18–19, 21.

43. List of feminist businesses compiled by the author.

44. Louis Hyman, *Debtor Nation: The History of America in Red Ink* (Princeton, N.J.: Princeton University Press, 2011), 192–202; Sharyn Campbell, *Women and Credit* (Washington, D.C.: National Organization for Women, 1973), 1–3; Margaret J. Gates, "Credit Discrimination Against Women: Causes and Solutions," *Vanderbilt Law Review* 27, no. 3 (1974): 412.

45. "Parrent, Joanne Elizabeth" and "Angers, Valerie Marguerite," in Love, *Feminists Who Changed America*, 352, 15; Enke, *Finding the Movement*, 89–90, 205–206; Beverly Buthwoman, FFCU Lansing office, memo, June 14, 1975, 1, Feminist Federal Credit Union Papers, MSS 251, Box 1, Folder 1, Special Collections Manuscripts and Archives, Michigan State University, East Lansing.

46. J. Carroll Moody and Gilbert C. Fite, *The Credit Union Movement: Origins and Development, 1850–1970* (Lincoln: University of Nebraska Press, 1971), 359; Patrizia Battilani and Harm G. Schröter, eds., *The Cooperative Business Movement, 1950 to the Present* (Cambridge: Cambridge University Press, 2012), 36; Maxwell S. Stewart, *Credit Unions—the People's Banks* (New York: Public Affairs Committee, 1940).

47. Buthwoman, memo; FFCU flyer, Feminist Federal Credit Union Papers, MSS 251, Box 1, Folder 2, Special Collections Manuscripts and Archives, Michigan State University, East Lansing; Grimstad and Rennie, *New Woman's Survival Catalog*, 174; "Special Report," 8; "Feminist Federal Credit Union: Cooperatives, Feminism, and Survival," *New Harbinger*, November 1976, 19.

48. FFCU flyer; Buthwoman, memo.

49. FFCU flyer; Buthwoman, memo; Grimstad and Rennie, *New Woman's Survival Sourcebook*, 29; "Lib Loan: Wasn't Easy, but Women Get Credit Unions," *Atlanta Constitution*, August 27, 1976, D18; Ann Crittenden, "Women's Banks: An Idea Whose Allure Has Faded," *New York Times*, August 4, 1980, B6; Susan Cheever Cowley, "Women Bank on September Start," *New York*, August 12, 1974, 50. In 1972, the average annual receipts for a woman-owned business with employees was $88,000 ("Table 1—Selected Statistics by Industry for Firms Owned by Women: 1972," in *Women-Owned Businesses 1972*, 17).

50. St. Joan, "Feminist Economic Seeds Split," 1.

51. Ibid., 1; Parrent, *Sowing the Seeds of Feminist Economic Revolution*, 10–12, 16–17.

52. "Special Report," 8–15; "Feminist Federal Credit Union," 19; Askins, "Old Lady, New Life," B1.

53. Jackie St. Joan, "The Detroit Conference: '. . . A Story of Money, of Being Organized, and of Values,'" *Big Mama Rag*, January 1, 1976, 11; "Special Report," 8.

54. "Special Report," 11.

55. Askins, "Old Lady, New Life," B1, B4; Enke, *Finding the Movement*, 217; "Feminists Open Club in Detroit," A3.

56. Enke, *Finding the Movement*, 241.

57. "Special Report," 8–15; Janis Kelly, Fran Moira, and Tanya Temkin, "Money on the Line," *off our backs*, March 1976, 10–11; St. Joan, "Feminist Economic Seeds Split," 1,

8–14; Bat-Ami Bar On, "Notes on a Feminist Economics," *Quest: A Feminist Quarterly* 2, no. 4 (1976): 46–58; Shelley, "What Is Fen?" 22; Enke, *Finding the Movement*, 241.

58. Enke, *Finding the Movement*, 247–248.

59. Brooke [Brooke Williams], "The Retreat to Cultural Feminism," in Redstockings, *Feminist Revolution* (New Paltz, N.Y.: Redstockings, 1975), 65–68. See also Echols, *Daring to Be Bad*, 6–9, 243–286. In contrast to Williams and Echols, several scholars have rejected the term *cultural feminism* as an inaccurate pejorative and have stated that virtually no activists used the term to describe themselves. See Taylor and Rupp, "Women's Culture and Lesbian Feminist Activism," 34, and Julie R. Enzer, "The Whole Naked Truth of Our Lives: Lesbian-Feminist Print Culture from 1969 Through 1989," Ph.D. diss., University of Maryland, College Park, 2013, 62.

60. Williams, "Retreat to Cultural Feminism," 65–68. In *Daring to Be Bad*, Echols echoes most of these critiques. For interpretations of feminist approaches to culture that do not conceptualize them as "cultural feminism," see Taylor and Rupp, "Women's Culture and Lesbian Feminist Activism," and Gayle Kimball, *Women's Culture: The Women's Renaissance of the Seventies* (Metuchen, N.J: Scarecrow Press, 1981).

61. Brooke L. Williams and Hannah Darby, "God, Mom, & Apple Pie: 'Feminist' Businesses as an Extension of the American Dream," *off our backs*, January–February 1976, 18–20, 26.

62. Janis Kelly and Wendy Stevens, "Better Business," *off our backs*, January–February 1976, 20.

63. "Letters," *off our backs*, March 1976, 26; Dorothychild, "Bookstores as Praxis," letter to the editor, *off our backs*, March 1976, 26, italics added; Jane Field, "Really Just Business," letter to the editor, *off our backs*, March 1976, 27, emphasis in original.

64. Elinor Lerner, "Basic Change," letter to the editor, *off our backs*, March 1976, 26–27.

65. Diana Press, Inc., Publications, "The Day Before," c. 1975, ALFA Collection, Box 11, Folder 24, Sally Bingham Center for Women's History and Culture, Duke University; "Fall Books 1976: From Diana Press," Diana Press Folder, ALFA Collection, Box 11, Folder 24, Sally Bingham Center for Women's History and Culture, Duke University.

66. Anne Mather, "A History of Feminist Periodicals, Part I," *Journalism History* 1, no. 3 (1974): 82; Travis, "The Women in Print Movement," 278–280; Hogan, *Feminist Bookstore Movement*, 29–35, 86–92. See also Simone Murray, *Mixed Media: Feminist Presses and Publishing Politics* (London: Pluto Press, 2004), and Kathryn Thoms Flannery, *Feminist Literacies, 1968–75* (Champaign: University of Illinois Press, 2005). On Lollipop Power, see Evans, *Tidal Wave*, 10–13.

67. Reid and Tomyris, "Diana Press," 1; Mickey Friedman, "A Feminist Publishing House That Refused to Die," *San Francisco Chronicle*, February 26, 1978, Scene-4.

68. Shelley, "What Is Fen?"; Reid and Tomyris, "Diana Press," 1.

69. Reid and Tomyris, "Diana Press," 1; Czarnik interview, May 12, 2015.

70. Janis Kelly, "trashing at diana press," *off our backs*, December 1977, 4.

71. Diana Press to ALFA, June 14, 1978, ALFA Collection, Box 11, Folder 24, Sally Bingham Center for Women's History and Culture, Duke University.

72. Reid and Tomyris, "Diana Press," 2; Czarnik interview, May 12, 2015.

73. Jeanne Cordova, "Lesbian Owned Businesses—Who's Surviving & How?" *Lesbian Tide*, September–October 1979, 6–7.

74. S. J. Diamond, "Efforts Not Appreciated: Feminist Credit Union Seeks to Disband," *Los Angeles Times*, September 28, 1978, D15; James J. Donahue Jr., "Feminist Credit

Union Closes," *Washington Post*, November 17, 1977, DC3; "Credit Union Closes Doors," *Big Mama Rag*, February 1979, 7; "Federal Feminist Credit Union Papers, 1973–1982: Historical Background," Michigan State University Libraries, http://find ingaids.lib.msu.edu/spc/index.php?p=collections/controlcard&id=289; "Collective Crisis and Internal Struggles at ICI—A Woman's Place," *Feminist Bookstores Newsletter* 6, no. 3 (1982): 13; Onosaka, *Feminist Revolution in Literacy*, 96–97.

75. "Has the Women's Movement Achieved Anything That's Made Your Life Better?" New York Times Women's Survey, November 11–20, 1983, data set USNYT1983-WOMEN; "As We Prepare to Enter the 1990s, Do You Think There Is a Need for a Strong and Organized Women's Movement to Work for Further Changes for Women, or Do You Think Changes Will Occur as a Matter of Course Without Any Organized Effort on the Part of Women?" Virginia Slims American Women's Poll, July 1989, data set USRSPVASLIMS1989-943-082; both data sets cataloged by the Roper Center for Public Opinion Research, http://ropercenter.cornell.edu/polls/dataset-collections/. On criticisms of feminists, see Evans, *Tidal Wave*, 184–190; Susan Faludi, *Backlash: The Undeclared War Against American Women* (New York: Crown, 1991); Susan Bolotin, "Voices from the Post-feminist Generation," *New York Times Magazine*, October 17, 1982, 28–36; Paula Kamen, *Feminist Fatale: Voices from the "Twentysomething" Generation Explore the Future of the Women's Movement* (New York: Fine, 1991), 1–6.

76. Onosaka, *Feminist Revolution in Literacy*, 109; "Burn Out," *Feminist Bookstores Newsletter* 5, no. 4 (February 1982): 7–8; Cordova, "Lesbian Owned Businesses," 6–7; Paul D. Doebler, "Recession: Moments of Truth and a Turning Point for Book People?" *Publishers Weekly*, October 8, 1979, 36–37; E. W. Nordberg, "Economic Outlook: Recession Looms for Publishing by Year-End," *Publishers Weekly*, April 9, 1979, 76.

77. "Enterprises Run by Women Widen Customer Base," *New York Times*, May 30, 1983, 37; Michael deCourcy Hinds, "Feminist Businesses See the Future and Decide It's Unisex," *New York Times*, November 12, 1988, 33; Vicki Moss, "Celebrating the 35th Anniversary of the New York and National Associations of Women Business Owners," March–April 1976, http://www.vfa.us/VickiMossNAWBO.htm; *The National Association of Women Business Owners Membership Roster, 1985–1986* (Chicago: National Association of Women Business Owners, 1985), A1–A12; Hinds, "Feminist Businesses See the Future," 33; Cowley, "Women Bank on September Start," 50. See also Claudia Dale Goldin, *Understanding the Gender Gap: An Economic History of American Women* (New York: Oxford University Press, 1990); Raymond F. Gregory, *Women and Workplace Discrimination: Overcoming Barriers to Gender Equality* (New Brunswick, N.J.: Rutgers University Press, 2003).

78. *Selected Characteristics of Women-Owned Businesses 1977*, 1; *1982 Economic Census*, 4; *1987 Economic Census*, 6–7; Hinds, "Feminist Businesses See the Future," 33; Michael K. Brown, Martin Carnoy, Troy Duster, Elliott Currie, and David B. Oppenheimer, "Introduction: Race Preference and Race Privileges," in *Whitewashing Race: The Myth of a Color-Blind Society*, ed. Michael K. Brown, Martin Carnoy, Troy Duster, Elliott Currie, and David B. Oppenheimer (Berkeley: University of California Press, 2003), 1–22; statistics from searches for use of the key terms *feminist business* and *feminist businesses* in *off our backs* in the ProQuest Central database.

79. Sue Levin, *In the Pink: The Making of Successful Gay- and Lesbian-Owned Businesses* (New York: Haworth Press, 1999); Grant Lukenbill, *Untold Millions: Positioning Your Business for the Gay and Lesbian Consumer Revolution* (New York: HarperCollins,

1995); Alexandra Chasin, *Selling Out: The Gay and Lesbian Movement Goes to Market* (New York: St. Martin's Press, 2000), 33–35; Katherine Sender, *Business, Not Politics: The Making of the Gay Market* (New York: Columbia University Press, 2004). On stereotypes, see Rosen, *The World Split Open*, 355–356; Jo Reger, *Everywhere and Nowhere: Contemporary Feminism in the United States* (New York: Oxford University Press, 2012), 163; Lynda Hart, *Fatal Women: Lesbian Sexuality and the Mark of Aggression* (Princeton, N.J.: Princeton University Press, 1994), 118.

80. Hogan, *Feminist Bookstore Movement*; Onosaka, *Feminist Revolution in Literacy*, 76–90.

81. Kimberly Springer, *Living for the Revolution: Black Feminist Organizations, 1968–1980* (Durham, N.C.: Duke University Press, 2005); Winifred Breines, *The Trouble Between Us: An Uneasy History of White and Black Women in the Feminist Movement* (Oxford: Oxford University Press, 2006), 117–149; Barbara Smith, "A Press of Our Own— Kitchen Table: Women of Color Press," *Frontiers: A Journal of Women Studies* 10, no. 3 (1989): 11–13; Barbara Smith, ed., *Home Girls: A Black Feminist Anthology* (New York: Kitchen Table,1983); Cherríe Moraga and Gloria E. Anzaldúa, eds., *This Bridge Called My Back: Writings by Radical Women of Color* (1981; reprint, New York: Kitchen Table Press, 1983); DeNeen L. Brown, "Books and Bonding: At D.C. Bookstore, Black Women Find Haven of Literature and Sisterhood," *Washington Post*, March 18, 1997, B1; Hogan, *Feminist Bookstore Movement*; Onosaka, *Feminist Revolution in Literacy*, 82–90.

82. Loraine Edwalds and Midge Stocker, "Part 2—Feeding and Watering: Growing Our Own Business," in *The Woman-Centered Economy: Ideals, Reality, and the Space in Between*, ed. Loraine Edwards and Midge Stocker (Chicago: Third Side Press, 1995), 111.

83. Carol Seajay, "Notes from the Computer Table," *Feminist Bookstore News* 16, no. 6 (1994): 1; "Books: 20 Years of Feminist Bookstores," *Ms.*, July 1992, 61.

84. John Baker, "The '80s: Reaching New Heights, It Was a Decade of Sometimes Reckless Growth," *Publishers Weekly*, January 5, 1990, 19; NPD Group, Inc., *1990/1991 Consumer Research Study on Book Purchasing* (New York: Book Industry Study Group, 1991), 58.

85. Hogan, *Feminist Bookstore Movement*, 145–178.

86. *1987 Economic Census*, 7.

5. NATURAL FOODS STORES

1. George Ohsawa, *Zen Macrobiotics: The Art of Rejuvenation and Longevity*, ed. Lou Oles (Los Angeles: Ignoramus Press, 1965), translation of George Ohsawa, *Zen-Macrobiotique* (Paris: Centre Ignoramus, 1958), 23, 46–65; Carol Liston, "FDA Investigates Diet Faddists in Boston Area," *Boston Globe*, June 22, 1966, 1, 4; "Cult Foods Seized in U.S. Raid Here—Linked to Diets Said to Have Caused Deaths," *New York Times*, June 3, 1966, 40.

2. William Shurtleff and Akiki Aoyagi, *History of Erewhon: Natural Foods Pioneer in the United States (1966–2011)* (Lafayette, Calif.: SoyInfo Center, 2011), 200; Paul Hawken, "Erewhon: A Biography," *East–West Journal*, August 1973, 11.

3. Shurtleff and Aoyagi, *History of Erewhon*, 22, 145, 201.

4. *Small Business Reporter: Health Food Stores* (San Francisco: Bank of America, 1972), 1; Shurtleff and Aoyagi, *History of Erewhon*, 54, 66; James F. Carberry, "Our Daily Bread: Food Faddism Spurts as Young, Old People Shift to Organic Diets," *Wall Street Journal*, January 21, 1971, 1. I define "natural foods stores" as businesses that

specialized in a wide range of vegetarian staples, especially fruits, vegetables, and grains produced without pesticides, processing, and preservatives. *Natural foods* was the prevailing term for such items for most of the 1960s, 1970s, and 1980s. On natural and organic foods, see Warren J. Belasco, *Appetite for Change: How the Counterculture Took on the Food Industry*, 2nd updated ed. (Ithaca, N.Y.: Cornell University Press, 2007); Samuel Fromartz, *Organic, Inc.: Natural Foods and How They Grew*, 1st Harvest ed. (Orlando, Fla.: Harcourt, 2007); Joe Dobrow, *Natural Prophets: From Health Foods to Whole Foods—How the Pioneers of the Industry Changed the Way We Eat and Reshaped American Business* (Emmaus, Penn.: Rodale Press, 2014); Michael Pollan, *The Omnivore's Dilemma: A Natural History of Four Meals* (New York: Penguin Press, 2006).

5. Judith Van Allen and Gene Marine, *Food Pollution: The Violation of Our Inner Ecology* (New York: Holt, Rinehart and Winston, 1972); Jack Lucas, *Our Polluted Food: A Survey of the Risks* (New York: Wiley, 1974). On the history of supermarkets and grocery stores, see Tracey Deutsch, *Building a Housewife's Paradise: Gender, Politics, and American Grocery Stores in the Twentieth Century* (Chapel Hill: University of North Carolina Press, 2010); Marc Levinson, *The Great A&P and the Struggle for Small Business in America* (New York: Hill and Wang, 2011); Susan Spellman, *Cornering the Market: Independent Grocers and Innovation in American Small Business, 1860–1940* (Oxford: Oxford University Press, 2016).

6. On humanistic psychology, see Jessica Grogan, *Encountering America: Humanistic Psychology, Sixties Culture, & the Shaping of the Modern Self* (New York: Harper Perennial, 2013).

7. E. F. Schumacher expressed the ideas that became the basis for his magnum opus *Small Is Beautiful: Economics as If People Mattered* (New York: Harper and Row, 1973) as early as 1960 (Barbara Wood, *E. F. Schumacher: His Life and Thought* [New York: Harper and Row, 1984], 266). Among Schumacher's admirers were Erewhon's early managers (Sherman Goldman and Bill Tara, "Changing Knowledge to Wisdom: An Interview with E. F. Schumacher," *East–West Journal*, November 1976, 14–18; Paul Hawken, introduction to E. F. Schumacher, *Small Is Beautiful: Economics as If People Mattered: 25 Years Later . . . with Commentaries* [Point Roberts, Wash.: Hartley & Marks, 1999], xii–xiv, xvii).

8. Adam D. Shprintzen, *The Vegetarian Crusade: The Rise of an American Reform Movement, 1817–1921* (Chapel Hill: University of North Carolina Press, 2013); Karen Iacobbo and Michael Iacobbo, *Vegetarian America: A History* (Westport, Conn.: Praeger, 2004); Brian C. Wilson, *Dr. John Harvey Kellogg and the Religion of Biologic Living* (Bloomington: Indiana University Press, 2014); Heather Addison, *Hollywood and the Rise of Physical Culture* (New York: Routledge, 2003); Marla Matzer Rose, *Muscle Beach: Where the Best Bodies in the World Started a Fitness Revolution* (New York: Macmillan, 2001).

9. *A World of Sense: The Life of Bob Rodale*, VHS (Emmaus, Penn.: Rodale Productions, 1994); Daniel Gross, *Our Roots Grow Deep: The Story of Rodale* (Emmaus, Penn.: Rodale, 2008), 69; Paul Keene, *Fear Not to Sow Because of the Birds: Essays on Country Living and Natural Farming from Walnut Acres* (Chester, Conn.: Globe Pequot Press, 1988), 26–27; George DeVault, "What Became of Walnut Acres," *Natural Farmer*, Spring 2006, 30–32.

10. Alan L. Olmstead and Paul W. Rhode, "The Transformation of Northern Agriculture, 1910–1990," in *The Cambridge Economic History of the United States*, ed. Stanley

L. Engerman and Robert E. Gallman (Cambridge: Cambridge University Press, 2000), 710; Linda Lear, *Rachel Carson: Witness for Nature* (New York: Houghton Mifflin Harcourt, 1997), 119.

11. J. I. Rodale, "15 Years," *Organic Farming and Gardening*, June 1957, 15; Belasco, *Appetite for Change*, 16, 97; Dobrow, *Natural Prophets*, 30–32, 103–104.

12. Aveline Kushi, with Alex Jack, *Aveline: The Life and Dream of the Woman Behind Macrobiotics Today* (Tokyo: Japan Publications, 1988), 165–181; Ronald E. Kotzsch, *Macrobiotics: Yesterday and Today* (Tokyo: Japan Publications, 1985), 106–110; Michio Kushi, "Food for Peace," *East–West Journal*, May 1975, 28, Kushi Collection, Box 84, Folder 4, National Museum of American History, Washington, D.C.

13. Kushi, *Aveline*, 174–175; Shurtleff and Aoyagi, *History of Erewhon*, 145, 185.

14. Paul Hawken, "History of Erewhon and Macrobiotics in America. Part I (Interview)," in Shurtleff and Aoyagi, *History of Erewhon*, 144; Kotzsch, *Macrobiotics*, 167–170; "Yin, Yang, and MB," *Newsweek*, April 5, 1965, 90, 92.

15. Robert Christgau, "Beth Ann and Macrobioticism," *New York Herald Tribune*, January 23, 1966, 10, 12–15; Douglas Robinson, "Public Is Warned Against Cult Diet: City Move Follows Death of Woman in Jersey," *New York Times*, November 13, 1965, 30; Shurtleff and Aoyagi, *History of Erewhon*, 187; Frederick John Stare, "The Diet That's Killing Our Kids," *Ladies Home Journal*, October 1, 1971, 72.

16. Shurtleff and Aoyagi, *History of Erewhon*, 22, 144; Kotzsch, *Macrobiotics*, 170; Hawken, "Erewhon," 16.

17. Kotzsch, *Macrobiotics*, 174; Shurtleff and Aoyagi, *History of Erewhon*, 201, 276–277; Paul Hawken, interviewed by the author, Sausalito, Calif., May 22, 2014; Michio Kushi, *The Order of the Universe: The Way of Life in the Age of Humanity* (Detroit: Artists' Workshop Press, 1967); Hawken, "Erewhon," 11–12.

18. Erewhon Trading Company, Inc., *Traditional Foods—Importers Processors Distributors, Wholesale–Retail Company*, catalog (Boston: Erewhon Trading Company, January 1970), Kushi Collection, Box 79: "Erewhon Catalogue, 1972–1977," Folder 11, National Museum of American History, Washington, D.C.; Hawken, "Erewhon," 12.

19. Shurtleff and Aoyagi, *History of Erewhon*, 145, 185; Hawken, "Erewhon," 12.

20. Fred Rohe, *The Complete Book of Natural Foods* (Boulder, Colo.: Shambhala Books, 1983), 1–2; Belasco, *Appetite for Change*, 96–97.

21. Thomas Jundt, *Greening the Red, White, and Blue: The Bomb, Big Business, and Consumer Resistance in Postwar America* (Oxford: Oxford University Press, 2014), 45–126, 158–192; Rachel Carson, *Silent Spring* (New York: Houghton Mifflin, 1962).

22. Murray Bookchin, "The Problem of Chemicals in Food," *Contemporary Issues* 3, no. 12 (1952): 206–241; (as Lewis Herber) *Our Synthetic Environment* (New York: Knopf, 1962); and *Post-scarcity Anarchism* (Berkeley, Calif.: Ramparts Press, 1971).

23. Jundt, *Greening the Red, White, and Blue*, 184–187, 209; Adam Rome, *The Genius of Earth Day: How a 1970 Teach-in Unexpectedly Made the First Green Generation* (New York: Hill and Wang, 2013); John Robert Greene, *America in the Sixties* (Syracuse, N.Y.: Syracuse University Press, 2010), 73; Fred Turner, *From Counterculture to Cyberculture: Stewart Brand, the Whole Earth Network, and the Rise of Digital Utopianism* (Chicago: University of Chicago Press, 2006), 81; Andrew Kirk, *Counterculture Green: The Whole Earth Catalog and American Environmentalism* (Lawrence: University of Kansas Press, 2007); Portola Institute, *The Last Whole Earth Catalog* (New

York: Random House, 1971), 32–58; Frank Zelko, *Make It a Green Peace! The Rise of Countercultural Environmentalism* (Oxford: Oxford University Press, 2013).

24. Jundt, *Greening the Red, White, and Blue*; J. R. McNeill, "The Environment, Environmentalism, and International Society in the Long 1970s," in *The Shock of the Global: The 1970s in Perspective*, ed. Niall Ferguson, Charles S. Maier, Erez Manela, and Daniel J. Sargent (Cambridge, Mass.: Harvard University Press, 2011), 263–278; Bookchin, *Post-scarcity Anarchism*, 66.

25. Lynn Ellingson, "If You Don't Dig Natural Foods, Maybe You Can Understand Pollution . . . ," *Freedom News*, December 1970, 35; Van Allen and Marine, *Food Pollution*; Lucas, *Our Polluted Food*; Garrett de Bell, *The Environmental Handbook: Prepared for the First National Environmental Teach-In* (New York: Ballantine Books, 1970), 306–307; Bookchin, *Our Synthetic Environment*, 61; *Spiritual Community Guide* (San Rafael, Calif.: Spiritual Community, 1972), 118–194.

26. Colin Spencer, *The Heretic's Feast: A History of Vegetarianism* (Hanover, N.H.: University Press of New England, 1996), 296–297, 310–311; Kotzsch, *Macrobiotics*, 106–107; Committee to Frame a World Constitution, *Preliminary Draft for a World Constitution* (Chicago: University of Chicago Press, 1948); Joseph Preston Baratta, *The Politics of World Federation: From World Federalism to Global Governance* (Westport, Conn.: Greenwood, 2004); Paul Feroe, "Vegetarian Movement Experiences Rapid Growth in US," *College Press Service*, April 21, 1975, 5; Frances Moore Lappé, *Diet for a Small Planet* (New York: Ballantine Books, 1971).

27. Peter Singer, *Animal Liberation: A New Ethics for Our Treatment of Animals* (New York: Random House, 1975), 98–99, 173–175. See also Stanley Godlovitch, Roslind Godlovitch, and John Harris, *Animals, Men, and Morals: An Enquiry into the Maltreatment of Non-humans* (London: Gollancz, 1971).

28. Robert Hughes Seager, *Buddhism in America* (New York: Columbia University Press, 2012), 112–134; Scott MacFarlane, *The Hippie Narrative: A Literary Perspective on the Counterculture* (Jefferson, N.C.: McFarland, 2007), 85–91; Martine Batchelor, *The Spirit of the Buddha* (New Haven, Conn.: Yale University Press, 2010), 99–102; Hawken, introduction to Schumacher, *Small Is Beautiful*, xii, xiv, xvii; Jack Garvey, "Running Your Own Natural Food Store," *East–West Journal*, October 30, 1972, 8–9; *Spiritual Community Guide*, 118–194; Hawken, "Erewhon," 11.

29. Hawken, "Erewhon," 14.

30. "For the People . . . Nutrition, a Final Revolution," *East–West Journal*, March 31, 1972, 7–8; Ambrose Blake, "The Organic Revolution," *San Francisco Examiner*, California Living, August 9, 1970, 8.

31. *Rodale Press, Inc. v. Federal Trade Commission*, 407 F.2d 1252 (D.C. Cir. 1968); Liston, "FDA Investigates Diet Faddists in Boston Area"; "Cult Foods Seized in U.S. Raid Here"; Hawken, "Erewhon," 14.

32. *Spiritual Community Guide*, 118–194; Carberry, "Our Daily Bread," 1; Shurtleff and Aoyagi, *History of Erewhon*, 54; Advest Co., *Erewhon, Inc.*, prospectus (Hartford, Conn.: Advest, 1972), 8, copy in author's files; Richard Martin, "Heard on the Street," *Wall Street Journal*, December 19, 1969, 31.

33. On the predominantly white natural foods community, see Kotzsch, *Macrobiotics*, 174, which makes observations borne out by the overwhelming majority of my research. The average age of Erewhon's employees in the late 1960s was twenty-two

(Shurtleff and Aoyagi, *History of Erewhon*, 201). On African Americans and natural foods, see Dick Gregory, *Dick Gregory's Natural Diet for Folks Who Eat: Cookin' with Mother Nature!* (New York: Harper and Row, 1973); Alvenia Fulton, *Vegetarianism: Fact or Myth? Eating to Live* (Chicago: CAMS, 1974); Elijah Muhammad, *How to Eat to Live* (Chicago: Muhammad's Temple of Islam No. 2, 1967), 1–6, 107, 114–116; Edward E. Curtis, *Black Muslim Religion in the Nation of Islam, 1960–1975* (Chapel Hill: University of North Carolina Press, 2006), 102–105, 214 n. 39; Haki Madhubuti (Don Lee), preface to Walimu, *A Food Guide for Afrikan People* (New Orleans: Ahidiana Work/Study Center, 1973), 1. Madhubuti also published Johari M. Kunjufu, *Commonsense Approach to Eating* (Chicago: Institute of Positive Education, 1975).

34. Elizabeth Lansing, "The Move to Eat Natural—New Converts to Organic Food Are Sprouting Up All Over," *Life*, December 11, 1970, 44–52; Advest, *Erewhon, Inc.*, 11; Shurtleff and Aoyagi, *History of Erewhon*, 11.

35. "Food Trip," *Good Times*, October 16, 1969, 10; Fred Rohe, *The NOT List* (San Francisco: Organic Merchants, 1971), in Shurtleff and Aoyagi, *History of Erewhon*, 60; Blake, "The Organic Revolution," 7–8; Hawken, "Erewhon," 14.

36. Lansing, "The Move to Eat Natural"; Carberry, "Our Daily Bread," 1; Shurtleff and Aoyagi, *History of Erewhon*, 187.

37. *Small Business Reporter*, 1–2, 5.

38. Paul Hawken, "Developing a Conspicuous Alternative," *East–West Journal*, October 30, 1972, 6; Lansing, "The Move to Eat Natural," 44–52; Hawken, "Erewhon," 14; Mary Daniels, "A Loaf of Whole-Grain Bread, a Jug of Bancha, and Thou," *Chicago Tribune*, August 1, 1971, F21.

39. Hawken, "Erewhon," 15; "Erewhon," *East–West Journal*, n.d. (c. 1970–1971), 10, Kushi Collection, Box 82, no. 619, National Museum of American History, Washington, D.C.; "Wholly Foods" and "The Rock Island Line Organic Food Trip," *Organic Morning Glory Message: The Magazine for Natural Living*, January 1971, Hippies Collection 1965–1975, Box 2, Folder 24, San Francisco History Center, San Francisco Public Library.

40. Council on Foods and Nutrition, "Zen Macrobiotic Diets," *Journal of American Medical Association* 218, no. 3 (1971): 397; Carol Phillips, "A Doctor Explodes Some Health-Food Myths," *Vogue*, June 1967, 121; Stare, "The Diet That's Killing Our Kids," 70–76; Frederick J. Stare and Margaret McWilliams, *Living Nutrition* (New York: Wiley, 1973), 127; Benjamin Rosenthal, Michael Jacobson, and Marcy Bohm, "Professors on the Take," *Progressive*, November 1976, 42–47; Joanne Slavin, "Whole Grains and Human Health," *Nutrition Research Reviews* 17, no. 1 (2004): 99–110; David R. Jacobs Jr., Mark A. Pereira, Katie A. Meyer, and Lawrence H. Kushi, "Fiber from Whole Grains, but Not Refined Grains, Is Inversely Associated with All-Cause Mortality in Older Women: The Iowa Women's Health Study," *Journal of the American College of Nutrition* 19, supplement 3 (2000): 326S–330S.

41. Schumacher, *Small Is Beautiful*; *Small Business Reporter*, 1–2, 5; Gene Arlin German, "The Dynamics of Food Retailing, 1900–1975," Ph.D. diss., Cornell University, 1977, 221.

42. John Curl, *For All the People: Uncovering the Hidden History of Co-operation, Cooperative Movements, and Communalism in America* (Oakland, Calif.: PM Books, 2009), 37, 90–102, 111–114, 164–191; Jessica Nembhard, *Collective Courage: A History of African American Cooperative Economic Thought and Practice* (University Park: Pennsylvania State University Press, 2014); Lizabeth Cohen, *A Consumers' Republic: The Politics*

of Mass Consumption in Postwar America (New York: Vintage, 2003), 25–50; Anne Meis Knupfer, *Food Co-ops in America* (Ithaca, N.Y.: Cornell University Press, 2013), 31–46; Patrizia Battilani and Harm G. Schröter, eds., *The Cooperative Business Movement, 1950 to the Present* (Cambridge: Cambridge University Press, 2012); Daniel Zwerdling, "The Uncertain Revival of Food Cooperatives," in *Co-ops, Communes, & Collectives*, ed. John Case and Rosemary C. R. Taylor (New York: Pantheon Books, 1979), 93–94; Jeff Singleton, *The American Dole: Unemployment Relief and the Welfare State in the Great Depression* (Westport, Conn.: Greenwood Press, 2000), 154–155.

43. Knupfer, *Food Co-ops*, 42; Nembhard, *Collective Courage*; Deutsch, *Building a Housewife's Paradise*, 148–150.

44. Curl, *For All the People*, 238, 197–198; Richard J. Margolis, "Coming Together the Cooperative Way," *New Leader*, April 17, 1972, 17–18.

45. Zwerdling, "Uncertain Revival of Food Cooperatives," 90–91; "Austin Community Project—Building a Cooperative Community," *Communities: A Journal of Cooperative Living*, March–April 1976, 44–47, Clippings File AF GROCERIES G4200 (65), Austin History Center, Austin Public Library.

46. "From the Beanery Paper," *Scoop*, May 1975, 32; Michael Foley, *Confronting the War Machine: Draft Resistance During the Vietnam War* (Chapel Hill: University of North Carolina Press, 2003), 32; "North Country Co-op Profile," *East–West Journal*, June 30, 1972, 1; William Ronco, *Food Co-ops: An Alternative to Shopping in Supermarkets* (Boston: Beacon Press, 1974), 1–20.

47. "People's Pantry," *Hundred Flowers*, May 15, 1970; Hans Elf, "Mill City," *Changes 21*, Summer 1972.

48. Craig Cox, *Storefront Revolution: Food Co-ops and the Counterculture* (New Brunswick, N.J.: Rutgers University Press, 1994), 47.

49. "From the Beanery Paper," 32–33; Jonathan Klein, "The Minneapolis Warehouse—Crises in the North Country," *New Harbinger: A Journal of the Cooperative Movement* 3, no. 1 (1976): 36; Cox, *Storefront Revolution*, 48, 102.

50. Hawken, "Erewhon," 11, 13; Rohe, *The NOT List*, in Shurtleff and Aoyagi, *History of Erewhon*, 60; Cox, *Storefront Revolution*, 89.

51. "The Minneapolis Warehouse," 34–41; "May PRB," *Scoop*, June–July 1975, 6–9; Cox, *Storefront Revolution*, 69–71.

52. Jon Collins, "When Twin Cities Co-ops Went to War Over Margarine," Minnesota Public Radio News, March 4, 2014, http://blogs.mprnews.org/cities/2014/03/when-twin-cities-co-ops-went-to-war-over-margarine/.

53. "From the Beanery Paper," 33; Charlene C. Price and Judy Brown, *Growth in the Health and Natural Foods Industry* (Washington, D.C.: U.S. Department of Agriculture, 1984), 26; Cynthia Cromwell, "Organic Foods—an Update," *Family Economics Review* (U.S. Department of Agriculture), Summer 1976, 8–9.

54. Nembhard, *Collective Courage*, 80–81; Dana Frank, *Purchasing Power: Consumer Organizing, Gender, and the Seattle Labor Movement, 1919–1929* (Cambridge: Cambridge University Press, 1994), 40–65; Florence E. Parker, "Labor Unions and Non-farm Cooperatives," *Monthly Labor Review*, October 1948, 388–389; Ronco, *Food Co-Ops*, 128.

55. Peter B. Levy, *The New Left and Labor in the 1960s* (Champaign: University of Illinois Press, 1994), 4–5, 19–22, 45–51, 65–66, 86–88, 94–95; Miller, *Democracy Is in the Streets*, 344. On New Left activists' hostility to unions, see also Jeffrey W. Coker, *Confronting*

American Labor: The New Left Dilemma (Columbia: University of Missouri Press, 2002), 19–22; Vocations for Social Change, *No Bosses Here: A Manual on Working Collectively* (Boston: Vocations for Social Change, 1976); Marten Estey, "The Grocery Clerks: Center of Retail Unionism," *Industrial Relations: A Journal of Economy and Society* 7, no. 3 (1968): 255.

56. Richard Warren Eivers, "From Alternative to Big Business: The Story Behind Erewhon's Unionization," *New Age*, November 1979, 33, 38.

57. Ibid., 31–40; "Unaffiliated Unions," *White Collar*, January–June 1982, xlii.

58. "Erewhon Fighting to Stay in Business," *Vegetarian Times*, February 1982, 83; Ronald E. Kotzsch, "Natural Foods Pioneer Erewhon," *East–West Journal*, February 1984, 26.

59. The material in this paragraph and the preceding three paragraphs comes from Eivers, "From Alternative to Big Business," 36–40.

60. Ibid., 39–40; "Erewhon Fighting to Stay in Business," 83; Advest, *Erewhon, Inc.*, 14; Michael Spielman, "Health Foods: Coming Into Their Own," *Health Foods Business*, June 1980, 60.

61. Doug Rossinow, *The Politics of Authenticity: Liberalism, Christianity, and the New Left in America* (New York: Columbia University Press, 1998), passim; Travis D. Stimeling, *Cosmic Cowboys and New Hicks: The Countercultural Sounds of Austin's Progressive Country Music Scene* (Oxford: Oxford University Press, 2011).

62. Ian Walker, "Take a Milk Run with Genius," *Austin People Today*, February 1975, 24, Clippings File AF GROCERIES G4200 (64), Austin History Center, Austin Public Library; David Frink, "Good Food Stores: Hard Work and a Taste for Natural Food Pay Off," *Austin American-Statesman*, November 1, 1976, Clippings File AF GRO-CERIES G4200 (64), Austin History Center, Austin Public Library; Mark Skiles, interviewed by the author, Austin, Tex., June 5, 2014; "Austin Community Project," 44–47. On the counterculture's interest in Tolkien (as in the name "Hobbit Hole"), see Rachel Rubin, *Well Met: Renaissance Fairies and the American Counterculture* (New York: New York University Press, 2012), 266–267.

63. Nick Paumgarten, "Food Fighter: Does Whole Foods' C.E.O. Know What's Best for You?" *New Yorker*, January 4, 2010, 39–40; Sam Gwynne, "Born Green: Behind the Whole Foods Empire Is a Texan Tale of Gastronomic Gumption," *Saveur*, May 26, 2009, 27–28; John Arlidge, "Peace, Love, and Profit: Meet the World's Richest Organic Grocer," *Guardian*, January 28, 2006, http://www.theguardian.com/life andstyle/2006/jan/29/foodanddrink.organics; Evan Smith, "John Mackey," in *Texas Monthly on . . . Food* (Austin: University of Texas Press, 2008), 191; John Mackey and Raj Sisodia, *Conscious Capitalism: Liberating the Heroic Spirit of Business* (Cambridge, Mass.: Harvard Business Review Press, 2013), 2–4.

64. John Mackey, "The Accidental Grocer," *The Whole Story: A Marketplace of Ideas*, September–October 1989, 7; Milton Moskowitz, Michael Katz, and Robert Levering, eds., *Everybody's Business Almanac: The Irreverent Guide to Corporate America* (San Francisco: Harper and Row, 1980), 115; "Safeway to Pacify Neighborhood Groups," *Daily Texan*, April 14, 1976, Clippings File AF GROCERIES G4200 (50), Austin History Center, Austin Public Library; Brenda Ball, "Safeway Can Become the Expensive Way," *Austin American-Statesman*, June 28, 1976, A7, Clippings File AF GROCERIES G4200 (50), Austin History Center, Austin Public Library.

65. Skiles interview, June 5, 2014; Gwynne, "Born Green"; Shurtleff and Aoyagi, *History of Erewhon*, 145; U.S. Bureau of Labor Statistics, "CPI Inflation Calendar," n.d.,

http://www.bls.gov/data/inflation_calculator.htm; Smith, "John Mackey," 187; Mackey, introduction to Schumacher, *Small Is Beautiful*, 4.

66. Dobrow, *Natural Prophets*, 79; Peter Barry Chowka, "Natural Foods: A Commodity in Crisis," *New Age*, July 1982, 38; Solomon J. Herbert, "When Ill Bodes Well," *Lawrence Journal World*, May 8, 1985, F.Y.I. 3.

67. Skiles interview, June 5, 2014; David Matthis and Karen Saadeh, interviewed by the author, Austin, Tex., June 5, 2014.

68. "Wise Buys," *Texas Monthly*, January 1981, 19; "Whole Foods Market—Extraordinary Food!" (advertisement), *Austin American-Statesman*, December 4, 1982, 70; "Product Quality: Unearthing the Issues," *Natural Foods Merchandiser*, November 1983, 34, quoted in Stephen Neal Theis, "Developing an Advertising Creative Strategy for a Whole Foods Store," M.A. thesis, University of Texas at Austin, 1983, 8.

69. *Food Policy Recommendations for the United States: Statement of Michio Kushi, September 21, 1977* (Boston: East West Foundation, 1977), 21; Steve Daniels, "The Growing Natural Foods Market," *East–West Journal*, November 1977, 39; David Gumpert, "Health Food Stores in 2 States Charged with Boycott, Told to Resume Purchases," *Wall Street Journal*, March 17, 1977, 7.

70. Kim Tyson, "SBA Office for Loan Applications Opens Today," *Austin American-Statesman*, December 28, 1991, E1; Whole Foods Market, "Whole Foods Market History," n.d., http://www.wholefoodsmarket.com/company-info/whole-foods-market-history; Kitty Higgins, Small Business Administration Freedom of Information and Privacy Act Office, to Joshua Davis, email, May 7, 2014, regarding emergency loan number 4490392004 to Whole Foods Market; "After the Flood," *Whole Foods Market Eaters Digest*, June 1982, 3; *Whole Foods Market General Information Handbook* (Austin, Tex.: Whole Foods Market, 1984), 5, and *Whole Foods Market General Information Handbook 1988* (Austin, Tex.: Whole Foods Market, 1988), 11, copies in author's files.

71. Shurtleff and Aoyagi, *History of Erewhon*, 181; Chowka, "Natural Foods," 38.

72. Jess Blackburn, "Health Boom Turns Natural Foods Into Big Business in Texas," *Dallas Morning News*, September 1, 1984, A39; Toni Mack, "Good Food, Great Margins," *Forbes*, October 17, 1988, 115; *Whole Foods Market General Information Handbook*, 5.

73. Don Moffitt, interviewed by the author, Durham, N.C., April 28, 2014; Dobrow, *Natural Prophets*, 181, quoting Peter Roy; Blackburn, "Health Boom Turns Natural Foods Into Big Business," A39; "Whole Foods Market Set to Buy Large Dallas Store," *Austin American-Statesman*, October 2, 1986, H1.

74. Mack, "Good Food, Great Margins," 113, 115; Dale M. Hudson, "Whole Foods Learns from Mistakes," *Austin American-Statesman*, February 6, 1989, 3; *Whole Foods Market General Information Handbook 1988*, 5; John Mackey, "The Accidental Grocer," *The Whole Story*, September–October 1990, 7. On supermarket industry profits, see "Fact and Fancy," *Wall Street Journal*, December 4, 1975, 18, and Roger Lowenstein, "Are Supermarket Aisles a Haven from Recession?" *Wall Street Journal*, September 19, 1990, C1.

75. "Profit Sharing," *Inner Views*, July–August 1981, 2–3; *Whole Foods Market General Information Handbook*, 2, 40; John Mackey, "The Accidental Grocer," *The Whole Story*, January–February 1990, 7; *Whole Foods Market General Information Handbook 1988*, 9; John Mackey, *Beyond Unions* (pamphlet) (Austin, Tex.: Whole Foods Market, 1992), 15; Mackey, "The Accidental Grocer," September–October 1990, 7;

"Employee Ownership Grows!" *Inner-Views Employee Newsletter*, July 1985, 3; Hudson, "Whole Foods Learns from Mistakes," 3. By 1988, however, profit sharing no longer was offered as an employee benefit (*Whole Foods Market General Information Handbook 1988*).

76. Marilyn Schwartz, "A Store Where Politics and Groceries Mix," *Dallas Morning News*, October 1, 1989, F1; "You Have Changed the World," *The Whole Story*, November–December 1990, 1; "Organizations That Are Changing the World," *The Whole Story*, November–December 1990, 3; "Working at Whole Foods Market," *Inner Views*, September 14, 1990, 2. On the history of the American and international dolphin-safe tuna movement, see James Brown, "An Account of the Dolphin-Safe Tuna Issue in the UK," *Marine Policy* 29 (2005): 39–46.

77. Berta Delgado, "4 Arrested During Grape Protest at North Lamar Grocery Store," *Austin American-Statesman*, November 12, 1988, B4; John Harris, "Protestors Sue City, Market, Officers," *Austin American-Statesman*, November 24, 1988, B6; Berta Delgado, "Union, Whole Foods Settle Case-Parties 'Committed' to Natural Grapes," *Austin American-Statesman*, October 7, 1989, B4.

78. James C. Maroney and Bruce A. Glasrud, "Introduction: The Neglected Heritage of Texas Labor," in *Texas Labor History*, ed. James C. Maroney and Bruce A. Glasrud (College Station: Texas A&M University Press, 2013), 1; Matthew Hermann, "Food Fight," *East Bay Express*, January 11, 1991, 1, 10; Mackey, "The Accidental Grocer," September–October 1990, 7.

79. "Report on Labor Dispute Between Whole Foods, Inc., and Locals #120 and #870," City of Berkeley Labor Commission, December 10, 1990, 22, copy in author's files; Jamin B. Raskin, "Does Whole Foods Market Lack Moral Fiber?" *Business and Society Review*, Summer 1992, 29; Hermann, "Food Fight," 19.

80. Hermann, "Food Fight," 11; L. A. Kauffman, "New Age Meets New Right: Tofu Politics in Berkeley," *The Nation*, September 16, 1991, 294; Raskin, "Does Whole Foods Market Lack Moral Fiber?" 30.

81. "Report on Labor Dispute," 1, 9.

82. Ibid., 20.

83. Kaufmann, "New Age Meets New Right," 296; "Report on Labor Dispute"; Hudson, "Whole Foods Learns from Mistakes," 3, 5–6.

84. Hudson, "Whole Foods Learns from Mistakes," 3; Hermann, "Food Fight," 13.

85. Mackey, "The Accidental Grocer," January–February 1990, 7; John Mackey, "The Accidental Grocer," *The Whole Story*, June–July–August 1991, 10–11; Mackey, *Beyond Unions*, 1, 16; Mackey and Sisodia, *Conscious Capitalism*.

86. Mackey, *Beyond Unions*, 16; Mackey, "The Accidental Grocer," September–October 1990, 7.

87. *Whole Foods Market General Information Handbook 1988*, 8, 10.

88. John Mackey, "The Accidental Grocer," *The Whole Story*, May–June 1990, 7; Mackey "The Accidental Grocer," January–February 1990, 7; John Mackey, "The Accidental Grocer," *The Whole Story*, March–April 1990, 11–12 (including the letter written by the African American customer); Cheryl Mott, "Beware the Inspired Feminist," *Inner Views*, April 5, 1991, 8; John Mackey, "An Answer to Cheryl Mott," *Inner Views*, April 19, 1991, 9.

89. Mackey and Sisodia, *Conscious Capitalism*, 4.

90. Milton Friedman and Rose Friedman, *Free to Choose* (New York: Harcourt, 1980); Mackey, "The Accidental Grocer," June–July–August 1991, 10, 11; John Mackey, "The

Accidental Grocer," *The Whole Story*, November–December 1990, 7; Mackey, "The Accidental Grocer," May–June 1990, 7; Carol Hughes, "Please Talk with Your Team Member Rep . . . ," *Inner Views*, May 15, 1992, 6.

91. Benjamin C. Waterhouse, *Lobbying America: The Politics of Business from Nixon to NAFTA* (Princeton, N.J.: Princeton University Press, 2013).

92. *Whole Foods Market: 1992 Annual Stakeholders Report* (Austin, Tex.: Whole Foods Market, 1992), 30; *"Whole Foods Market, Inc.," International Directory of Company Histories* (Chicago: St. James Press, 1998), 525, 523; *Whole Foods Market: 1994 Annual Stakeholders Report* (Austin, Tex.: Whole Foods Market, 1992), 30–31, F11; Lex Alexander, interviewed by the author, Chapel Hill, N.C., April 15, 2014.

6. PERSEVERANCE AND APPROPRIATION

1. Whole Foods Market, "Growth of the Organics Industry," n.d., https://www.whole foodsmarket.com/mission-values/organic/growth-organics-industry; John Mackey and Raj Sisodia, *Conscious Capitalism: Liberating the Heroic Spirit of Business* (Boston: Harvard Business Review Press, 2013); Greenpeace, "2014 Seafood Retail Scorecard," n.d., http://www.greenpeace.org/usa/Global/usa/planet3/photos-oceans/CATORank ings.pdf; "Energy Performance," *Better Buildings: U.S. Department of Energy*, n.d., http://betterbuildingssolutioncenter.energy.gov/energy-data/Whole%20Foods; *Whole Foods Market's Green Mission Report* (Austin: Whole Foods Market, 2012), 5–6, 33–50; Whole Foods Market, "Education and Public Participation," n.d., http://www .wholefoodsmarket.com/mission-values/core-values/sustainability-and-our-future.

2. "Whole Foods Founder John Mackey on Fascism and 'Conscious Capitalism,'" National Public Radio, January 16, 2013, http://www.npr.org/sections/thesalt/2013/ 01/16/169413848/whole-foods-founder-john-mackey-on-fascism-and-conscious-capi talism; Julie Dermansky, "What the Keystone Pipeline Protest Looks Like in Texas," *Atlantic*, February 18, 2013, http://www.theatlantic.com/national/archive/2013/02/ what-the-keystone-pipeline-protest-looks-like-in-texas/273261/.

3. Whole Foods Market, "Our Core Values," n.d., http://www.wholefoodsmarket.com/ mission-values/core-values; Whole Foods Market, *General Information Guide— Mid-Atlantic Region* (Austin, Tex.: Whole Foods Market, 2013), 14; Hayley Peterson, "We Compared Whole Foods' Prices to Those of Its Biggest Competitor—and What We Found Was Shocking," *Business Insider*, November 20, 2015, http://www.busines sinsider.com/whole-foods-prices-compared-to-kroger-2015-11; Katy Osborne, "This Is How Much More You'll Spend at Whole Foods vs. Trader Joe's," *Time*, August 27, 2015, http://time.com/money/4013394/trader-joes-whole-foods-prices/; Tracy McMillan, "Can Whole Foods Change the Way Poor People Eat?" *Slate*, November 19, 2014, http://www.slate.com/articles/life/food/2014/11/whole_foods_detroit_can_a_gro cery_store_really_fight_elitism_racism_and.html; Matt Welch and Nick Gillespie, "Whole Foods Health Care," *Reason Foundation*, December 15, 2009, http://reason. org/news/show/whole-foods-health-care.

4. McMillan, "Can Whole Foods Change the Way Poor People Eat?"; Evan Smith, "John Mackey," in *Texas Monthly on . . . Food* (Austin: University of Texas Press, 2008), 189.

5. Kroger, *Notice of Annual Meeting of Shareholders: Proxy Statement and 2014 Annual Report* (Cincinnati: Kroger, 2015), A4; Safeway, *Annual Report* (Pleasanton: Calif.: Safeway, 2014), 12; Barbara Farfan, "2014 World's Largest Grocery Stores, Top 100 Supermarket Retail Chains," August 15, 2016, https://www.thebalance.com/top-super

market-retail-chains-2892136; Whole Foods Market, *General Information Guide—Mid-Atlantic Region*, 17; "How Much 70 Big Companies Plan to Give This Year," *Chronicle of Philanthropy*, July 17, 2014, 10; Susan Adams, "American Companies That Give the Most Back," *Forbes*, October 21, 2011, http://www.forbes.com/sites/susan-adams/2011/10/21/american-companies-that-give-back-the-most/#2b42aadf3ed9.

6. Nancy H. Koehn and Katherine Miller, *John Mackey and Whole Foods Market*, Case 9-807-111 (Cambridge, Mass.: Harvard Business School, 2007), 7; Lisa Marshall, "Crafting a New Future for Independent Natural Retail," *Natural Foods Merchandiser*, July 5, 2016, http://newhope.com/managing-your-retail-business/crafting-new-future-independent-natural-retail; Whole Foods Market, "Company Info," n.d., http://www.wholefoodsmarket.com/company-info; Whole Foods Market, *2015 Annual Report—Whole Foods Market* (Austin, Tex.: Whole Foods Market, 2015), 34; "Grocery Store Chains Net Profit—Percent of Sales," *FMI: The Voice of Food Retail*, June 2016, http://www.fmi.org/docs/default-source/facts-figures/grocery-store-chains-net-profit.pdf?sfvrsn=2; *International Directory of Company Histories* (Chicago: St. James Press, 1998), 523–552; "Top 100 Retailers Chart 2014," *National Retail Federation*, n.d., https://nrf.com/2014/top100-table; Whole Foods Market, "Fast Facts," n.d., http://media.wholefoodsmarket.com/fast-facts/ and http://www.wholefoodsmarket.com/stores/lamar; Barbara Farfan, "World's Largest U.S. Retail Chains in 2015," October 12, 2016, https://www.thebalance.com/largest-us-retail-chains-2892857.

7. Examples of head shops with names that connect to peace and nonviolence include the World Peace Smoke Shop in Huntsville, Texas; the Peace of Sunshine head shop in Catonsville, Maryland; and the Chillin' Out Smoke Shop in Scotch Plains, New Jersey. *High Times* today produces far fewer wide-ranging political analyses than it did in the 1970s. For examples of such analyses, see Glenn O'Brien, "I Remember Civil Defense: How We Survived the Apocalypse," *High Times*, May 1977, 62–66, 75–78, 90–92; Robert Singer, "The Rise of the Dope Dictators: How the Dope War Replaced the Cold War—a Study in U.S. Foreign Policy," *High Times*, March 1977, 52–58, 84–90, 108–114; and Douglas Kelley, "The $350-Billion Arms Trade," *High Times*, November 1978, 65–69.

8. Jessica Bennett, "In Colorado, a Rebranding of Pot Inc.," *New York Times*, October 3, 2014, ST-1; Joshua Greene, "Cannabusiness," *Atlantic*, April 2009, 23.

9. Shawn E. Rhea, "Buy the Book," *Black Enterprise*, February 1999, 175; Judith Rosen, "African American Booksellers Look for a Turnaround," *Publishers Weekly*, February 14, 2014, http://www.publishersweekly.com/pw/by-topic/industry-news/bookselling/article/61078-african-american-booksellers-look-for-a-turnaround.html; Paula Woods, "Black-Owned Shops Fight to Survive Super Bookstores," *Emerge*, February 1999, 104–105; Karen E. Quinones Miller, "Memories of Old School Black Bookstores," *Philadelphia Sun*, November 29, 2014, http://www.philasun.com/local/memories-of-old-school-black-book-stores/; Tom Bradshaw and Bonnie Nichols, *Reading at Risk: A Survey of Literary Reading in America—Research Division Report #46* (Washington, D.C.: National Endowment for the Arts, 2004), ix–x; Gwen Richardson, "Top Ten Reasons Why African American Bookstores Are Closing," African American Literary Book Club, AALBC.com, September 27, 2010, http://aalbc.com/reviews/top_ten_reasons_why.html; Troy Johnson, "Death of the Black-Owned, Independent Bookstore," African American Literary Book Club, March 25, 2012, http://aalbc.com/blog/index.php/2012/03/25/death-of-the-black-owned-independent

-bookstore/; Troy Johnson, "Only 54 Black Bookstores Remain in America," African American Literary Book Club, March 31, 2014, http://aalbc.com/blog/index. php/2014/03/31/54-black-owned-bookstores-remain-america/.

10. Jasmine Johnson, "Harlem's Hue-Man Hopes Past Is Prologue for Black Booksellers," *Colorlines*, July 24, 2012, http://colorlines.com/archives/2012/07/harlems_hue-man _hopes_the_past_is_prologue_for_black_booksellers.html.

11. Rebecca Bowe, "Marcus Books of San Francisco Evicted," *San Francisco Bay Guardian*, May 8, 2014, 13.

12. Candice Reed, "Society and Credit Unions Have Come a Long Way, Baby," *Credit Union Times*, December 12, 2012, http://www.cutimes.com/2012/12/12/society-and-credit-unions-have-come-a-long-way-baby; Karla Mantilla, "Feminist Bookstores: Where Women's Lives Matter," *off our backs* 37, nos. 2–3 (2007): 50; Anjali Enjeti, "The Last 13 Feminist Bookstores in the U.S. and Canada," *Paste*, May 9, 2014, http:// www.pastemagazine.com/blogs/lists/2014/05/the-last-13-feminist-bookstores-in-the-us-and-canada.html.

13. *The 2014 State of Women Owned Businesses Report* (New York: American Express OPEN, 2014), 2; *Women Owned Businesses 1972* (Washington, D.C.: U.S. Department of Commerce, Bureau of the Census, 1976), 1.

14. Andi Zeisler, *We Were Feminists Once: From Riot Grrrl to CoverGirl®, the Buying and Selling of a Political Movement* (New York: Public Affairs, 2016); Dorothy Sue Cobble, Linda Gordon, and Astrid Henry, *Feminism Unfinished. A Short, Surprising History of American Women's Movements* (New York: Norton, 2014), 185–189, 218–219; Sheryl Sandberg and Nell Scovell, *Lean In: Women, Work, and the Will to Lead* (New York: Knopf, 2013).

15. Kate Losse, "Feminism's Tipping Point: Who Wins from Leaning In," *Dissent*, March 26, 2013, http://www.dissentmagazine.org/online_articles/feminisms-tipping-point-who-wins-from-leaning-in; bell hooks, "Dig Deep: Beyond Lean In," *Feminist Wire*, October 2013, http://thefeministwire.com/2013/10/17973/; Linda Gordon, "Confidence Game: The Problem with *Lean In*," *Huffington Post*, August 25, 2014, http:// www.huffingtonpost.com/linda-gordon/problem-with-lean-in_b_5698220.html; "Linda Gordon Says the Feminist Movement Has Become Very Individualist," *Village Voice*, March 18, 2015, http://www.villagevoice.com/news/linda-gordon-says-the -feminist-movement-has-become-very-individualist-6706729. See also Cobble, Gordon, and Henry, *Feminism Unfinished*, 197–200.

16. *Food Co-op Directory* (Albuquerque, N.Mex.: Co-op Directory Association, August 1978), 10–79; "Food Co-op Directory," *Cooperative Grocer Network*, n.d., http:// www.grocer.coop/coops; Patrizia Battilani and Harm G. Schröter, "Introduction: Principal Problems and General Development of Cooperative Enterprise," in *The Cooperative Business Movement, 1950 to the Present*, ed. Patrizia Battilani and Harm G. Schröter (Cambridge: Cambridge University Press, 2012), 1, 3; Ann Hoyt and Tito Menzani, "The International Cooperative Movement: A Quiet Giant," in Battilani and Schröter, *Cooperative Business Movement*, 37; *Cooperative Businesses in the United States . . . a 2005 Snapshot* (Washington, D.C.: National Cooperative Month Planning Committee, 2005), 4; Mondragon Corporation, "FAQs—How Many of Your Employees Are Cooperative Members and How Many Are Not? What Areas Do Non-members Usually Work In?" n.d., http://www.mondragon-corporation.com/ eng/co-operative-experience/faqs/.

17. Panu Kalmi, "The Disappearance of Cooperatives from Economics Textbooks," *Cambridge Journal of Economics* 31, no. 4 (2007): 625, 632, 641.

18. Milton Friedman, "The Social Responsibility of Business Is to Increase Its Profits," *New York Times Sunday Magazine*, September 13, 1970, 33, 122–125. See also Angus Burgin, *The Great Persuasion: Reinventing Free Markets Since the Depression* (Cambridge, Mass.: Harvard University Press, 2012); Daniel Stedman Jones, *Masters of the Universe: Hayek, Friedman, and the Birth of Neoliberal Politics* (Princeton, N.J.: Princeton University Press, 2012); David Harvey, *A Brief History of Neoliberalism* (Oxford: Oxford University Press, 2005); David M. Kotz, *The Rise and Fall of Neoliberal Capitalism* (Cambridge, Mass.: Harvard University Press, 2015).

19. A. B. Cochran, "Small Business Mortality Rates: A Review of the Literature," *Journal of Small Business Management*, October 1981, 57–58; Small Business Administration, Office of Advocacy, "Frequently Asked Questions," March 2014, 3, https://www.sba .gov/sites/default/files/FAQ_March_2014_0.pdf.

20. Paul Hawken, *The Next Economy* (New York: Holt, Rinehart and Winston, 1983), *The Ecology of Commerce: A Declaration of Sustainability* (New York: Harper Collins, 1993), and *Natural Capitalism: Creating the Next Industrial Revolution* (New York: Little, Brown, 1999); Paul Hawken and KQED-TV, *Growing a Business*, VHS (New York: Ambrose Video, 1988); Fred Turner, *From Counterculture to Cyberculture: Stewart Brand, the Whole Earth Network, and the Rise of Digital Utopianism* (Chicago: University of Chicago Press, 2006), 176–188.

21. Directory search for B corporations, buying clubs, collectives, community-development credit unions, consumer cooperatives, fair trade, and worker cooperatives in *Solidarity Economy Map and Directory*, http://solidarityeconomy.us; Ethan Miller, "Solidarity Economy: Key Concepts and Issues," in *Solidarity Economy I: Building Alternatives for People and Planet—Papers and Reports from the 2009 U.S. Forum on the Solidarity Economy*, ed. Emily Kawano, Thomas Neal Masterson, and Jonathan Teller-Elsberg (Amherst, Mass.: Center for Popular Economics, 2009), 33–35, 26–28. See also Ash Amin, *The Social Economy: International Perspectives on Economic Solidarity* (London: Zed Books, 2009); Jenna Allard, Carl Davidson, and Julie Matthaei, eds., *Solidarity Economy: Building Alternatives for People and Planet* (Chicago: U.S. Solidarity Economy Network, 2008); Red Emma's, "About," http://www.treasurecitythrift.org/about-us; "The Cheapest Thrift Store in Austin," *Treasure City Thrift—Solidarity Not Charity*, n.d., http://www.treasurecitythrift.org/about-us. On the anarchist tradition of infoshops, see Joel Olson, "The Problem with Infoshops and Insurrection: U.S. Anarchism, Movement Building, and the Racial Order," in *Contemporary Anarchist Studies: An Introductory Anthology of Anarchy in the Academy*, ed. Randall Amster, Abraham DeLeon, Luis Fernandez, Anthony J. Nocella II, and Deric Shannon (New York: Routledge, 2009), 35–45; and Chris Atton, "Infoshops in the Shadow of the State," in *Contesting Media Power: Alternative Media in a Networked World*, ed. Nick Couldry and James Curran (Lanham, Md.: Rowman and Littlefield, 2003), 57–69. On Democracy Collaborative, see democracycollaborative. org and *Conversations on Community Wealth Building: Interviews by Steve Dubb for the Democracy Collaborative* (Washington, D.C.: Democracy Collaborative, 2016).

22. Janine S. Hiller, "The Benefit Corporation and Corporate Social Responsibility," *Journal of Business Ethics* 118, no. 2 (2013): 287–301; Gar Alperovitz, *What Then Must We Do? Straight Talk About the Next American Revolution* (White River Junction, Vt.: Chelsea Green, 2013), 39–40; Benefit Corporation, "State by State Status of

Legislation," n.d., http://benefitcorp.net/policymakers/state-by-state-status; "Find a B-Corp," n.d., https://www.bcorporation.net/community/find-a-b-corp?search=&field _industry=&field_city=&field_state=&field_country=United+States; "Find a Benefit Corp," n.d., http://benefitcorp.net/businesses/find-a-benefit-corp?field_bcorp_ certified_value=&state=All&title=king+arthur&op=Go&sort_by=title& sort_order=ASC; "King Arthur Flour Becomes a Founding B Corporation," February 12, 2008, https://www.kingarthurflour.com/press/founding-BCorporation.html; Kate Cooney, Justin Koushyar, Matthew Lee, and Haskell Murray, "Benefit Corporation and L3C Adoption: A Survey," *Stanford Social Innovation Review*, December 5, 2014, http://ssir.org/articles/entry/benefit_corporation_and_l3c_adoption_a_survey.

23. BALLE: Business Alliance for Local Living Economies, "About Us," n.d., https:// bealocalist.org/about-us, https://bealocalist.org/Board-of-Directors and https://bealocalist.org/History; Judy Wicks, *Good Morning, Beautiful Business: The Unexpected Journey of an Activist Entrepreneur and Local Economy Pioneer* (White River Junction, Vt.: Chelsea Green, 2013), 33–44; Jennifer Rockne, letter to the editor, *The Nation*, April 11, 2005, 31; "Ten New Studies of the Local Economic Premium," October 2012, http://www.amiba.net/resources/studies-recommended-reading/local-premium; American Independent Business Alliance, "Our Affiliates," n.d., http://www. amiba.net/about_ibas/our-affiliates/. On the National Federation of Independent Businesses, see Patrick Akard, "Corporate Mobilization and Political Power: The Transformation of U.S. Economic Policy in the 1970s," *American Sociological Review*, October 1992, 602–603.

24. J. Gregory Dees, "The Meaning of 'Social Entrepreneurship,'" presentation at the Kauffman Center for Entrepreneurial Leadership, Ewing Marion Kauffman Foundation, Stanford University, October 31, 1998; "Gregory Dees: Social Capitalist," *Economist*, December 24, 2013, http://www.economist.com/blogs/schumpeter/2013/12/ gregory-dees; O. C. Ferrell, John Fraedrich, and Terry Gable, *Managing Social Responsibility and Growth at Ben & Jerry's* (Albuquerque: Daniels Fund Business Ethics Initiative, University of New Mexico, 2011), 2–3; Fred "Chico" Lager, *Ben & Jerry: The Inside Scoop—How Two Real Guys Built a Business with a Social Conscience and a Sense of Humor* (New York: Crown, 1994), 186–190, 221–226; Ben & Jerry's, "Our SEAR Reports," n.d., http://www.benjerry.com/about-us/sear-reports. The concept of "social entrepreneurship" also emerged out of broader debates as early as the 1950s on the issue of "corporate social responsibility." See Archie B. Carroll, "Corporate Social Responsibility: Evolution of a Definitional Construct," *Business & Society* 38, no. 3(1999): 268–295.

25. Skoll World Forum on Social Entrepreneurship, "Organization Directory," n.d., https://skollworldforum.org/organizations/; Frederik O. Andersson, "Social Entrepreneurship as Fetish," *Nonprofit Quarterly*, April 11, 2012, https://nonprofitquarterly .org/2012/04/11/social-entrepreneurship-as-fetish-2/; Ruth McCambridge, "Hybrids, Hybridity, and Hype," *Nonprofit Quarterly*, March 7, 2014, https://nonprofitquar terly.org/2014/03/07/hybrids-hybridity-and-hype-2/; Daniel Flynn, "Social Enterprise Confusion," *Pro Bono Australia*, May 21, 2014, http://www.probonoaustralia .com.au/news/2014/05/social-enterprise-confusion#; Catherine A. Ramus and Ivan Montiel, "When Are Corporate Environmental Policies a Form of Greenwashing?" *Business & Society* 44, no. 4 (2005): 377–414; Ray Hennessey, "All Entrepreneurship Is 'Social' Entrepreneurship," *Entrepreneur*, June 9, 2015, http://www.entrepreneur .com/article/247137.

26. Turner, *From Counterculture to Cyberculture,* 3–6, 141–142; Fred Turner, "Bohemian Technocracy & the Countercultural Press," in *Power to the People: The Graphic Design of the Radical Press and the Rise of the Counter-Culture, 1964–1974,* ed. Geoff Kaplan (Chicago: University of Chicago Press, 2013), 132–159. See also John Markoff, *What the Dormouse Said: How the Sixties Counterculture Shaped the Personal Computer Industry* (New York: Penguin, 2005); Walter Chen, "Bosslessness: What It Is and Why It's All the Rage in Silicon Valley," *Entrepreneur,* November 22, 2013, http://www.entrepreneur.com/article/229977; Rachel Emma Silverman, "Who's the Boss? There Isn't One," *Wall Street Journal,* June 19, 2012, B1; Danielle Sacks, "The Sharing Economy," *Fast Company,* April 18, 2011, http://www.fastcompany.com/1747551/sharing-economy; Neil Howe, "Open Offices Back in Vogue—Thanks to Millennials," *Forbes,* March 31, 2015, http://www.forbes.com/sites/neilhowe/2015/03/31/open-offices-back-in-vogue-thanks-to-millennials/; Meghan M. Biro, "5 Reasons Why Workplace Flexibility Is Smart Talent Strategy" *Forbes,* August 18, 2013, http://www.forbes.com/sites/meghanbiro/2013/08/18/5-reasons-why-workplace-flexibility-is-smart-talent-strategy/#2715e4857a0b27a311355361; Dorian Zandbergen, "Fulfilling the Sacred Potential of Technology: New Edge Technophilia, Consumerism, and Spirituality in Silicon Valley," in *Things: Religion and the Question of Materiality,* ed. Dick Houtman and Birgit Meyer (Bronx, N.Y.: Fordham University Press, 2012), 356–378; Lizzie Widdicombe, "The Higher Life: A Mindfulness Guru for the Tech Set," *New Yorker,* July 6, 2015, 40, 42–47.

27. Baba Ram Dass, *Be Here Now* (San Cristobal, N.Mex.: Lama Foundation, 1971), 63–64; Walter Issacson, *Steve Jobs* (New York: Simon and Schuster, 2013), 18, 34–36, 41.

28. Issacson, *Steve Jobs,* 328–332.

29. Perla Ni, "America's Least Philanthropic Companies," *Stanford Social Innovation Review,* June 20, 2007, https://ssir.org/articles/entry/the_least_philanthropic_companies; Andrew Ross Sorkin, "The Mystery of Steve Jobs's Public Giving," *New York Times,* August 29, 2011, http://dealbook.nytimes.com/2011/08/29/the-mystery-of-steve-jobss-public-giving/; George Packer, "Change the World," *New Yorker,* May 27, 2013, 44–55; Paulina Borsook, *Cyberselfish: A Critical Romp Through the Terribly Libertarian Culture of High-Tech* (New York: PublicAffairs, 2001); Andrew Leonard, "Tech's Toxic Political Culture: The Stealth Libertarianism of Silicon Valley Bigwigs," *Salon,* June 6, 2014, http://www.salon.com/2014/06/06/techs_toxic_political_culture_the_stealth_libertarianism_of_silicon_valley_bigwigs; Kentaro Toyama, *Geek Heresy: Rescuing Social Change from the Cult of Technology* (New York: PublicAffairs, 2015); Mark Zuckerberg, "Zuckerberg's Letter to Investors," Reuters, February 1, 2012, http://www.reuters.com/article/2012/02/01/us-facebook-letter-idUSTRE8102MT20120201; Keith A. Spencer, "Why the Rich Love Burning Man," *Jacobin,* August 25, 2015, https://www.jacobinmag.com/2015/08/burning-man-one-percent-silicon-valley-tech/; Steven W. Thrasher, "Burning Man Founder: 'Black Folks Don't Like to Camp as Much as White Folks,'" *Guardian,* September 4, 2015, https://www.theguardian.com/culture/2015/sep/04/burning-man-founder-larry-harvey-race-diversity-silicon-valley; Nick Bilton, "A Line Is Drawn in the Sand: At Burning Man, the Tech Elite One-Up One Another," *New York Times,* August 21, 2014, http://www.nytimes.com/2014/08/21/fashion/at-burning-man-the-tech-elite-one-up-one-another.html. For a more positive assessment, see Fred Turner, "Burning Man at Google: A Cultural Infrastructure for New Media Production," *New Media & Society* 11, nos. 1–2 (2009): 73–94.

30. Robert Putnam, *Bowling Alone: The Collapse and Revival of American Community* (New York: Simon and Schuster, 2001); Dora Costa and Matthew Kahn, "Understanding the American Decline in Social Capital, 1952–1998," *Kyklos* 56 (2003): 17–46; Jean M. Twenge, W. Keith Campbell, and Nathan T. Carter, "Declines in Trust in Others and Confidence in Institutions Among American Adults and Late Adolescents, 1972–2012," *Psychological Science* 25 (October 2014): 1–12; Jean M. Twenge, W. Keith Campbell, and Brittany Gentile, "Increases in Individualistic Words and Phrases in American Books, 1960–2008," *PLOS One* 7 (2012): 1–5.

CONCLUSION

1. Lizabeth Cohen, *A Consumers' Republic: The Politics of Mass Consumption in Postwar America* (New York: Vintage Books, 2003); Jennifer Delton, *Racial Integration in Corporate America, 1940–1990* (Cambridge: Cambridge University Press, 2009); John P. Fernandez, with Jules Davis, *Race, Gender, and Rhetoric: The True State of Race and Gender Relations in Corporate America* (New York: McGraw-Hill, 1999); Katherine Turk, *Equality on Trial: Gender and Rights in the Modern American Workplace* (Philadelphia: University of Pennsylvania Press, 2016), 200–208; Martha E. Reeves, *Women in Business: Theory, Case Studies, and Legal Challenges* (New York: Routledge, 2010), 10–12; Bradley S. Greenberg and Jeffrey E. Brand, "Minorities and the Mass Media: 1970s and 1990s," in *Media Effects: Advances in Theory and Research*, ed. Jennings Bryant and Dolf Zillmann (Hillsdale, N.J.: Lawrence Erlbaum, 1994), 290–292; Bradley S. Greenberg, Dana Mastro, and Jeffrey E. Brand, "Minorities and the Mass Media: Television into the 21st Century," in *Media Effects: Advances in Theory and Research*, 2nd ed., ed. Jennings Bryant and Dolf Zillmann (Mahwah, N.J.: Lawrence Erlbaum, 2002), 333, 339; Scott Coltrane and Melinda M. Messineo, "The Perpetuation of Subtle Prejudice: Race and Gender Imagery in 1990s Television Advertising," *Sex Roles* 42, no. 5 (2000): 375, 382, 385–386.

2. Gary Dymski, "Discrimination in the Credit and Housing Markets: Findings and Challenges," in *Handbook on the Economics of Discrimination*, ed. William M. Rodgers III (Cheltenham, U.K.: Edward Elgar, 2006), 240.

3. On questions of the impact of online activism, see Mark Engler, "The Limits of Internet Organizing," *Dissent*, October 5, 2010, https://www.dissentmagazine.org/blog/the-limits-of-internet-organizing; Geert Lovink, *Networks Without a Cause: A Critique of Social Media* (Cambridge: Polity Press, 2011); Henrik Serup Christensen, "Political Activities on the Internet: Slacktivism or Political Participation by Other Means," *First Monday: Peer-Reviewed Journal on the Internet*, February 2011, http://firstmonday.org/ojs/index.php/fm/article/view/3336/2767.

4. World at Work, *Survey on Workplace Flexibility 2013* (Scottsdale, Ariz.: World at Work, 2013), 3, 18–19, http://www.worldatwork.org/adimLink?id=73898.

Index